Enter His Courts with Praise!

Old Testament Worship
for the New Testament Church

ANDREW E. HILL

Star Song
PUBLISHING GROUP
Nashville

Star Song Publishing Group, a division of Jubilee Communications, Inc.
2325 Crestmoor, Nashville, Tennessee 37215.
Printed in the United States of America.

First Printing, June 1993

Library of Congress Cataloging-in-Publication Data

Hill, Andrew E.
    Enter his courts with praise / by Andrew E. Hill. — 1st ed.
        p.   cm.
    Includes bibliographical references and indexes.
    ISBN 1-56233-034-9 : $12.99
    1. Public worship—Biblical teaching.   2. Worship in the Bible.
3. Bible. O.T.—Criticism, interpretation, etc.   4. Judaism
(Christian theology)   I. Title.
BS1199.P93H55   1993
248'.3—dc20

                                                            93-13581
                                                            CIP

1 2 3 4 5 6 7 8 9 10 — 99 98 97 96 95 94 93

FOR

Jordan Robert
AND
Jim and Jeanne Wendt

May you always worship God with the same expression
of energy, enthusiasm, devotion, and artistry as displayed in
your finely crafted reconstruction of the Mosaic Tabernacle!
(Lev. 26:2, 11–12)

Contents

    What Is Worship?
    Why the Recent Interest?
    What Forms the Basis of Hebrew Worship?
    Why Study Old Testament Worship?

    Words of Worship
    What Is Your Vocabulary Rating?

    Personal Piety: What Are Its Characteristics?
    Personal Piety: How Is It Demonstrated?
    False vs. True Worship
    The Holy, the Clean, and the Unclean
    The Sacred vs. the Secular

    Patriarchal Period
    Mosaic Period
    Davidic and Solomonic Periods
    Exilic and Restoration Periods

Preface

FOR SEVERAL YEARS NOW I have polled students in my Old Testament survey courses on a variety of topics. Included among those questions is one addressing worship, framed something like this: "How would you describe the worship experience in your home church?" Invariably, and now predictably, the majority of students answering summarize their worship experience in one, six-letter word beginning with *b*—"Boring!" Little wonder many of the young people raised in traditional evangelical churches abandon their "religious roots" once they have severed the parental tether. They prefer to seek meaning, relevance, and participation in other worship traditions. I have observed a general pattern in this "worship pilgrimage," with students gravitating in one of two directions: either into churches emphasizing the form of liturgy or into churches emphasizing the freedom of charismatic expression.

This trend is but one symptom of a malady diagnosed by Leith Anderson as *Dying for Change*.[1] His astute, even prophetic analysis of current realities in the church leads to one basic conclusion—churches must change and change quickly in order to contend with the rapid pace of transformation in our technological society. Spiritual renewal, including worship, is one of several areas in which Anderson challenges churches and church leaders to catch the vision and make a decision for meaningful change in their church or parachurch organization.

Enter His Courts with Praise! does not pretend to be the antidote for this spiritual malady plaguing the church today. Rather, this book should be regarded as one ingredient necessary to concoct a serum for worship renewal in the church. Indeed, the Old Testament has much to teach us about worship. While the needs of individual churches differ, all approaches to worship renewal must be comprehensive enough to consider the biblical, historical, and theological sources of Christian worship.

This contribution primarily focuses on the biblical source of
Christian worship. Specifically, our discussion is limited to the worship of the ancient Hebrews as recorded in the Old Testament. My
guiding premise has been the understanding that the Old Testament
has much to teach the New Testament Christian about worship, at
least implicitly by theological principle, if not by explicit example
and direct application. This is true because the Old Testament is
the foundation on which the New Testament was written and the
Christian church established.

Typically, the modern study of religion describes religious beliefs
and practices by means of academic methodologies. The three most
common approaches include the *anthropological* (religion = a shared
experience, ever evolving in living communities), the *sociological* (religion = group identity, providing a worldview for the individual),
and the *psychological* (religion = the projection of the powers of the
human mind).[2] These and other academic methodologies have one
thing in common. They all reduce religion to a strictly human phenomenon, since they can only study what is "empirically verifiable."

The approach here may be identified as biblical, historical, and
theological. Biblical in that the Old Testament and the New are
affirmed as divinely revealed, ultimate truth, and foundational to
our knowledge and worship of God. Historical in that the religious
beliefs and practices of the ancient Hebrews were prompted by divine intervention in the events of human history (like the call of
Abram and the exodus from Egypt). And theological in that this is
a study of ancient Hebrew religion from the "inside." This means
accepting the Old Testament as a unified whole (rather than the
archaic atomizing of the Old Testament into an alphabet of literary
sources characteristic of the majority of works on Hebrew worship)
and reading it from the viewpoint of Christian faith (Gen. 15:6; cf.,
Gal. 3:6).

Consequently, the application of this knowledge about God and
Hebrew religion in the Old Testament is deemed valuable to Christian behavior (ethics) and Christian worship (liturgy) because the
new covenant in Christ is the fulfillment of the old (Matt. 5:17;
26:28; cf., Jer. 31:31–34).

This book has been designed to serve as a reference work or manual on Old Testament worship. While there is continuity of theme

and logical chronological progression from the worship of the Mosaic tabernacle period to the worship of Herod's temple, each of the twelve chapters stands on its own as a self-contained unit. In keeping with the pattern of educational practice in Old Testament times, those areas of overlap are not only cross-listed but also welcomed, given the value of repetition for learning. I am optimistic the book will prove equally valuable to the individual seeking to enhance her or his private devotion and the worship leader or church worship committee planning worship renewal in the local church.

I have attempted to document each chapter in such a way that through the endnotes, plus additional bibliography (at times annotated), the serious student and/or worship leader may expand and deepen their probe of a given topic. Scripture references are profuse throughout the book—I trust not to the point of distraction! Do not disparage these citations to the primary source of Old Testament worship. It is my firm belief that worship renewal can only occur as we begin to catch glimpses of God in his holy temple (Hab. 2:20); the text of the Old Testament provides these "divine flashes."

The theological implications of Old Testament worship for Christian worship, as well as the practical suggestions for implementing principles of Old Testament worship gathered at the conclusion of each chapter are illustrative, not exhaustive. Be creative! Personalize the ideas presented here, develop them, refine them, and invent additional categories for applying the concepts of Old Testament worship to contemporary worship in the church. Use this text as a resource for and as a bridge into worship renewal!

I have consciously excluded certain issues and topics from this discussion as secondary to the primary goal of investigating Old Testament worship as a means for worship renewal in the church. For instance, I have said little about the role of women in Old Testament worship. Although the ancient Hebrews were a patriarchal society, the Old Testament contains numerous examples of women worshiping God (Miriam, Exod. 15:20–21; Hannah, 1 Sam. 1:9–10, 19). The principle of universal giftedness envisioned by the prophet Joel and realized at Pentecost suggests both male and female may participate as equals in the service of worship (cf., Joel 2:28–32; Acts 2:16–21). Of course, the constraints of culture and one's own worship tradition may condition this ideal. My advice here is do not let gender issues become a barrier to worship renewal.

As you encounter God as Creator and Redeemer in the Old Testament, indeed the very fountain of life, may you see the light of worship renewal in his light (Ps. 36:9). And finally, may God's good Spirit lead you on a level path into worship renewal so that you might truly *Enter His Courts with Praise!* (Ps. 143:10).

Andrew E. Hill
Wheaton, Illinois

Acknowledgments

I AM INDEBTED to my colleague, Dr. Robert E. Webber, who first suggested I write a book on the topic of Old Testament worship, encouraged me to see it through to completion, and was instrumental in securing the publisher for the manuscript.

I am also grateful to Rev. L. Ted Johnson of the Midwest Baptist Conference who arranged my participation in a worship workshop with conference church representatives. Their enthusiastic response to my "experiment" in Old Testament worship confirmed the viability of the project and motivated me to press on with my ideas.

David West, Matt Price, and the rest of the staff of the Star Song Publishing Group are to be commended for ably supervising and coordinating every phase of production in the process of transforming the debris of a manuscript into the polished art form of a book.

Thanks as well to Hugh Claycombe. I benefited personally from our collaborations on the idea of worship in the Old Testament, and his excellent illustrations both enhance the text aesthetically and complement the instruction pedagogically.

The author acknowledges with gratitude those who have provided the charts and tables included herein. The sources for these figures are identified where the items appear in the text.

As always, my family remains my primary concern and my greatest source of inspiration apart from the Scriptures themselves. May God reward their patience and loyalty as accomplices in the weariness of writing and the vanity of publishing. If this feeble study enables the wife of my youth, Terri, and me to impart the legacy of worship to Jennifer, Jesse, and Jordan, then it will have succeeded!

Foreword

AS I READ *Enter His Courts with Praise!*, I was impressed by two initial observations.

First, I was reminded of how little has been written on Old Testament worship. The renewed concern for worship which has been fueled first by the promulgation of the Catholic document *The Constitution on the Sacred Liturgy*, and by the charismatic movement has produced numerous works on worship, but to my knowledge no full-blown treatment of Old Testament worship has been produced. In this sense *Enter His Courts with Praise!* is a pioneer work!

Secondly, I was struck by how much of contemporary renewal, particularly the charismatic renewal and the current theme of praise and worship music draws on Old Testament themes and images. I subscribe to a number of worship magazines which frequently contain articles on worship in the Old Testament, particularly studies in tabernacle worship, Davidic worship, and worship in the Psalms. Again, what amazes me is that no one has sat down and taken the time to write a book on Old Testament worship. Until now!

I not only welcome *Enter His Courts with Praise!* for the reasons cited above, but for other reasons as well.

First of all, *Enter His Courts with Praise!* is a work of inspirational and devotional reading. I have read numerous books on worship. Many of them simply put more information on the table and increase the menu items. I like more information, and *Enter His Courts with Praise!* has plenty of information to digest. But what I like about this book and the reason I think you will like it as well is that while I read its words and chapters, I was stimulated to worship. Very few books on worship do that. And that alone sets this work aside as an important and invaluable work.

I also like to read books that are organized well. I don't like to stop and ask "How does this fit with what precedes?" I want the interior argument of the book to flow forth in a clear and well-ordered way. That's another reason why I can commend *Enter His Courts with Praise!* It *develops* its subject and carries the reader's interest from beginning to end.

I also want to know whether an author writes out of knowledge. Sometimes I get the impression that a writer hasn't done his or her homework. But not so with *Enter His Courts with Praise!* Dr. Hill writes out of two decades of study and teaching and writes with the confidence of a scholar who has studied sources and knows whereof he speaks.

I welcome *Enter His Courts with Praise!* It opens up Old Testament worship and makes this world of thought and practice which helped to shape early Christian worship available to me.

I feel confident that you will experience the same thing I did— a reading that is spiritually energizing, clear and accessible, and rooted in the finest of biblical worship.

Robert E. Webber

Introduction

THE BEST-SELLER *Megatrends* by John Naisbitt offered readers of the eighties insightful analysis of social, political, and economic currents shaping the future, at least the nineties. Among coming changes observed by Naisbitt were shifts from short-term to long-term orientations in education and employment. He forecasted a return to the ideal of a generalist education—lifelong learning for lifelong employment.[1]

In his sequel *Re-Inventing the Corporation,* Naisbitt ventures these long-term perspectives on employment will result in a new ideal about work—that work should be fun, even fulfilling.[2] He dared to predict contemporary education and affluence will change peoples' expectations to the point where the "work should be fun" ethic will displace the Puritan work ethic (i.e., work is honorable and valuable but inherently possesses an element of drudgery).

While the jury is still out on many of Naisbitt's prognostications, we can speak with certainty about another kind of employment. A. W. Tozer called this employment *worship.* In fact, he vigorously maintained worship is the normal employment of human beings. God originally created man and woman to worship and commune with him (Isa. 43:7). Later, according to God's redemptive plan, Jesus Christ entered human history "in order that He might make worshipers out of rebels; in order that He might restore us again to the place of worship we knew when we were first created."[3]

Like Naisbitt's futuristic analysis of employment trends, I assume education will change our expectations. My analysis of how the Hebrew people of Old Testament times went about the normal employment of worshiping their God Yahweh should change our expectations about Christian worship. By learning from their example, we as individual Christians and a Christian church corporately may enrich our understanding and improve our practice of this kind of employment, the worship of God. We will then be better equipped for fulfilling what Tozer called the moral imperative of human beings—worship. What's more, we will be duly prepared for an eternity of employment in the worship of God, Jesus Christ, and the Holy Spirit in the heavenly kingdom (Rev. 7:15).

What Is Worship?

No doubt most of us assume we know what the word *worship* means. Whether or not the reader belongs to a religious movement generally or a Christian tradition specifically he or she has probably had occasion to hear, read, utilize in a conversation, or experience personally worship. Whether or not we are churchgoers most of us have seen media portrayals (or caricatures!) of worship services in feature films, television shows, or dramatic productions. Perhaps some, out of sheer curiosity, have viewed a worship telecast from a well-known cathedral, church, or synagogue on TV. And should all else fail, we can always consult *Webster's Dictionary* for the precise meanings of the word *worship*—revere, pay homage, idolize, adore, esteem worthy.

And yet, defining worship proves difficult because it is both an attitude and an act. Any definition of worship must be both simple and complex because worship is a concept as well as a relationship. Robert Schaper has noted that worship belongs in that category of human experience that possesses a certain intuitive simplicity and philosophical complexity. He elaborates that worship

> . . . is like love. We may spend a great deal of time and mental energy defining and explaining it. And after we have gotten through, we will know what it is, though probably not as a result of the explanation. Worship is like that because it is basically the expression of a relationship. Such a relationship is always simple and complex at once, since it is a relationship between persons.[4]

Definitions of worship abound in literature. Even a cursory reading of a sampling of books treating the topic of worship demonstrates the extreme difficulty in pinning down the exact nature and character of this relationship between the Creator and his creatures. For example, Evelyn Underhill defines worship as "the response of the creature to the Eternal."[5] Yet despite the simplicity of this definition, it proves inadequate because there are many responses a human being might make that would not constitute worship.

John Huxtable understood worship as "a dialogue between God and his people."[6] It is true that worship involves such dialogue. But to describe worship as dialogue alone suggests the Creator and his creatures are equals, and surely true worship is more than mere dialogue. Leslie Flynn regards worship as "adoring contemplation of God."[7] This definition too falls short in that worship is cognitive, affective, and behavioral. Even Robert E. Webber's understanding of worship as "a meeting between God and his people"[8] implies worship is only a scheduled and corporate experience, with no mention at all of a faith response.

By the same token, attempts at thorough and theologically precise definitions of worship may prove equally inadequate. For instance, compare Robert Rayburn's definition of worship:

> Worship is the activity of the new life of a believer in which, recognizing the fullness of the Godhead as it is revealed in the person of Jesus Christ and His mighty redemptive acts, he seeks by the power of the Holy Spirit to render to the living God the glory, honor, and submission which are his due.[9]

Although formal and precise, the beauty and simplicity of worship as a concept is obscured by the verbiage. Note too how the relational aspects of worship between God as the initiator and human beings as the respondents gets lost in the jargon of theological correctness.

So where does all this leave us in our attempt to define the simple yet profound experience of worship? For our purposes perhaps Schaper best captures the idea and ideal of worship when he characterizes the event of worship as a Spirit-led reaction to what we believe God has said and done. This prompts him to define worship "as the expression of a relationship in which God the Father reveals himself and his love in Christ and by his Holy Spirit administers grace, to which we respond in faith, gratitude, and obedience."[10] This definition is best suited for framing our study of worship because it emphasizes the relational nature of worship, affirms God as initiator of the worship response by his word and deeds, outlines the proper worship responses, and recognizes the agency of the Holy Spirit in true worship.

The purpose then of our study of Old Testament worship will be to inform both the definition and the practice of proper worship responses, while all the time keeping in mind Schaper's observations that worship is the expression of a relationship, always simple and complex at once.

Why the Recent Interest?

According to Geoffrey Wainwright, the churches in our century have joined a "liturgical movement seeking a renewal of Christian worship."[11] Evidence of this liturgical movement is widespread. You only need to visit a bookstore, religious or otherwise, and peruse the plethora of titles on worship, its history, practice, and revitalization. In fact, Robert E. Webber, a leading figure in worship renewal among evangelicals, actually found it necessary to justify the publication of another book on the topic of worship.[12] Such was hardly the case two decades ago!

Other signs of this liturgical movement abound. In addition to this raft of new books on the subject of worship, magazine articles and even periodicals devoted entirely to worship topics are common-place. Growing interest in worship renewal is also attested by the numerous seminars and workshops around the country designed to bring a new vibrancy in worship to both clergy and laity. Perhaps even a more telltale sign of this resurgence in Christian worship is the changes now occurring in Bible college and seminary curricula. The demand among the laity for instruction on worship has now reached such proportions academic institutions have begun to supply not only course work on worship topics, but also complete degree programs encompassing the idea, history, and practice of Christian worship. Indeed, Christians and the Christian church are seeking to recover that missing jewel—worship.

But how are we to explain this widespread interest in worship renewal? And what factors or combination of variables have prompted the Christian church to ask how modern people should meet with God in worship?

Like any social or political movement in history, religious movements are most often a complex series of interrelated circumstances, events, and extraordinary personalities. The current so-called liturgical movement proves no exception.

At the risk of reductionism let me simply summarize several of those significant factors contributing to the quest in today's church for worship renewal. First, shifts in formal church polity may impact the idea and practice of worship. The documents of Vatican II (1963–1965) have required a substantial rewriting of the Roman Catholic liturgical books. Second, social change usually spawns religious change. The experimentation of the sixties and seventies resulted in experimentation in worship too, and issues like gender and "political correctness" shape liturgical practice today. Third, emphasis on individual involvement and fulfillment in contemporary society has triggered the long overdue reaction to the passive nature of corporate worship, especially in Protestantism, where the notion of the "frozen chosen" has given way to large-scale lay involvement in worship, particularly in respect to the use of spiritual gifts. And fourth, the "me, here, now, there is no more" philosophy of post-World War II existentialism has run its course. Today people everywhere are seeking an experience with the "transcendent" to bring meaning and perspective to this life. There has been an explosion of religious interest of all sorts, including the classic world religions, the New Age movement, and the assorted cults and "isms" receiving media attention due to some bizarre teaching or practice.

These factors, among many others, have helped bring about today's liturgical movement, which attempts to combine order and freedom, structure and spontaneity, and old traditions with spiritual innovation.[13]

More important than the causes of the liturgical movement are its outcomes or effects. James White has identified five irrevocable effects of the religious experimentation of the past two decades.[14] They include: more inclusive thinking about the people who worship God, the recognition of the importance of imagination in the planning of worship, the developing approaches to worship that maximize our humanness by involving our whole being, awareness of the ecumenical nature of worship, and lastly, the growing realization that worship must be connected to a display of social responsibility.

A complete survey of the current liturgical situation even in the United States proves impossible. If this was true for James White writing on the subject twenty years ago, how much more so today?[15] However, discernible megatrends have emerged as both Protestants and Catholics engage in recovering the riches from earlier traditions and also experiment in balancing freedom and order in worship. These significant trends in worship renewal include

- an emphasis on personal piety and the relationship of individual worship to "body life" and corporate worship.
- the necessity of congregational participation in corporate worship. This movement toward active rather than passive worship may take on a liturgical form combining Word and sacrament, or the manifestation of spiritual gifts as members of the church congregation worship God and minister to each other, or even some combination of the two.
- an investigation of and a return to the traditions of Christian worship in earlier periods of church history.
- the importance of corporate worship designed for the entire family.
- the rejection of one-dimensional, traditionally rational, intellectual worship for more holistic worship that involves all the senses in the spirit of celebration, with priority given to the place of the arts in worship.
- the willingness to accommodate liturgy and church life to surrounding culture.
- the recognition of direct ties between worship and service, including outreach in evangelism and involvement in issues related to social justice.
- the tendency toward ecumenism in worship permitting a sharing in both forms of liturgy and worship theology.

Happily, all these current trends in the worship renewal movement are firmly rooted in the Hebrew idea and practice of the worship of Yahweh in the Old Testament.

What Forms the Basis of Hebrew Worship?

The God of Israel

The question is probably better phrased, "Who is the basis for Hebrew worship?" The reader barely need turn the pages of the opening book of the Old Testament to encounter the object of Hebrew veneration. Israelite worship and devotion were focused solely on the God of creation (Gen. 1:1–2), the God of covenant revelation (Gen. 12:1–3), and the God of redemptive acts in history (Exod. 20:2–3).

Who is the God of the Old Testament that merits the unequivocal worship of humanity? Above all, this God is a holy God (Ps. 99:3–9). Indeed, a favorite epithet of the Old Testament writers for God is "the Holy One of Israel" (2 Kings 19:22; Ps. 71:22; Isa. 1:4). The holiness of God emphasizes his otherness or transcendence, his inaccessibility and unapproachableness, and his mysterious and inscrutable nature. But if this alone were true about God, why worship such a terrible and awesome deity?

Not only is God holy and transcendent, God is "the Holy One in the midst of thee" (Hos. 11:9 KJV). God is the one who dwells "in a high and holy place, but also with him who is contrite and lowly in spirit" (Isa. 57:15). God merits worship because he is able to answer those who call to him and to forgive their wrongdoings (Ps. 99:8). The abiding presence of a holy God dwelling with Israel made them a holy people and raised their consciousness of sin and need for forgiveness (Isa. 6:4–5). It was also the intimate presence of a holy God that prompted heartfelt praise and worship (Ps. 99:3) and the keen desire for holy living (Lev. 19:2).

And yet, this was not enough if God was not sovereign in all of his creation. The sovereignty of God indicates his absolute authority and power over all creation for the purpose of accomplishing his divine will. God's sovereignty is essentially the application of his attribute of omnipotence—utter and unlimited power—to the created order, including the natural world and human history. Israel's redemption could only have been executed by a God who is "majestic in power" (Exod. 15:6). Otherwise the Hebrews would have been little better off than the rest of the nations.

The Old Testament knows only one God who could deliver his

people from their enemies—the Lord who triumphed over Pharaoh and Egypt and redeemed his people (Exod. 15:13), the same Lord who delivered King Hezekiah from the Assyrians (Isa. 37:30–38). The God of Israel alone rules forever (Exod. 15:18) and accomplishes his sovereign plan among the nations (Isa. 14:24–27).

Finally, the holiness of God, the holy immanence of God, and the sovereignty of God make him unique. For the prophet Isaiah the uniqueness of God constituted a call to worship the Lord as King and Redeemer of Israel: "I am the first and I am the last; apart from me there is no God. Who then is like me? . . . Is there any God besides me? No, there is no other Rock; I know not one" (Isa. 44:6–8). The only proper response to this unique God is to assemble before him, turn to him in repentance for salvation, and bow in worship in his presence (Isa. 45:20–23).

The Exodus Event

A. S. Herbert has identified two additional features of Hebrew worship: the idea of salvation history associated with Yahweh's deliverance of Israel in the Exodus and the notion of Israel's covenant relationship with Yahweh, especially the lovingkindness (*hesed*) or constant love of God for his people.[16]

Practically speaking, the mighty deeds of Yahweh demonstrated during the Hebrew exodus from Egypt were responsible for thrusting a monotheistic worship system upon the Hebrew nation.

The Old Testament writers freely conceded that other gods may exist (Deut. 7:4; 8:19). These gods are variously identified as foreign gods (Judg. 10:16), other gods (2 Kings 17:7), false gods (Ps. 40:4), strange gods (Ps. 44:20 KJV), or even new gods (Deut. 32:17 KJV). And though the psalmist decried these gods of the peoples as idols (literally worthless or insignificant things), they were a very real threat to the exclusive worship of Yahweh by the Israelites (Ps. 96:5).

The confrontation between Moses and the magicians of Pharaoh evidenced both the existence and power of the false gods, as these devotees of the Egyptian moon god Thoth were able to duplicate some of the divine signs performed by Moses (Exod. 7:8–13). According to Old Testament and New Testament teaching, these false gods and their idolatrous religious systems are energized by demonic forces (Deut. 32:16–17; Ps. 106:36–37; 1 Cor. 10:20). This demonic enablement included counterfeit signs and wonders (Exod. 7:22; 8:7) and even extended to the foretelling of the future on a limited basis (cf., Acts 16:16–18; 2 Thess. 2:8–12).

However, through the events culminating in the Hebrew exodus from Egypt, Yahweh executed divine judgment on the gods of Egypt (Exod. 12:12) and publicly demonstrated his superiority over all the gods of the people (Exod. 15:11).[17] A. S. Herbert has noted that the activity of these other gods "is so limited and their subordination to Yahweh so complete that, *provided men wholly acknowledge Yahweh's sovereignty*, they can be ignored. For Israel, there is only one source of power, authority, and creativity; and that is Yahweh the Saviour and Redeemer" (italics added).[18]

The response of Jethro, Moses' Midianite father-in-law, typified the desired response to Yahweh's deliverance of Israel when he rejoiced,

> Blessed be the LORD, who has delivered you out of the hand of the Egyptians and out of the hand of Pharaoh. Now I know that the LORD is greater than all gods, because he delivered the people from under the hand of the Egyptians. (Exod. 18:10–11 RSV)

Perhaps more important was Jethro's offering of burnt offerings and sacrifices to God (Exod. 18:12). The Exodus was designed to prompt worship in those who witnessed and among those who heard the account of Yahweh's dealings with the Egyptians. Elsewhere in the Old Testament this ability of Yahweh to deliver his people from their enemies marks the God of the Hebrews as the one truly omnipotent God among all gods (Deut. 3:23–24; Isa. 36:11–20; 37:30–38).

Since this same God who humbled Pharaoh and the Egyptian gods rules our world today, how can our response be anything but that contained in the psalmist's lyric, "I will meditate on all your works and consider all your mighty deeds. Your ways, O God, are holy. What god is so great as our God?" (Ps. 77:12–13).

Covenant Relationship

A third basis for Hebrew worship in the Old Testament is Yahweh's covenant relationship enacted with Israel at Mt. Sinai after the Exodus. The salvation experienced in the exodus event was intended to be an initiation rite into community life and a continuing affiliation with God. In fact, as Elmer Martens describes, the community "at which deliverance aims is a special kind of community, a covenant people under God, as depicted in the statement: 'I will take you for my people, and I will be your God' (Exod. 6:7a RSV)."[19] Thus Yahweh's covenant consists of both a promise—"I will be your God"—and a stipulation or demand—"you will be my people."

According to George E. Mendenhall, the purpose of covenant is to create new relationships, whereas the purpose of law is to regulate existing relationships by ordering means.[20] This new relationship obligated the Israelites to love the Lord God completely (Deut. 6:4–5), worship him alone (Exod. 20:3–4), and love others as themselves (Lev. 19:18). This relationship includes rewards and punishments in the form of blessings and curses attached to covenant law (Deut. 28:1–46). But more importantly, it afforded Yahweh the opportunity to demonstrate his covenant love (ḥesed) to Israel in pardoning iniquity and passing over transgression (Mic. 7:18–20; cf., Isa. 44:21–23).

To sustain this new relationship, divinely ordained legislation was also incorporated into the covenant ceremony. This divine law expressed the extremely perfect moral character of Yahweh, and as such the law laid out the essential principles governing the Hebrew covenant community. The basic purpose of covenant law was to provide instruction for the Israelite community in holy worship and holy living, so that they might be faithful keepers of Yahweh's covenant and enjoy the blessing of his presence (Lev. 26:1–13). Thus Israel, as the people of Yahweh, was prepared to fear God and worship him and to avoid sin (i.e., be holy, Exod. 22:20).

Why Study Old Testament Worship?

The Authority of the Bible

The reasons for studying Old Testament worship are directly linked to the Christian's rationale for studying the Old Testament itself. According to the apostle Paul, the Bible is "inspired" or "breathed out" by God (2 Tim. 3:15–17). The Scriptures (at the time of Paul's writing this referred to the Old Testament only and by implication was later applied to the New Testament canon) have their source and origin in the very person of God. The Bible not only contains the record of God's living Word to humankind, the person and work of Jesus Christ, but also it is God's self-revelation breathed out to men and women through the culture and personality of particular people chosen by God and motivated to speak and write by the Holy Spirit (2 Pet. 1:19–21).

Hence, the doctrine of inspiration makes God the ultimate author of the Bible and the Bible the authoritative word of God's self-disclosure. By authoritative I mean that the Bible has the inherent right to command and enforce obedience based on an intrinsic power that dictates respect for and confidence in the Bible as a source that may be appealed to in support of action or belief. The Bible is the sure, reliable, and trustworthy Word of God. The great *Westminster Confession* of 1647 states, "The authority of the holy Scripture, for which it ought to be believed and obeyed, depends not upon the testimony of any man or church, but wholly upon God (who is truth itself), the Author thereof; and therefore it is to be received, because it is the Word of God" (chapter I, article IV).

Not only are the Scriptures inspired, but Paul further informs us that the Bible is profitable. That is, it is useful, beneficial, advantageous, and valuable for the Christian. Specifically, the apostle wrote that Scripture is useful for teaching or instruction, for conviction or rebuke, for correction and restoration, and lastly for upbringing or guidance in justice and righteousness (2 Tim. 3:16). This means both testaments are profitable for instruction in the sense that they are the positive source for Christian doctrine, including teaching on the worship of God. The work of conviction and correction includes repentance, a necessary prerequisite for worship and proper guidance that prevents false worship. As for training in uprightness the Bible serves as the manual for constructive education in personal piety and Christian living, the foundation for true worship of God.

Finally, the study of the New Testament alone leads to an inadequate picture of God's self-disclosure and his purpose for creation. The two covenants, old and new, are one divine record of God's progressive and redemptive revelation to humankind. The promise of the older covenant finds its fulfillment in the better covenant (Heb. 12:21–24). Emphasis on one covenant over another produces an imbalance, robbing the Word of God of its full force and distorting its one message of salvation accomplished by God within the confines of human history. Following the instruction of the writer to the Hebrews, we too must look to the example of Old Testament worship as an essential part of our Christian heritage as we offer to God acceptable worship with reverence and awe (Heb. 12:28–29).

The Foundation of the New

The New Testament writers appealed to the Old Testament for illustrative examples of instruction and exhortation and for models of faith in God. For instance, the apostle Paul indicated the Old Testament Scriptures were written for our instruction and encouragement (Rom. 15:4–6). The words and deeds of exhortation in the Old Testament are intended to engender hope in the believer so that Christians may live in harmony with one another (one aspect of personal piety) and glorify God with one voice (corporate worship). By referring to the Old Testament example Paul reminds the Christians in Rome that unity and harmony in worship are the by-product of unity and harmony in life.

Elsewhere, Paul drew from episodes of Israelite history during the post-exodus desert trek as warnings to the New Testament church against impious personal behavior and idolatry in worship (1 Cor. 10:1–13). The negative example of Hebrew personal piety and corporate worship after the Exodus served to admonish the church in Corinth, lest they too experience the judgment of God. This passage becomes extremely important for our understanding of the value of the Old Testament for the New Testament church, as Paul assumed the facts of Israel's history had significance for the Corinthians. Paul clearly understands Israel's history in the Old Testament as having "a typical sense, that is, there are real events, but those events also have meaning for a later generation."[21]

And finally, the New Testament commends the reader to carefully consider the models of faith in God found in the Old Testament. Paul singles out Abraham as a prime Old Testament example of faith in God and uses him as supporting evidence for the central doctrine of Christianity—justification by faith in Jesus Christ (Rom. 4). Jewish Christians facing persecution in Jerusalem were encouraged to hold fast their confession of Christ, given their heritage of faith documented in the Old Testament (Heb. 11). Faith in God is one of the characteristics of personal piety and is foundational to genuine worship. In Hebrews 11 the faith of three individuals is specifically connected with acts of worship—Abel in verse 4, Abraham in verse 17, and Moses in verse 28. These examples of faith pointed to Christ as the pioneer and perfecter of our faith, warned believers against apostasy, and encouraged the continual sacrifice of praise and good deeds in the name of the Lord (Heb. 12:2; 13:9, 15–16).

Christ-centered Worship

According to Robert E. Webber, Christian worship takes place in and through Jesus Christ, who is the eternal praise of God the Father because of his perfect work of redemption.[22] The worship of the church is an offering or sacrifice of praise and thanksgiving to God through the Son who secured our salvation (Heb. 13:15–16). Thus, Christ's ministry of redemption mediates our worship to the Father and the blessings and grace of the Father to us (Eph. 1:13–14; 1 Pet. 1:3).

The Christ-centered nature of our worship is indeed self-evident, which raises the question how does the Old Testament factor into the worship principles for the church of Jesus Christ? Although the character of Hebrew worship in the Old Testament is essentially theocentric, the New Testament writers understood the older covenant to foreshadow the person and work of Jesus Christ in a variety of ways. For example, the writer of the letter to the Hebrews identified Jesus Christ as the fulfillment of the Old Testament tabernacle, priesthood, and sacrificial system (Heb. 6; 9; this method of biblical interpretation—establishing historical correspondence between Old Testament events, persons, objects, or ideas and similar New Testament events, persons, objects, or ideas—is labeled *typology*). (See Chapter 12.) Moreover, Jesus himself taught the disciples that the Old Testament was the book of the Messiah and that he was the Messiah of Israel (Luke 24:44–46).

The study of Old Testament worship then, yields two important benefits for the individual Christian and the church of Jesus Christ in respect to the Christocentric nature of Christian worship. First, the study of the Old Testament as the book of the Messiah contributes to our understanding of Jesus of Nazareth's fulfillment of that promise and thus enhances our comprehension of Christology, or the doctrine of Jesus Christ. In turn, our improved knowledge of the person and work of Jesus Christ in light of Old Testament predictions fosters a greater appreciation for and a deeper recognition of the truly Christocentric nature of Christian worship. All of this may revitalize the truth that "Christ is all, and is in all" (Col. 3:11).

Hebrew Anthropology

True worship must be a response of the whole person to the God of creation and redemption. The holistic emphasis of Hebrew anthropology in the Old Testament has long been recognized. While Hebrew anthropology affirms the individual is comprised of distinguishable physical and spiritual elements, there is no systematic distinction between the material and the immaterial, the physical and the spiritual in the Old Testament. According to the pattern of ancient Hebrew thought, a human being is an indivisible totality or unity.[23] Thus, it is the whole person, not just the immaterial, or spiritual, essence of an individual, that blesses the holy name of the Lord (Pss. 84:2; 103:1).[24]

This synthetic understanding of the nature and constitution of humanity in the Hebrew Old Testament proves most valuable for the study of the relevance of Israelite worship for contemporary Christianity.

First, grasping the biblical truth that we are indivisible unities in the image of God combining both the material and immaterial elements of life is a potent antidote for the far-reaching effects of the Platonic dualism within Western thought.[25] Acknowledging the interrelatedness of the physical and the spiritual in human beings prevents the false dichotomy of the sacred from the secular from undermining Christian beliefs, values, and practices. Hebrew anthropology teaches that all facets of life lived out under God are sacred—work, play, and worship.[26]

Second, the holistic emphasis of Hebrew anthropology encourages participatory worship, permitting a "whole person" response to God's self-disclosure. The individual believer is truly free to worship God with his or her total being—mind, emotions, will, personality, senses, body. (See Chapter 7.)

And third, the study of Hebrew anthropology as recorded in the

Old Testament fosters the notion that the individual is essentially a member of society at large. This sense of corporate identity or belonging to the organic unity of humanity has important implications for worship. As a member of the people of God, whether Israel in the Old Testament or the church in the New Testament, the individual belongs to a society, a worshiping community. Ultimately, that worshiping community brings depth and meaning to the worldview and life of the individual.[27] Thus individual and privatized worship finds its completion in corporate and public worship (Heb. 10:25).

Judeo-Christian Worship

The Old Testament accounts depicting the life of the Israelite nation provide the pattern for public worship in both Judaism and Christianity. Specifically, the covenant ceremony between God and the Hebrews at Mt. Sinai "contains the most basic structural elements for a meeting between God and his people."[28] These five elements constitute the very substance of corporate public worship in both the Jewish synagogue and the Christian church:

1. God called his people to meet with him.
2. The entire congregation had responsibility in the worship of God.
3. God proclaimed his divine Word, revealing his person, will, and purpose to the Hebrews through his covenant law.
4. The Israelites accepted the covenant with Yahweh and submitted to his authority. The worshiping community would be continually involved in the experience of covenant renewal with Yahweh (essentially the purpose of the Eucharist or Lord's Table in the New Testament—covenant renewal in the proclamation of the Lord's death, 1 Cor. 11:17–32).
5. God sealed his covenant with Israel by blood sacrifice, a foreshadowing of the supreme sacrifice of Jesus Christ as the Lamb of God (John 1:29; Heb. 9:23—10:10).

◆ 1 ◆

Increase Your Word Power
An Old Testament Worship Vocabulary

OVER THE DECADES the editors of *Reader's Digest* have challenged readers to expand their knowledge of the English language by means of a twenty-question vocabulary quiz, titled "It Pays to Enrich Your Word Power." The monthly multiple-choice vocabulary quiz sometimes focuses on a topic or theme and is always educational and entertaining. However, the underlying premise of this brainteaser is simply stated—words are power. There is an assumed correlation between one's control of words and the shape of his or her destiny. As Peter Funk notes, "The words in a well-developed vocabulary are like the sturdy rungs of a ladder, helping you to make life's climb easier, as well as more pleasurable and successful."[1]

Words were power in the mind of the ancients as well. Among the Assyrians, Babylonians, and Egyptians the word represented more than the mere expression of thought. The spoken or written word was regarded as a living force, a concrete entity that possessed an intrinsic and powerful dynamic. This was especially true of the divine word, the word responsible for creating and sustaining all things.[2]

The exact understanding of the nature of this inherent potency of the word is difficult to assess, because this concept varied among the cultures of the ancient Orient. Today biblical scholars agree the effectiveness of the word in Hebrew thought differed substantially from that found in ancient Near Eastern sources. The efficacy of the divine word in Old Testament times was not intrinsic or peculiar to the word itself. Nor was it rooted in primitive magical practices and superstitions, as in the case of the Egyptians and Mesopotamians.[3] Rather, the vitality and power of the word of the Hebrew God is a function of his conscious and moral personality. Thus, the power and authority of the divine word in the Old Testament are rooted in the very person of Yahweh and as such are the reflection of the totality of his divine nature, character, and attributes.

Words reflect the totality of a person's nature and character at the human level too. Indeed, our words often reveal (or even betray) human motive, personality, and character more than we care to admit. The Bible affirms this dimension of word power. For instance, the Old Testament sages recognized that the foolish and the wicked tended to multiply words (Prov. 10:19; Eccles. 10:14), while the wise and the righteous restrained their words (Prov. 17:27; Eccles. 5:2). Also, Jesus stated that the words of the mouth proceeded directly from the heart, thus exposing the true nature of the person speaking (Matt. 15:10–20). More than the food we eat or the literature we read, "we are what we say"; we are known by our words.

Like the New Testament, the Old Testament employs several different terms all translated by our English word *worship*.[4] Just as our speech reveals motive, personality, and character, so too understanding the words describing Old Testament worship is helpful for understanding the nature of Hebrew ritual. The words of worship used by the biblical writers reveal several important aspects of Israelite religious belief and practice. In the following pages these Hebrew vocabulary items are arranged alphabetically by root. As you increase your Old Testament word power, this introduction to the key ideas associated with Israelite worship will build an essential database for understanding the topics developed in subsequent chapters.

Words of Worship

Worship As Spiritual Inquiry

The Hebrew root DRŠ (*dārash*) may be rendered "worship" in English (Ezra 4:2; 6:21 RSV), but more often the term is translated "seek" or "inquire" (Pss. 24:6; 69:32; Isa. 11:10). The word has singular implications for worship in the Old Testament since it addresses the issue of personal desire and heartfelt intent on the part of the suppliant. Genuine worship is a quest for God not out of obligation or duty but freely and earnestly in gratitude for his goodness (Pss. 27:4, 8–9; 63:1–4). Hence, the worship of the God-seeker is unfeigned, not like the worship of those who honor the Lord with their lips while their hearts remain cold and distant (Isa. 29:13).

The prophet Hosea likened this seeking after God to a hunter pursuing the prey as he exhorted Israel to "press on" to know the Lord (Hos. 6:3; the same thought is echoed in Paul's prayer in Phil. 3:12–14). This desire to seek, know, and worship the Lord of Hosts may be prompted by distress and trouble, as in the laments of the psalmist (Ps. 9:9–10), or by love and adoration in thanksgiving for God's goodness to the righteous (Ps. 119:2, 10, 68). In either case the God-seeker's quest is not in vain because the Lord responds to those who pursue him, giving pardon for sin, the blessing and hope of salvation, and deliverance from enemies (Pss. 69:32; 70:4; Jer. 5:1).

Worship As Reverent Obedience

Our English vocabulary includes the word *revere*, which means "to venerate" or "to fear" with a sense of awe and respect. In the Old Testament, the Hebrew word YR' (*yārē'*) describes this kind of fear and awe for the Lord of Israel by his people (Exod. 14:31; Deut. 31:12–13). The righteous fear or revere Yahweh because of who he is as a unique, holy, just, loving, and merciful God (Pss. 86:11; 103:11; 112:1) and for what he does as Creator, Covenant Maker, and Israel's Redeemer (Lev. 19:32; Ps. 27:1; Hab. 3:2).

This fear of the Lord is tinged with a reverence bordering on terror and dread. The Lord God is to be feared above all gods (Ps. 96:4) because he has the authority to both deliver the righteous (Isa. 43:1, 5) and judge the wicked (Joel 2:31; Mal. 1:6). This is especially true as Israel anticipates the Day of the Lord, when God will place fear in the hearts of his faithful for their own good (Jer. 32:38–41). But the rebellious and faithless ones who possess no fear of God will be consumed in his wrath (Zeph. 3:1–8).

This fearful reverence for God Almighty motivated both worship and service on the part of the righteous, according to the Old Testament (Deut. 6:13; 10:20; Pss. 22:23; 135:20). The covenant-keeping Israelite was charged to "fear God" and "serve him" (Eccles. 12:12). This call to reverent obedience was characterized by a constant passion for doing God's commandments and walking in his ways (Deut. 8:13, 22). For the Hebrews it was the fear of the Lord that ultimately led to life (Prov. 19:23).

According to James Crenshaw the fear of the Lord was "religious devotion in the richest sense of the phrase. It meant purely and simply, that which every human being owes the Creator."[5] This devotion incorporated both the idea of appropriate awe in the face of divine mystery and observing the covenant obligations of the divine law given to Israel (Deut. 5:29; 8:6; 17:19; Job 25:2; Ps. 25:12, 14). Thus, worship as reverent obedience marked the practical outworking of the fear of God in the life of the community of faith—formally in proper religious service (2 Chron. 19:9–10; Pss. 2:11; 76:11) and informally in right living (Job 1:1; Prov. 3:7; 16:6).

Worship As Loyal Service

The basic meaning of the Hebrew root 'BD ('ābad) is "work" or "service" (Exod. 5:18; Num. 8:25). However, the term can mean "worship" when used in the context of performing a service to false gods (Jer. 16:13) or the God of Israel (Exod. 3:12; Isa. 19:21, 23). The central idea of the word as it relates to worship is the notion of obedience to a set of divine commands, whether prescriptions for religious rites or rules governing behavior (Deut. 10:12, 20; Josh. 22:5). Service in this context is submission to the will of the deity and compliance with his divine directives.

The close relationship between service and worship is emphasized in the Mosaic sermons of Deuteronomy (4:19; 8:19; 17:3). In the Old Testament the service rendered to God constituted worship in that it demonstrated a faithfulness and loyalty which issued from the human will (Deut. 10:12, 20; 30:15–20). This obedient service was demanded by God as Israel's sovereign to the point of "clinging" (literally, being "welded" or "soldered") to him in utter dependence and swearing an oath of allegiance by his name. Repeatedly the Hebrews were challenged consciously to choose between loyal service to the gods of the nations and allegiance to Yahweh as their covenant God (Josh. 24:14–15).

The Hebrew prophets recognized that the service of worship to God was polluted by the divided loyalties among the Israelites. The exchange of loyalties in service from Yahweh to the baals of the nations was an abomination to the Lord (Deut. 7:25; 27:15). As Israel's covenant maker and guarantor he had every right to expect uncompromised fidelity to his covenant stipulations (Deut. 4:31; Ps. 111:5). Sadly, Israel's history was a constant replay of treachery and deceit (Ps. 78:56–58). Try as they might, the Hebrews could never escape the haunting rebuke of Elijah, "How long will you waver between two opinions?" (1 Kings 18:21). Of course, Jesus later instructed his disciples on the folly of attempting to give allegiance to two masters (Matt. 6:24; cf., 4:10).

Worship As Personal Ministry

The ministry of worship belonged to the Levitical priesthood in the Old Testament (Deut. 10:8). The Hebrew word ŠRT (shārat) describes this priestly ministry of worship and is usually translated "attend" (Gen. 39:4, in the context of serving human rulers) or "minister" (Deut. 18:5–7; Ezek. 44:12, in the context of serving idols or God). In one instance the Revised Standard Version translates ŠRT (shārat) as "worship," in association with Israel's penchant to serve the wood and stone idols of the nations (Ezek. 20:32).

This word may indicate a higher order of service than the Hebrew 'BD ('ābad), since it is applied to the personalized and specialized service of attendants to important personages (2 Chron. 22:8), the service of the priests to the Lord (Jer. 33:21–22), and even the angels who do God's bidding (Ps. 103:21). The notion of official or formal authorization may factor in here too, as all three categories of ministers were appointed or commissioned to render particular service to their master or Lord.

The implications of the word ŠRT (shārat) for Old Testament worship are numerous and profound. First, the idea of a divine charge or commission to minister as a priest before God suggests solemn responsibilities. The priest not only represented the people of Israel in the presence of the Lord of the covenant (Deut. 10:8), but also stood as God's official representative in the covenant community to teach, interpret, and enforce God's covenant law (Num. 16:9). Old Testament law demonstrates the seriousness of this priestly responsibility in that anyone who defied Levitical authority was punishable by death (Deut. 17:12). Likewise, the priest who acted presumptuously in ministry before God risked the death penalty (cf., the story of Aaron's sons in Lev. 10:1–11).

In addition, this worship term signified a type of quality control for priestly ministry by the Levites within the Israelite community. Even as the special garments peculiar to the priesthood distinguished them as ministers to the Lord (Exod. 28:25, 43; 35:19; 39:1, 26, 41), so their service to God was to be marked by blameless precision in performing the divinely appointed duties of Hebrew religious practice (Num. 1:50–54, 3:31; Ps. 101:6). The integrity and competence of Levitical service before Yahweh was the benchmark by which all Israel (Isa. 61:6), and eventually all Gentiles (Isa. 56:6–7), would stand and minister as priests before God.

Finally, the ministry of worship for the Levitical priesthood was a lifelong calling of selfless personal service to God (Num. 8:23–26). For this reason the tribe of Levi received no inheritance of land in Canaan when the tribal allotments were made after the conquest of the land of promise (Josh. 14:3–5). The inheritance of the Levites was God himself—to keep the ark of the covenant and to stand before the Lord to minister to him and to bless his name (Deut. 10:8–9).

Worship As Genuine Humility

The Hebrew term ŠHH (shāhâ) is the most widely used Old Testament word for worship. English Bibles understand the expression in a variety of ways, including: bow down (low or deeply, Gen. 18:2; 47:31), prostrate oneself or do homage (Isa. 49:7), or worship (Gen. 24:26; Exod. 12:37). The literal meaning of the verbal root is the act of falling down and groveling or even wallowing on the ground before royalty (2 Sam. 14:22; 1 Kings 1:16) or deity (Exod. 34:8; 2 Sam. 12:20; 2 Kings 19:37).

Whether in the context of doing obeisance to the king or worshiping a deity, the basic idea conveyed is unworthiness and humility. The word pictures an inferior being in the presence of a superior being. This relationship of an inferior to a superior may include that of the creature before the Creator (Ps. 95:6), the Old Testament faithful before a holy and righteous God (Josh. 5:15; Ps. 25:6–10), or a loyal subject before his or her king (1 Kings 1:16; 2 Chron. 20:18). In each case, the issue is the honest appraisal of one's place or station in relationship to deity, civil authorities, and other people. Thus worship springs from an attitude and posture of humility prompted by the recognition of one's rank or standing in the order of God's creation (Ps. 8:3–8).

More importantly, genuine humility is the sacrifice acceptable to God (Ps. 51:17). The Lord turns his face and extends his favor to the humble and contrite of heart (Isa. 66:2). The God of heaven and earth abases the proud, but he saves the humble (Job 22:29). For this reason the prophet Micah exhorted the Israelites "to walk humbly with your God" (6:8). Jesus Christ is the ultimate example of humility before God, for "he humbled himself and became obedient to death" (Phil. 2:8).[6]

Worship As Prostration in Prayer

There is one Aramaic term for worship used exclusively in the story of King Nebuchadnezzar's golden image and the fiery furnace recounted in the book of Daniel, chapter three. The root SGD (sĕgid) means to "do homage" or "prostrate oneself in worship" (Dan. 3:5–7, 10–12, 14–18, 28). The expression is used in conjunction with the verb NPL (nāpal), "to fall on one's face" or "fall down." In this context worship is equated with a position of prostration before the deity, much like the Hebrew ŠḤH (shāḥâ). More than reverence, the word connotes the subservient relationship of a feudal tenant or vassal to the overlord. The act of prostration signifies the vassal's submission and loyalty to the authority of the overlord. In the case of Nebuchadnezzar's golden image, religious homage to the god was tantamount to political homage to the king of Babylon.

The Hebrew cognate SGD (sāgad) may be a loan word from Aramaic as it occurs only in Isaiah 44:15, 17, 19, and 46:6. In context the term implies prostration in prayer before a deity (worthless idols, cf., Isa. 44:10), as the worshiper thanks his god for daily provisions and petitions his god for deliverance (Isa. 44:17). Bowing or kneeling in prayer was also an acknowledgment of weakness, dependence, and inability on the part of the worshiper. Normally the custom in the ancient Near East was to stand for public prayer, so prostration in prayer became a symbol of abject humility before God on the part of the suppliant.[7]

Worship As Nearness to God

Finally, a cluster of Hebrew verbs, associated with the practice of Old Testament worship, is frequently used in the context of Israelite religious observance and includes terms like: *BW'* (*bô'*, "to come, enter"), *HLK* (*hālak*, "to go, walk"), *NGŠ* (*nāgash*, "to approach"), and *QRB* (*qārab*, "to draw near"). While none of these words is formally translated "worship" in the English Bible, they are often paired with the vocabulary for Old Testament worship discussed above (2 Kings 16:12–13; Ps. 69:18; Isa. 58:2; Ezek. 44:15–16).

For instance, the word *NGŠ* (*nāgash*) suggests worshiping God is analogous to approaching a person of high rank or a king. Approaching such an exalted personage required formal invitation or appointment (Lev. 9:6–7; Num. 4:19; Jer. 30:21), the careful observance of appropriate protocol (Exod. 19:10–15), and the performance of proper rites of purification (Exod. 19:22; 20:21).

The idea of drawing near to God in worship also implies an intimate relationship in spirit with the deity, since both *NGŠ* (*nāgash*) and *QRB* (*qārab*) may be used figuratively to signify sexual relations between a man and a woman (Gen. 20:4; Exod. 19:15; Deut. 22:14). The Old Testament prophets clearly understood that "drawing near to God" was more than mere spatial proximity. Zephaniah acknowledged this expression of spiritual intimacy in his coupling of drawing near to God with trust in the Lord (Zeph. 3:2), whereas both Isaiah and Jeremiah linked approaching God with genuine, heartfelt devotion, not hollow lip service (Isa. 29:13; Jer. 12:2). Even the Hebrew sage advised it is better to "go near to listen rather than to offer the sacrifice of fools," underscoring the quality of relationship and not the obligatory performance of religious rites (Eccles. 5:1).

Both *NGŠ* (*nāgash*) and *QRB* (*qārab*) also have a technical meaning related to the Old Testament ritual of animal sacrifice. Most often the terms are translated "offer" (Lev. 1:3; Mal. 1:7–8). The sacrifices may be presented by the priest (Lev. 7:8; 16:6) or by a member of the covenant community (1 Chron. 16:1; Ezra 8:35). These words commonly describe the offering or presentation of specifically designated sacrifices necessary for approaching the Holy One of Israel (the burnt offering, Lev. 1:10; the cereal offering, Lev. 2:14; the peace offering, Lev. 3:1; etc.). When used in the context of sacrificial ritual, these supplemental Old Testament worship words connote the careful step-by-step adherence to the detailed instructions prescribed by Mosaic Law for the offering of animal and grain sacrifices (the cereal offering in Lev. 6:14–23). Essentially then, they convey the idea that the process of offering sacrifices to God as part of Hebrew worship was every bit as important as the final product—a complete sacrifice pleasing to the Lord (Lev. 1:9, 13, 17; cf., Malachi's indictment of Israel for profaning the process of sacrifice, 1:6–14).

Last, and perhaps most important, these worship words indicate the Lord is indeed an approachable God. He not only invites his people to draw near to him so that they might live (Deut. 4:7; HLK [hālak], "come" in Isa. 55:1, 3), but he also draws near to all those who call on his name (Lam. 3:57). Specifically, the Lord draws near to the brokenhearted and delivers them from their troubles as a divine helper or ally (Ps. 34:17–18). The most practical demonstration of the nearness of God for the Hebrew people was the revealed word or covenant commandments of the Lord and the divine enablement permitting them to keep his statutes (Deut. 30:11–14). Of course, the ultimate proof of the nearness of God was to come much later, at the initiation of the new covenant when the "Word became flesh and made his dwelling among us" (John 1:14).

What Is Your Vocabulary Rating?

The *Reader's Digest* vocabulary quiz always includes the list of correct answers on the following page. Those with the self-discipline to take the quiz without peeking ahead are rewarded with immediate feedback. Although not a formally structured quiz, the intent of this study of Old Testament worship vocabulary is similar to that of "It Pays to Enrich Your Word Power" in at least two, and, perhaps, three ways. First, the investigation and analysis of the Hebrew words for worship improves our understanding of the nature and character of Israelite religious belief and practice. Second, our examination of the terminology describing Old Testament worship provides the opportunity for the joy of discovery. This is true both for identifying the key ideas and concepts foundational to Hebrew worship and for thoughtfully considering the ramifications of the Old Testament worship for the contemporary Christian church. And third, like the enthusiastic reader of "It Pays to Enrich Your Word Power," who anxiously awaits the challenge of a new quiz in the next month's issue, perhaps your recently acquired worship word power will pique your interest in continuing the study of Hebrew worship in the Old Testament.

So in summary, what do the words used by the biblical writers teach us about the nature, character, and practice of Old Testament worship as spiritual inquiry, reverent obedience, loyal service, personal ministry, genuine humility, prostration in prayer, and nearness to God? Here is a brief catalog of key ideas and important principles:

- Worship is a response to a person—God as Creator and Redeemer.
- Worship involves the whole person—body, intellect, volition, emotion, etc.
- Worship is complex, diverse, and may be highly specialized.
- Worship is a relationship more than a function or ritual.
- Worship is an active, not a passive, experience.[8]
- Worship may be true or false.
- Worship may be formal or informal, structured or spontaneous.
- Worship is "serious business."
- Worship is a life-style more than an act or event.
- The act of worship reinforces the attitudes of service, loyalty, and humility necessary for true worship.
- True worship of God is motivated by love, not duty.

◆ 2 ◆

The Fear of the Lord Is Clean

The Place of Personal Piety in Worship

THE DEFINITIONS OF WORSHIP presented in the Introduction and Chapter 1 all possess a common denominator: worship is essentially spiritual, an attitude and habit of the heart. Since the heart or inner person is the wellspring or fountainhead of the worship of God, it is necessary to have a right heart before God in order to offer right or true worship. Personal piety concerns this right heart before God, and thus is directly related to the worship of the Lord in the Old Testament (and the New Testament for that matter). Personal piety then is the one necessary precondition for all Hebrew worship, the formal and the informal, the spontaneous and the structured, the individual and the corporate.

According to William Dyrness, if worship is the response of the believing heart to God, then piety in the Old Testament "is the response of the heart to God's self-revelation."[1] The Old Testament frequently equates piety with the fear of the Lord (Prov. 14:2). True piety is rooted in the attitudes of reverence, submission, and obedience to a personal God. Piety is an active response of the whole person to divine self-disclosure, and it encompasses the entirety of the human experience. The characteristics of Old Testament piety are discussed below and include the fear of the Lord, faith in God, separation from the world, consecration to God, and personal holiness.

J. I. Packer has identified obeying the gospel (Rom. 10:16) and holiness (1 Thess. 4:3) as the essence of piety in the New Testament.

Further, the piety God commends in the New Testament includes

> the practical expression of faith in a life of repentance, resisting tempta-
> tion and mortifying sin; in habits of prayer, thanksgiving and reverent
> observance of the Lord's Supper; in the cultivation of hope, love, gener-
> osity, joy, self-control, patient endurance and contentment; in the quest
> for honesty, uprighteousness and the good of others in all human rela-
> tions; in respect for divinely constituted authority in church, State, fam-
> ily and household.[2]

There is considerable overlap between the old and new covenants on what it means to have a right heart before God. Indeed,
the Teacher's injunction to "fear God and keep his commandments"
(Eccles. 12:13) finds its complement in John's summary of the distinctive features of Christian piety—namely, faith in Christ, keeping
God's commands, and showing love toward fellow Christians (1 John
3:22–24).

Personal Piety: What Are Its Characteristics?

Fear of the Lord

The fear of the Lord has already been defined theologically in
Chapter 1. The concern here is the practical outworking of the fear
of Yahweh within the community of the upright for living well as
servants of God. The concept of the fear of the Lord is especially
prominent in Hebrew wisdom literature, and according to Elmer A.
Martens, "it is heralded as . . . the means to life. The fear of Yahweh
is not terror but a reverence for God which expresses itself in positive
responses to God and his Word."[3]

The book of Proverbs equates the fear of the Lord with the
knowledge of God (2:5–6). In the Old Testament, the knowledge of
God is associated with the experience of covenant relationship with
Yahweh (Hos. 6:1–3). Since God alone possesses wisdom and dis-
penses understanding to humanity (Prov. 2:6–8), only those who
know God through the experience of covenant loyalty will find wisdom's hidden treasures—righteousness, justice, equity, and every
good path (Prov. 2:4, 9; 3:3).

It is the idea of the fear of the Lord that bridges the human and
the divine is such a way that God's storehouse of wisdom for living

in favor with God and others is available to his saints (Prov. 2:7–10, 20; 3:4). The fear of Yahweh in Old Testament wisdom literature is a response of attitude and will that molds human behavior in conformity with the commandments of God. Specifically, the acquisition of the fear of the Lord as described by the Hebrew sages involves

- the desire to "get understanding" stemming from a choice grounded in the human will (Prov. 1:29; 2:5).
- awe and reverence for the God of creation and redemption, which elicits genuine worship and willing obedience to his commands (Prov. 24:21).
- dread at God's holiness and trepidation of his divine judgment (Eccles. 12:13–14).
- faith and trust in God's plan for human life, and a rejection of pride and self-reliance (Ps. 115:11; Prov. 3:5–6; 14:26).
- hating and avoiding evil, and refusing to envy sinners (Prov. 3:7; 8:13; 16:6; 23:17).
- disciplined instruction that instills wisdom, humility, and honor (Prov. 15:33; 22:4).

So then, while the fear of the Lord is an attitude that includes the emotion of reverence and awe for a unique, holy, all-powerful, and all-knowing God, it is primarily "a way of life based on a sober estimate of God's presence and care."[4] This fear of Yahweh fostered an awareness among the Hebrew faithful that God is clearly above all, providentially "ensuring the outcomes of a personal life in accordance with one's character and action."[5] Thus, the upright may live in quiet confidence, knowing that the blessing of Yahweh rests on the head of the righteous (Prov. 10:6).

Finally, the fear of the Lord provides the basis for the worship of God in the Old Testament. Only the fear of Yahweh preserves the inscrutable nature of God (Eccles. 3:11) and maintains the profound mystery of life (Eccles. 3:12–15). True worship of God springs from our inability to answer two simple questions posed by a biblical understanding of the fear of the Lord: (1) O God, who is like you in power, righteousness, mighty deeds, and in pardoning sin (Ps. 71:18–19; Mic. 7:18–20)? and (2) what are woman and man that

God should look down from heaven and care for them and lift them up to sit with princes (Pss. 8:4; 113:5–8)?

Faith in God

The prophet Habakkuk declared "the righteous will live by his faith" (2:4). These words were proclaimed to the doomed nation of Judah, not long before the destruction of Jerusalem by the Babylonians in 587 B.C. (ca. 600 B.C.). This is a rare Old Testament passage where *faith* signifies the religious response to God on the part of humankind. A contemporary paraphrase taken from the counter-culture movement of the sixties captures the gist of the prophet's oracle: "Keep the faith, baby!" What did it mean for the ancient Hebrews to keep the faith?

The Hebrew word for *faith* occurs infrequently in the Old Testament. (The word *faith* is found only twice in the KJV, eleven times in the NIV, and eighteen times in the RSV.) However, the rarity of the word in the Old Testament does not mean the concept was unimportant. To the contrary, the profuse distribution of synonyms like *believe, hope, trust,* and *wait* indicates the idea was central to Hebrew religion (Pss. 25:2; 31:6; 38:15; 78:22). Faith in the Old Testament has been succinctly described by Ronald Youngblood, as "both subjective and objective, it is both an attitude and an action, it is both believing and receiving. As an attitude, true faith may be described as complete dependence on a dependable and trustworthy God."[6]

This attitude and the action of faith may be seen in the psalmist's exhortation to the righteous,

> Trust in the LORD and do good:
>   dwell in the land and enjoy safe pasture.
> Delight yourself in the LORD
>   and he will give you the desires of your heart.
> Commit your way to the LORD;
>   trust in him and he will do this . . . .
> Be still before the LORD and wait patiently for him.
>   (Ps. 37:3–5, 7a)

Without question the poet appeals to the righteous to live an upright life by advocating an attitude of trust in the Lord and an active response of right living before God. In commenting on this psalm William Dyrness understands faith as the "voluntary surrender to God for guidance."[7]

Faith is the attitude and the action of absolute trust or reliance in God. Indeed, God and his flawless character, his mighty works, and his sure word are the only legitimate objects of faith recognized by the Old Testament writers. The faith and trust of the righteous during Old Testament times was but a response to Yahweh's faithfulness in keeping his covenant promises to Israel (Ps. 111:8; Lam. 3:23). Perhaps King David best represents this faith response of the upright in heart when he wrote, "Because your steadfast love is before my eyes, I walk in faithfulness to thee" (Ps. 26:3). And yet, repeatedly the Old Testament likens the Israelites to a faithless wife who has scattered her "favors" among the nations by forsaking the commandments of the Lord (Jer. 3:11–20; cf., Ps. 119:158).

Thankfully, however, faith and repentance are closely related in the Old Testament Scriptures. The prophet Jeremiah could condemn the "faithless wife" Israel and then call her to repentance all in the same breath: "Return, faithless people; I will cure you of backsliding" (Jer. 3:22). The reluctant preacher Jonah could only acknowledge a gracious God who accepted the Ninevites when they believed God and turned from their evil ways (Jon. 3:5–10; 4:2). Even more important though, the reward of repentance coupled with faith is atonement for iniquity (Prov. 16:6) and salvation provided by the Lord (Pss. 13:5; 24:5; 40:10).

Despite continued misperceptions the upright in the Old Testament were not redeemed by their deeds of righteousness (Ps. 14:1–3; Isa. 64:6; Ezek. 3:20; 18:24). Again David illustrates the true nature of "saving faith" in the Old Testament when he prayed for divine vindication on the basis of his trust—"I have trusted in the LORD without wavering" (Ps. 26:1). He appealed to his integrity, or deeds of righteousness, as evidence of his faith in God, knowing full well that redemption was found in Yahweh's steadfast love and grace alone (26:3, 11). Thus, the life of faith in the Old Testament was the life of obedience to the law of the Lord, again prompting the psalmist to proclaim, "I have chosen the way of truth; I have set my heart on your laws" (Ps. 119:30).[8]

The Old Testament states, "Abram believed the LORD, and he credited it to him as righteousness" (Gen. 15:6). In the New Testa-

ment the apostle Paul upholds the Hebrew patriarch as Exhibit A
for the defense of the doctrine of justification by faith alone (Rom.
4:1–15). As Paul develops his arguments it becomes clear there is
great continuity between the old and new covenants when it comes
to faith in God. Faith remains both an attitude of trust and the action of obedience to God's word (Rom. 4:10–12); faith is grounded
in the same object—the personal God of biblical revelation (Rom.
4:20–21); and faith has the same reward in both covenants—hope
in sharing the glory of God (Rom. 5:2). All this prompts Ronald
Youngblood to conclude, "'Believing God' is the definition of faith
that is at once its simplest and its most profound. Although at an
earlier period and from an alien perspective, the saints of the Old
Testament shared a confidence in God's promises that was remarkably akin to ours."[9]

Separation from the World

The intention of Yahweh's theocratic charter with Israel at Sinai
was to make the Hebrews a distinct people group, separate from the
other nations (Lev. 20:24, 26). Their call to priestly holiness was
designed to mark them as God's special possession as a sign of his
ownership of all nations and the entire earth (Exod. 19:5–6). The
later history of Israel in the Old Testament is essentially a recounting
of the Hebrew success or failure in maintaining this priestly holiness
as a separate people.[10]

The vehicle for establishing Israel as a distinct and holy people
was the covenant law instituted by the Lord at Mt. Sinai and ratified
by the Hebrew community (Exod. 24:1–8). The stipulations or laws
of God's theocratic charter with Israel regulated all aspects of Hebrew life, including diet and personal hygiene (Lev. 11; 13), morality
(Lev. 18; 20), the civil and judicial realms (Exod. 21—23), the calendar (Lev. 25), and the religious and ceremonial realms (Lev. 1—7).
All this was written so that the Hebrews would not follow the ways
of their neighbors in Egypt and Canaan (Lev. 18:3). This separation
from the world on the part of the Hebrews permitted Yahweh to be
their God and to live and move among them as his people (Isa.
52:11; Jer. 31:31; Ezek. 37:27).

Of course, this command to be a separate people is reiterated in
the New Testament, as Jesus called his disciples to be in the world

but not of the world (John 15:19; 17:14–16). And Paul warned the Corinthian church that righteousness has no accord with iniquity, and thus to "come out from them and be separate, says the Lord" (2 Cor. 6:14–18).

Consecration to God and Personal Holiness

A fourth characteristic of personal piety in the Old Testament is that of consecration to God and personal holiness. By *consecrate* the Old Testament means to dedicate or set apart for service to God (Deut. 15:19; Jer. 1:5) or to sanctify or make holy (Exod. 30:29–30). Most often the act of consecration was associated with the sanctifying or setting apart of certain persons or objects for special roles or purposes in the worship of Yahweh, like the priests (Exod. 29:1–9) and the tabernacle furniture (Exod. 30:22–38). Unlike the surrounding pagan nations who consecrated themselves to Baal or other deities (Hos. 9:10), the Hebrews were a people consecrated to God for worship and service. Much of the sacrificial system instituted by the Lord reminded the Israelites of the reality of this fact on a regular basis. All firstborn sons were consecrated to the Lord (Exod. 13:11–16), symbolizing divine redemption of families at the Exodus). The firstborn of the flocks were also consecrated to God (Deut. 15:19–23), lest the Hebrews forget the divine origin of their material bounty, and the priesthood was consecrated for service to God on behalf of the whole nation (Lev. 8:1–13), recalling the covenant mandate for the entire nation to be a kingdom of priests.

The act of consecration to God took on several forms in the Old Testament, including ritual washing and abstaining from sexual relations (Exod. 19:10–15), prayer and sacrifice (Lev. 7:37), anointing with oil (Exod. 30:30), and the taking of particular vows (e.g., the Nazirite vow, Num. 6:1–21). The performance of these external acts served the dual purpose of symbolically demonstrating the internal and spiritual dimensions of consecration to the religious community and reinforcing the willful choice of the individual choosing to consecrate himself to God.

This consecration to God on the part of the Hebrews was not optional given the nature of covenant relationship to Yahweh. Since he was the Lord God who delivered them from Egypt, they were commanded to consecrate themselves to the Lord by divine decree

(Lev. 20:7). The goal of consecration to God was personal holiness. Israel was charged to "consecrate yourselves and be holy, because I am holy . . . I am the LORD who brought you up out of Egypt to be your God; therefore be holy, because I am holy" (Lev. 11:44–45).

As in the case with the injunction to be separate from the world, this truth about personal holiness bridges both covenants as well. Jesus called his disciples to "be perfect, therefore, as your heavenly Father is perfect" (Matt. 5:48), and Peter exhorted the first-century Christians not to conform to the former evil desires but to "be holy in all you do" (1 Pet. 1:15–16). Despite contemporary tendencies to the contrary, God's holiness remains a constant in divine revelation on either side of the cross of Christ. This is why the four living creatures praise God day and night with the never-ending chant, "Holy, holy, holy is the Lord God Almighty, who was, and is, and is to come" (Rev. 4:8; cf., Ps. 99:9).[11]

Personal Piety: How Is It Demonstrated?

Piety is an active response of the heart of the righteous to the self-revelation of God and in the Old Testament is primarily identified with the fear of the Lord. Even a casual study of this phrase, *the fear of the Lord,* in the books of the old covenant, especially Proverbs, reveals that this aspect of personal piety is essentially behavioral (Prov. 2:9–10). What are the "activities" of a right heart before God? Five habits of personal piety in the Old Testament are examined below, including repentance and the avoidance of sin, praise and thanksgiving, prayer, glorifying God, and a life-style of covenant obedience. This list is representative, not all inclusive. Nor should this list suggest that personal piety is the result of a rigid and mechanistic system of cause and effect in human behavior patterns. This uprightness of heart is the lifeblood of the righteous.

> Whom have I in heaven but you?
> And earth has nothing I desire besides you.
> My flesh and my heart may fail,
>   but God is the strength of my heart and my portion forever . . .
> But as for me, it is good to be near God.
> I have made the Sovereign LORD my refuge;
> I will tell of all your deeds. (Ps. 73:25–26, 28)

Repentance and Avoidance of Sin

No man or woman may stand before a just and holy God without a repentant heart. The idea of redemption for the Hebrews was contingent upon repentance and the washing clean of sin and evil (Isa. 1:16, 27). The alternative was the death penalty, facing the lethal weapons of a righteous Judge (Ps. 7:10–16). By repentance the Old Testament means a turning away from sin and a forsaking of all evil and wickedness (Ezek. 18:30–31). Repentance is an about-face from previous sinful behavior by an act of the will as well as emotional sorrow for wrongdoing (1 Kings 6:47–48). True repentance prompts the forgiveness of God and creates a new heart and spirit within the penitent (note the rewards of repentance outlined by Moses in Deuteronomy 30:1–10). This "new heart" is the spirit of piety which hates every false way (Ps. 119:104, 128, 163) and takes pains to avoid evil (Prov. 16:6).

Praise and Thanksgiving

Perhaps the most prominent expression of personal piety in the Old Testament is praise and thanksgiving. Moses reminded the Israelites that praise was first and foremost a person—"He is your praise; he is your God" (Deut. 10:21). Yahweh's flawless character and mighty acts of grace in fulfilling his covenant promises to the Hebrews instilled the righteous with an overwhelming sense of trust and confidence in the Lord God of Israel (Ps. 22:3–5). In turn, this inspired profound delight and great jubilation among the people of God because joy is found both in the presence of God (Pss. 16:11; 97:10–12) and in the salvation of the Lord and his preservation of the upright (Isa. 29:19; Hab. 3:18). Of course this links repentance with praise, for sin robs the God-fearer of the joy of salvation, but the broken heart of repentance restores the wayward to the joy and gladness of renewed relationship with the Lord (Ps. 51:7–12).

The joy and gladness of the Lord's salvation generates spontaneous praise and thanksgiving among the people of God. The psalmist says, "it is fitting for the upright to praise him" (Ps. 33:1). This praise "came to be associated with the joyous recounting of God's gracious work as an expression of the gratitude of the worshiper."[12] Most often the praise of the Hebrews focused on Yahweh's redemption of Israel at the Exodus (Exod. 15:1–3; Deut. 26:5–11) or his

great faithfulness in keeping his covenant with his chosen people
(Pss. 89:1–5; 98:1–3). Frequently in the Old Testament thanksgiving
is coupled with praise (1 Chron. 23:30; 2 Chron. 5:13; Ezra 3:11).
Exalting the goodness of God as Israel's creator, redeemer, and king
served to underscore the mercy of the Lord and the unworthiness
of the upright in the divine bridging of utter holiness and human
sinfulness (Mic. 7:18–20). Happy indeed are those "whose transgressions are forgiven, whose sins are covered" (Ps. 32:1).

Praise and thanksgiving for the Hebrews involved noisemaking
and raucous shouting (Pss. 27:6; 32:11; 33:3), singing and playing
musical instruments (Pss. 66:2; 71:22; 100:2), hand-clapping and
dancing (Exod. 15:20; Pss. 149:3; 150:4), and merrymaking in general (1 Chron. 16:1–6; Neh. 12:43). This praise issuing from the
personal piety of the righteous contributed much to the jubilant,
triumphant, and exuberant nature and spirit of Hebrew worship (see
Chapter 10). It was to this end that God chose a people for his name
that they might declare his praise (Isa. 43:21). Gerhard von Rad has
aptly commented, "Praising and not praising stand over against one
another like life and death: praise becomes the most elementary token of being alive that exists."[13] Small wonder the psalmist pleads
with God, "Let me live that I may praise you" (Ps. 119:175).

Prayer

A third manifestation of personal piety in the Old Testament is
prayer. Prayer is communion or fellowship with God, and many are
persuaded it is the most lofty work of the human spirit.[14] Prayer expresses the broadest spectrum of response to God, including praise
(1 Sam. 2:1), thanksgiving (Dan. 6:10), loving adoration (Ps. 116:1),
devotion issuing in a prayer or vow (1 Sam. 1:11), communion (Ps.
42:8), confession (Dan. 9:4, 20), petition or supplication (1 Sam.
1:22), and intercession (Exod. 8:29–30; Num. 21:7). But most of all,
prayer is worship in that "the ultimate object of prayer in both the
Old and New Testaments is not merely the good of the petitioner
but the honor of God's name."[15]

Prayer is the private and spontaneous expression of trust in and
devotion for God. Whether prayer is verbal (2 Kings 19:14–19) or
nonverbal (as in the case of Hannah's distress before God, 1 Sam.
1:10–11), it evidences the intensely personal bond between God

and his people. Prayer springs naturally from covenant relationship with Yahweh for several reasons. First, prayer is rooted in the knowledge of God as mighty Creator and merciful Redeemer (Neh. 1:4–11). Second, knowledge of the holy God raises the consciousness of sin and inability in the heart of the righteous (Ps. 25:4–7). For this reason, Old Testament prayers often begin with lament and confession for sin and covenant violation. Finally, prayer is frequently associated with sacrifice in the Old Testament (Gen. 13:4; 26:25). "This offering of prayer in a context of sacrifice suggests a union of one's will with God's will, an abandonment and submission of the self to God."[16] Here is the direct connection between personal piety and prayer, and this is why the Lord delights in the prayer of the upright (Prov. 15:8, 29).

Of course, the personal and spontaneous prayer of the righteous Hebrew was the catalyst for communal prayer among the Israelites. Again, William Dyrness states, "in the Old Testament, private and communal prayer are always complementary."[17] In fact, the genuine life of prayer in Israel was marked by a childlike simplicity, sincerity, and confidence toward God. Here Walther Eichrodt has noted, "There is no need for real and living piety to take refuge in private prayer, but real adoration and lively religious feeling lend force even to public worship."[18] It was this kind of "living piety" that the prophet Isaiah envisioned when he predicted the Lord's temple would be a "house of prayer for all nations" (Isa. 56:6–7; see Chapter 7).

Glorifying God

The psalmist associates both praise and glorifying God with the fear of the Lord (Ps. 22:23). Elsewhere, the Old Testament connects glorifying God with the divine deliverance and salvation of the righteous (Ps. 50:15; Isa. 44:23). Thus glorifying God is another important manifestation of personal piety among the upright of heart since it is a response to the Lord's self-revelation. But what does it mean to "glorify God"?

The basic idea of the Hebrew root meaning "glory" or "glorify" is "heaviness" (KBD, kābēd). When applied to persons or to God in the Old Testament, the word group connotes the honor, worthiness, and splendor ascribed to one of distinctive character and impeccable reputation (Exod. 24:16–17; Deut. 5:24; 1 Chron. 16:10, 24, 28–29, 35). It has been well said that God's "glory is his holiness revealed."[19] Yet the psalmist expands this to include the uniqueness of God as well (Ps. 86:8–10). So by virtue of possessing the attributes of holiness and uniqueness, Almighty God is also a glorious being (Pss. 76:4; 145:4–7).

The created order also reflects this glorious nature of God's character. Again the psalmist sings, "the heavens declare the glory of God" (Ps. 19:1), and the prophet Isaiah pronounces "the whole earth is full of his glory" (6:3). Humanity too, as the pinnacle of creation, reflects the glory and honor of the glorious Creator (Ps. 8:5). Finally, as the special possession of the Lord God, Israel was created for his glory (Isa. 43:7). Their worship of the Lord was intended to glorify his name (Lev. 10:3), serve as a beacon of salvation to the nations (Isa. 49:6), and point to the eschaton when the glory of God will fill the earth (Isa. 4:5; Hab. 2:14).

In his reflection upon the relationship between praise and glorifying God in the Psalms, C. S. Lewis wrote, "In commanding us to glorify him, God is inviting us to enjoy him."[20] To glorify God is to enjoy his personal presence and esteem him with the honor and worthiness he is due as a unique and holy Sovereign. Further, to glorify God is intensely personal rejoicing in his works of creation and redemption—especially his covenant love (Ps. 86:12–13). Finally, to glorify God is to proclaim the year of the Lord's favor and to testify to the reality of the good tidings of God's salvation! (Isa. 61:1–4).

Covenant Obedience

The covenant ceremony at Mt. Sinai after the Exodus gave the Israelites the opportunity to accept or reject the terms of Yahweh's agreement to make them his possession among the nations (Exod. 24:7). This choice was given to each succeeding generation of Hebrews, a choice ultimately of life and death for the Israelite people (Deut. 30:15–16; Josh. 24:14–15). Keeping covenant with Yahweh and obeying his commandments meant the Hebrew people would enjoy the blessing of God's presence and the benefits associated with living in the land of the promise (Deut. 28:1–14). By contrast, disobedience to the Lord's covenant stipulations would bring the divine curse, evil, and death upon the Israelites (Deut. 28:15–46; Jer. 11:3).

Moses summarized the covenant demands in one great requirement, "to observe the LORD's commands and decrees" (Deut. 10:13). Obedience to the statutes, ordinances, and commandments of the Lord's covenant law issued in a life of practical holiness for the nation. This holiness set them apart from the other surrounding nations and made them a kingdom of priests to the Lord.

Obedience to Yahweh's covenant law was intertwined with other aspects of personal piety as well, including repentance, the nearness of God, the answering of prayer, and the fear of the Lord (Deut. 4:6–8; 13:3–4). More importantly, a life-style of covenant obedience was a sign or demonstration of genuine love for the Lord God on the part of the righteous (Deut. 30:19–20; cf., the charge of Jesus in John 14:15, "If you love me, you will obey what I command"). Consequently, Samuel condemned Saul's disobedience in offering sacrifices outside the will of God, since "to obey is better than sacrifice" (1 Sam. 15:22).

False vs. True Worship

False worship during Old Testament times is most commonly associated with the pagan idolatry of the foreign nations surrounding Israel (Deut. 7:3–6). This false religion was usually characterized by homage to graven images and gross misconduct, including ritual prostitution and human sacrifice (Lev. 18:6–30). This religion of idols was banned by Mosaic decree as a detestable and abhorrent practice before the Lord God (Deut. 7:23–26). However, within one generation after the death of Joshua the Israelites left the Lord God of their fathers and followed the baals. The book of Judges documents this cycle of apostasy, as the Hebrews turned away from Yahweh to the false religion of baalism, were oppressed by foreign nations and experienced deliverance through the leadership of divinely appointed judges, only to lapse into apostasy in the subsequent generation (Judg. 2:11–23).

The psalmist recorded their folly—those who make idols will be like them (Ps. 115:2–8). The prophets too warned Israel about idolatry, a fatal attraction for the people of God (Ezek. 14:3–7). Unfortunately the biting sarcasm of God's messengers, who decried these images that had to be nailed to shelves to prevent them from toppling over, fell on deaf ears, as deaf as the idols they had fashioned (Isa. 41:5–7; Hab. 2:18–20). In the end these stumbling blocks of wood, stone, and precious metal could not save Israel (Isa. 44:9–20, especially v. 17). The full measure of Yahweh's wrath eventually fell upon the Hebrews, resulting in the national destruction and foreign exile the prophets of God had forecast (2 Kings 17:23; 24:2).

And yet, there is a more subtle and profane type of false worship denounced in the Old Testament. This kind of false religion takes on two distinct forms, religious syncretism and hypocrisy. Religious syncretism is a process of assimilation which incorporates elements of one religion into another.[21] As a result, the basic tenets and character of both religions are fundamentally changed. For the Hebrews during Old Testament times, this religious syncretism usually involved the union of Mosaic Yahwism and Canaanite baalism. The pre-exilic prophets were especially active in their condemnation of this false religion among the Hebrews, as both the Israelite and Judean monarchies found it politically expedient to sanction the religion of Yahweh and the religion of Baal (see particularly the book of Hosea; cf., 1 Kings 12:25–33).

Hypocrisy is a pseudo-pietism that pays "lip service" to covenant keeping and social justice (Jer. 12:2) while exhibiting all the external trappings of true worship of Yahweh (Hos. 8:3).[22] However, this worship is godless, being based on rules formulated by human teachers (Isa. 29:13). Additionally, this false piety is also lawlessness, in that it multiplies sacrifices while it tramples the poor (Amos 5:11, 21–24). The impious and insincere nature of this worship is further characterized by a consistent pattern of infidelity to Yahweh's covenant (Jer. 12:10). Much later, Jesus described religious hypocrisy as playacting (Matt. 6:2, 5, 16) and godlessness (worshipers who were outwardly pious but inwardly profane, Matt. 23:13–29). Nonetheless, their end is the same; the pseudo-pious and the hypocritical worshiper are rejected and judged severely by Almighty God (Jer. 14:11–12; Matt. 23:35).

By contrast, true worship and service acceptable to God Almighty issues from the genuine personal piety of the righteous. Worship pleasing to God must be unfeigned and transparent, offered in a broken spirit and with a contrite heart (Ps. 51:16–17). The Lord esteems or looks with favor on those who worship and serve him with a humble and penitent heart (Isa. 66:2). Apart from this posture of approach to an exalted and holy God, the worshiper bringing sacrifices, offerings, and prayers is no better than a murderer or an idolater (Isa. 66:3–4). Only those with clean hands and a pure heart may ascend the mountain of the Lord and stand in his holy place (Ps. 24:3–4).

According to the Old Testament writers, worship acceptable to the Lord was also marked by deeds of true social service—keeping justice, doing righteousness, and holding fast to Yahweh's covenant (Isa. 56:1, 6–7). The prophet Isaiah proclaimed that true worship loosens the bonds of wickedness, sets the oppressed free, and liberally extends aid to the socially disadvantaged (58:5–7). The poets of Israel, especially King David, linked the true worship of Yahweh to blameless living centered in obedience to the Law of the Lord (Pss. 19:7, 11–14; 20:3, 7; 119:108). Thus, as the people of God rejected his words and the teachings of his law, so too the Lord rejected their burnt offerings and sacrifices—their worship (Jer. 6:19–20).

Jesus commended right worship in his conversation with the Samaritan woman (John 4:23–24). All true worshipers worship God in "spirit and truth." That is, true worship takes place on the inside, in the heart or spirit of the worshiper (Pss. 45:1; 103:1–2). Only as the Spirit of God touches the spirit or heart of the worshiper can genuine worship occur. This is why Willard Sperry declared, "worship is a deliberate and disciplined adventure in reality. It is not for the timid or comfortable. It involves the opening of ourselves to the dangerous life of the Spirit."[23]

But this is not enough. Worship "in truth" connects the heart or spirit of worship with the truth about God and his work of redemption as revealed in the person of Jesus Christ and the Scriptures. Again, King David understood the importance of worshiping in truth and the necessary association between truth and the word of God when he wrote, "Teach me your way, O LORD, and I will

walk in your truth; give me an undivided heart, that I may fear [YR']
your name" (Pss. 86:11; 145:18). The true worship of God is essentially internal, a matter of the heart and spirit rooted in the knowledge of and obedience to the revealed word of God.[24]

The Holy, the Clean, and the Unclean

Ultimately, the idea of personal piety shaped the Hebrew
worldview. Yahweh's covenant ceremony with Israel at Mt. Sinai after the exodus from Egypt was intended to create "a kingdom of
priests" (Exod. 19:5-6). As the people of God the Israelites were to
reflect and represent the very essence of their Lord—holiness. This
divine charge for holy worship and holy living is summarized in the
command, "consecrate yourselves, and be holy, because I am holy"
(Lev. 11:44-45). In fact, the basic purpose of the book of Leviticus
was to provide instruction for translating the notion of Yahweh's holiness to the sphere of daily living, so that the Hebrew community
might be faithful keepers of the Lord's covenant and enjoy the blessing of his presence (Lev. 26:1-13).

The Old Testament word group for "holiness" essentially means
the separation from the mundane for service and/or worship of God,
who is totally separate from his creation. However, the legislative
holiness of covenant law, as expressed in a book like Leviticus, could
prove effective only as Israel implemented the ideal of "the holy"
into everyday human experience. At issue was discerning between
the holy and the common, between the clean and the unclean (Lev.
10:10-11). Here personal piety for the Hebrews entailed the application of the concepts of the holy, common, clean, and unclean to
the physical, moral, and spiritual realms of life. Distinguishing the
holy from the common and the clean from the unclean allowed the
Israelites to order their relationship to the natural world in such a
way that they might indeed be holy as the Creator is holy.

According to Gordon Wenham, everything in life was either
holy or common for the Hebrew people, including persons, creatures, foods, and objects. Those things determined common were
subdivided into categories of clean and unclean (not "dirty" but con-
taminated by physical, ritual, or moral impurity and thus rendered
ceremonially unfit). Clean things might become holy through the

process of sanctification, accomplished by the blood sacrifice of animals (Lev. 8:22–24) or unclean through pollution (sin and disease, Lev. 15:4–6). Holy things may be profaned by sin and disease and become common or even unclean (Lev. 22:4–8). Unclean things must be cleansed before they can become clean again, and they must be consecrated or sanctified before they can become holy (Lev. 12:1–8).[25]

$\leftarrow$ *sanctify* $\leftarrow$ $\leftarrow$ *cleanse* $\leftarrow$

HOLY   CLEAN   UNCLEAN

$\rightarrow$ *profane* $\rightarrow$ $\rightarrow$ *pollute* $\rightarrow$

Common or clean things or persons devoted to God become holy through the mutual efforts of human activity in sanctifying (or consecrating through sacrifice) and the Lord as the sanctifier (Lev. 21:8). Uncleanness may be caused by disease, contamination, infection, or human sin. Uncleanness can be cleansed only by ritual washing and sacrifice. Hence the importance of the instructions regarding the various sacrifices and offerings in the book of Leviticus. Since the very presence of the holy God resided in the Israelite camp within the tabernacle precinct, it was imperative to prevent the unclean from coming into contact with the holy (Lev. 7:19–21; 22:3; Num. 5:22–23). Failure to do so resulted in death (Num. 19:13, 20; cf., Num. 15:32–36; Josh. 7).

The emphasis on practical holiness in the Old Testament had a dual function according to J. I. Packer.[26] Negatively speaking, ritual holiness and moral cleanness identified the Hebrews as a nation separated from the world by God. It also pointed out the seriousness of sin before a Holy God and the need to avoid or purge away all evil and uncleanness. Positively speaking, the pursuit of practical holiness on the part of the Israelites demonstrated loyalty and faithfulness to Yahweh's covenant and testified of the gracious, merciful, just, and holy nature of God Almighty to all who observed the character and conduct of his people. It is this imitation of God's perfection or call to practical holiness that unites the ethical teachings of both the old and new covenants (Matt. 5:48; 1 Cor. 11:1).

Paul understood atonement in a similar way. All human beings are unclean because of inherited sin due to the fall of Adam (Rom. 5:6–14). The redemptive work of Jesus Christ washes (elevating to cleanness) and sanctifies (makes holy) the repentant sinner (1 Cor. 6:9–11). Thus believers in Christ are "saints" or holy ones positionally in the Savior (Phil. 1:1). The exhortation to practical holiness (1 Pet. 1:16) can be realized only as the believer in Christ yields to the Spirit of God in obedience to the teachings of righteousness found in Scripture (Rom. 6:15–23; 8:12–17; 2 Cor. 7:1). "Without holiness no one will see the Lord" (Heb. 12:14).[27]

Sadly, by New Testament times this application of the concepts of the holy and common to the physical, moral, and spiritual realms of Jewish life had degenerated into a hollow and lifeless legalism. Perhaps this is best evidenced by Jesus' condemnation of the Pharisees, who cleansed the outside of the cup while the inside remained stained with greed and extortion (Matt. 23:25–26). Regrettably, the principle of the Old Testament instruction concerning the holy and the common had been obscured by the preoccupation with the literalness of covenant law. The issue was not one of food and drink; these only served as illustrations or types of the true defilement or uncleanness, that of the unclean heart.[28] Jesus Christ taught that food and drink do not defile or make a person unclean; sin from within defiles (Mark 7:18–23). Paul affirmed that all things are clean for the Christian (Rom. 14:20) and that everything in life is clean and good for the believer as it is received in thanksgiving and consecrated or sanctified by the Word of God and prayer (1 Tim. 4:4–5).

The Sacred vs. the Secular

Finally, personal piety as understood and expressed by the Hebrews negated any notion of separating the sacred (holy in relationship to God) from the secular (a way of life and thought without reference to God), a view of life commonly accepted in contemporary society, even within the Christian subculture. Unlike Greek philosophy (later reinforced by Renaissance humanism and Enlightenment rationalism), which made sharp distinctions between matter and spirit, the ancient Hebrew worldview dismissed any idea of compartmentalizing human life into sacred (worship) and secular (the routine of daily living). In fact, William Dyrness has observed,

"There can be no split between the sacred and profane spheres of life; at least potentially every moment can be sacred unto the Lord."[29]

This holistic approach to personhood and life on the part of the Israelites was grounded in two basic arenas of divine activity: creation and covenant making. The creation of God reflects his glory and goodness (Ps. 19:1–4), thus making the physical environment sacred in the sense that God is still personally and providentially involved in his world (Gen. 50:20; Pss. 37:17, 24; 119:116). Human life (Gen. 2:9; Job 4:9; Dan. 5:23) and the routine of human existence are considered gifts from God (Eccles. 2:24–26; 5:18–20). Hence they too are sacred in that human life and endeavor find their origin in the personal Creator. The idea of covenant relationship with this source of life binds human beings, their labors, and the created order together so that "all of life takes on the character of a response to God."[30]

◆ 3 ◆

From Abraham to Ezra
The Historical Development of Hebrew Worship

THE OLD TESTAMENT SCRIPTURES were compiled over a period of ten centuries, roughly the millennium between Moses (ca. 1400 B.C.) and Ezra (ca. 400 B.C.). Actual Hebrew history extended beyond this some six centuries earlier to the time of Abraham (ca. 2000 B.C.). During these many centuries of Hebrew history God continued to make himself and his covenant purposes known to the Israelites. This sequential self-disclosure of God's divine character and redemptive plan for humanity is usually understood as "progressive revelation."

This unfolding of God's design for the Israelites and their role among the nations was primarily the expansion and refinement of the basic covenant promises made to Abraham: land, numerous descendants, and divine blessing (Gen. 12:1–3). As the history of Israel advanced so too Old Testament theology and the beliefs and practices of Hebrew worship evolved. For instance, Old Testament teaching on the doctrine of resurrection from the dead is scant. While Job (19:25; 29:18) and David (Pss. 16:9–10; 23:6) seem to affirm the idea implicitly, it is not until the time of Isaiah (eighth century B.C.; 26:19) and Daniel (sixth century B.C.; 12:2) that explicit reference is made to the resurrection from the dead.

The same is true for the development of covenant themes through Old Testament history. God's initial promise to Abraham included a tract of land, Canaan, as a perpetual inheritance for his descendants. Yet the office of king is not mentioned until Jacob's deathbed blessing of his son Judah (Gen. 49:10). The divine right of kingship ultimately belongs to the family of David (2 Sam. 7:1–14). Much later, the exilic prophets Jeremiah and Ezekiel indicate the Davidic kingship was but a foreshadowing of an even greater messianic ruler who would govern the land of promise (Jer. 33:14–21; Ezek. 33:23–24). Of course, the New Testament writers make clear that the old covenant found its fulfillment and completion in the new covenant and the person and work of Jesus Christ (Matt. 5:17; Heb. 8:13).

The development of Hebrew worship in the Old Testament parallels this progression in theological teaching and covenant revelation. This chapter briefly charts the growth of Israelite religion through four distinct eras or time periods. Each one marks the introduction of significant new elements and institutions in Hebrew worship. The Patriarchal Period (ca. 2000–1700 B.C.) was the age of Yahweh's early covenant dealings with the Hebrew patriarchs and matriarchs. The Mosaic Period (ca. 1400–1000 B.C.) witnessed the birth of Israel as a nation through the covenant law instituted by Yahweh at Mt. Sinai. Divine law ordered Israel's civil and religious life, established a worship center—the tabernacle, and ordained a priesthood to lead Hebrews in worship and a religious calendar to regulate Hebrew life. The Davidic and Solomonic Period (ca. 1000–600 B.C.) saw the construction of a permanent worship center, the division of responsibility among the temple personnel, and the rise of the prophetic movement in response to state control of the religious center. The Exilic and Restoration Period (ca. 600–400 B.C.) brought renewed emphasis on ritual law and the role of the priesthood in Hebrew worship in response to the catastrophe of foreign exile. (See also Appendix A.)

Patriarchal Period (ca. 2000–1700 B.C.)

The beginnings of the Hebrew nation are usually traced to God's call of Abram to leave the city of Haran in northwestern Mesopotamia for the land of Canaan (Gen. 12:1–9). Right from the start, two ideas extremely important to the nature and practice of Hebrew worship emerge. First, worship is divinely initiated and motivated; the key phrase here is "the LORD had said to Abram" (Gen. 12:1). The worship of God only occurs as he chooses to reveal aspects of his divine purpose and character to human beings through word and deed. Second, the worship of God is a response to this divine self-disclosure. Worship may be the expression of praise and thanksgiving for God's revelation or the act of obedience to some divine directive. In Abram's case his initial act of worship was obedience to God's command—"so Abram left" (Gen. 12:4).

One of the first worship responses of Abram recorded in the Old Testament was the building of an altar at the oak of Moreh in Shechem in Canaan (Gen. 12:7). God "appeared to Abram" and spoke to him, and Abram responded. The exact nature of the Lord's appearance is unclear, but it included the promise of the land of Canaan as perpetual inheritance. The erection of an altar may have included a sacrifice of some kind, but the text is silent here.[1] Abram's altar marked the site as holy because of the Lord's appearing and demonstrated Abram's reverence before God and his thanksgiving for the divine word of promise.

The building of altars to God was to become a key element of patriarchal worship. Abraham erected altars at Bethel (Gen. 12:8), Hebron (Gen. 13:18), and Mt. Moriah (Gen. 22:9); Isaac built an altar at Beersheba (Gen. 26:25); and Jacob did the same at Luz (Gen. 35:7). In addition to the offering of sacrifices, altar building as worship was associated with prayer or "calling on the name of the LORD" (Gen. 12:8; 26:25). No doubt this was praise and thanksgiving spoken in gratitude for promises of blessing. On two occasions altar building precipitated the changing of a place name as a result of the utterance of an important and dramatic word of God (Jehovah Jireh, Gen. 22:14; El-Bethel, Gen. 35:7).

Altar building and the offering of sacrifice are linked on three occasions in the patriarchal narratives. Twice Jacob worshiped God by presenting sacrificial offerings of an unspecified nature (Gen. 31:54; 46:1). More troublesome is Abraham's attempt to offer Isaac as a human sacrifice at the command of the Lord in Genesis 22. And yet, this narrative is crucial to the development of Hebrew religion for several reasons.

One, it demonstrates God's willingness to accommodate his revelation to cultural conventions. Human sacrifice was practiced in ancient Mesopotamia, and Abraham was no doubt familiar with the ritual since he came from Ur of the Chaldees (Gen. 11:31).

Two, the episode highlights what Walter Brueggemann labels "the mystery of testing and providing." Both the Old and New Testaments illustrate the tension between the testing of God on the one hand and the provision of God on the other. It is this contradiction "between the sovereign freedom which requires complete obedience and the gracious faithfulness which gives good gifts" that elicits the faith response in the people of God.[2]

Three, the purpose of worship in the Old Testament is the glorification of God, not the commendation of any human faith response (such as Abraham's willingness to offer Isaac). The point of biblical narrative is to praise Yahweh as the faithful provider for his people (Gen. 22:14).

And four, the abruptness of the divine intervention and the gracious provision of a substitute in the story of Abraham's testing both register's Yahweh's protest against this worship practice of human sacrifice prevalent during that day and affirms the validity of his unique covenant relationship to Abraham as the forefather of the Hebrew people.

This unique covenant relationship between God and the Hebrew patriarchs was made manifest through varied forms of divine revelation. Prominent among these different aspects of divine self-disclosure were the theophanies or appearances of God (Gen. 17:1; 26:2; 35:9), the promises of descendants and land secured by covenant pacts sealed with animal sacrifice (Gen. 12:1-3; 15:12-21), and the many divine names and titles by which God revealed his character, personality, and purposes to the Hebrew patriarchs. (God made himself known to Abram as a shield after he had routed the kings of the plain in battle [Gen. 15:1].) (See Appendix B.)

In addition to altar building and the offering of sacrifices (Gen. 33:20), the book of Genesis describes several other expressions of patriarchal worship, including the erection of stone pillars and the pouring of libations (a sacrifice of liquid or drink offering, 28:18, 22; 35:14), the taking of vows in response to divine revelation (28:20; 31:13), ritual purification in preparation to meet God (35:2), the rite of circumcision as a sign of covenant obedience (17:9-14), and prayers of praise and thanksgiving (12:8; 13:4), petition (24:12; 25:21), and intercession (18:22-33; 20:7).

Conspicuous by its absence from patriarchal worship is the mention of any priesthood. During this time the Hebrew fathers apparently functioned as priest for the clan by virtue of their position as eldest male and head of the family. The lone exception is Abram's encounter with Melchizedek, that mysterious priest-king of Salem (Gen. 14:17–24). Melchizedek led Abram in worship after he had defeated Chedorlaomer and the kings of the plain and rescued his nephew Lot (Gen. 14:1–16). This meeting between the obscure priest-king of God Most High and Abram foreshadowed several important features of later Hebrew worship, including a priestly figure presiding over the worship, the pronouncement of a priestly blessing, and the giving of a tithe to the priest of God.

The book of Job confirms much of this assessment of pre-Mosaic religion among the Hebrews. The date of the literature of Job notwithstanding, the cultural and historical background of Job's testing certainly reflects the patriarchal age. Like the Hebrew patriarchs, Job has the role of priest for his clan as head of the family and offers sacrifices on their behalf (Job 1:5). Confession and repentance (Job 42:6), and petition and intercessory prayer (Job 6:8–9; 42:8–9) were routine practices for Job as a blameless and upright man. Even the internal attitude of worship represented by the fear of God (Job 2:3) and the life-style response of obedience as seen in Job's defense (Job 31) parallel the patriarchal worship experience.

By way of summary, what have we learned about Old Testament worship from this earliest period of Hebrew history? First and foremost, worship is primarily a response to the revelation of God. Worship is an active and not a passive response to the disclosure of God's message and purpose. Patriarchal worship was largely informal and spontaneous, not restricted by time and place, and permitted a variety of ritual acts as appropriate expressions of devotion to God. In his assessment of Hebrew worship during the patriarchal period, Ralph Martin concludes even "at this early offering of thankful worship to Yahweh, the basic elements of Israel's worship form were present. From its nomadic beginnings Israel's worship included theophanies, promises of the land, the practice of marking important places with an altar, the figure of a high priest, and a cultic celebration using bread and wine."[3]

Mosaic Period (ca. 1400–1000 B.C.)

The Mosaic Period (ca. 1400–1000 B.C.) is widely recognized as the formative era of Israelite worship and history. Hebrew religious consciousness and worship practice was largely shaped by the dramatic events of the Exodus, attested by the profuse distribution of the epithet for Yahweh as the God "who brought Israel up out of the land of Egypt" in the rest of the Old Testament: Joshua 24:17; Judges 2:11; 1 Samuel 10:18; etc. Likewise, the covenant ceremony at Mt. Sinai was the vehicle by which God established Israel as his "treasured possession" (Exod. 19:5). The divine law attached to the covenant pact became the instrument that both molded and preserved Israel's identity as the people of God and chartered Israel as a theocratic kingdom of priests (Exod. 19:6). Whereas the events of the exodus from Egypt bonded Israel together as a worshiping community, the covenant ceremony at Mt. Sinai resulted in a constitution which created the nation of Israel (Deut. 4:32–40).

The Divine Name

Divine self-disclosure played a prominent role in the development of Hebrew religion during the Mosaic Period. The revelation of the name Yahweh (or Jehovah) to Moses as the divinely appointed deliverer of Israel marked a new stage in God's progressive revelation to the Hebrew people. The name is usually translated "I Am" and connotes the personal, eternal, and all-sufficient aspects of God's nature and character.[4] The psalmist celebrated this generosity of Yahweh during the desert trek after the exodus when he sang, "He . . . satisfied them with the bread of heaven" (Ps. 105:40).

In addition to being the all-sufficient provider, the revelation of Yahweh also introduced to the Hebrews the transcendence and holiness of their God. Moses responded by removing his sandals and hiding his face (Exod. 3:6). The people of Israel were commanded to consecrate themselves in preparation to meet God (at the risk of death! Exod. 19:10–15). These acts of reverential awe before a holy God represent the beginnings of the idea of the fear of the Lord in Hebrew worship. Perhaps more important, they are object lessons teaching the importance of preparation before entering the presence of God in worship.

The covenant legislation enacted at Mt. Sinai prohibited the Hebrews from attempting to represent Yahweh's likeness with an image (Exod. 20:3-4). The question of the existence of other gods, Egyptian or Canaanite, was not at issue. The Hebrews acknowledged the existence of foreign deities, or better the reality of "demons which are not God" (Deut. 32:16-17; Ps. 106:36-37; 1 Cor. 10:20). The sole task of the Hebrews was to worship Yahweh and serve him alone. In this sense the revelation of the divine name Yahweh during the covenant experience at Mt. Sinai initiated what F. F. Bruce has called "practical monotheism" among the Hebrews.[5]

Theophanies

The unveiling of the divine name Yahweh was not the only way in which God revealed himself to Israel during the exodus experience. Several other types of theophanies occurred. For example, Yahweh revealed his nature and person as well as his will and divine purposes for Israel by means of the angel of the Lord (Exod. 3:2; 14:19) and other angelic agents (Exod. 23:20; 33:2), miraculous event (Exod. 8:16-19), a flame in a bush (Exod. 3:2), fire, smoke, thunder, and lightning at Sinai (Exod. 19:18-20), vision and dream (Num. 12:6-8), voice and direct communication (Exod. 24:1), the cloud of glory (Exod. 16:10), the cloud of guidance and pillar of fire (Exod. 40:34-36), and even a face-to-face encounter with Moses (Exod. 33:11, 20-23).

More important than the variety of divine manifestations to the Hebrews was the theology they relayed to Israel about this covenant God, Yahweh. He was a God who remembered his previous covenant obligations (Exod. 2:24), a God of judgment and deliverance (Exod. 12:27), a transcendent yet immanent God (Exod. 19:10-15; 25:1-9), a God who rules the nations for the providential benefit of his elect, Israel (Exod. 15:4-6, 13-18), a unique and holy God, far above and far more powerful than the gods of the nations (Exod. 15:11; 18:10-12), and a gracious and merciful God who relents of anger and responds favorably to intercessory prayer and repentance (Exod. 32:11-14).

The Exodus Event

The Old Testament celebrates the Passover and Exodus as the supreme act of divine judgment and deliverance in Hebrew history (Exod. 6:6; 15:13; Deut. 7:8; 13:5). As such it furnished the seedbed for the growth and development of the Israelite theological language of redemption. The exodus event exalted the covenant God, Yahweh, who redeemed Israel (Ps. 78:12). It stood as a perpetual reminder to successive generations that redemption inevitably leads to the worship of Yahweh (Exod. 15:18).

Given this context, the institution of the Passover meal (as recorded in Exodus 12) was both a memorial feast commemorating the Hebrew deliverance accomplished by the mighty arm of Yahweh and a call to worship the Lord for his mercy in sparing the firstborn in the Israelite homes sprinkled with the Passover blood. Ultimately, the purpose of the Passover animal sacrifice was to instruct the Israelites in the principles of God's holiness and his unique role as redeemer, revealing human sinfulness and the need for a substitutionary death to cover human transgression and for repentance, which leads to cleansing and renewed fellowship within the community and with Yahweh.

Mosaic Law, given at Mt. Sinai, now legitimized and standardized the form and the institutions of Israelite worship. The forms or media of worship included specific types of animal and grain sacrifices and offerings (the burnt, cereal, peace, sin, and guilt offerings of Leviticus 1—7), ritual cleansing (Deut. 21:6), prayer (Exod. 30:7–10), instruction in and recitation of the word of God (Lev. 10:11; Deut. 6:4–9), and the giving of tithes and offerings to the Lord (Num. 18:21-24). The formal institutions of Hebrew worship ordained by God included the tabernacle or tent of meeting and the Levitical priesthood (Exod. 29:1-9; 35:1-19). (See Chapter 4 for a discussion of the forms of Hebrew worship and Chapter 8 for a discussion of the Hebrew priesthood).

The exodus event and covenant pact at Mt. Sinai reshaped Hebrew understanding of time and reordered Hebrew life according to a new religious calendar. The Decalogue command to observe one day in seven as holy to the Lord established the connection between the Sabbath and original creation (Exod. 20:11). The "rest" in God's presence on the Sabbath day typified the goal of redemption in Old Testament revelation—rest in Yahweh's presence in the land of covenant promise. According to William Dumbrell, "Sabbath and rest coalesce as factors expressing the purpose and result of the exodus"—the transformation of the promised land into Eden.[6]

The divinely ordained covenant prescriptions for holiness in Hebrew life extended even to the calendar. Six annual festivals and holy days were inaugurated as part of Mosaic legislation (Lev. 23). They included: the Passover (and Feast of Unleavened Bread), the Feast of Firstfruits, the Feast of Pentecost, the Feast of Trumpets, the Day of Atonement, and the Feast of Tabernacles. These great religious festivals and holy days corresponded to the major seasons of the agricultural cycle of the land of Palestine so that the Israelites might acknowledge Yahweh as their provider and sustainer. Three of the festivals required pilgrimages of all Israelite males to appear before the Lord at the central sanctuary (Passover/Unleavened Bread, Pentecost, and Tabernacles; Exod. 23:17). This assembling of the Hebrews for worship reinforced the ideals of covenant community and personal piety and reminded the Israelite nation that physical and spiritual well-being were solely dependent on the covenant love of Yahweh. (See Chapter 6 and Appendix C.)

The Settlement Period

"Then choose for yourselves this day whom you will serve" (Josh. 24:15). Joshua's challenge to the nation of Israel illustrated the very real dilemma faced by the Hebrew people as they prepared to settle in the land of covenant promise. Life in Canaan would severely test Israelite loyalty to Yahweh, their deliverer and provider. The competition stemmed from two principal sources, the Mesopotamian deities of the Hebrew ancestors and the gods of the local Amorites (or Canaanites).

The chief god of the Canaanite pantheon was Baal, the son of El and Asherah. He was the rain and storm god whose foremost concerns were agricultural fertility and sexual reproduction among animals and humankind. Mot, the god of sterility and death, was Baal's eternal rival. According to Canaanite mythology, the seasons of rain and plenty and drought and famine were the consequence of the perpetual conflict between Baal and Mot. To aid Baal in his struggle against the god Mot, Canaanite worship of the storm god included human sacrifice and ritual prostitution (Deut. 23:17; Ps. 106:34–41).[7]

These gods or baalim of the indigenous Canaanite populations posed a great threat to the Hebrew religion of Yahweh for several reasons. First, the gods of the Canaanites were firmly entrenched along geographical lines in ancient Palestine. The Amorite migrations, which populated much of Palestine, occurred early in the second millennium B.C. This meant the gods of the Amorites had been worshiped in Canaan centuries before the arrival of the Hebrews. Moses well knew the only way to circumvent the ideological power base of the local Canaanite deities was the eradication of Canaanite religion (Deut. 7:1–7).

Second, the religion of Yahweh and the religion of the Amorites represented two completely different life-styles. The God of Moses was well-suited for the needs of nomadic desert wanderers; the Amorite or Canaanite deities were gods of a settled people. In the minds of many Hebrews it remained to be seen whether Yahweh could adapt to meet the needs of the sedentary life awaiting the Israelites in the land of Canaan (Deut. 4:32–40).

Third, life in Canaan introduced the Hebrews to a new seasonal calendar and a different agricultural system. For centuries the Israelites labored in rich fields irrigated by the annual flooding of the Nile River and enjoyed the abundant produce of a stable agricultural cycle. Now, the natural life cycle depended solely on the early and later rainfalls off the Mediterranean Sea. The Canaanite worship of the storm god Baal had proven effective. Again, the Hebrews remained skeptical over Yahweh's ability to duplicate the life-giving powers of Baal (Judg. 2:1–5).[8]

Regrettably, the golden calf episode in the desert shortly after the Hebrew exodus from Egypt was only the early warning sign of the cancer of idolatry that continued to fester during the settlement period. The writer of the book of Judges paints a grim picture of Hebrew religious life during this era. Incomplete conquest and intermarriage with the Canaanites led to religious syncretism and outright apostasy. Preferring idolatry and its attendant immorality, the Hebrews abandoned the Lord and served the Baals and Ashtoreths (Judg. 2:13). Earlier Joshua had chided the Israelites, "You are not able to serve the LORD" (Josh. 24:19). Unhappily for Israel he was correct.

Davidic and Solomonic Periods
(ca. 1000 B.C.–600 B.C.)

The Davidic Period

David is credited as the king who organized the nation of Israel into a worshiping covenant community. Perhaps more than any other Old Testament figure, King David exemplified the true worshiper of Yahweh (Ps. 51). Despite all of King David's success as Israel's premier statesman and general, it is God's declaration of David as "a man after God's own heart" that endeared him to the Hebrew people (1 Sam. 13:14; Acts 13:22). This dimension of David's character singled him out as the prototype of the Messiah, the greater "Son of David" (Ezek. 34:23–24; Matt. 1:1; 9:27; 12:23; etc.).

David's zeal for Yahweh was never demonstrated so boldly as when he brought the ark of the covenant into Jerusalem and reestablished sacrificial worship (much to the chagrin of his wife Michal, 2 Sam. 6:12–19). Other contributions of King David to the development of Hebrew worship included the purchase of a permanent home for the ark, which later became the temple site (2 Sam. 24:18–25), the stockpiling of resources for the eventual construction of the temple of the Lord (1 Chron. 22:2–5), and the assigning of duties to the Levites, priests, gatekeepers, and other personnel for the temple liturgy (1 Chron. 23–24; 26).

However, King David's most significant contribution to the practice of Hebrew religion was the formation of professional musical divisions to accompany the sacrificial ritual of temple worship (1 Chron. 25). These musical guilds were responsible for composing and directing the songs of praise and thanksgiving used in the temple celebrations and worship services. These songs of praise were gradually compiled into a hymnal for Hebrew temple worship, now known as the book of Psalms. David contributed heavily to the worship songbook; seventy-three psalms are attributed to the "sweet psalmist" of Israel (2 Sam. 23:1 RSV). It seems likely that the first two collections or books of the Psalms were completed during David's reign or shortly after his death, since they are almost entirely Davidic compositions (Pss. 41:13; 72:18–20).[9]

God rewarded David's faith and genuine worship by enacting a covenant granting perpetual kingship over Israel to his descendants (the so-called Davidic covenant, 2 Sam. 7:4–17). This prophetic utterance had tremendous significance for the future of Hebrew religion, as it combined the offices of king and priest in messianic figure (Ps. 110). (See Chapter 10.)

The Solomonic Period

King Solomon's legacy to the worship of Israel was the actual building of the temple of Yahweh and the development of sacrificial worship (1 Kings 8:1–13). His temple for the Lord was one of the architectural marvels of the ancient world. The temple represented Israel's gratitude and thanksgiving for Yahweh's covenant blessings on the grandest of scales (1 Kings 8:22–26). Solomon's reign also ushered in the "golden age" of Israelite history. As king he was "loved by God" (the meaning of the name Jedidiah, 2 Sam. 12:24–25) and divinely gifted with wisdom (1 Kings 3:3–15). He brought unprecedented peace, wealth, and glory to Israel during his tenure on the throne (1 Kings 10:14–29) and achieved international renown as a sage and student of the arts and sciences (1 Kings 4:29–34; 10:23).

Sadly, Solomon's notoriety as a covenant breaker outstripped all his fame and glory. The royal historian records that the latter years of Solomon's rule were marked by steady political decline and religious and moral decay. Ironically, Solomon fell prey to the seductions of the foreign women within the royal harem (1 Kings 11:1–3). Consumed by sensuality and materialism, he was unable to avoid the snare about which he had repeatedly warned others (Prov. 5:1–14; 7:6–27). The biblical writer correctly attributes the division of Israel's united monarchy to Solomon's sin of idolatry (1 Kings 11:33, perhaps foreshadowed in 1 Kings 3:3). However, the collapse of the empire was merely the regrettable by-product of years of gross mismanagement of the affairs of state.

Predictably, the religious syncretism and idolatry of Solomon's reign set the tone for the subsequent histories of the divided monarchies of Israel and Judah. Only eight of the forty or so kings of the two monarchies served the Lord by obeying his covenant stipulations.[10] The Hebrews turned to false gods in their stubbornness and rebellion before the Lord and became false themselves (2 Kings 17:14-15). God had no choice but to destroy the Hebrew monarchies and send his people into captivity for rejecting the word of his covenant (Lam. 2:18).

The Prophetic Response

The birth of the Hebrew monarchy prompted the emergence of a parallel prophetic movement in Israel. God established the prophetic office to ensure covenant keeping among the Israelites now that his theocratic rule over Israel had ended. In a very real sense the prophets of God were history-makers and king-makers in ancient Israel, serving as a check and balance against the inherent limitations and inbred liabilities of human kingship. Foremost among the functions of the prophet was that of public spokesperson for the Lord God. This included both commentary on contemporary events and the forecasting of future events (e.g., Ahijah in 1 Kings 11:26-40). The prophet also served as a spiritual and political advisor to the king, usually with little success (cf. Jer. 38:1-6). And finally, God's prophet courageously ministered to the nation in respect to covenant morality (e.g., Elijah confronting Ahab, 1 Kings 18:20-40).

The prophets of the pre-exilic period frequently cast their message to king, priests, and people in a standard, four-point outline that consisted of (1) the indictment for covenant violations (Hos. 4:1-3), (2) the pronouncement of judgment and exile according to the curses attached to Yahweh's covenant stipulations (Hos. 5:8-12), (3) the instruction, including a call to repentance (Hos. 6:1-3), and (4) the aftermath, including the promise of future restoration to a remnant of Israel (Hos. 14:4-8).

Significant for the study of Hebrew worship are the prophetic characterizations of Israelite worship that often constitute part of the indictment of the leaders and the people. Without exception the prophets condemned religious hypocrisy and social injustice, the basic symptoms of breaking covenant with Yahweh. (The classic prophetic responses to the hypocrisy of Hebrew worship include Isa. 1:10-17; 58:1-7; Jer. 7:1-17; 10:11-18; 11:1-13; Amos 5:18-24; and Mic. 6:6-8.) Isaiah's call for the people of God to "wash and make yourselves clean" and "learn to do right" (10:16–17) echoes loudly in the book of James, who writes that pure religion before God is the visitation of widows and orphans and a life-style of righteousness in a corrupt world (1:27).[11]

Exilic and Restoration Periods (ca. 600–400 B.C.)

The Hebrew Exile

The fall of Jerusalem to the Babylonians in 587 B.C. and the subsequent deportation of thousands of Hebrews to Mesopotamia profoundly impacted the religious life of Israel. The institutions of state and cult, including kingship and sacrificial worship, were overthrown and dissolved. The forfeiture of the land of promise as a result of continued covenant violations signaled Yahweh's curse of divine wrath for disobedience. What had seemed impossible to the Hebrews was now reality; the Lord had indeed scorned his altar, disowned his personal sanctuary, and handed over his own people to the enemy (Lam. 2:7).

However, neither the loss of the temple nor the relocation in Babylon caused the worship of Yahweh to cease. The focus of Hebrew religion merely shifted from the sacrificial to the nonsacrificial aspects of worship. If the books of Lamentations and Psalms are any indication, corporate worship of the temple period gave way to a greater emphasis on individual worship highlighting confession, lament, prayer, and praise, especially in song and hymn (Ps. 137; Lam. 3:19–27). The prophetic voices of the day reinforced this more personalized approach to worship with their teaching about individual responsibility before God for sin and repentance (Ezek. 18:1–20).

Many biblical scholars contend that the exilic period also gave birth to the synagogue, the most important religious institution of later Judaism. Although Ezekiel attests to an "assembly of the elders" who gathered at the prophet's home during the Babylonian exile, the references are too cryptic to warrant such conclusions (Ezek. 8:1; 9:6; 14:1). Certainly though, by the time of Ezra and Nehemiah, these "officials and elders" do constitute the civil and religious power structure of post-exilic Jerusalem (Ezra 6:7–14; 10:8).

Apart from the question of the origin of the Jewish synagogue,

the exilic prophets did infuse Hebrew worship with hope for covenant renewal and the restoration of temple worship. The sacrificial
worship of Yahweh had been postponed only for the years of Sabbath
rest for the land of the promise (2 Chron. 36:20–21; Jer. 25:12).
The legacy of both Jeremiah and Ezekiel to the Hebrew captives in
Babylon was the marvelous expectation that God would regather his
people, make a new covenant with them, establish Davidic rule in
the land of the promise, cleanse the priesthood, and reinstitute sacrificial worship (Jer. 31:23–37; Ezek. 34:11–24; 40—48).[12]

The Restoration of Jerusalem

The later reordering of Hebrew society under Ezra and Nehemiah also had immediate and far-reaching implications for civil and
religious life. Two primary concerns shaped the reform of the restoration community. The first was the prevention of another Hebrew
exile, since another loss of the land of covenant promise was un-
thinkable. The second was the preservation of the ethnic identity
of the Hebrew people while they languished beneath the Persian
yoke in a fringe province surrounded by hostile foreign nations.

Specific measures taken by Ezra and Nehemiah to ensure Israelite possession of the land of the promise included: the covenant ceremony (Neh. 9:38—10:27), the rehabilitation of the priesthood (Ezra
10:18–44), the reinstitution of temple ritual and Sabbath observance (Neh. 8:13–18; 13:15–22), and the introduction of the Law
of Moses as the rule of community life (Neh. 8:1–12). Attempts to
maintain the ethnic purity of the post-exilic Israelite community
included social and economic reforms based on covenant principles
(Neh. 11:1–2; 13:10–14), renewed emphasis on the ceremonial purity of the entire populace of Jerusalem (Neh. 10:28–39), and the
divorce and expulsion of foreigners from the assembly of God (Ezra
10:1–8; Neh. 9:1–5; 13:1–3).

The immediate consequences of these reforms had considerable
impact on the nature and structure of the post-exilic community.
Israel's identity as the people of God took on new meaning as temple
and priest replaced state and king as the stabilizing institutions of
Hebrew society. The Law of Moses became the charter or constitution that reorganized society into a priestly temple-state. Religious,
social, and economic policy was now determined by Mosaic Law,

bringing a new emphasis on Hebrew exclusiveness and separation from the Gentiles and their polluted world systems.

Perhaps even more significant was the metamorphosis that took place in the offices of priest and scribe. In the pre-exilic period a scribe was a high-ranking cabinet member of the state bureaucracy (2 Sam. 20:24–25; 2 Kings 18:18; 22:3; Isa. 22:15; 36:3; Jer. 36:12) and never functioned as a priest. But with the arrival of Ezra in Jerusalem the role of the scribe was redefined. As a priest-scribe he became the model for a later class of religious professionals whose sole task was the study and exposition of the Old Testament Scriptures (Ezra 7:10).

Jesus' Response

The long-term ramifications of the restructuring of Hebrew society emerged in the attitudes and teachings of later Judaism. Unfortunately, the consequences for Hebrew religion were mostly negative. Yet the historical and theological developments traced from the post-exilic period through the intertestamental period contribute greatly to the understanding of the New Testament, especially Jesus' encounters with the religious elite of first-century Palestine.

For example, the zealous but misguided appeal to Mosaic law for community rule eventually led to a pharisaical legalism which tithed pepper seeds with ruthless calculation but ignored the very essence of Torah—faith, justice, and mercy (Matt. 23:23). To maximize community obedience to covenant stipulations related to personal purity the Mosaic code was supplemented by a legal hedge called the oral law or "tradition of the elders" (Matt. 15:1–9). Gradually however, the supplemental code displaced the primary code of Moses, prompting Jesus to decry a religion that neglected the law of God to cling to the traditions of men (Mark 7:1–9).

The idea of Hebrew exclusiveness fostered by Ezra slowly degenerated into an unhealthy preoccupation with separation from the "unclean" life-style of the Gentiles. Consequently, the majority of the Jews were blinded to their divine commission as a light to the nations (Isa. 42:6; Luke 2:32) and desensitized to their spiritual bankruptcy (Luke 5:27–31; 10:25–37).

Finally, the study and teaching of the Law of Moses continued to be divorced from the priesthood. For their part the priests were

more concerned about political and economic issues resulting from
the influence of Hellenism on the ruling aristocracy of Jerusalem.
By New Testament times however, a professional class of scribes or
lawyers had usurped the priestly role as spiritual leaders of the people. But Jesus condemned them as little more than "blind guides"
and "whitewashed tombs" (Matt. 23:16, 27).

◆ 4 ◆

I Will Show Myself Holy!
Hebrew Worship As Sacred Form

"LIKE A PRINCE I would approach him" (Job 31:37b). Job protests his innocence before God for the final time and reveals the essence of his sin. Granted Job was blameless and upright, and God initiated the testing of his faith without cause (2:3). Yet, as the story unfolds, Job's faith clearly is flawed. Job doubts God can overcome his worst fear (3:25). Only divine discipline will remedy the situation.

Symptoms of Job's "malady" surface regularly during his dialogues with his friends. For example, Job believed if he could only get a day in court with God he should be vindicated without question (9:32–33; 13:2–3). Later Job accused God of being a bully and again demanded the opportunity to argue his case before the Almighty—a case he would surely win (23:1–7). Thus, in his last soliloquy Job has now convinced himself that he could approach God as an equal, "like a prince," and earn acquittal by means of legal finesse and oratory skill (31:35–37).

Though innocent at the outset of his ordeal, Job's sin of pride is now fully disclosed. When given the chance to take the witness stand before God, he covers his mouth in shame and silence (40:4–5).

The questions posed at this divine interrogation also betray the root issue—Job's pride in assuming he could dialogue with God on equal footing. Will Job impugn God to vindicate himself (40:8–9)? Or is God Almighty indebted to Job on account of Job's righteous behavior (41:11)?

Unable to respond to this divine cross-examination, Job drops

all indictments against God (42:1–4) and affirms experiential faith
in God over intellectual knowledge about God (42:5–6). The
Creator-creature relationship is reestablished (9:1–12). And despite
the arrogance of Elihu's speech to the suffering Job, he was correct:
"The Almighty is beyond our reach and exalted in power; in his
justice and great righteousness he does not oppress. Therefore, men
revere him, for does he not have regard for all the wise in heart?"
(Job 37:23–24).

Job discovered he was not a windbag (8:2) or a worm (25:6), nor
was he a prince who could make demands on God (31:37). Rather,
Job learned he was a human being, a creature who must approach
the Almighty Creator in a particular way. Job then appropriately
responded to God in humility, with repentance and worship, and
even the service of prayer for his friends (42:6–8). So the Lord accepted Job's prayer (42:9) and restored him (42:10).

The truth of Job's discovery is illustrated even more tragically in
the lives of Aaron's two sons, Nadab and Abihu (Lev. 10:1–7). As
priests they failed to perform their duties according to Levitical pre-
scription (Lev. 10:8–11). For this breach of liturgical protocol they
were consumed by fire from the presence of the Lord. "This is what
the LORD spoke of when he said, 'Among those who approach me
I will show myself holy; in the sight of all the people I will be honored'" (Lev. 10:3). Our God's holiness and glory is made manifest
to all through the means for worship. This chapter discusses the
forms of Hebrew worship in the Old Testament and the implications
for contemporary worship in the Christian church.

Were the Ancient Hebrews a Cult?

Typically, books on Old Testament worship refer to the Hebrew
"cultus" or to the "cultic activity" and "cultic" institutions of Israel.[1] Today the word *cult* usually has negative connotations. Images
come to mind of fanatical quasi-religious groups promoting strange
teachings and even more bizarre behavior under the leadership of
some self-proclaimed and dictatorial "holy man" (or woman). Were
the ancient Hebrews a cult?

The Latin word *cultus* originally meant worship. Until recently,
the use of the word *cult* in the study of worship denoted the worship

practices of a particular group or religion. Of late, the term *cult* has been applied to the adherents of the group itself.

Thus, the ancient Hebrews were cultic in the sense that as an identifiable group they participated in specific worship practices. When speaking of Israel's cult biblical scholars are referring to those worship institutions and practices distinctive to the corporate worship of the Hebrews.

However, the ancient Hebrews were not a cult in the modern application of the term. Ernst Troeltsch (quoted by I. Hexham) classified a cult as "a mystical or spiritual form of religion that appeals to the intellectuals and educated classes. At the heart of the cult is a spirituality which seeks to enliven a dead orthodoxy."[2] Evangelicals tend to further define the cult based on their heretical doctrines and the immoral and unethical practices of its leaders.

I have opted not to use the term *cult* in this study of Hebrew religion, given the pejorative overtones of the word. Yet, the implications of the term do apply to this study. William Dyrness understands cult as "simply the form of Israel's response to the revelation of God."[3] The form of worship is defined as *ritual*, again, a Latin term essentially meaning "the form or manner of religious observance."[4] Since all of life was under divine authority, God carefully prescribed the Hebrew worship rituals or forms. Our interest lies in the character and purpose of these divinely ordained manners or formal structures peculiar to the worship of God in the Old Testament.

Form in Old Testament Worship

The necessity of structural form in worship stems from two related biblical truths. The first is the absolute transcendence and holiness of Almighty God. Since he is totally "other" as Creator, we as his creatures may not approach and address him in a cavalier manner. Human beings must approach and address God in ways that acknowledge his glory and holiness (Lev. 10:3). As finite and fallen creatures we are incapable of grasping the infinite magnificence of God's person and character and unfit by virtue of our sin to enter his presence. Consequently, God defines the way of approach in worship.

Second, because we are human and finite, our thoughts, values, emotions, attitudes, imagination, and beliefs require conventional and tangible modes of expression. William Dyrness reminds us "belief strives for embodiment. . . . Part of what it means to be . . . created in the image of God relates to our ability to make concrete objects and actions symbolic of our values."[5]

Yet we must recognize that the concrete objects and physical actions of our worship are more than mere visible representations and illustrations of our humanness. According to A. S. Herbert, acts of worship were (and are) "symbolic acts," which both stimulated an attitude of worship and possessed intrinsic power to fulfill what they symbolized.[6] We are likely to miss or misunderstand the importance of the symbolic significance of worship for the ancients. "All these visible things [i.e., the elements of Hebrew ritual] were soaked with symbolic meaning; and for that reason they signify not an unimportant or secondary, but a necessary and essential activity of religious experience."[7] Hebrew worship confirmed and reinforced their faith and commitment, and the worship forms communicated the reality of God.[8]

Finally, despite the restrictions inherently imposed by formal structures in worship, in them we are reminded of our created state. As creatures we are unable to approach and address God apart from some type of framework that instills meaning and order. As fallen creatures our sin necessitates a formal structure by which we approach and address God. As sinners and rebels we are unfit and unworthy to enter into God's presence (Pss. 15; 24). Ultimately, "atonement and redemption . . . are really at the heart and core of Old Testament worship."[9]

Patterns in Old Testament Worship Forms

At least three distinct worship patterns may be identified in the Old Testament. These include the sacrificial liturgy, the covenant renewal liturgy, and the temple liturgy.

1. The Sacrificial Liturgy (Lev. 8:14–9:22; 2 Chron. 29:30–36; see also Chapter 7)

   • atonement for sin—symbolized in the sin and guilt sacrifices (which included music and worship—bowing down before

God; 2 Chron. 29:2ff.) and implying penitence, confession, forgiveness, and cleansing
* consecration and devotion to God—symbolized by the burnt and cereal offerings, including praise, reverence, worship proper, and personal vows
* fellowship and communion with God—symbolized in the peace offerings and implying rejoicing, thanksgiving, and dialogue

2. The Covenant Renewal Liturgy (Neh. 9—10)
* preparation, including fasting and sackcloth (and even ritual washing and abstinence from sexual relations, Exod. 19:10–15)
* confession of sin
* reading of Scripture (Torah)
* confession and repentance
* worship (getting low before God)
* blessing God (with praise and thanksgiving)
* prayer and recitation (of Scripture and Israelite history)
* covenant-sealing ceremony
* response of obedience (Neh. 13; 2 Kings 23)

3. The Temple Liturgy (Ps. 95)
* entrance implying preparation, confession, forgiveness, and cleansing (Ps. 95:1a; cf., Ps. 24:3–6)
* enthusiastic praise (Ps. 95:1b–5)
* worship proper (getting low before God, Ps. 95:6–7ab)
* response of obedience (in service, Ps. 95:7c–11; cf., Ps. 15)

The Dangers of Form in Worship

The notions of "sacred" and "secular" are really false dichotomies in the worldview of the ancient Hebrews (see Chapter 2). Jacques Ellul has correctly observed that during the course of church history the elevation of form in worship (or any visible object for that matter) has often led to the paganization of the church. He cautions, "The visible object is typical of the sacral world and very quickly becomes sacred itself."[10] The worship of the visible creates potential dangers for the utilization of formal structures in worship in at least four ways: accretion, ritualism, idolatry, and anti-formalism.

Accretion. The word *accrete* means "increase by natural growth or by gradual external addition." A. S. Herbert recognized that "ritual tends to grow unless it is violently interrupted, perhaps because the original rite needs further explication to convey its meaning to the worshiper."[11] Often this leads to worship forms and practices whose original significance have been either forgotten by the contemporary worshiper or so modified that they are unrecognizable.

This idea of accretion in worship is perhaps best illustrated by Franz Kafka's satirical parable "Leopards in the Temple." "Leopards break into the temple and drink to the dregs what is in the sacrificial pitchers; this is repeated over and over again; finally it can be calculated in advance, and it becomes a part of the ceremony."[12]

Ritualism. Sometimes called *externalism*, ritualism occurs when the worshiper is no longer able "to participate knowingly, actively, and fruitfully."[13] In other words, the worshiper no longer recognizes and appropriates the form or liturgy of worship as his or her personal expression of faith. Thus, participation in the outward form of worship is devoid of inward reality.

Craig Erickson further defines ritualism as "a dysfunctional relationship among persons, church, and liturgy. . . . Devotion to God is eclipsed by a sole recourse to ritual which thereby becomes excessive because the reality behind the ritual has 'fallen away.'"[14] While less technical in their description, the Old Testament prophets also encountered ritualism. "These people come near to me with their mouth and honor me with their lips, but their hearts are far from me. Their worship of me is made up only of rules taught by men" (Isa. 29:13).

Idolatry. Idolatry means "the worship of an idol or of a deity represented by an idol, usually as an image."[15] The visible forms of worship may become an end in themselves; in that sense the liturgy may become an idol or image. When the liturgy becomes the concrete reality of divine mystery, the form itself is deemed sacred. The formal structures then become objects of reverence and worship rather than symbols serving to facilitate the meeting of God with his people.

The ancient Hebrews were especially susceptible to this type of idolatry. For example, King Saul assumed the liturgy of sacrifice was sufficient to ensure victory over the Philistine armies, apart from proper attitudes of the heart and priestly officiating (1 Sam. 13:8ff.). For Saul, the ritual of sacrifice was akin to stroking a rabbit's foot. This presumption in equating the performance of liturgy with the worship of God reached its height during the days of Isaiah the prophet. God's prophet decried the mockery and let it be known that the Holy One of Israel would not accept the substitution of form for true worship.

> "The multitude of your sacrifices—what are they to me?" says the LORD. . . . "I have no pleasure in the blood of bulls and lambs and goats. When you come to appear before me, who has asked this of you, this trampling of my courts? Stop bringing meaningless offerings! Your incense is detestable to me. New Moons, Sabbaths and convocations—I cannot bear your evil assemblies. Your New Moon festivals and your appointed feasts my soul hates. They have become a burden to me; . . . When you spread out your hands in prayer, I will hide my eyes from you; even if you offer many prayers, I will not listen." (Isa. 1:11–15)

Anti-formalism. Of course, excesses in the application of form and structure to the practice of worship may precipitate an anti-ritual response. Frequently, this reaction is rooted in issues of Christian doctrine related to particular aspects of the liturgy. Various movements and denominations have attempted to reform worship in the church by rejecting all or part of traditional worship liturgies. However, in these "free" or "open" services, even non-order has the tendency to become liturgy, imposing some sense of form and structure to the worship.

Freedom in Worship

Even as the formal structures of worship practice are rooted in God's holiness, so too spontaneous worship emanates from the nature and character of God. On the one hand, "God is a covenanting God who enters into binding relationships with God's people. Yet

God is also a Sovereign, free Spirit who is elusive, not to be taken for granted, hidden, wholly other."

God is free to reveal himself at the times and places of his choosing. These so-called theophanies usually spawned impromptu worship on the part of the recipient(s) of the revelation (Gen. 35:14; Judg. 13:19–21). Since God is everywhere present (Ps. 139:7–12), the upright may praise him at all times and in every situation (Ps. 146:2).

Likewise, the Spirit of God who creates and renews life (Ps. 104:30) also lives in the midst of the faithful of Israel and creates praise on the lips of the righteous (Isa. 57:19; 63:1).

Finally, God's power, glory, righteousness, and invisible nature are manifest in the handiwork of his creation (Pss. 19:1–4; 50:6). His creation is ever singing his praise and revering his name (Pss. 96:11–13; 98:7–9; 148). Indeed, the very angels worship him continually (Ps. 89:5–8; Rev. 4:8). It is only natural, then, for those who are upright in heart and righteous (Ps. 97:11) to spontaneously burst into jubilant music and worship (Ps. 98:4). As creator and covenant redeemer (Ps. 100), our God is deserving of this praise and worship "day after day" (Ps. 96:2) and through the night (Ps. 149:5). On this aspect of spontaneous worship C. S. Lewis has commented:

> I had not noticed either that just as men spontaneously praise whatever they value, so they spontaneously urge us to join them in praising it. . . . The Psalmists in telling everyone to praise God are doing what all men do when they speak of what they care about. . . . I think we delight to praise what we enjoy because the praise not merely expresses but completes the enjoyment; it is its appointed consummation.[16]

This paradox of God's immanence and transcendence means the "tension between freedom and structure [in worship] is an inevitable one."[17] God's presence is experienced in both ritual and prophecy. By prophecy Erickson means that gift of the Holy Spirit prompting the faithful to respond spontaneously, whether in revelation and instruction (Amos 3:8; Mic. 3:8) or in worship (Isa. 43:19–20; 61:11). Erickson summarizes, "The modes of ritual and prophecy reflect the difference between.

predictability	and	experience
comfort	and	discomfort
familiarity	and	unfamiliarity
composition	and	improvisation
the habitual	and	the fresh
corporate	and	individual creativity."[18]

Worship that truly represents the fullness of the Godhead must balance structure and freedom, since it is the same Spirit of God who inspires his people to respond formally in liturgy and spontaneously through the course of daily life. But this spontaneous worship response may also be allowed in the corporate worship of the church. Craig Erickson has labeled this kind of corporate worship response "spontaneous involvement." Thus, "true spontaneity originates with God's free Spirit."[19] As Christians yield to the indwelling Holy Spirit, the charismata or gifts of the Spirit are unleashed for the edification of the church, in this case gathered for worship (1 Cor. 14:26).

Two ingredients are essential for nurturing this kind of spontaneous involvement in the church: time and space. George Mallone affirms spontaneous involvement in corporate worship with his principle of "multi-gifted participation."

> It is not just the trained professionals who have prepared for the corporate gathering, but the entire church is prepared to give. They come as participants and not as spectators. Worship is not a program staged before an audience by one who has polished the fine art of communication, but rather a Spirit-inspired painting produced through a community of multi-gifted people who bring their own hues and colors to the service. However, this can only happen as the church leadership provides sufficient time for multi-gifted participation in worship.[20]

The second essential ingredient for spontaneous involvement is space—an environment where worshipers feel free to share their Spirit-motivated gifts and worship responses with the entire congregation. Again, Erickson observes, "Social pressure and judgment, as well as narrow views of liturgical decency and order, can inhibit the development of this free space."[21] Spontaneous involvement introduces the elements of risk and unpredictability into the worship. Yet

God is a risk-taker (in making us free moral agents) and unpredictable (in the timing and methods of divine revelation). Our God is a God of surprises. "Oh, the depth of the riches of the wisdom and knowledge of God! How unsearchable his judgments, and his paths beyond tracing out! . . . For from him and through him and to him are all things. To him be glory forever! Amen" (Rom. 11:33, 36).

Sign and Symbol in Worship

Belief strives for embodiment in conventional and tangible modes of expression. Both signs and symbols communicate the reality of God to the worshiper. Here are some definitions and illustrations of sign and symbol in the Old Testament.

Robert Schaper understands symbolism as an object, act, or word that stands for, suggests, or represents something else. A symbol refers "to an idea or reality beyond or more than itself."[22] Schaper suggests a sign is something practical and visible that essentially conveys information leading to personal action.[23]

A sign may be (or become) a symbol when that sign conveys a particular message or meaning. For example, the sign of circumcision in Hebrew males points to the idea of covenant revelation and relationship with Yahweh through Abraham (Gen. 17:11; Deut. 10:16). However, Vernon Kooy more precisely discerns between sign and symbol in the Old Testament when he states, "The religious symbol points beyond itself to reality, participating in its power, and makes intelligible its meaning. As such it goes beyond a sign or an image."[24] Thus, the sign may represent reality, whereas the symbol embodies it.

Sign in the Old Testament

Signs in the Old Testament are primarily visual and oftentimes miraculous in character. The significance of signs in the Old Testament is that they reveal God's nature (power, glory, holiness, etc.) and publicly display his credibility or that of his agents and messengers.[25] W. Stewart McCullough has identified nine specific ways in which signs function in the Old Testament:

1. A physical sign (perhaps a portent). The celestial bodies are signs as to direction, calendar, weather (Gen. 1:14), or extraordinary celestial activity is a portent of the Day of the Lord (Jer. 10:2; Joel 2:30).
2. An identifying mark. The blood on the doorposts of the Hebrew houses distinguished them from the Egyptians during the tenth plague (Exod. 12:13).
3. A declaration. The rainbow pointed to God's covenant with Noah (Gen. 9:13); circumcision pointed to God's covenant with Abraham (Gen. 17:11).
4. A warning. The altar covering was a warning to Israel (Num. 16:38), and Aaron's rod was an omen against the rebellious (Num. 26:10).
5. A proof or assurance. Rahab was given sign of safety (Josh. 2:12). There may be accompanying signs affirming God's word or a prophet's message as true (Exod. 3:12; 1 Kings 13:3, 5).
6. A reminder. The Passover recalled the Hebrew exodus from Egypt (Exod. 13:9); the Sabbath recalled God's work of creation (Exod. 31:17). Israelites even wore God's law as a sign on the hand to prevent forgetfulness (Deut. 6:8).
7. A portent or object lesson. The prophet Isaiah was a sign to Judah (Isa. 8:18; cf., Ps. 71:7); the idolater was a sign of God's judgment (Ezek. 14:8).
8. An omen. The prophet was an emblem or omen of God's favor (Ps. 74:9). (This category seems indistinguishable from number 3.)
9. A witness or testimony. The heap of stones at the Jordan River attested God's deliverance of Israel according to his promise (Josh. 4:6); or the myrtle tree was a memorial to God's covenant blessing of Israel (Isa. 55:13).[26]

Symbol in the Old Testament

Symbolism has been a part of biblical religion from its beginnings because it is the vehicle of revelation and the language of faith. As vehicles of revelation symbols summarize and interpret human experience and interaction with the divine. As part of the language of faith symbols interpret the holy, the eternal, and the grace

and righteousness of the divine. Vernon Kooy has identified several
key categories of symbolism.

1. Symbolic words. An example would be the naming of a child
   (Immanuel means "God with us," Isa. 7:14; Lo-Ammi means
   "not my people," Hos. 1:9) or the blessings and curses of covenant (Deut. 27—28). In the ancient Near East the word
   spoken or written was "a symbol, a dynamic, living reality
   embodying the power, authority, and purpose of the speaker
   (Isa. 55:11; Jer. 28:9). . . . Once the word has been spoken,
   the effect becomes assured."[27]

2. Symbolic persons. Abraham was the patriarch of biblical
   faith (Gen. 15:6; Rom. 4:1–5); Moses was the lawgiver (Deut.
   18:15; Hos. 12:13; Heb. 3:1–6); Elijah was the forerunner of
   the Messiah (Mal. 4:5; Matt. 16:14); David was a messianic
   prototype (Ezek. 34:23; Matt. 21:9).

3. Symbolic objects. The ark of the covenant was equated with
   the presence of God in Israel (Exod. 25:10–22); the altar of
   incense symbolized prayer (Ps. 141:2); and the tablets of the
   Law given at Sinai represented God's holiness (Deut. 10:1–5;
   Heb. 9:1–5).

4. Symbolic places. Sodom was the epitome of immorality and
   wickedness (Isa. 1:10; Ezek. 16:46); Egypt was the place of
   slavery, oppression, and evil (Hos. 11:5); Jerusalem was the
   holy city and God's dwelling place (Isa. 24:23; Zech. 8:3);
   Sheol was a place of separation from God (Ps. 16:10).

5. Symbolic actions. The prophet Ahijah tore his garment in
   twelve pieces, foreshadowing the division of Solomon's empire (1 Kings 11:30–32). Hosea's marriage to the prostitute
   Gomer depicted God's relationship to Israel (Hos. 1—3). Jeremiah wore the oxen yoke, symbolizing Judah's servitude to
   Babylon (Jer. 27:2–7, 10–12).

6. Religious or cultic symbolism, profuse in ancient Israelite religion. Examples include the offering and sacrifice, the priesthood, the tabernacle and later the temple, the Sabbath, the
   festivals, and holy days.[28]

The Value of Sign and Symbol in Christian Worship

This study of Old Testament worship has continually under-scored the fact that worship entails more than form and order. First and foremost, worship is internal—heart, mind, will, and emotions focused on God (and his Son and the Holy Spirit in the New Testament). However, sign and symbol are important components of liturgy or form in worship because they are useful in preparing us to meet with God. As Christian signs and symbols call attention to the person of God and his work of redemption through Jesus Christ, so the worshiper is drawn away from self to a more full consideration of God in all his glory.

Sign and symbol function as preparatory steps to worship because they have the "ability to elucidate; to compress into a simple meaningful whole, readily grasped and retained."[29] Modern advertising agencies certainly know the potential of well-conceived symbols and logos for selling products to consumers. They also exploit the staying power of these symbols in the minds of the consumer; just witness how many times you or your children have been unconsciously triggered to recite a commercial jingle or visualize an ad symbol.

Likewise, Christian religious symbols compress biblical and spiritual truth into a form easily comprehended and assimilated by the worshiper. Consider for example the most common of all Christian symbols, the cross of Jesus Christ. What truth embodied in those two slabs of lumber—the redemption of humanity. What assurance conveyed to the believer, even the Christian martyrs through the centuries—"I have overcome the world." And what staying power in the mind of the worshiper, whether atop a church steeple or visualized in utility poles along a roadside—"the cross is foolishness to those who are perishing, but to us who are being saved it is the power of God" (1 Cor. 1:18).

Given our video culture, how much more should the church explore the uses of Christian sign and symbol both to elucidate Christian truth and provide that recall mechanism for the worshiper?

Signs and symbols in the Old Testament were also revelatory vehicles, but always in conjunction with an interpretive word from God.[30] Thus, accompanying words of instruction and interpretation regarding Christian signs and symbols are necessary on a regular basis. Otherwise, succeeding generations may forget the theological significance of a given sign or symbol or perpetuate misinterpretations of that sign or symbol.

Sign and symbol had value in the Old and New Testaments. For example, the plagues against Egypt demonstrated Yahweh as superior to the Egyptian pantheon (Exod. 18:10–11), while the miraculous works of Jesus were intended to instill and confirm faith (Luke 7:18–23). Symbols developed in association with these signs implanted the remembrance of divine word and sign. They also served as testimonials or witnesses to the veracity of divine revelation and the certitude of divine fulfillment of covenant promises in human history, the very same purposes of the Christian Eucharist or Lord's Table: "Do this in remembrance of me," and in so doing "you proclaim the Lord's death until he comes" (1 Cor. 11:25–26).

Yet Bernhard Anderson cautions that false signs may undermine the value of divine signs and symbols as in the case of those counterfeit signs of Pharaoh's magicians (Exod. 7:11–13; 8:22) or false sacrifice and worship of Baal (Hos. 10:1–2). He further warns, "Signs and wonders did not lead irresistibly to faith" in the New Testament.[31]

But sign and symbol are valuable in a different way as well. Often Christian signs and symbols are like parables in that they are ambiguous in character. They may serve to confirm and assure the faithful (Matt. 11:2–6), pique curiosity in the uninitiated or uninformed, leading to repentance and knowledge of God (Luke 19:1–10), or even be misunderstood to the point of eliciting anger, hostility, and rejection (Exod. 17:7; John 11:47; 12:37).

Since sign and symbol are so potent, church leadership responsible for worship must employ sign and symbol primarily for instruction and edification of the believing worshiper. Yet, they must recognize the potential for evangelism among the curious (especially children) and even the possibility of hostile response on the part of those who do not have eyes to see or ears to hear (Mark 4:21–25).

Of course, Christian sign and symbol can never be a substitute for personal faith in the person and work of Jesus Christ as God's Messiah. It was for this reason that Jesus refused to give an unambiguous sign (until his resurrection) to those who clamored for one, lest their love of the miraculous sign take precedence over true faith (Luke 11:29–32).

Nor should these signs and symbols be regarded as conclusive evidence or proof that either compels belief in God or renders faith unnecessary. Again, recall the parable of Jesus about the rich man, his brothers, and Lazarus. "If they do not listen to Moses and the Prophets [the Old Testament Scriptures], they will not be convinced even if someone rises from the dead" (Luke 16:31).

And finally, as noted above in connection with specific forms in worship, sign and symbol may degenerate into idolatry when they become an end in themselves. In the last days the Antichrist will perform all manner of bogus signs and wonders that will deceive the people (2 Thess. 2:9–11).

Form and Freedom in Christian Worship

Andrew Blackwood once remarked that worship is "the finest of the fine arts . . . the whole should be better than any of its parts."[32] For this to occur worship leaders must be "spiritually prepared and psychologically attuned to the needs" of the worshipers.[33]

How do worship leaders prepare and organize an order of worship to ensure meaningful and spiritually satisfying worship experiences? First, it is essential that the local church leadership clearly identify the nature and character of their congregations. Expectations for the form of worship are in large measure determined by the "personality" of the local church. Five church personality types may be identified, each representing a particular worship emphasis:

1. Relational (worship is telling another person what and how you feel about God);
2. Charismatic (worship necessitates the release of all the gifts of the Spirit, moving to one collective charismatic outpouring);
3. Reflective (contemplation and silence are viewed as the pathways to truly reverence God);
4. Doctrinal (the essence of worship is biblical exposition); and
5. Aesthetic (worship must involve all the senses, and this is best accomplished liturgically).

Of course, most local churches demonstrate multiple personalities. This means effective leadership must provide a variety of worship experiences to meet the needs of the different personality types in the church.

Second, local church leadership must develop and refine a theology of form in worship suited to the needs of the congregation and consistent with the Bible and the heritage of their theological tradition. Since forms are symbols of spiritual reality and relationship to God, it's important the worshiper understands why the worship response is structured in a specific form. Robert E. Webber roots a theology of form in three basic Christian doctrines[34]:

1. Creation. Since God created the natural order, he can be known in and through it.

2. Revelation. God communicates his power and glory through natural creation (Ps. 19:1; Rom. 1:19–20). God also makes himself known through word and deed (Heb. 1:1). Certain revelations concerned the Hebrew institutions and practices of worship, for example, the tabernacle and the priesthood. The New Testament understands these Old Testament forms of worship as "shadows of the good things that are coming" (Heb. 10:1). However, it is important to recognize that while the New Testament abrogates particular forms of Old Testament worship, it does not deny the principle that earthly forms may communicate spiritual truths.

3. Incarnation. "The doctrine of the Incarnation is the focal point for a theology of form."[35] The truth of the Word of God becoming flesh and living among us affirms the principle that eternal truths may be made manifest through physical or earthly forms (John 1:14). Thus, "the physical creation . . . has a place in worship." As a meeting between God and his people worship must have a beginning and an ending and as an enactment of salvation history it should follow the sequence of divine redemption in human history. Worship responds to this work of God in history.[36] Meaningful ritual or form in worship must be a cooperative interplay between the church leadership, the worshipers, and the liturgy—all

orchestrated by God's Holy Spirit. Craig Erickson describes this cooperative working relationship as "synergistic ritual." This proper interaction between the worshiper and the prescribed forms of worship occurs only "when worshipers, by the power of the Spirit, participate knowingly, actively, and fruitfully in the liturgy."[37]

◆ 5 ◆

Remove Your Sandals!
Hebrew Worship As Sacred Place

THE BOOK OF EXODUS recounts the story of Moses at the burning bush near Horeb, the mountain of God (Exod. 3:1–6). Yahweh visited this place in the form of the angel of the Lord. Because of Yahweh's holy presence, Moses was commanded to remove his sandals and to keep his distance. Overcome by fear, Moses tried to hide his face from God—not an uncommon response to the divine presence of the Creator (even the seraphs hide their face in God's presence, Isa. 6:2).[1]

The idea of the "sacred place" was not peculiar to the Hebrews in the ancient world. The Old Testament indicates the Canaanites and other people groups also worshiped their deities at particular holy sites (Num. 21:29; 35:52; 1 Kings 11:5–8). These sacred locations were often associated with mountainous or elevated regions because the gods were believed to gather and hold sessions on the summit of the great mountain of assembly.[2] By analogy then the Canaanite shrines were located in the high places, above ordinary life and nearer the very dwelling of the gods. Here we examine the ancient Hebrew understanding of the "sacred place," its effect on their relationship to the real world, and its implications for contemporary Christianity.

Highest Heaven Cannot Contain You

Unlike the pagan deities worshiped by ancient Israel's neighbors, the Hebrew God Yahweh may not be contained within any particular sphere of creation or local geographical region. The Israelites understood their God to dwell in the heavens (Ps. 115:3). In fact, one of the epithets for Yahweh in the Old Testament is God of heaven (Dan. 2:18–19; Jon. 1:9). In another place God is called the Most High who parts the heavens in his visitations to earth (Ps. 18:7–15; Isa. 64:1).

Symbolically, the very throne of God from which he ruled over all his creation was established in the heavens (Pss. 11:4; 123:1; Isa. 40:22). And yet King Solomon recognized that since even the highest heaven cannot contain the Lord God, how much less the meager temple he had built (1 Kings 8:27; 1 Chron. 6:18). The glory of the Lord God actually extends beyond the heavens, and from this vantage point he looks down on both the heavens and the earth (Ps. 113:4–6). It is for this reason the prophet Isaiah reminded those Israelites who would reduce God to their level of understanding and ability that Yahweh's ways and thoughts are infinitely higher than those of mortals (Isa. 55:9).

On a more human note the psalmist also experienced the vastness of God's Spirit in all his creation when he acknowledged in a rhetorical query, "Where can I flee from your presence?" (Ps. 139:7). Here the poet affirms the divine attribute of omnipresence and confesses the awesomeness of the all-pervasive and inescapable scrutiny of the God of heaven. But Yahweh is not a distant and uncaring God, remotely stationed in the heavens and removed from his creation. Rather, Yahweh is a most personal deity who not only registers the birth and birthplace of all the peoples (Ps. 87:5–6), but also is the God of heaven who stoops down to help the poor and bring relief to the needy (Ps. 113:7–8).

The truth of God's pervasive presence in creation has profound implications for worship. Since God is everywhere present, the spontaneous and informal worship of the Lord of heaven knows no restriction of space or time. The righteous may rejoice in God's presence continually (Pss. 16:8; 34:1). Moreover, this kind of continual praise is infectious—as praising the splendor of the God of heaven instills hope which in turn elicits even more praise (Ps. 71:8, 14–15). In fact, according to the psalmist this continual praise and worship of God is the whole purpose of life (Pss. 63:4; 119:75). For this reason the Hebrew poet bids all of God's creation (Ps. 145:10, 21), everything that has breath (Ps. 150:6), to praise the Lord!

The Lord Will Choose a Place for His Name

Isaiah the prophet captured the true mystery of this great God of heaven when he affirmed,

> For this is what the high and lofty One says—he who lives forever, whose name is holy: "I will live in a high and holy place, but also with him who is contrite and lowly in spirit, to revive the spirit of the lowly and to revive the heart of the contrite." (Isa. 57:15) This text harmoniously blends two opposite and distinct attributes of the Godhead. First, God is "high and holy," or transcendent. This means God is detached and self-existent from his creation. God is far removed from his creatures, including humanity, in his essential being. But secondly, God is also immanent. This includes God's nearness to and pervasive indwelling of everything he created—the world, its creatures, and its processes. God is at the same time the external sovereign creator and judge of his world and the intimate indwelling one who is in all things, holding all things together. (Acts 17:24–28; Col. 1:15–17)[3]

This attribute of divine immanence gives rise to the notion of "sacred place" in the Old Testament. Figuratively speaking, the earth serves as God's footstool even as the heavens are his throne (Isa. 66:1; affirmed in Matt. 5:35; Acts 7:49). The footstool was the symbol of royal authority in the ancient world. As creator of the earth it is only appropriate for God's dominion to extend over its entirety (Ps. 24:1; Job 41:11; Ps. 97:5).

Theophany in the Old Testament

As the story of salvation history unfolds in the Old Testament, God at times chooses to make himself known in special ways to those who seek him.[4] Since human beings are finite, God accommodates this human limitation by disclosing features of his divine character and aspects of his divine will for humankind at specific geographical locations. Of course, the creation story in Genesis offers a glimpse of this idealized relationship between the Creator and his creatures in their direct communion in the garden (Gen. 3:8).

Sadly, those first humans doubted God's goodness and succumbed to the temptation offered by the serpent (Gen. 3:1–13). God's judgment of the man's and woman's disobedience included curses making life more difficult and banishment from the Garden of Eden—the very presence of God (Gen. 3:14–24). Yet, God chose to overcome the sin barrier and restore the severed relationship with humanity by revealing himself in visible and/or auditory manner to his fallen creatures. This divine manifestation is initiated by God himself and is called a *theophany*. These self-disclosures by God included a voice (Gen. 4:9; 6:13), a dream (Gen. 15:12), a flame in the burning bush (Exod. 3:2–6), the lightning and thunder on Mt. Sinai (Exod. 19:18–20), the pillar of cloud and fire (Exod. 40:34–38), and even the angel of the Lord in human form (Judg. 13:8–20). The actual physical and external details of these divine manifestations are usually somewhat obscure because the emphasis is primarily on the person and character of God and his message to the hearers (Gen. 12:1–3). (See Chapter 3.)

These sacred sites associated with some kind of divine manifestation were usually identified with landmarks. For example, often altars built for worship at the location of God's appearance served as a landmark (Gen. 12:8; 13:18; 22:9), while elsewhere stone pillars and stelae, or engraved standing stones, were erected to commemorate the place of divine revelation (Jacob's stone pillar at Bethel, Gen. 35:14; the twelve stones at Gilgal, Josh. 4:1–9; or the plastered stelae of the Ebal ceremony, Josh. 8:32). In some instances natural geographical features functioned as the landmark denoting the sacred site, as in the case of the oak trees at Shechem and Mamre (near Hebron, Gen. 12:6; 18:1).

The purpose of these landmarks designating a particular geographical site as sacred was threefold. First, the establishment of a permanent marker at the place of a divine visitation served as both a worship response to God and a tangible sign confirming the theophany for the recipient. Second, marking the site provided a geographical reference permitting a later return or pilgrimage to the place of divine revelation (whether a covenant renewal experience, Josh. 24:26; or even a grave site, Gen. 35:20). And third, the landmark often became a teaching memorial by which the Israelites instructed successive generations in the knowledge of Yahweh's covenant (Josh. 4:20–24, likely by analogy to the exodus Passover, Exod. 13:8).

Even as the exodus event secured divine redemption and energized Israelite worship of Yahweh, so Yahweh's covenant code standardized the media and legitimized the institutions of Hebrew worship during the Old Testament period (see Chapter 3). Equally as important, the Israelite covenant ceremony at Sinai also witnessed the crystallization of the idea of the sacred place in the Hebrew religion of Old Testament times.

First, Mt. Sinai (or Mt. Horeb) itself became revered as the holy mountain of God (Exod. 19:9–25). The sacred place was associated with the awesome presence of God, seismic disturbances, and covenant lawgiving. Elsewhere the Old Testament venerates the Lord God as the "One of Sinai" (Ps. 68:8) and commemorates the mountain site as the place where the earth shook during God's initial visitation to the nation of Israel after the Exodus (Deut. 33:2; Judg. 5:5; Neh. 9:13). On at least one occasion Mt. Sinai was the site of a pilgrimage by the prophet Elijah for the purpose of spiritual enlightenment (1 Kings 19:8).

Second, divine revelation included the provision of a permanent holy place within the camp of the Israelites (Exod. 25—40). The tabernacle or tent of meeting was designed to be the very precinct where God would literally dwell with his people (Exod. 25:8). In particular, the holy presence of Yahweh was identified with the ark of the covenant (Exod. 37:1–9). The cloud of glory and the pillar of fire were the visible symbols representing Yahweh's sacred presence among his people (Exod. 40:34–38). Since the tabernacle and the ark of the covenant were portable, the sacred place of the Lord's presence could travel with the Hebrews on their desert trek to the land of covenant promise—Canaan. (See Chapter 8.)

Third, later revelation at the second covenant lawgiving in Moab indicated the sacred place of divine presence would not always be mobile. God specified very clearly through Moses that once the Israelites possessed the land of the promise, he would choose a place where his name might be permanently established (Deut. 12:5, 11, 21; 14:23; 16:2, 6, 11; 26:2). This site was to be the place of worship for the tribes of Israel. Until such time as the permanent location for Yahweh's name had been secured (ultimately the site of Mt. Zion in Jerusalem, 2 Sam. 6:1–11), the travels of the tabernacle eventually gave rise to numerous sacred religious places, including Mts. Ebal and Gerizim (Deut. 27:1–14), Shechem (Josh. 24:1), Shiloh (Josh. 18:8–10; Judg. 18:31), and finally the threshing floor of Araunah the Jebusite (2 Sam. 24:18–25).

The Sacred Place and Hebrew Worship

The implications of the notion of sacred place for Hebrew worship may be as numerous as the plethora of holy sites in Old Testament religious history. However, these five seem primary: (1) the necessity of preparation as a precondition for worship, (2) the importance of pilgrimages for Hebrew faith, (3) the sacred place as a teaching memorial, (4) the value of place-specific worship, and (5) the development of the theological truth of "God with us."

Preconditions for worship. The recognition of sacred places in the Old Testament underscored the importance of personal piety as a precondition for the worship of Yahweh (see Chapter 2). Embedded within the idea of the sacred place was the reality of God's holiness. Even as the visitation or manifestation of God to the righteous sanctified a particular geographical location, so too the worshiper must sanctify himself or herself in order to enter into the presence of God. In some cases this preparation included physical activity, such as ritual washing, a change of garments, abstaining from sexual relations, and the offering of animal sacrifices (Exod. 19:9–16). However, in every case this preparation was spiritual, thus the psalmist admonishes that only those who have a pure heart (Ps. 24:3–6) and a blameless life-style (Ps. 15:1–5) may stand in the sacred place.

Pilgrimages. A pilgrimage is defined as "a journey made to sacred place as an act of devotion." The pilgrimage was a part of Israel's religious life from the very beginning, attested by the patriarchal journeys to holy sites like Bethel (Gen. 12:8; 31:13; 35:18). One such important site was Shiloh, where the ark of the covenant resided (Judg. 21:19). The story of Elkanah and Hannah indicates that devout Hebrews made annual pilgrimages there for the covenant feast (1 Sam. 1:3). Later, the three pilgrimages to the central sanctuary legislated by the Mosaic covenant code became a fixed element of the religious calendar (the Feast of Unleavened Bread as part of the Passover, the Feast of Harvest or Weeks, and the Feast of Ingathering or Tabernacles/Booths, Exod. 23:14–17).[5] According to Abraham Bloch, the festival of Sukkot or Feast of Tabernacles is especially important to Jews as a symbol of homelessness.[6] The festival recalled Israel's desert wandering after the exodus.

As an act of worship the pilgrimage was intended to be an event of great joy and celebration in homage to the living God (Ps. 84). The pilgrimage also afforded opportunity to teach a new generation of Israelites about the holiness of Yahweh and the demands of covenant relationship with him (Pss. 15; 24:3–6; Isa. 33:14–16). The recollection of past pilgrimages to Zion's temple with the faithful of Israel that helped renew the psalmist's faith in the midst of deep distress (Ps. 42:4). Indeed, only a journey to God's holy mountain will vindicate the cause of the righteous against the assaults of the ungodly (Ps. 43:1, 3–4).

After the time of David the pilgrimage to Jerusalem became an important symbol of the unity and solidarity of the Hebrew tribes (Ps. 122:3–5). The political ramifications of such journeys were obvious and immediately recognized by King Jeroboam after the split of the united monarchy. He established rival cult centers and decreed alternative pilgrimages (to Dan and Bethel) in order to complete the separation of the Northern Kingdom from the Southern Kingdom and to consolidate the tribes of the Northern Kingdom (1 Kings 12:25–33). By the time of Josiah the problems of idolatry and religious syncretism associated with some of the ancient sacred places were so severe that Jerusalem became established as the only legitimate site for pilgrimages (2 Kings 23:1–25). With the Babylonian exile the dispersed Israelites regarded pilgrimages to Jerusalem as a sacred dream and duty. It is likely the "Pilgrim Songs" or "Songs of Ascents" (Pss. 120—134) represent a collection of musical poems sung by the Hebrew pilgrims as they ascended the holy mountain of the Lord (Isa. 30:29). (See Chapter 10.)

Teaching memorials. The Israelite practice of identifying sacred places with landmarks contributed greatly to the covenant catechism of the next generation. These tangible markers affirmed the historical reality of God's intervention in the natural order and functioned as teaching memorials for successive Israelite generations.

Yahweh actually did disclose covenant revelation and perform great acts of redemption for his people in history (unlike the religious myths of Israel's neighbors, Ps. 105). This rehearsal of history at sacred places taught essential truths about God (his holiness, his power, etc.; cf., Josh. 24:1–15) and the promises and obligations of his covenant (Gen. 35:1–15). The active participation in the re-membrance of Yahweh's past words and deeds at the sacred site was intended to instill responsible covenant obedience and implant a sense of loyalty in the religious community and its heritage.

Place-specific worship. Israelite worship at the sacred religious sites fostered attitudes and responses of loyalty on two different planes. On the vertical level individual and corporate worship at the sacred place encouraged loyalty to Yahweh. The act of worship at the location served as a reminder that God in his grace had met with his people. The carefully preserved tradition of those past visitations ensured God's continuing gracious revelation (Deut. 4:21–40). On the horizontal level the act of worship at the sacred place strengthened the covenant bonding of the religious community. The corporate and public identification with Yahweh at the sacred site heightened awareness of the obligations for loyalty and service to each other as common members of the covenant community (Exod. 23:1–9). It is not surprising then that the Hebrew prophets were quick to pronounce words of vehement condemnation against the Israelites for their worship of pagan deities at "false" sacred sites (Hos. 4:12–13, 15–16; Amos 5:4–5). This false worship not only violated covenant loyalty with Yahweh, but also eroded the moral and social covenant structures of the religious community (Hos. 4:1–3).

"God with us." Finally, and perhaps most important, the idea of the sacred place in the Old Testament restored the possibility of intimate fellowship enjoyed by God and man and woman in the garden prior to the Fall (Gen. 3:8). A key outcome of the covenant agreement between Yahweh and Israel was the very presence of God "dwelling in the midst of his people" (Exod. 25:8). The tabernacle structure described in Exodus 25—40 was designed to symbolize the active and continual presence of the Lord among the Hebrews. The tabernacle was also called the tent of meeting because there God met with Israel, through the holy priesthood ordained to represent the Hebrew people before Yahweh (Lev. 1:1).[7]

Whether associated with this portable shrine or "contained" in the later permanent edifice of Solomon's temple, one sober reality conditioned the presence of Yahweh among his people. The sin of idolatry meant "divine abandonment," and was the necessary corollary to the blessing of "divine presence" of covenant obedience.[8] This truth became a painful part of Hebrew history with the fall of Shiloh (cf. 1 Sam. 4) and the fall of Jerusalem (cf. Ezek. 8—10), as the "glory of the Lord departed from Israel." For this reason Isaiah looked for that day when Immanuel, "God with us" in the flesh, would establish justice and righteousness in the land and permanently secure the divine presence of God among his faithful remnant and all nations (Isa. 7:14; 9:7; 11:9).

Sacred Stones and Wooden Idols

Jeremiah's oracle (7:1—8:3) is usually identified as the prophet's great "temple sermon." Here the man of God denounced the people of Jerusalem for trusting these deceptive words, "This is the temple of the LORD" (7:4). By this he meant the "temple theology" pedaled by the deluded priesthood and national leaders who understood God's temple to be a symbol of Judah's inviolability. Since Yahweh himself had chosen this site to establish his name in Israel, God's presence represented by the temple guaranteed security and prosperity. Jeremiah attacked this supposition as little more than idolatry—the substitution of nearness to a sacred place for nearness to God. The prophet merely had to rehearse Hebrew history to substantiate his argument. God could dispense with the temple in Jerusalem as easily as he ruined Shiloh for the wickedness of Israel (Jer. 7:8–15).

The hazard of exchanging loyalty to Yahweh for loyalty to a sacred place has been well documented. For example, William Dyrness observes, "The danger was always present that Israel would believe that God was limited to these [sacred] places."[9] The Hebrews had to continually learn and relearn that there was no necessary connection between Yahweh and the place(s) where he revealed himself to his people. This meant the sacred place could never serve as a talisman or good-luck charm to avert either evil or divine judgment.

The prophet Ezekiel countermanded this fallacious notion of sacred place in his vision (Ezek. 1—3). There he disclosed that the very throne of God rested on a magnificent carriage, signifying his presence in any location (Ezek. 1:15-28). The Hebrew captives in Babylon needed to know Yahweh was not parked in Jerusalem.

In this chapter I have used the words *sacred* and *sanctified* or *holy* somewhat interchangeably. The idea of the sanctified or sacred place in Christian theology can only be a vehicle for the demonstration of the divine mystery and God's ultimate hiddenness. It can never serve as a visible or concrete reality of God's revelation since that would make the sacred place an object of reverence and worship—an end in itself and a form of idolatry. R. K. Harrison has commented that God demands conversion of mind and heart and actions as the basis of peace and security, not superstitious veneration of a stone building or a traditionally sacred site.[10]

The assent to the notion of the sacred place in Hebrew religion naturally gave rise to corresponding sacred objects (furniture, vessels, and the like). In fact, such objects had been ordained by Yahweh to be an integral part of the ritual and worship associated with the Lord's tabernacle (Exod. 35:30—39:43). Unfortunately, the Israelites continually had difficulty distinguishing between those sanctified objects utilized in the worship of Yahweh and sacred objects worshiped as idols instead of Yahweh.

The awesome holiness of God demanded that the Hebrew nation, the Levitical priesthood, and all the objects that contributed to the worship of Yahweh in the tabernacle be sanctified or consecrated for service (Lev. 11:44-45; 19:2). The book of Exodus recounts the consecration of the people at Mt. Sinai (19:10-15), the consecration of the priests for liturgical service (29:1-10; Lev. 8:1-29), and the consecration of the tabernacle by Moses (39:32-43). But even though the tent of meeting and all its furniture and implements were sanctified by sacrificial ritual, these manmade objects were not to be worshiped (Exod. 29:36; 30:29; 40:9). Yahweh alone merited the worship of Israel (Exod. 22:20). The holy or sanctified objects were only symbols of his divine presence and pictures of his absolute holiness (see Chapter 2).

Despite the forthright prohibitions against the worship of other gods and sacred objects of any kind, the Israelites were easy prey to the snare of idolatry (Exod. 20:2-4; Deut. 4:15-20). The Hebrew prophets understood the Israelites had been deluded and led astray by a "spirit of prostitution" (Isa. 44:20; Hos. 4:12). Habakkuk pointedly described this deception or seduction as being like the idol maker who "trusts in his own creation" instead of in the Creator God (Hab. 2:18).

Examples of Israelite worship of idols and sacred objects are numerous in the annals of Old Testament history. The citation of specific episodes of this idolatrous behavior prove instructive because two distinct categories of false worship emerge. First, there is the danger of sanctified objects becoming sacred objects. For instance, the ark of the covenant was eventually mistaken for a talisman that insured deliverance and protection from Israelite enemies. Only by permitting the Philistines to defeat the Israelites at Shiloh and capture the ark could God demonstrate the reality of his power and the impotence of misplaced faith (1 Sam. 5—6).

On another occasion, the bronze serpent sanctified by Moses as the instrument of deliverance from the plague of serpents during the wilderness wanderings evolved into an idol (Num. 21:2-9). King Hezekiah had the relic destroyed because it was linked to false worship (2 Kings 18:4). Of course the real hazard for the Israelites was that they assumed that they were still practicing true covenant religion simply because they used the divinely approved props for worship. The ever-present risk was to unconsciously transfer faith and loyalty from Yahweh to the sacred symbols representing him.

The second category of false worship included the idols and cultic objects borrowed from the pagan religions of surrounding neighbors. Even a casual reading of the Hebrew prophets produces a lengthy catalog of these symbols and images of false gods consulted by the Israelites (Isa. 2:20; Ezek. 6:5-7; 8:7-13; Hos. 4:12; etc.). Those kings who heeded the prophetic warnings and reformed Israelite religion totally demolished these insidious "sacred objects" of the pagan religions (2 Kings 18:1-9; 23:4-14). The purification of Hebrew religion was possible only in direct proportion to the measures the righteous took to eradicate the alien influences contaminating covenant faith. Israelite history proves time and again that the people of God cannot "waver between two opinions"; they must serve God alone or the baals (1 Kings 18:21).

The chiding, even biting, sarcasm of Elijah echoes through the messages of the later Hebrew prophets. These servants of God stood fast against the folly of idolatry. These sacred objects could neither see nor hear (Isa. 44:9–20; Hab. 2:18–19), let alone stand, without being tacked down for fear of their falling over (Isa. 41:7; 46:7). How much less able were these impotent "gods" to deliver their worshipers in the face of calamity and divine judgment (Isa. 45:20; 57:13)? And yet, despite the Israelite penchant to worship "wood and stone," the prophets knew there would come a day when the name of Yahweh would no more be profaned (Ezek. 20:30–31, 39–40).

Implications for Christian Worship

The Christian church worships the same God as those Israelites of Old Testament history who made pilgrimages to sacred places in Canaan, the land of covenant promise. The God of Abraham, Isaac, and Jacob is also the God of the apostles John, Peter, and Paul (Gal. 3:6–9). What lessons then, might the contemporary church glean from the Hebrew understanding of the sacred place?

Prepare to Meet Your God!

We have already learned that personal piety or a right heart is the one necessary precondition for the Hebrew worship of Yahweh in the Old Testament (see Chapter 2). Attaining this right heart for worship meant careful preparation according to the meticulous written prescriptions for entry into God's presence (2 Chron. 35:4–6). Even as the people of Israel gave strict attention to how they approached God in worship, so too the Christian church must acknowledge the holiness and worth of God. Since public worship is no ordinary experience, some guidelines for ensuring the transcendent and mysterious quality of Christian worship are in order. Robert E. Webber has outlined practical procedures by which the Christian worshiper might prepare to meet God, including silence, the procession, the greeting, the invocation, the acknowledgment of God's glory, and repentance.[11]

Silence, an expression of awe at the majesty and holiness of God (Hab. 2:20), "evokes feelings of transcendence and puts one in touch with the otherworldly character of reality."[12]

The processional symbolizes entry into a place or an event. No doubt its roots are traceable to the idea of pilgrimages in the Old Testament. The procession is a visible and tangible act that reminds the worshiper of his or her entry into the very presence of the living God.

The greeting initiates the formal act of God meeting with his people. The greeting may be a prayer or Scripture reading that invites a congregational response. As a salutation the greeting also serves to draw attention to the common bond the worshipers share in Christ's covenant community.

The invocation is prayer that humbly admits that Christians worship God the Father only through the agency of Jesus Christ his Son and by the power of the Holy Spirit. This "call" or "plea" acknowledging the presence of the Triune God and utter inability in human strength is usually made with the congregation standing in reverence.

The affirmation of God's glory is an acclamation of God's essential being and character, glory and holiness (Ps. 29:3). This hymnic outburst of praise traces its origins to the angelic host who lauded the birth of Immanuel in Bethlehem (Luke 2:14). The early church developed a hymn now universally known as the "Gloria in excelsis Deo" for extolling the Godhead, but any hymn of praise is appropriate.[13]

Finally, like Isaiah before the throne of God (Isa. 6:5) or the tax collector at prayer (Luke 18:13), the worshiper beseeches God for mercy and cleansing from sin in an act of repentance. Often a Scripture reading, an Old Testament psalm, or a Christian hymn is used to convey the full expression of contrition before God.

Highways to Zion in Your Heart

The practice of journeying to sacred places was not limited to the Hebrew religion of Old Testament times. By the second century A.D. Christian pilgrimages to the Holy Land of Palestine were very popular. The retracing of Jesus' movements during his last week or Passion Week in Jerusalem became especially significant.[14] Later, travels to the graves of martyrs and saints, sites where miracles had been performed, and other holy cities (Rome, Canterbury, etc.) were added to the Christian tradition of pilgrimages. The church encouraged pilgrimages as a means of penance, since travel in the ancient world was undertaken with considerable risk of hardship and sacrifice. The significance of the pilgrimage for Christianity was demonstrated militarily with the medieval Crusades, ordered by the church in part to make the Holy Land free and safe for pilgrim travels.[15]

Despite the views of prominent critics over the centuries (like John Chrysostom, Jerome, and Erasmus), pilgrimages to the Holy Land and elsewhere remained an important feature of piety in many Christian traditions. Alternatives to these treks to specific sacred sites of Christianity have gained popularity recently. These mock pilgrimages may include the re-creation of the Bethlehem advent scene or the stations of the Way of the Cross at Easter. The more liturgical Christian traditions view the worship processional as a re-enactment of the pilgrimage to Zion, while some Christians understand their weekly journey to their local church or parish as a type of pilgrimage. In other instances, travels to local church reunions and anniversaries, baby dedications or baptisms, or the revisiting of the site of one's conversion prompt the same spiritual reflection and renewal associated with the pilgrimage experience.

More important to the New Testament writers was the equation of the Christian life with the pilgrimage of Hebrew tradition. Even as Jacob considered his life a "sojourn" of one hundred thirty years (Gen. 47:9), so the life of faith is a pilgrimage to the heavenly country (Heb. 11:13–16). For this reason, the New Testament refers to Christians as "aliens and refugees" (1 Pet. 2:11) whose citizenship is in heaven (Phil. 3:20). The psalmist had a similar understanding of the life of faith when he blessed all those who set their hearts on pilgrimage embracing the hardships of daily living (Ps. 84:5). Likewise, the Christian's earthly life is but a long pilgrimage to that city whose maker and architect is God (Heb. 11:10). Thus Paul compared this spiritual pilgrimage to the life of a soldier on a mission who refuses to entangle himself in civilian affairs (2 Tim. 2:3–4). The Christian should be separated from the corruption of the world to live a righteous life before pagans to the glory of God (1 Pet. 2:12).

What Do These Stones Mean?

According to Walter Brueggemann, the Christian church could benefit greatly by adapting some of the Old Testament ideas of education.[16] The Israelites were concerned about the binding of the generations in the religious community. Education in ancient Israel capitalized on the curiosity and yearning of the youth to know and belong to the "secret" held so precious by the adult covenant community. In this context, Brueggemann understands teaching as "the shrewd management of that secret, having an acute sense of when and in what ways it is appropriate to conceal and when to reveal."[17]

One way the Hebrews taught the next generation was by talking about Yahweh during ceremonies and festivals or at landmarks commemorating past historical events (the Passover meal, Exod. 12:26; 13:8, 14; the Mosaic covenant, Deut. 6:20–21; 27:2–3; the pillar of stones at the crossing of the Jordan, Josh. 4:6, 21). The rituals associated with the ceremonies or markers were designed to evoke a teachable moment by means of a catechism of questions and answers. The adult would respond to the children's questions articulating a creedal formula or stylized testimony of faith in Yahweh (the recital of Yahweh's acts at the stone pillars of the Jordan, Josh. 4:6, 21). This recital introduced the new generation to the baseline of identity for the religious community and reinforced that normative baseline for the adult generation.[18]

Brueggemann calls the church to an imaginative reclamation of this Hebrew educational model. The Eucharist and Christian baptism are obvious examples of New Testament ceremonies that would be teachable events (1 Cor. 11:17–34; Rom. 6:1–4). The cross as the universal symbol of Christianity could also be used most effectively as a teaching memorial. Of course, the wealth of material related to Old Testament belief and practice of the Israelites and later Judaism could also be mined rewardingly for significant ceremonies and observances. In addition, creative appeal to outstanding personages and events from the rich tradition of church history as well as important symbols, objects, and works from the world of Christian art might evoke that teachable moment as well.[19]

A Spiritual House

The New Testament understands the church of Jesus Christ to be the assembly of people who meet in particular locations on a regular basis for worship (1 Pet. 2:4–10). For better or (usually) worse, church history has tended to regard the local church building as a sacred place by analogy to the Old Testament tabernacle and temple. However, there are benefits for the church (the holy assembly of people) in recognizing the physical location and superstructure as a "sanctified" place. Much like the Israelite tent of meeting, the church building helps reinforce the corporate identity of the local congregation. This regular collective gathering of God's people is mandated by Scripture and is designed to foster true community bonding in Christ (Heb. 10:23–25). Paul understood this as "Carry each other's burdens, and in this way . . . fulfill the law of Christ" (Gal. 6:2).

This kind of covenant community life is intended to promote love and unity in the faith (Eph. 4:10–16). The regular assembly of the church instills a sense of anticipation and expectancy for the redemptive work of God in his creation (1 Cor. 14). This mutually encourages believers and engenders hope during present distress (Rom. 15:4). The church gathered at its sanctified place also affords the opportunity for public renewal of vows to covenant loyalty in Christ (understanding the Eucharist, in part, as a covenant renewal ceremony). And when the church scatters for its week of work, play, mission, and ministry, the "sanctified place" remains a silent witness to the possibility of true reconciliation by the power of God.

And You Are That Temple!

The New Testament announces the realization of the Old Testament theme of God's presence among humankind with John's declaration, "The Word became flesh and made his dwelling among us, full of grace and truth" (John 1:14). Perhaps this return of the divine presence to Israel fulfilled Haggai's prophecy about the latter glory of the temple being far greater than the glory of the former (Solomon's) temple (Hag. 2:9; Luke 2). Regardless, the promise of the old covenant was now accomplished in the new covenant. The gospel writer Matthew certified as much when he interpreted the birth of Jesus as the fulfillment of the Immanuel oracle of Isaiah: "The virgin will be with child and will give birth to a son, and they will call him Immanuel—which means, God with us" (Matt. 1:23).

The divine presence and abandonment motif resurfaces for the final time in Jesus' farewell address to his disciples (John 13—16). Jesus must first depart and return to the Father, but he will send the Holy Spirit as the abiding presence of God in the life of the believer (John 16:4–15). The spiritual and invisible presence of God will one day give way to the eternal, physical, and visible presence of God within his creation (Rev. 22:1–5). During the interim, the Holy Spirit indwells the individual believer in Christ (1 Cor. 3:16–17). For the Christian this means the human body now becomes a temple (literally "inner sanctum") of the Holy Spirit of God (1 Cor. 6:19–20), thus reflecting the presence of God on earth as the "light of the world" and "letters from Christ, known and read by everybody" (Matt. 5:14; 2 Cor. 3:1–3).

Your God Is Too Small

J. B. Phillips in his book *Your God Is Too Small*[20] addresses the dangers of confusing the sacred with the sanctified. Two chapters of this Christian classic are especially pertinent. In Chapter 3 Phillips notes how the idea of the "sacred" has encouraged the old-fashioned concept and eventually "fossilized" God and the worship response in a previous historical context.[21]

In Chapter 7 he describes how the "denominationalizing" of the sacred has divided God and established "monopolies of God's grace."[22] Thus the outsider views the Christian church and its God as factional and irrelevant. These are ever-present perils if the Christian church fails to adequately discern the distinction between the sacred and the sanctified.

Right worship of God in "spirit and truth" (John 4:24) demands doctrinal integrity. Malcolm Muggeridge has suggested that the blurring of the sanctified and sacred in Christendom has encouraged religious syncretism, not religious separatism and distinctiveness. In his satirical commentary on the ecumenical movement associated with the World Council of Churches, Muggeridge remarks, "They [the World Council at Uppsala, Sweden] were able to agree about almost anything, because they believed almost nothing."[23] Muggeridge ironically noted that one of the few sensible observations of the session came from a Russian Orthodox Nicodim who asked how a dialogue between Christians and Marxists might occur given the inseparable ideological abyss between the two groups.[24]

The reaction of Jesus to the Samaritan woman at the well proves instructive here. Granted, the Samaritans worshiped at a sacred place on Mt. Gerizim. However, they worshiped in ignorance because they rejected the revealed truth about God in the Hebrew Scriptures (John 4:21–22). Paul also understood the importance of sound doctrine or teaching to Christian life-style and worship. He admonished his co-workers to instruct believers in sound doctrine and refute those who oppose it (Titus 1:9). He knew full well that people would gravitate to teaching that sated their natural evil desires (2 Tim. 4:2–3). This is why the book of James interprets "pure religion" as an unflagging commitment to social justice and an uncompromising stand against defilement by the world (James 1:27).

◆ 6 ◆

Ask Now About
the Former Days
Hebrew Worship As Sacred Time

WHILE I WAS PREPARING this chapter I overheard a student respond to the inquiry of a bystander who asked what he was doing. "Oh, just killing time," was the reply. Harmless enough, right? In fact, most of us have no doubt glibly uttered this same cliche as we too have frittered away time for one reason or another. But the phrase rings strangely true for many in our popular culture, perhaps unconsciously. There is a line from a pop tune that mirrors current thinking in our post-Christian modernist culture—"Time is a river rolling into nowhere."[1] Time is meaningless; time marches toward no goal.

However, as Christians we do care about time. Our God as the Father of Abraham, Isaac, and Jacob is the Lord of the past (Exod. 3:6). As the Father of our Lord Jesus Christ, our God is the Lord of the present (Rom. 15:6). And as the one who alone possesses immortality, our God is the Lord of the future (1 Tim. 6:16). Time has both a purpose—the redemption of creation (John 1:29), and a goal—the kingdom of God (Acts 1:6–11).

This chapter sets forth a biblical theology of time, explaining what time is as understood in the Old and New Testaments. Primary attention is devoted to the worship theme, specifically the relationship of time and worship, and more important, what the ancient Hebrew understanding of time and worship may teach the Christian about time and worship at the end of the twentieth century.

Old Testament Perspectives

The vocabulary of the Old Testament contains numerous words for expressing the idea of time. For instance, the *Revised Standard Version Analytical Concordance* cites more than twenty Hebrew words that are rendered "time" in the Revised Standard Version and the New Revised Standard Version.[2] In addition, the language of the Old Testament possesses a cadre of words for time units, like hour, day, night, morning, noonday, week, month, year, generation. This study highlights only a few of the key Old Testament terms for time.

Among the dozens of Hebrew words for time and time units in the Old Testament, these nine represent the range of perceptions held by the ancient Hebrews:

- *'îshôn*—the time of night and darkness (Prov. 7:9; 20:20);
- *zĕmān*—specific time, hour, regular time as in the "time for this" and the "time for that" in the "time poem" of Ecclesiastes 3:1-9;
- *yôm*—day (time, Gen. 8:22), twenty-four-hour day (Gen. 1:5), daily (Gen. 39:10), year (1 Sam. 1:21), lifetime (Gen. 47:8), today (2 Sam. 18:20), unspecified extended period of time (Prov. 31:25);
- *mōneh*—time, as in separate occurrences (Gen. 31:7, 14);
- *môʻēd*—fixed day (Exod. 9:5), appointed time (1 Sam. 9:24), determined span of time (Dan. 12:7);
- *'ôlām*—long time (Gen. 13:15), all (coming) time or forever (Gen. 13:15; 1 Chron. 23:25), lifetime (1 Sam. 27:12), dim past (Gen. 49:26);
- *'ēt*—a point in time (Gen. 24:11), a lapse of time (Eccles. 9:11), the (right) time (Jer. 5:24);
- *paʻam*—time, as in separate occurrences (Exod. 8:28; Prov. 7:12); and
- *regaʻ*—while, period of time (Isa. 26:20; 54:8), moment or instant of time (Exod. 33:5), every moment (Isa. 27:3).

Biblical scholars are quick to point out that a scriptural doctrine of time must emerge from careful study of the biblical words for time in their contexts. Furthermore, modern Western scientific and philosophical categories must not be imposed on any interpretation of Hebrew concepts of time in the Old Testament. The text of the Bible must be given the freedom to speak for itself.[3]

The Old Testament terms for time demonstrate knowledge of linear and chronological time. However, Hebrew has no specific word for abstract time. Despite the flexibility of many of these words in English translation, the focus or emphasis is on the content of time, not time as a dimension. The ancient Hebrews did recognize endless time or eternity quantitatively, but the Old Testament does not equate eternity with timelessness in a qualitative sense. Thus, the Bible "stresses not the abstract continuity of time but rather the God-given content of certain moments of history."[4] Of course, broad-based generalizations may foster misperceptions. Three common misinterpretations of the biblical understanding of time are clarified below.

Correct Time, Please

Hasty and imprecise linguistic analysis of the Old Testament terms for time have spawned faulty interpretations of the Hebrew understanding of time. The Old Testament employs no specific term for time in the abstract, that is the indefinite and continuous duration of time. While it is true that biblical Hebrew has no distinct vocabulary word for *time* in the abstract, like the Greek *chronos* (time as duration), there are ways in which the language of the Old Testament can express the equivalent idea.

For example, the Hebrew word for "day" (*yôm*) can mean an extended period of time, as in Numbers 20:15 where Moses recalled the Israelite sojourn in Egypt lasting a "long time" (NRSV). The same expression is found in Joshua 23:1 describing the duration of Hebrew conquest in Palestine.

The Hebrew *'ôlām*, "always, forever," may also be used to express the duration of time. Here the examples include the perpetual covenant between Yahweh and Israel (Exod. 31:16), the perpetual right of the Levites to redeem their property (Lev. 25:32), and even the "days of old," when God established the nations (Deut. 32:7).

And finally, the Hebrew word *yôm* may be coupled with other words to form phrases that convey the duration of time. Perhaps the most well-known illustration is the "Day of the Lord." This "day" is understood as a period of time in the future when God will judge the nations, restore his people Israel, and re-create the heavens and the earth (Isa. 13:6; Jer. 46:10; Amos 5:18; Zeph. 1:7, 14; etc.). Other similar expressions indicating this eschatological duration of time include "that day" (Joel 3:18), "the day of the Lord God of hosts (Jer. 46:10 RSV), "the day of calamity" (Hab. 3:16), and "the day of vengeance/wrath" (Isa. 61:2; Zeph. 1:15).

So then, although the Hebrews had no specific *word* for time in the abstract, it is incorrect to say that the Old Testament has no *concept* of time in the abstract (or time in duration).

A second misunderstanding growing out of studies on the Hebrew words for decisive moments in time is the notion of linear time in the Old Testament. Frequently, the ancient Hebrews are credited with a linear concept of time, whereas their pagan counterparts (as well as the later Greeks) are usually accused of having a cyclical view of time. But it is erroneous to assume that linear time and cyclical time are mutually exclusive. The ancient counterparts of the Hebrews had both a cyclical view of time founded in the regularity of the agricultural seasons and a linear view of time as demonstrated in their genealogical and historical records (like the chronologically precise Assyrian annals).

Likewise, the Old Testament evidences the ancient Hebrews also understood linear or chronological time in their genealogical and historical records (the sequential arrangement of the history of the Hebrew kings or the ordering of prophetic oracles chronologically; 2 Kings 16:1; 17:5; Hag. 1:1; 2:1). However, parts of the Old Testament indicate the ancient Hebrews also understood time cyclically, like their neighbors. Examples include the Levitical or liturgical calendar, which clearly patterned the religious festivals after the seasonal agricultural cycles of planting and harvest (Lev. 23). Elsewhere, the book of Ecclesiastes manifests a cyclical view of time in the repetition of natural events and the passing of human generations, so much so that the sage finds the cycles of time empty, wearisome, and full of despair (Eccles. 1:1–11; 3:1–11).

The important issue is not the distinction between cyclical and linear time. Rather, it is the content of time and the purpose or destination of time that is crucial. The Old Testament affirms both cyclical and linear time, and that time is not devoid of intention or meaning. The Bible warns that time, at least in human history as we know it, will come crashing to a halt. The continuum of history stops abruptly with the Day of the Lord. More importantly, time in the Old Testament is not chaotic, random, or meaningless. God has infused time with a redemptive purpose so that the original goodness of creation and humanity might be restored (Isa. 43:18–21).

Last, the divine epithet El Olam or Eternal God (Ps. 90:2; Isa. 40:28) has been misconstrued by some who assert God stands outside of time. In part, this is a philosophical issue that cannot be fully developed here. Suffice it to say God is not timeless. Granted, God is not affected by time in the same way we are—that is God does not age. Nor does he process time as we do; as the psalmist notes, a thousand years is like yesterday to God or even a watch in the night (a mere four hours, Ps. 90:4; cf., 2 Pet. 3:8).

Perhaps the best illustration of God's presence in time is another Old Testament epithet, the God of Abraham, Isaac, and Jacob (Exod. 3:15). God is Lord of the past (Exod. 20:2), the present (Ps. 139:7–12), and the future (Jer. 31:33). God's activity in the past, present, and future does not mean he exists in all three at once. Rather, he is a personal God who has the ability to intervene in time for each generation as they participate in his redemptive plan through covenant relationship (Mic. 7:18–20).

Former Time—Conceptions of Time in the Old Testament

The Old Testament primarily understands time "as the limited succession of days in which human experience of the world flows."[5] The emphasis in the Old Testament is not so much on the measuring of time in duration as on the action, responses, and events in moments of time. Four essential aspects of the Old Testament conception of time are outlined here: God and time, the human lifetime, moments of time in history, and future time.

God and time. Although the Old Testament contains no systematic teaching about God and his relationship to time, several theological principles may be adduced from the analysis of key texts:

- God is Lord over time as Creator (Gen. 1:5; Jer. 31:35);
- Time has a beginning, time can be measured from a starting point (Gen. 1:1);
- Time is inherently good as part of God's original creation, but was later corrupted by the Fall (Gen. 3:14–19);
- Earthly time will end and be absorbed into God's eternity (Isa. 60:19–20), yet time continues in the new creation (Isa. 65:20; 66:23);
- God has limitless existence in time, but he is not timeless (Isa. 40:28; 44:6);
- Temporality, that is time in the sense of past, present, and future, distinguishes the creature from the Creator (Ps. 90:4);
- God rules and overrules time in his creation on both the macro and the micro levels (the nations, Isa. 60:22; Jer. 18:7, 9; and the individual, Pss. 31:15; 39:5); and
- God rules and overrules time for specific purposes related to his plan of redemption for all creation (Gen. 12:1–3; Ps. 74:12; Isa. 49:6; 52:10).

The human lifetime. Human beings were divinely created in time, as the measurement of time (day/night) was already operative (Gen. 1:3–5). Human sin against God as recounted in the Genesis narrative of the fall of man and woman had a profound impact on humanity's experience in time (Gen. 3). First, physical death was now a reality in God's good creation (Gen. 3:19; Ps. 104:29). In addition, the divine mandate to subdue the earth became grievous toil because the harmony between humanity and nature had also been violated (Gen. 2:15; 3:17–18). And soon the cumulative effects of sin shortened human life spans (Gen. 5—6).

The Old Testament also teaches that our time is not our own as God's creatures. God controls the destiny of individuals as well as the plight of nations (Job 33:4; Pss. 31:15; 139:16; Isa. 60:22; Dan. 2:20–23). In fact, God controls the life of every living thing (Job 12:10). Further, he has divinely allotted each one the number of years in a lifetime (normally 70–80 years, Ps. 90:10). Hence, in the Old Testament, long life is considered a blessing from God (1 Kings 3:10–14), whereas a shortened life may be the result of divine judgment upon the wicked (Eccles. 7:17).

Since life is short, a mere breath (Job 7:7, 16; Pss. 39:5–6; 90:4; 144:4), and there is no advantage in time to the wise or the rich (Ps. 62:9), it is always the right time to seek the Lord (Hos. 10:12). Human plans perish apart from God (Ps. 146:4; cf., Ps. 127:1–2), and the cycles of time in human life can be vexation and weariness (Eccles. 1:8; 2:23; etc.). But the righteous understand time as a gift from God (Ps. 139:16). In wisdom they use each day to bless and praise God (Pss. 34:1; 71:15, 18, 24; 89:16; 90:12; 118:24; 119:164). They enjoy the divinely appointed labor of "subduing" God's creation (Eccles. 2:24–26; 5:18–20), knowing they will be required to give an account for their use of God's gift of time (Eccles. 12:12–14).

Moments of time in history. God also demonstrates himself as Lord over time by injecting "his promise (Isa. 40:8), his salvation (Isa. 45:17), redemption, and righteousness (Isa. 51:6, 8), his goodness (Isa. 54:8), and his covenant (Isa. 55:3) into the transitory creation as eternal values."[6] In so doing, God's self-revelation in time affirms both the dignity and worth of temporal humanity and his free sovereignty as Creator.

This revelation of grace by the Creator in history demands a response from the creature. Time cannot be held in suspension, nor is time reversible. This is why the Bible emphasizes "now" as the expedient time for a faith response to God. The divine appeal echoes through the Scriptures from voices like that of Moses ("this day . . . choose life," Deut. 30:11–19), Joshua ("choose for yourselves this day whom you will serve," Josh. 24:15), Elijah the prophet ("if the LORD is God, follow him," 1 Kings 18:21), Jesus ("As long as it is day, we must do the work of him who sent me. Night is coming, when no one can work," John 9:4), and the apostle Paul ("now is the day of salvation," 2 Cor. 6:2).

The certainty of God's gracious promise of redemption and the effectiveness of his salvation is as sure as time itself. If the covenant with day and night could be broken, then God's covenant to restore humanity would be null and void (Jer. 33:19–22; cf., 31:35–36). Here Ernst Jenni reminds us that "time and history are, therefore, in the Old Testament not a matter of indifference, but are of decisive importance, because they must afford the means of salvation."[7]

Future time. The Old Testament teaches that even though history as we know it will end, time will not cease (Dan. 11:40; 12:4). Rather, time will be re-created as a part of the new heavens and earth established by Yahweh (Isa. 65:17–25). Human experience in time is blessed by God in such a way that distress and suffering are remembered no more (Isa. 65:19), labor is sweet and lifetimes are graciously extended (Isa. 65:20–23), and all nature is at peace (Isa. 65:25).

Although the nature and measure of time units is changed in the new creation (no extremes in the seasons and no day/night distinctions, Zech. 14:6–7), the focus of the human experience will remain on the contents of time. Then humankind will fill time with the continual praise and worship of God, as he had originally intended (Zech. 14:20–21; Isa. 43:7). Then humankind will be able to actually perform the worship response required by God—doing justice, loving mercy, and walking humbly with God (Mic. 6:8).

Ultimately, the Old Testament reveals that the Hebrews "understood time as something qualitative, because for them time is determined by its content."[8] Another summary of Old Testament teaching on time has been offered by Abraham Heschel who said, "To understand the teaching of the Bible, one must accept its premise that time has a meaning for life which is at least equal to that of space; that time has a significance and sovereignty of its own."[9] Rabbi Heschel identifies Israelite religion in the Old Testament and later Judaism as "a *religion of time* aiming at the *sanctification of time*" (italics added).[10]

The Fall—Serving Time

It is important to remember that the ravages of sin that entered God's good creation at the Fall have perversely affected human perceptions of time as well (Gen. 3:1–24). The divine curse pronounced on the physical creation and humanity established adversarial relationships between humanity and the natural order, including time. The phrase "all the days of your life" in Genesis 3:17 indicates human existence is now bound by time. Even more than this, the human experience in relationship to time is now characterized by servitude and suffering.

The idea of the duration of time was soon tainted as well because human thought and inclination tended only toward wickedness continually (Gen. 6:5). This corruption brought death, as God prohibited humanity from "living forever" (Gen. 3:12). Now divine judgment became necessary to purge the creation of its great wickedness and violence with the great Flood (Gen. 6:11–13). The combination of these two truths, death and judgment, led the Teacher to despair over the human life, as nothing but emptiness (Eccles. 3:16–18; 6:1–7; 11:8; 12:8).

However, the "evil times" (as they are described by the prophets, Amos 5:13; Mic. 2:3), leading to death and judgment may be overcome. Despite the great troubles weighing heavily on humanity bound in time, the Teacher also recognized "there is a proper time and procedure for every matter" (Eccles. 8:6). Interestingly, his twofold solution to the human predicament in relationship to time embodies the essence of worship in the Old Testament: "fear God" and "keep his commandments" (Eccles. 12:13).

As we learned in Chapter 1, the fear of God is an attitude of reverence and worship that prompts the worship response of obedience to God. As such, the fear of the Lord constitutes a position or stand toward the idea of time on the part of the righteous.

Thus, the evil nature and character of the human experience in the duration of time, that is, human lifetime in human history, may be tempered or even overcome. More precisely, the attitude of worship generated by the fear of God brings divine perspective to human life and human history. Only this kind of reverence for the Lord God permits a proper understanding of his nature and character as revealed within time. He alone is the God who created the sequence of time (Gen. 1–2), rules over time in his sovereignty (Dan. 2:20–23), overrules time providentially (Gen. 50:20), and maps out a redemptive plan for all creation (Jer. 29:11–14).

Likewise, as the worshiper stops doing evil and learns to do good, justice and righteousness will sweep over evil like a flood (Isa. 1:16–17; Amos 5:23–24). These worship responses—acts of justice and mercy in the time-bound human experience—trigger God's gracious activity (Amos 5:14–15). In turn, this both anticipates and escalates the time when justice and righteousness spawn peace and quietness under the King of Righteousness (Isa. 32:1, 16–20; 35:1–10)—the time of the new creation that knows no time (Isa. 65:17–25; Zech. 14:6–7), only the continuous worship of God (Zech. 14:16–21).

The duration of time was no longer empty and meaningless for the righteous. A lifetime is really a gift from God affording the opportunity to do justice and righteousness, instilling a sense of sacredness to continuous time since divine purposes of judgment and redemption are being accomplished in creation (Deut. 4:9–14; Eccles. 3:11; Isa. 14:26–27; Dan. 2:20–23).

For this reason, the Hebrew poets assured the Old Testament faithful that it will be well with those who fear God, despite all appearances and circumstances (Pss. 84:10; 118:9–10; Eccles. 8:12; Prov. 15:16). Of course, the exodus is the prime Old Testament example of a moment-in-time event giving meaning to the duration of time in human life and history (Exod. 12—14). At that time God established his supremacy among the deities, redeemed his people with a mighty hand, and initiated covenant relationship (Exod. 19:1–6). All this was a type foreshadowing that ultimate act of redemption—the cross of Jesus Christ (1 Cor. 5:7).

New Testament Perspectives

The New Testament teaching on the biblical concept of time endorses that of the Old Testament. Although the Greek language of the New Testament employs specific vocabulary for definite linear time (*chronos*, Matt. 25:19), indefinite linear time (*kairos*, Acts 24:25), and time in the abstract (*aion*, Matt. 28:20), the emphasis is still on the content of time. Specific examples of this qualitative understanding of time include Luke's Gospel prologue citing the "events" or "things" that have been fulfilled among us (Luke 1:1, NRSV) and the frequent appeal on the part of the New Testament writers to the events of the Old Testament as central to the ministry of Christ (Acts 7; 26).

As does the Old Testament, the New Testament asserts a singular purpose for time and history—redemption (Luke 1:68–79). Thus the New Testament writers view the Old Testament as important preparation history for discerning the person and work of Jesus of Nazareth as Messiah (Rom. 15:4; 1 Cor. 10:11). In fact, the apostle Paul observed that Jesus Christ entered time just when human history was "ripe" (literally "full" or "fulness") for God's redemption (Gal. 4:4). Here in this same section of his letter to the Galatians, Paul identifies the purpose of Old Testament law as that of tutor or disciplinarian in escorting people to the biblical truth of justification by faith (Gal. 3:24). So Paul interprets the events of Old Testament time as the necessary prelude to the fulfillment of justification by faith in Jesus Christ (Gen. 15:6; Hab. 2:4).

Likewise, the New Testament represents God as the Lord of eternity, possessing limitless existence and the Creator of time (1 Tim. 6:16; Heb. 1:10–12). The New Testament also declares God as the Lord of time, ruling and overruling time in history to accomplish his redemptive purpose (Acts 2:22–24; 3:17–26; Gal. 4:4; Heb. 1:1–2). Remarkably, this immortal God entered human history as the Word who became flesh to live among humanity and reveal God the Father (John 1:14–18). This extraordinary thought is best captured in the lyrics composed by a contemporary Christian songwriter who penned,

> And so the Light became alive
> And manna became Man
> Eternity stepped into time
> So we could understand.[11]

The New Testament also concurs with the Old Testament assessment that time has been corrupted by the Fall. Indeed, the whole world is in the power of the Evil One (1 John 5:19). The New Testament exhorts Christians to make the most of time because the days are evil (Eph. 5:15; Col. 4:5). "The Christian's stewardship of time as God's priceless commodity is the teaching here."[12] Since every moment is a precious gift from God, the believer is called to redeem the time through acts of worship and service, especially doing good, prayer, and evangelistic outreach (Gal. 6:10; Eph. 5:15–20; Col. 4:2; 2 Tim. 4:2).

Finally, the New Testament projects a similar picture of time in the eschaton. Time will not cease, for the months and ages of time continue (Eph. 2:7; Rev. 22:2). However, the mode of experiencing time changes, for there are no longer time units of day and night (Rev. 21:23, 25; 22:5). The centerpiece of this new creation is the

Lord God, who dwells among mortals and makes all things new (Rev. 21:3, 5, 22). And most important, the curse is overturned so that humanity may occupy its time with continual worship, praise, and service to God (Rev. 7:14–17; 22:3).

Time and Worship

Ordinary Time?

Over the centuries the Christian church has developed a "church year" or liturgical calendar. This expression "church year" refers to the regular sequence of cycles, seasons, festivals, and fasts in the calendar of the Christian church. The succession of events in the church year is ordered independently from the civil calendar, although church year dates are reckoned according to the civil (Julian) calendar for the sake of convenience.[13]

The beginnings of a liturgical calendar in the Christian church can be traced to the third century A.D.[14] The church year was largely patterned after the Jewish religious calendar, with the key events of Jesus Christ's redemptive ministry replacing the exodus and Passover events of Old Testament redemptive history.[15] Eventually the liturgical calendar grew by accretion to include a complex rotation of church seasons and festivals. The Western church—Roman Catholic and Anglican—adopted a chronological scheme highlighting two cycles of time in the church year: Advent and Easter. The Eastern church—Byzantine and Orthodox—divided the church year into three cycles of time: the Menaia (Cycle of Fixed Feasts, beginning September 1), the Octoechos (Cycle of Eight Tones), and the Triodion and Pentekostarion (Easter Cycle).[16]

The purpose of the church year is to sanctify time within the yearly experience of church life. The celebration of Christ's life, teaching, death, resurrection, ascension, and sending of the Holy Spirit was designed to bring spiritual renewal to the church through "a vibrant reliving of the paschal mysterious."[17] Due to abuses that crept into the observance of the liturgical calendar during the medieval period, the Reformers abandoned the practice.[18] Today, the idea of a church year is foreign to many Protestant worshipers.

Of course, abuse remains a potential danger in the celebration of a church year. The most common problem associated with the liturgical calendar is the dichotomy it invites between "sacred" and "secular" time. For instance, the periods of time between the festival cycles in the church year are usually referred to as ordinary time or non-festive time, as neither special nor demanding the same intensity of spiritual participation.[19] Here Jacques Ellul has addressed the gist of the problem when he writes, "very quickly some days of the week . . . come to rank as sacred."[20] And soon sacred versus secular distinctions blur the perception of time.

However, the Old Testament knows no such distinction between sacred and secular time. All time is God's gift to humanity (Pss. 31:15; 139:16; Isa. 60:22), and each season or cycle of time has its appropriate place within the divinely ordered sphere of human experience in time (Eccles. 3:1–9; Song of Sol. 2:12; Hos. 10:12). For the ancient Hebrew each day was a special or sacred day because it could be used to fulfill creation's purpose of worshiping and praising God (Pss. 34:11; 118:24; Isa. 43:7).

The Hebrew religious calendar did not mark special festival days and seasons in order to separate them as sacred from ordinary or non-festive time. Instead, the Hebrew liturgical year marked all time in the annual cycle as sacred, with the special festival days and seasons celebrated as extra-festive times. The annual cycle of special festivals in the Hebrew religious calendar was a type of "time insurance" guaranteeing the daily celebration of all time as God's gift and the arena of divine activity.

Sabbath Time

A thorough exploration of the history and significance of the Sabbath in the Old Testament and later Judaism lies outside the scope of this study of Old Testament worship, since the topic of the Sabbath has generated a massive volume of literature.[21] Thankfully, our study is limited to the Sabbath's impact on the Old Testament understanding of time and worship. The primary source of information is Rabbi Abraham Heschel's classic essay on the Sabbath as a "palace in time."[22]

Sabbath in the Old Testament. The Mosaic legislation for holiness in Hebrew life extended even to the calendar. The great religious festivals were ordered according to the agricultural calendar of Palestine so that the Israelites might acknowledge Yahweh as their provider and sustainer (Lev. 23:4–44). The command to observe one day in seven as a Sabbath rest to God prefaced this religious calendar (Lev. 23:1–3).

This Sabbath ordinance reminded Israel that God was the Creator; he fashioned his work of creation in six days and rested on the seventh day (Exod. 20:8–11; cf., Gen. 1:31—2:3). The Sabbath brought a sense of timelessness to the worship of Yahweh and a sense of holiness to the human idea of time. Keeping one day holy to God certainly meant rest and refreshment to both humankind and beasts of burden. But more important, the Sabbath rest sanctified the human endeavor so that in the other six days of the week men and women might truly "eat, drink, and find enjoyment in their labor" as a gift from God (Eccles. 2:24–26; 5:18–20).

In the book of Exodus the Sabbath was a covenant sign between Yahweh and Israel denoting Israel's special relationship with God and testifying that her holiness was rooted in the Holy One, not in law and ritual (Exod. 31:12–17; Lev. 26:2). According to the prophet Jeremiah, it was the neglect of the sabbatical laws and consequent rejection of the covenant instruction inherent in the commands that was responsible for the fall of Jerusalem and the Hebrew exile to Babylon (Jer. 25:8–14; 2 Chron. 36:17–21). By the time of Jesus the practical and humanitarian benefits of the Sabbath had been obscured if not forfeited by the legalism of Judaism (Matt. 12:1–4). Such was the case that Jesus deliberately performed miracles of healing on the Sabbath to reassert the original intent of Sabbath for humanity, not humanity for Sabbath (Mark 2:23–28; 3:1–6; 7:1–13).

Rabbi Heschel's basic premise is that twentieth-century technological civilization has led humanity to pawn "the world of time" for power and control over "the world of space." The remedy for our time malady according to Heschel is the Bible (the Old Testament for this late Jewish scholar). "The Bible is more concerned with time than with space . . . to understand the teaching of the Bible, one must accept its premise that time has a meaning for life which is at least equal to that of space; that time has a significance and sovereignty of its own."[23]

More specifically, Rabbi Heschel appeals to the religion of Judaism and the Jewish Sabbath as the antidote for humankind's time-space disorder. The religion of Judaism instructs one "to be attached to *holiness in time,* to be attached to sacred events, to learn how to consecrate sanctuaries that emerge from the magnificent stream of a year" (italics added).[24] Even more than the Jewish religious festivals, the Sabbath is the synthesizing factor for humanity seeking to piece together the components of civilization caught between space and time. Thus he affirmed,

> The meaning of the Sabbath is to celebrate time rather than space. Six days a week we live under the tyranny of things of space; on the Sabbath we try to become attuned to *holiness in time.* It is a day on which we are called upon to share in what is eternal in time, to turn from the results of creation to the mystery of creation; from the world of creation to the creation of the world. (italics added)[25]

Accordingly, those who truly observe the biblical Sabbath build "a sanctuary in time." Worship is the primary focus of the Sabbath experience, but "the Sabbath is not dedicated exclusively to spiritual goals. It is a day of the soul as well as of the body . . . . man in his entirety, all his faculties must share its blessing."[26] The Sabbath celebrates God and his creation, so worship, prayer, and praise, as well as family, friends, food and drink, rest and recreation, festivity and solitude, conversation and study are all a part of the Sabbath experience.

The Sabbath also bridges the two worlds, this world and the one to come. "For the Sabbath is joy, holiness, and rest; joy is part of this world; holiness and rest are something of the coming world."[27] The Sabbath is an island or harbor sheltering people from the storms of life lived out in time and space.

What then is the Sabbath? Rabbi Heschel responds, "spirit in the form of time" and a realm in which to abide.[28] The Sabbath orders human life so men and women may complete their divinely assigned tasks: conquering space ("subduing the earth," Gen. 1:28) and sanctifying time ("becoming holy," Lev. 11:44).

Sabbath Year and Jubilee. The Hebrew religious calendar provided a Sabbath of rest for the land of the covenant promise as well. After six years of sowing, cultivating, and harvesting, the land was to lie fallow in the seventh year (Lev. 25:1-7). Practically speaking, the poor and socially disadvantaged were the beneficiaries of the sabbatical year, as they could glean the produce of the fallow land (Exod. 23:11). The laws of Deuteronomy expanded the sabbatical program to include the cancellation of debts, generous relief to the poor, and the release of Hebrew slaves (Deut. 15:2-18). The sabbatical cycle culminated in the Jubilee, or year of emancipation (Lev. 25:8-24). After seven sabbatical-year cycles, the land was sanctified in the fiftieth year. In addition to the enforcement of the sabbatical year sanctions, this Jubilee year stipulated the reversion of all property to the original owners.

The Sabbath and sabbatical-year ordinances were designed to foster social and economic equality and inculcate important covenant community principles in Hebrew society, including thanksgiving for past provision and faith in God's continued sustenance during the fallow year, forgiveness in the remission of debts, respect of persons created in the image of God in the freeing of slaves, and the practice of generosity and the idea of stewardship in the redistribution of the covenant land.

Sacred Times

The divine mandate for sacred times or festival times is found in Leviticus 23 and 25. This Mosaic legislation actually constitutes ancient Israel's religious calendar. The major festivals appointed for celebration at special worship times included the Sabbath, the Passover and Feast of Unleavened Bread, the Offering of Firstfruits, the Festival of Weeks, the Festival of Trumpets, the Day of Atonement, the Festival of Booths, Sabbath Year, and the Year of Jubilee. (A complete outline of the major and minor religious festival times in the Hebrew liturgical calendar with Julian calendar equivalents may be found in Appendix C.)

The order of major festival times of the Israelite liturgical calendar reflects the seasonal rhythms of nature, since most of the ancient calendars were originally based on the agricultural cycles of planting and harvesting. Unlike their Canaanite predecessors, however, the Hebrew religious festivals and appointed sacred times "have been historicized—that is they have received their content and meaning from the history of redemption."²⁹ This means that the Hebrew sacred times were not bound inextricably with the annual cycle of the agricultural seasons. Rather, the Hebrew religious calendar was linked to those redemptive events in Israelite history, especially those connected with the exodus from Egypt.³⁰

Thus, the Passover/Unleavened Bread Festival was celebrated at the time of the spring barley harvest, since according to tradition the Hebrew exodus from Egypt occurred at that time. The Feast of Pentecost or Weeks recalled Yahweh's giving of the Law to Moses at Mt. Sinai at the time of the fall wheat harvest. In the same manner, the Feast of Tabernacles or Booths marked the beginning of the fall vintage (wine) and olive (oil) harvests. Roland de Vaux correctly observes that these feasts and other appointed special times in the Hebrew religious calendar celebrates the various events of human life and especially the redemptive events of Israelite history.³¹ All this serves to further underscore the importance the Hebrews attached to the content of time.

What then was the purpose of this religious calendar in ancient Israel? First, the liturgical calendar was "a dramatic replay of history, done every year to bring home its meaning for the present."³² In other words, the replay of redemptive history through the special festival times of the liturgical calendar was designed to both instill and affirm faith in the Israelite covenant community. This annual cycle of special religious times reminded all Israel that it was the Lord God who delivered them from Egypt and established his covenant with them (Lev. 23:43).

William Dyrness identifies three additional purposes for the sacred times of the Hebrew religious calendar: (1) the seasons of feasting and religious celebration reminded the Hebrews that all good gifts come from God; (2) by remembering God's good gifts in the rhythm of nature and the cycle of redemptive history they showed obedience to God; and (3) the festival times of the religious calendar celebrated their God-given dominion over nature (Gen. 1:28).³³ That the liturgical calendar was an integral part of Israelite religious and social life is seen in Hosea's prophecy against the Northern Kingdom. As the Lord puts an end to the feasts, new moons, Sabbaths, and appointed times, so Israel is laid waste and vanquished (Hos. 2:11-13).

Finally, what was the significance of these special festivals for time as perceived and experienced by the Hebrews? Here again Dyrness has already highlighted the salient points:

1. These special or sacred times were an annual reminder that all time is in God's hands.
2. These special times were both reminders and demonstrations (through reenactment) that God was working in time by means of specific event and the natural process to show his goodness and save his people.
3. The liturgical calendar was an expression of confidence that Israel's life possessed a divine order, direction, and purpose.
4. The liturgical calendar assured Israel that God would continue to show his goodness and deliver his people in the future.[34]

New Testament Time and Worship

The early church was initially an assembly of Hebrew Christians, Jews who had confessed Jesus of Nazareth as Messiah. This Judeo-Christian heritage of the church has important ramifications for the New Testament understanding of time. Essentially, the New Testament church continued to perceive and experience time in the same way as the Hebrews of the Old Testament era. Hellenistic influence notwithstanding, Robert Banks condenses New Testament teaching on time to these two basic principles: "a discerning approach to time" and "alertness not busyness."[35] In connecting the New Testament conception of time with the Old Testament, Banks further observes,

> The ancient Hebrews had a distinctive awareness of their presence in time and history, and this was a direct consequence of their experience of God. The early Christians took over and intensified this approach to time and, through Christianity, it came to have an important place in Western thought.[36]

The book of Acts records formal daily worship in the early church, both in the temple (Acts 3:1; 5:12) and in private homes (Acts 2:46; 12:12). The morning and evening sacrifices of the temple liturgy no doubt influenced the daily corporate worship of the first-century Jewish Christians. It is unclear how long this formal daily worship continued in the early church.[37] However, the tradition of daily formal worship continued into the fifteenth and sixteenth centuries in many church traditions.[38]

One thing is clear; the principle of informal worship was important and became a distinctive mark of the New Testament Christian. The believers in Christ were to be a living sacrifice to God (Rom. 12:1–2), continually worshiping the Lord in their hearts (Eph. 5:18–20; Col. 3:16–17). In fact, the admonition not to forsake corporate assembly coupled with the exhortation for a worship life-style in the book of Hebrews suggests there is a complementary relationship between the two (Heb. 10:23–25; 13:15–16).

The New Testament also makes reference to Christians and the Christian church observing special worship times on a weekly, monthly, and seasonal or yearly basis. For example, the book of Acts portrays Christians worshiping and celebrating both the Jewish Sabbath and the Lord's Day (or first day of the week, Acts 13:14; 18:4; 20:1; 1 Cor. 16:2; Rev. 1:10).[39] Church history reveals some segments of the Christian church observed the Jewish New Moon and other religious festivals well into the fourth century A.D. (Col. 2:16).[40] The apostle Paul condemned the legalistic observance of the Jewish festival days, fearing such practice promoted a doctrine of human works over divine grace (Gal. 4:10). The key issue here is firm personal conviction and absolute devotion to the Lord Jesus Christ in religious practice, whether or not one celebrates special sacred days and seasons (Rom. 14:5–8).

In summary, the New Testament affirms in principle the idea and practice of informal daily worship. The celebration of special worship times or sacred days and seasons is a matter of personal conviction, as the Christian or Christian church is led by the Holy Spirit and biblical teaching in view of given historical and cultural circumstances.

Time for Reflection and Application

What have we learned? What does the biblical teaching about time mean for the Christian today, living in a "now box"? My desire is to provoke thought and prompt action by identifying categories for the reader's consideration yet leave room for exploration and expansion so the reader may personalize her or his own Christian response to time and worship

Time for Time

Augustine of Hippo (A.D. 354–430) well understood the problems associated with not only grappling with time philosophically but also experiencing time pragmatically. Quipped this great theologian of the early church, "Time never takes time off" (*Confessions*, Book XI, Chapter 14.17). Time waits for no one; neither can time be pushed or speeded ahead. Time moves at its own pace. According to Niels-Erik Andreasen, the key to living in time is learning to move with time and learning to wait for time.[41] The secret is recognizing that living in time is more "being" than "doing."[42] Time is for "becoming" holy, even as God is holy (Lev. 11:44) or becoming Christlike, as Paul exhorts the new covenant believer (1 Cor. 11:1).

The tenets catalogued below constitute a summary of the biblical teaching on time discussed above. These principles are offered as a foundation upon which the individual or church may build a personal theology of time—a theology that gives priority to "becoming" in time.

- All time is God's gift (Pss. 31:15; 139:16).
- Human life is short and people are frail (Pss. 39:4–6; 90:3–10; 103:15–16).
- Men and women must learn to number their days, or make the most of the time, because our days are short (Ps. 90:12), and the days are evil (Eph. 5:16).
- Time is not an abstract measurement, but consists of the contents or events that fill it (Exod. 20:2; Luke 1:1–4; Rom. 15:4; Gal. 4:4; 1 Cor. 10:11).
- People must act in time even as God has acted in time; people are called to make decisions and choices (Deut. 30:19; Josh. 24:15; 2 Cor. 6:2).
- The essence of time is worship, praise, joy, thanksgiving, and service (Pss. 71:5, 18, 24; 89:15–16; 118:24; 119:164, 175; Isa. 43:7; John 10:10; Gal. 6:10; Eph. 5:15–20).

- Special (worship/festival) times give meaning to daily time (Exod. 20:8–11).
- Time, as we perceive and experience it, will end; future time should shape present behavior (1 Thess. 5:6–11; 2 Pet. 3:11–12; Rev. 22:10–11).
- Since all time is sacred in that it is divinely granted, the Christian is called to balance all the dimensions of life's time (work, play, and worship) into a unified and holistic life-style response to God (1 Cor. 6:12–13; 10:23–24).
- God is gracious; his goodness overshadows all who wait on him; he enables the righteous to make the most of the time by his Holy Spirit (Pss. 31:19–24; 90:13–17; 143:10; 145:13; 147; Rom. 5:15; Eph. 5:18; 2 Pet. 3:7, 10; James 4:4–6). (See bibliography for further works devoted to biblical perspectives on time and the Christian use of time.)

C. S. Lewis once remarked, "Christians will usually seem to have a lot of time; you will wonder where it comes from."[43] It is my prayer that these thoughts outlining a theology of time will help you experience Lewis's observation: a lot of time, time for everything, time for work and rest, worship and meditation, leisure and recreation, family and friends, and service to Christ's church and others.

Time for Space

The Jewish Sabbath celebrates holiness in time rather than in space. For six days a week humanity lives under the tyranny of things of space. The Sabbath day is a day of freedom and independence from technology and civilization, from the things of space and the chase after things. The Sabbath nurtures the proper attitude toward things, possessions, the world of space—"to have them and be able to do without them."[44]

Biblical teaching about time should impact Christians in a similar way when it comes to the world of space. In his excellent book *Freedom of Simplicity*, Richard Foster articulates principles that seek to balance inward simplicity—particularly personal piety and worship—with outward simplicity—a biblical approach to the world of space. Especially important is the discipline of "the single eye of simplicity toward God."[45] This means learning how to renounce possessions and the world of space and to learn detachment—a detachment from things that liberates the Christian from the control of others, "no longer manipulated by the people who hold our livelihoods in their hands."[46]

Gordon Dahl challenged Christians to this kind of detachment from the world of space in his prophetic essay of the seventies, *Work, Play, and Worship in a Leisure Oriented Society*. He proposed the ABC's of Christian life-style and called the church to

> A—Abandon. Let go of things. Travel light. Be willing to give away all possessions to become Christ's disciple (Luke 14:33).
> B—Take time to enjoy the beauty of God's creation in nature and human culture. Slow down. Cultivate an aesthetic appreciation for the timely beauty in all that God has made and done (Eccles. 3:11).
> C—Celebrate life. Let the celebration of redemption in worship spill over into daily life in such a way that you can truly rejoice in each day that God has made (Ps. 118:24).[47]

Of course, all this does not mean the Christian forsakes or neglects the original mandate of creation: "Fill the earth and subdue it and have dominion over [it]" (Gen. 1:28 RSV). Again, Dahl argues the opposite is true. The "kingly ministry" of the Christian church must address issues of authority, distribution of power, control of technology, and the production and consumption of resources and goods. Dahl called upon the church to actively participate in the management process of our world, a world of space and things. The Christian and the Christian church has a divinely granted responsibility to be "earthkeepers" in the very best sense of the term, biblically and ecologically.[48]

Time for Worship

Worship is the key to a Christian understanding of life and time. Only worship can place all of human experience in the larger context of life's ultimate purpose and meaning. For the Christian, all of life is a response to a loving and gracious God. Thus, "the worship that God expects . . . involves a continuous response of gladness and hope through every experience of life—including its work and play—and a daily discipline of service and self-examination in the context of the Law's claim upon us and the Gospel's call to freedom and maturity."[49]

Stop the clock! I want to worship! How many times have you heard a wristwatch beep or chime at 12:00 noon during Sunday morning worship service? True worship is a meeting of the human and divine that transcends time.[50] I fear we have been conditioned to approach corporate worship much like the factory clock. We punch in, put in our time, and then wait for the whistle to blow quitting time. "If worship is to be an integral part of church life we must have time to do it."[51] Formal worship requires time—time for confession and repentance, time for praise and thanksgiving, time for the Word of God and the Eucharist, time for responding to the Word and the Table, and time for the spontaneous ministry of the spiritual gifts represented within the body of believers for the edification of the church.

Get a life . . . style! Not only do we need time for genuine formal worship of God as a corporate body, as a church; we also need worship to pervade our time—all of it. Since time is a divine gift, making all time sacred, worship is a life-style.

> We may speak in jest about going to church when you're hatched, matched, and dispatched, but that does not destroy the reality of the place of the worshiping community at all high points of life. . . . we will discover that virtually every Christian tradition feels the necessity of a congregational and liturgical response to the mountain peaks of our lives.[52]

This regular corporate worship celebrating major events of a lifetime is vital to the experience and expression of the Christian community or body life. But Schaper emphasizes "We go from the service of corporate worship into the service of individual worship, never away from the presence of God, never to be called anything less than the incarnation of His love and the vehicle of His will."[53] The continuing reality is the "body language" of unceasing spiritual worship offered to God (Rom. 12:1–2).

This worship as a way of life both permits and demands the Christian to "make the most of every opportunity" (Eph. 5:15–17; Col. 4:5–6). For Jacques Ellul this means the work of "preservation," preserving God's creation by God's methods and "salvation," redeeming a world burdened with sin and separation from God with Christ's gospel. The Christian places herself or himself "at the point of contact between two currents: the will of the Lord, and the will of the world."[54]

Let's get liturgical! We have already discovered that the purpose of special worship or festival times marking key events in Israel's redemptive history in the Old Testament was to bring meaning and celebration to all time. This principle of religious time transfers to the New Testament as well. The key redemptive events for the Christian church are Christ's birth, manifestation, baptism, death, resurrection, ascension, bestowing of the Spirit at Pentecost, and his second coming. This series of events brings meaning to all time in the Christian era. Like the Hebrew religious calendar, the application of Christian "event-time" to all time gives a certain transcendent meaning to all of life.[55]

Since our relationship to event-time determines our relationship to all time, I concur with Robert E. Webber when he advocates a return to the observance of the church year by evangelicals.[56] Whether one's church celebrates a liturgical year or not, individuals and families benefit from marking time on a daily, weekly, and yearly basis. (See Webber's helpful suggestions for developing a simple liturgical calendar that accents the major events of Christ's life and ministry.[57])

Especially important for the Christian is the weekly celebration of time. Robert Lee has challenged the church to consider the concept of "Sabbath time" for the Christian Sunday. This means recognizing a weekly cycle of time in which one day revitalizes life during the other six. He calls upon the contemporary Christian church to relearn the significance of Sunday as understood in the early church. He suggests three meanings for Sunday in the early church that we might recover profitably for our day:

1. Sunday as the day of light—light was created on the first day of the week, and Christ, the light of the world, arose from the dead on the first day of the week.

2. Sunday as the day of resurrection—a sign of the new covenant in Christ.

3. Sunday as the day of the Spirit—the day the Holy Spirit descended upon the first Christians, the birthday of the church.[58] Perhaps the appropriation of this early church teaching about Sunday would help us recapture the enthusiasm Tertullian had for the Sabbath. That great second-century Christian apologist proclaimed: "Sunday we give to joy!" (Ad Nationes, 13; De Oratione, 23).

Let all the earth keep silence! The prophet Habakkuk's charge to the nation of Judah, facing imminent destruction by the pagan Babylonian hordes of King Nebuchadnezzar, is no less forceful today. "But the LORD is in his holy temple; let all the earth be silent before him" (Hab. 2:20). Holiness in time through worship is possible only because God is indeed holy. In turn, God's holiness exposes our smallness, inability, frailty, and mortality. As we hush before the Lord in his holy temple we are reminded that God is sovereign in time. This assures the Christian of salvation and divine redemption in human history (Ps. 4:4–8). It also keeps the believer in Christ from apathy and cynicism because the personal involvement of our Holy God in creation preserves the sense of mystery and wonder of time, of a lifetime.

The silence of worship is equally as important as the noise of worship. Silence takes the worshiper out of time and into God's eternity—"Be still, and know that I am God" (Ps. 46:10). Silence is valuable in Christian worship because it is disturbing, arresting. We feel uncomfortable, helpless; we are no longer in control. The silence we spend in God's eternity brings perspective to our life in several ways. First, theologically, silence heightens communication with God because it provides a framework for hearing his word. Second, spiritually, the silence of worship leads the Christian to maturity in Christ because in silence we learn obedience to God.[59] And third, sociologically, the silence of worship teaches compassion for others because we are no longer attempting to "devour people with our words."[60]

The discipline of silence also instructs the worshiper in what it means to "wait upon the Lord." The psalmist vowed, "For God alone my soul waits in silence" (Ps. 62:1, 5 NRSV). Waiting on the Lord in silence renews the physical and spiritual strength of the faithful (Ps. 27:14; Isa. 40:31), breeds genuine humility, instills a practical hope that sustains the righteous in the present (Pss. 130:5–6; 131:1–3), reveals the will of God to those who are patient (Pss. 25:4–5; 37:7), and perhaps most important, reminds us that our times are in God's hands—not our own (Ps. 31:15).

Remember the Sabbath. The legacy of the Old Testament Sabbath for the Christian church is a day of rest and worship.[61] Augustine understood Sabbath rest as a rest of the heart, the peace and tranquility of a good conscience before God (*On the Gospel of John*, Tractate 20, Chapter V. 19.1). Sabbath rest is the application of Sabbath time to all of life in God, to all of time—all our senses alive in the joy and celebration of Sabbath worship. The human and divine encounter of Sabbath worship transcends time "so that in our ministry in time we may extend such transfigured life into the daily world without becoming lost in it."[62]

Today, the question is not what *is* Sabbath rest or Sabbath worship. There are a multitude of resources available describing and defining the essence of Sabbath time, several discussed in this very study. Our question is how do we participate in Sabbath rest and worship meaningfully, consistently? Here I think Robert Lee offers at least a partial solution. He contends Christians need to rediscover the difference between holy day and holiday.[63] The holy day celebrates in worship (or solemn and penitential quiet) past events. By contrast, the focus of the holiday is essentially the celebration of the present, having a good time now. The Christian celebration of a holy day is not marked by a red number on the calendar. Rather, it is a posture toward time and history, toward divine mystery and revelation in space and time.

Sabbath rest also had a humanitarian dimension, as it recalled the rest the Hebrews achieved when God delivered them from slavery in Egypt (Deut. 5:12–15). This prompts Tilden Edwards to observe, "Judeo-Christian sabbaths provide remembrances and signs of who we are in God's sight; ultimately equal and free from human subservience."[64] For Edwards this freedom invites the liberation of time for "appreciating rather than manipulating life."[65] Indeed,

Sabbath time tutors the Christian in doing justice and loving mercy at all times (Mic. 6:8).

Sabbath rest points to a time when the principles of justice and righteousness inherent to divine rest will pervade God's creation (Isa. 32:15–17). Recognizing that the Christian belongs to two cities, Ellul calls upon all those who belong to the heavenly city to practice a revolutionary Christianity. By this he means a life-style characterized by the power of Christ which unleashes biblical justice and righteousness—the kingdom of God, if you will—in this present order.[66] May your Sabbath rest and Sabbath worship enable you to celebrate time today in light of time in that day to come!

For further reference on the relationship between time and worship see the section on time in the Old Testament Bibliography in the back of this book.

◆ 7 ◆

In Your Name I Will Lift up My Hands!
Hebrew Worship As Sacred Actions

ONE OF THE TRENDS identified in the current worship renewal movement is participatory or active worship. There is widespread agreement today that the whole congregation should participate in worship, engaging all the varied ministries and gifts of the Spirit. Worship is no longer construed as a passive experience in which the people function as an audience while the clergy "performs" or "leads" them in acts of worship. Rather, worship in the Christian church is now viewed as a corporate act with each member contributing to the liturgy—the work of the people in worship.

Two books given solely to the idea of participatory worship have done much to help move Christian churches toward a more active celebration of worship.[1] A key feature of both texts is the appeal for balance with respect to the intellectual, emotional, and physical aspects of worship. This is not simply a knee-jerk reaction to the numbing affects of Enlightenment rationalism in Christian worship either. Rather, both authors present well-informed cases for participatory worship that is rooted in the biblical traditions of the Old and New Testaments and the practice of church history. This chapter discusses the theology of participatory worship in the Old Testament, outlines the range of worship actions employed by the ancient Hebrews, and explores the implications of their active worship for the New Testament church.

Active Worship and Hebrew Culture

The ancient Hebrews understood a human being as an indivisible totality. Thus, almost by definition, Hebrew worship in the Old Testament was participatory. Their synthetic understanding of the nature and constitution of the human being demanded that the whole person respond to Yahweh in worship, not just the spirit and soul.

This functional integration of the person is nowhere more evident than in the Psalms. Here, in one breath, the poet expresses the yearning of his entire being for God: "O God, you are my God, / earnestly I seek you; / my soul thirsts for you, / my body longs for you" (Ps. 63:1). Biblical commentators unanimously agree that soul (Heb. *nepesh*) and body (Heb. *bāśār*) simply denote David's whole person.[2] It is only quite natural then, when the psalmist offers worship to God, that the mind ("and beheld your power and your glory," Ps. 63:2), the lips and will ("my lips will glorify you," v. 3), and the body ("in your name I will lift up my hands," v. 4) all respond to the Lord in one accord. Examples of this kind of holistic worship abound in the Old Testament (1 Kings 8:22; 2 Chron. 29:30; Pss. 27:6; 47:1; 141:1-2; 149:1-3).

Active, whole person worship of the Lord God is not only implicit given the Hebrew worldview but also is implicit in the divine commandments regulating Israel's covenant relationship with Yahweh. The Great Commandment or *Shema* of later Judaism demanded a response of love to the God who delivered the Hebrews from bondage in Egypt: "Hear, O Israel: The LORD our God, the LORD is one. Love the LORD your God with all your heart and with all your soul and with all your strength" (Deut. 6:4-5).

Traditionally, Christian interpreters have understood the heart (or mind), the soul, and strength (or spirit) as complementary aspects of the human personality. Patrick Miller comments that the three phrases—heart, soul, and strength—express a totality. "The most important word, therefore, in its character as a demand that shapes our identity is, Love the Lord your God wholeheartedly, with your whole self, with all your capacity."[3] Ultimately, the oneness of the Lord God is to be matched by the holistic response of his worshipers.

Worship Actions and Old Testament Theology

A word of caution is appropriate, lest the significance of bodily movement in worship be misunderstood. Jacques Ellul reminds us of the potential danger in associating personal piety with only the visible. "The visible object is typical of the sacred world and very quickly becomes sacred itself."[4] When related to worship, Ellul's warning serves notice that physical movement and bodily gestures are not to become the goal or end of our worship experience.

The Old Testament prophets knew all too well the reality of a liturgical formalism devoid of any genuine spiritual understanding or commitment. For example, Isaiah observed, "These people come near to me with their mouth and honor me with their lips, but their hearts are far from me. Their worship of me is made up only of rules taught by men" (Isa. 29:13). In light of Isaiah's rebuke, perhaps Leslie Flynn's summary statement on the physical side of worship best captures the need for balancing the internal and the external aspects of our worship.

> Bodily movements are not necessarily acts of worship, nor do they guarantee that their significance will automatically occur. Unless the spirit is lifted to the Lord, actions will be mere conformity to custom. Yet we must not overlook the potential reciprocal relation between bodily action and soul faith. Through physical movement, commitments can be made, vows declared, and the challenge of faith accepted.[5]

Given this reciprocal relationship between what Flynn calls "bodily action" and "soul faith," what is the theological purpose of movements and gestures in worship? For the Hebrews several important reasons for movement of the body in worship may be identified.

1. Movement fulfills the divine imperative to worship God with the whole person (Deut. 6:4–5).
2. Worship actions permit a holistic response to God consistent with the Hebrew understanding.
3. Movement affirms and demonstrates faith. Robert E. Webber describes this as "enactment," the retelling and dramatic portrayal of a story, in this case, God's redemptive acts in human history, especially the exodus event in the old covenant and

the Christ event in the new covenant.[6] Enactment in worship revitalizes faith, instructs the faithful in the history of God's redemptive work, fosters the idea of participation in a community of faith, and builds disciplined behavior patterns in obedience to God.

4. According to A. S. Herbert, acts of worship serve to express the desire of human beings to communicate with God, to maintain and restore relationship with God, and to model worship practices for the next generation in the community of the faithful.[7]

5. Worship action may have the practical effect of inducing penitence (Isa. 32:11; Jon. 3:5–8), confirming or sealing a vow (Gen. 31:13; Num. 15:3), or serving as a reminder of God's gracious deeds in the past (Deut. 6:4–9).

6. Movement can give educational value through symbolism. This may be historical, as in the Passover festival (Exod. 13:3–10), or theological, as in substitutionary animal sacrifice (Exod. 34:20; Lev. 16:6–10).

7. Bodily movements in worship serve to mirror God's approach to humanity by means of both word and deed, for example, the exodus event and the covenant ceremony at Sinai. God has acted in history and spoken to humanity through the written and living Word. People of faith in both the Old and New Testaments in turn respond to God in word (recitation) and act (ritual or drama).[8]

Worship Actions in the Old Testament

A brief reminder is in order here before we examine the worship actions of the Hebrews as documented in the Old Testament. First, it is important to remember that the Old Testament spans a vast historical period, nearly two millennia of Hebrew history. Obviously, the practice of Hebrew worship was a long process comprised of various formative stages (see Chapter 3).

Second, this catalog of Hebrew worship responses makes no distinction between the spontaneous actions of private worship and the structured forms of public worship; these worship responses were appropriate in either context.

And third, this analysis of Hebrew worship does not pretend to be comprehensive or exhaustive but rather a representative sampling of how the ancient Hebrews responded to their God in worship.

According to Robert E. Webber's theology of enactment, worship is a dramatic retelling of the relationship between God and ourselves.[9] But worship is more than the simple re-creation of redemptive events in history; it is a personal encounter with God. God has acted, and people of faith respond. Enactment as a worship response occurs through recitation and ritual (or drama).

Worship As Recitation

Before we explore recitation as a worship response for the Hebrews, it is important for our discussion to clearly define the word *liturgy*. Literally this Greek word means the "work of the people" in worship. Specifically the term refers to the structure and sequence of events and actions of a particular worship service. This study catalogs various liturgical practices generally, not always systematically according any one given worship service.

Liturgical responses. The Old Testament records several occasions where congregational recital was either orchestrated by the priests or spontaneously evoked given the particular nature of the worship context. For example, after the recital of the hymn of praise celebrating the entry of the ark of the covenant into Jerusalem, all the people said "Amen!" (1 Chron. 16:36). Sometimes the "Amen" response is repeated, especially in the Psalms (Pss. 41:13; 72:19; 89:52). In other instances, "Amen!" as a liturgical response is coupled with "Hallelujah!" or "Praise the Lord!" (Ps. 106:48). In fact, the word *Amen* has several theological functions in Old Testament worship. In addition to a formal liturgical praise response in public worship as in 1 Chronicles 16:36, "Amen" confirms a wish, command, or prophecy (1 Kings 1:36). "Amen" also marks the acceptance of the consequences associated with a divine curse (Num. 5:22; Deut. 27:15–26; Neh. 5:13). The "Amen" is often a spontaneous expression of praise and worship in response to God's grace and mercy (Neh. 8:6), and in one case the "Amen" is used almost like a nickname for God, literally "the Amen God" (Isa. 65:15), usually translated "God of Truth" or "God of faithfulness" in English. Other liturgical responses utilized as a part of recital in Hebrew worship included phrases like "Hallelujah!" or "Praise the Lord!" (Pss. 105:45; 106:48; 117:1; etc.) or "Great is the Lord!" (Pss. 48:1; 145:3). At times these kinds of liturgical responses were sung, chanted, or shouted in the form of a litany, for example, the refrain "for his steadfast love endures forever" after each line of Psalm 136. Creedal recitations were also part of Israel's audible response to God, often in conjunction with covenant renewal ceremonies (Josh. 24:16–18). A credo is a confessional statement of belief(s) basic to sustaining a common faith in the religious community. Several early Hebrew creeds have been identified in the Old Testament, including passages like Deuteronomy 6:4, 20–24; 26:5–9 and Joshua 24:2–13.

Singing. Music is both worship and an aid to worship. Music was a vital element of Hebrew worship in the Old Testament as evidenced by the role of the singers, minstrels, and musical guilds associated with temple worship (1 Chron. 25) and the presence of the Psalter in the Old Testament canon. (The significance of this songbook for ancient Israel is treated separately in Chapter 9. The role of music in Hebrew worship is dealt with in detail in Chapter 11.)

Singing was a favorite Hebrew worship response. Whether the songs were sung by an individual (Exod. 15:20–21; Ps. 51:14), in unison or responsively by the whole congregation (Num. 21:17; Ezra 3:11), or by the temple choirs and minstrels (1 Chron. 15:27; 2 Chron. 23:13; Ps. 68:25), it was good for the people of God to sing praises to him (Pss. 92:1; 147:1).

This form of recital traces its origins to the Mosaic covenant (Exod. 15:1; Deut. 32:1–44). The song of Moses actually served as a witness for the Hebrews of their covenant relationship with and obligation to Yahweh (Deut. 31:19–22). For this reason the psalmist sings to God as long as he lives as a sign of covenant fidelity (Pss. 61:8; 104:33; 146:2). Several types of singing as a worship response may be identified in the Old Testament. Five categories of songs recited in worship have been broadly defined:

1. The song of praise or hymn, extolling the perfection and magnificence of God's person and character (Pss. 29:1-2; 40:3; 95:2; 147:1).
2. The song of thanksgiving, recounting specifically the past deeds of redemption and blessing performed by God for his people (Neh. 12:8, 46; Pss. 27:6; 42:4).
3. Joyous songs, perhaps a variation of the song of thanksgiving (Ps. 107:22), or even a hybrid combining the hymn of praise and the song of thanksgiving (Pss. 47:1; 98:4).
4. Victory songs or hymns, commemorating Yahweh's deliverance of Israel and/or the righteous from enemies (Exod. 15:1-18, 21; Judg. 5:1-31; Ps. 118:15).
5. Glad shouts, a variation of the victory hymn, perhaps the chanting of particular words or phrases of the victory song (Pss. 42:4; 118:15).
6. Other types of songs for recital in worship gradually became a part of the Hebrew repertoire as the book of Psalms expanded over the centuries. These psalmic types included laments (Ps. 3), storytelling psalms (Ps. 105), songs of trust (Ps. 16), royal psalms (Ps. 2), wisdom psalms (Ps. 110), liturgy psalms (Ps. 15), Torah psalms (Ps. 119), covenant renewal liturgies (Ps. 81), penitential psalms (Ps. 51), and mixed types or hybrids (Pss. 34; 36; 52). These additional psalmic types are discussed at length in Chapter 9.

Prayer. Prayer in the Old Testament should not be equated with the superstitious incantations and magical chants of the Hebrews' pagan neighbors (cf., the prayers of the priests of Baal in 1 Kings 18:20-29). For the ancient Israelites prayer was always a personal encounter with God rooted in his divine self-revelation and covenant relationship with Israel. Whether audible (Dan. 9:4) or silent (1 Sam. 1:13), prayer was understood as direct communication with a responsive deity—a God in Zion who hears prayers (Ps. 65:1-2).

Walter Liefeld is correct when he identifies the several aspects of prayer as overlapping with worship because they lead to the glory of God.[10] These distinct but related expressions of prayer may be defined as follows:

1. Worship—ascribing God the glory due his name (Ps. 29:1–2).
2. Praise—preoccupation with who God is and what he has done (Ps. 135:1–7).
3. Thanksgiving—specifically acknowledging the goodness of God (Ps. 136:1–26).
4. Adoration—personal, loving worship (Ps. 73:25).
5. Devotion—prayer resulting in a vow (1 Sam. 1:11).
6. Communion—emphasizes relationship with God and two-way communication and fellowship in prayer (Pss. 5:3; 42:8; 94:19).
7. Confession—individual or corporate admission of sin and guilt before God, a necessary prerequisite for prayer and worship (Ezra 9:6–15; Neh. 9:1–3).
8. Petition or supplication—presenting personal needs, concerns, cares, complaints to God (1 Sam. 1:17; Ps. 20:5).
9. Intercession—petition or supplication for another individual or group (2 Sam. 12:16; Exod. 32:11).

The Old Testament mentions appointed times for prayer. Specifically, the Psalms speak of the faithful praying in the morning (5:3), even before dawn (119:147). Elsewhere the psalmist utters prayers of lament in the morning, at noon, and in the evening (55:17). Perhaps this text served as Daniel's inspiration for praying three times a day facing Jerusalem (Dan. 6:10). Also, it seems morning and evening prayers were common, patterned after the morning and evening sacrifices of the temple liturgy (1 Chron. 23:30; cf., 1 Chron. 16:40). Finally, much like the apostle Paul's injunction to "pray without ceasing" (1 Thess. 5:17), the psalmist likewise invoked praying continually (Pss. 72:15; 105:4).

Several different prayer postures are mentioned in the Old Testament, including standing (2 Chron. 20:5), kneeling with the arms outstretched (1 Kings 8:54; note Solomon began this prayer kneeling, 1 Kings 8:22), kneeling (Ezra 9:5), head bowed (Neh. 8:6), prostrate (Josh. 7:6), with uplifted hands (Ps. 28:2), sitting (2 Sam. 7:18), and bowing with the face between the knees (1 Kings 18:42). While particular postures and gestures in prayer were optional, they were always conditioned by the mood, content, and circumstance of the prayer.

Vows. Vows are solemn promises or pledges to God. Vows may include the pledge to perform some deed or enter some form of special covenant to Yahweh or some other kind of response that alters current behavior, living conditions, or vocational situation. Whereas one might swear an oath to another person, vows are made to God (or other deities). Thus, in the Old Testament vows are usually made in the context of prayer.

According to Mosaic legislation, vows for the ancient Hebrews were voluntary but binding (Lev. 27; Deut. 23:23; Eccles. 5:4–5). A vow may be made by an individual (Jacob, Gen. 28:20) or taken by an entire group or community (Israel, Num. 21:2). Often vows in the Old Testament are conditional in nature, usually the result of personal distress or national calamity.[11] That is, a vow is taken contingent upon God's prior fulfillment of a specific request made by the worshiper (Jephthah's problematic vow, Judg. 11:30).[12] In some cases, one might take a vow for another person as in the case of the Nazirite vows (Hannah's vow regarding Samuel, 1 Sam. 1:11; cf., Num. 6:1–21). Usually an animal sacrifice was prepared as a gift or votive offering to the Lord when God had answered the request of the worshiper making a conditional vow (Lev. 27:9; Num. 15:8).

The taking and fulfilling of vows was important to both personal piety and corporate worship during the course of Israelite history. For the psalmist especially vow making was an essential part of personal worship in covenant relationship with God (Pss. 50:14; 56:12; 61:5, 8). Vows were an act of faith for the righteous, a testimony or witness of fidelity to the congregation, and a tribute to the God who answers prayer (Pss. 65:1; 66:13–19; 116:14, 18).

Yet the Old Testament prophets understood that vows made to God apart from covenant faith and obedience were useless and an abomination to God. Jeremiah condemns the people of Judah for their perfunctory vows, making promises to God while continuing their "vile deeds" (Jer. 11:14–17). Likewise, Malachi rebuked those in Jerusalem who made vows to God but responded in worship with inferior offerings (Mal. 1:14). As with the other worship responses studied thus far, vow making must be accompanied by a heart of faith in God and a proper attitude demonstrated by deeds of covenant love and obedience to have any spiritual significance.

Preaching/teaching. The public reading of Yahweh's covenant history and legislation began at Mt. Sinai (Exod. 24:7). This public reading of the Law to the congregation of Israel was decreed every seventh year (Deut. 31:9–13). The purpose of these public readings was to recite the history of Yahweh's redemptive deeds for Israel for the sake of instructing a new generation of Hebrews. The event also afforded the covenant community an opportunity to renew their covenant faith and reaffirm their vow of obedience. As in the case of King Josiah's reform the reading of the Law could also bring rebuke, prompt repentance, and inspire covenant renewal (2 Kings 23:1–3).

One clear example of biblical exposition surfaces from the postexilic period of Israelite history. In conjunction with the reforms initiated by Ezra and Nehemiah in Jerusalem, Ezra read the law of God. In addition, a group of Levites interpreted or gave "the meaning so that the people could understand what was being read" (Neh. 8:3–8).

This exposition of Mosaic readings was probably both a translation from Hebrew into Aramaic, then the lingua franca, and an interpretation or explanation of the meaning of the texts addressing covenant relationship with Yahweh. Since the pre-exilic prophets indict the priesthood for their failure to instruct the Hebrew people in the knowledge of God (Hos. 4:4–6; Mic. 3:11), it seems reasonable to conclude that this kind of exposition was intended to be part of the ongoing ministry of the Levites (1 Chron. 26:32; 2 Chron. 31:2–4).

Related to the reading and exposition of Mosaic Law is meditation. The Hebrew word for "meditation" means literally "to ponder by talking" or "muttering to oneself." So meditation for the Hebrews was not necessarily a silent practice. Joshua's charge to the Israelites included meditating on the book of the law day and night (Josh. 1:8). The purpose of his injunction was to inculcate habits of obedience to the commands of God. Meditation on the law of God was crucial to covenant relationship with Yahweh and the receiving of its attendant blessings.

The psalmist too knew the value of frequent meditation on the law of God (Ps. 1:2). The Torah psalm, Psalm 119, indicates that the righteous will meditate on God's precepts, statutes, and promises—his word—and his wondrous works (119:15, 23, 27, 48, 78,

148). Meditation produces an inner strength and joy since it is motivated by love (Ps. 119:97–99). Meditation takes place in the heart
and the mind, the centers of emotional and rational life. The truly
righteous meditate upon the law of God because they desire their
thoughts and attitudes to approach the standard of holiness Yahweh
approves (Ps. 19:14).

Implicit in this practice of meditation is memorization. The biblical world placed a high premium on oral communication, including the memorization of genealogies, history, and literature.[13] Given
the limited availability of written copies of the Old Testament Scriptures, it is only natural the Hebrews would devote themselves to the
task of memorizing God's revelation. The Great Commandment or
Shema of later Judaism reinforces the practice of memorizing the law
of God. The Hebrews were directed to teach (literally "repeat") the
instructions of God to their children (Deut. 6:6–9). Specific times
for this memory work were suggested, including times when the family sits together at home, in travel, and in the morning and evening
of each day. Disciplining the mind by memorizing the past words
and deeds of God also functioned to produce practical obedience to
the commands of God.

Worship As Ritual Drama

Sacrificial worship. In addition to prayer (Jer. 29:12) and repentance and contrition (Isa. 66:2), the ritual sacrifice was another way
the Hebrew people might approach their God Yahweh. The idea of
sacrifice was not unique to the Hebrews in the ancient world, as
animal, grain, and drink offerings to deities were common to the
religious cults of Mesopotamia and Syro-Palestine. Whereas the parallels between Israelite and ancient Near Eastern sacrificial practices
attest the universal need for humanity to placate the gods, the Hebrew sacrificial system was distinctive in that it was divinely revealed
and was directed toward the goal of personal and community
holiness.

Mosaic law stipulated that the sacrificial victims offered to the
Lord were to come from the categories of clean animals and birds
(Gen. 7:2–8; Lev. 27:9–13). These included bulls, oxen, goats, rams,

sheep, doves, and pigeons. Non-blood offerings were to be choice agricultural staples (Lev. 2:1, 4).

Certain requirements were attached to the sacrificial offering, including the preference of male animals (Lev. 1:2, 10), unblemished animals at least eight days old (Lev. 22:17–30), and animals actually owned by the worshiper (Lev. 1:2, wild animals were unacceptable sacrifices).

Five basic types of sacrifices or offerings were instituted as part of formal, corporate worship and personal celebration in Hebrew religious expression: cereal or grain, fellowship or peace, burnt, sin, and guilt or trespass offerings. These sacrifices, described in Leviticus, fell into two categories: (1) those offered spontaneously to God in praise and thanksgiving for blessings received or favors granted (the cereal or grain offerings and the three types of peace offering, Lev. 2:1–16; 3:1–17); and (2) those demanded by Yahweh on the occasion of sin in the Hebrew community (the burnt, sin, and trespass or guilt offerings, Lev. 1:3–17; 4:1–5:13; 5:14–6:7). The former were grateful responses to the goodness of God, and the latter were necessary to atone for or cover the sin committed, accomplish reconciliation with Yahweh, and restore the penitent sinner to fellowship with other persons and God. (See Appendix D.) The ritual for the major altar sacrifices of Leviticus 1–5 is described in formulaic terms. The sacrifice comprised six basic steps or acts, three performed by the worshiper and three by the officiating priest. First, the worshiper brought his sacrifice or offering to the entrance of the sanctuary (Lev. 1:3), placed his hand upon the head of the animal (Lev. 1:4), and slaughtered the sacrificial victim (Lev. 1:5; 3:2, 8). Then the priest collected and sprinkled the blood on the altar (Lev. 1:5; 3:2) and burned the appropriate portions of the sacrifice (Lev. 1:6–9; 3:3–5), leaving the remainder of the offering to be eaten by the priest (and/or the worshiper) as a sacrificial meal (Lev. 6:16, 26; 10:14).

Several biblical texts indicate there was a proper order for the offering of these altar sacrifices: First the sin and guilt offerings; second the burnt offerings; finally the cereal and peace offerings followed in succession (see Lev. 8:14–9:22; 2 Chron. 29:20–36). The procedural sequence of the sacrifices reflects Old Testament teaching on how the worshiper approached the holy God. First the worshiper atoned for sin (the sin and guilt offerings), then consecrated himself in devotion to God (the burnt and cereal offerings), and then fellowshiped and communed with God in worship (the peace offerings).

The Hebrew word for atonement (Lev. 4:26, 31) is part of the word group related to the Hebrew term *kāpar*. This root word conveys the ideas of appeasement and reconciliation in contexts related to animal sacrifice (Exod. 32:30). The word may mean ransom or atonement money in connection with the sanctuary tax (Exod. 30:12–16). William Dyrness has noted two elements basic to the Israelite sacrificial system: (1) the humiliation of the worshiper (symbolized by laying hands on the victim), along with reparation to God by the sacrifice of personal property in the form of animals or produce; (2) the transference from a state of sin and guilt to a state of cleanness and purity, emphasizing the objective standards of God's justice and the appropriate process for approaching God in worship.[14] Ultimately, the purpose of Hebrew sacrifice was didactic. The enactment of the ritual atonement or "covering of sin" was designed to instruct the Israelites in the principles of God's holiness, human sinfulness, substitutionary death to cover human transgression, and the need for repentance leading to cleansing and renewed fellowship within the community and with God.

Seasonal festivals. In addition to the altar sacrifices, Mosaic Law prescribed sacrifices for the seasonal festival, including Passover and Unleavened Bread, Firstfruits, Tabernacles, and Day of Atonement. (See Appendix D.)

Daily morning and evening sacrifices were also offered by the priest, and sacrifices of a more private nature were permitted as well: personal dedication (1 Kings 3:1); fulfillment of a vow (1 Sam. 1:3, 21); consecration (1 Sam. 16:3); veneration of God (Judg. 13:19).

Connected to the sacrifices were the festival liturgies of the Hebrew religious calendar. Our interest here are the worship responses and related activities associated with these festivals. (The historical backgrounds of these religious holy days and their significance for the Hebrew concept of time has been discussed in Chapter 6; see also Appendix C.) By the time of the New Testament seven major festivals were observed annually in the Jewish calendar. For the most part these festivals were connected with the important historical events of early Israelite history. The specific ritual reenactments associated with each festival not only dramatized Hebrew history but also evoked memories of God and his covenant relationship to Israel. This liturgical symbolism was employed didactically for the theological education of the religious community in the divine works of deliverance and redemption. The key elements of the ritual reenactment for each of the seven major festivals are outlined below.

1. Feast of Unleavened Bread and Passover (Exod. 12:21–27; 23:14–15; Lev. 23:4–5; Deut. 16:1–8). The Feast of Unleavened Bread and Passover are the first of the major feasts in the liturgical calendar and the most significant historically and theologically for the Hebrews. Passover reenacted the Israelite deliverance from slavery in Egypt. A special meal and family service embodied the Passover celebration. The sacrifice of the Passover lamb and the blood ritual which preserved the Hebrew firstborn during the tenth plague demonstrated the practice of substitutionary sacrifice. This principle characterizes much of Hebrew worship in the Old Testament. The ritual questions of the children around the Passover table afforded the opportunity for instruction on the great redemptive event of the old covenant, the Israelite exodus from Egypt. The seven-day Feast of Unleavened Bread connected with Passover symbolized the years of sorrow and bitterness the Israelites spent languishing in bondage to the Egyptian taskmasters and their hasty flight from Egypt. First and foremost, the Passover feast was a proclamation and an affirmation of God's redeeming grace to the Hebrew people.[15]

2. Feast of Weeks or Pentecost (Exod. 23:6; Num. 26–31; Deut. 16:9–12). Also called the Feast of the Harvest or Day of Firstfruits, this feast celebrated the completion of the barley harvest. The festival was also called Pentecost because it was placed on the calendar fifty days after the beginning of the barley harvest, *pente* meaning fifty. This was a time for great rejoicing before the Lord and a time for bringing freewill offerings to God from the harvest. The giving of the firstfruits of harvest was a symbolic reminder that the Lord had provided the bounty of agricultural produce and all really

belonged to him. Later, the giving of the Law at Sinai was also connected with Pentecost, infusing the festival with ideas and practices related to covenant renewal as well.

3. Feast of Booths or Tabernacles (Lev. 23:33–43; Num. 29:12–40; Deut. 16:13–17). Mosaic legislation called for the Israelites to construct some type of temporary shelter—booth, tent, lean-to—and presumably live in it for all or part of the seven-day festival. As part of a fall harvest celebration the booth dramatized dependence on God. The festival was also connected with the wilderness wanderings after the Exodus, so the booth hearkened back to the temporary homes of the Israelites during that desert trek. Today the Feast of Tabernacles or Sukkot serves as a symbol of homelessness in Judaism. The move from one's permanent home to a temporary shelter both admonishes the affluent to consider charity for the socially disadvantaged and instructs all in reliance on God.

4. Feast of Trumpets, later Rosh Hashanah or "New Year" (Lev. 23:24–25; Num. 29:1–6). The blowing of the ceremonial trumpet, the *shofar*, marked the beginning of the new religious year for the Israelites, in contrast to the calendar year. The day was a solemn Sabbath and afforded an opportunity for the worshiper to reorder his or her religious life at the beginning of a new liturgical year. In later Judaism the New Year is a day of divine judgment as God distinguishes between the righteous and the wicked and seals their fate on Yom Kippur, the Day of Atonement. The reading of the Torah and giving gifts to the poor were New Year's customs instituted by Ezra the scribe (Neh. 8:9).

5. Day of Atonement or Yom Kippur (Lev. 16). The Day of Atonement was the national day of repentance and sacrifice for sin in ancient Israel. This was the only required fast day in Mosaic legislation. On this special day the high priest entered the Holy of Holies to make atonement for the priests and people. The annual scapegoat ceremony reminded the people of God's holiness and the seriousness of sin. Especially important was the symbolic transference of community sin to the head of the scapegoat before it was sent off into the wilderness (Lev. 16:22). Here again the substitutionary character

of Hebrew sacrificial worship is graphically demonstrated. Unlike the joy and celebration associated with many of the other Hebrew festivals, the Day of Atonement was a day of sorrow, mourning, and self-mortification over personal and community sin.

6. Feast of Purim (Esther 3:27; 9:20–32). This festival celebrates the deliverance of the Hebrews in Persia under King Xerxes by Queen Esther. One of Xerxes' royal princes, Haman, plotted to have all the Jews in Persia exterminated by royal decree. Through a providential series of events, along with Mordecai's wisdom and Esther's courage, the Jews were spared destruction in Haman's pogrom. Today the Feast of Purim is observed by prayer and fasting on the first day, since by prayer and fasting the Jews were able to overturn Haman's wicked scheme. The second day of the feast is given to the reading of the book of Esther in synagogue services, including denouncing wicked Haman with boos, noisemakers, and foot-stomping when his name is read. The third day of Purim is given to joyous celebration, feasting, dressing in costumes, exchanging gifts with friends, and charitable distribution to the poor.

7. Feast of Dedication or Lights (1 Macc. 4:36–58; 2 Macc. 10:1–9; cf., John 10:22–39). This feast commemorates the cleansing and dedication of the second temple by Judas Maccabeus in 164 B.C. The celebration is known as Hanukkah today and is marked by the lighting of candles for eight straight days, symbolizing the miracle of oil. According to Jewish tradition, this small measure of oil burned for eight days in the golden lampstand after the cleansing of the temple. The light of the candles symbolized the divine light of God's revealed word to his people (Pss. 27:1; 36:9; 119:105) and to the world (Isa. 42:6; 49:6).

Several important points for our consideration emerge from this overview of the Hebrew religious festivals. First, God ordered Jewish worship in such a way that there were cycles of exciting worship celebrations at regular intervals during the year. Second, these festivals connected the worship of God with concrete historical events of divine intervention on the part of Yahweh for his people. Third, joyous celebration was balanced with sober reflection. And fourth, the festivals offered a variety of participatory worship experiences. Robert Schaper summarizes this way, "The festivals were elaborate, they were demanding, they were joyous for the most part, and they were interesting."[16]

Pilgrimage festivals. Three festivals were pilgrimage festivals—Passover, Pentecost, and Tabernacles. Israelite males were required to appear before the Lord at the central sanctuary (Exod. 23:14–17; Deut. 16:16–17). With the construction of a permanent temple by King Solomon, this location was Jerusalem. Mosaic legislation also stipulated that the Israelite worshiper would appear before the Lord empty-handed, indicating sacrificial offerings were to be brought and presented to the Lord God. The topic of pilgrimages has already been dealt with at length in Chapter 5. In summary, pilgrimages embodied the principle of "uprootedness" for the ancient Hebrews. In the midst of the joy and celebration of families and clans traveling to worship God, there was the constant reminder of the alien quality of biblical faith. Life is short, life is a difficult journey, community is essential to success in the journey, and dependence on a gracious God who sustains and upholds his people is the essence of life (Pss. 73:25–26; 90).

Incense offerings and libations. The offering of incense was another ritual act common to worship in the ancient world. Only the Hebrew priests were permitted to make incense offerings to the Lord (Num. 16:35). Two specific types of incense offerings are prescribed in the Old Testament: (1) the burning of incense upon the altar of incense in the tabernacle precincts, and later the temple, every morning and evening (Exod. 30:7–9); and (2) the annual censer offering of the high priest in the Holy of Holies of the sanctuary during the Day of Atonement ritual (Lev. 16:12–13).

The recipe for the incense burned by the Israelite priests in the worship of the Lord was revealed to Moses as part of the Mt. Sinai covenant (Exod. 30:34–38). The compound was made by perfumers and was forbidden for secular use. Frankincense, a chief ingredient in the incense mixture, was also burned with vegetable offerings (Lev. 2:1–2, 15–16; 6:15), accompanied the bread upon the show-

bread table in the sanctuary (Lev. 24:7), and was burned as a spontaneous expression of joy and devotion (assuming the incense offering
is performed correctly, Lev. 10:1). The sweet aroma of the incense
offering both enhanced the worship experience aesthetically and
provided a cloud of incense smoke serving as a symbolic shield protecting the worshipers from contact with the holy (Lev. 16:13; Num.
16:46–48).

Elsewhere in the Old and New Testaments the burning of incense is symbolic of the prayers of the saints (Ps. 141:2; Rev. 8:3–5).
The gift of frankincense to the Christ child by one of the magi was
both a statement of his deity and a symbol of his future priestly ministry (Matt. 2:11). It is possible Paul's reference to the gospel as the
"aroma of Christ" is an allusion to the incense offering of the old
covenant (2 Cor. 2:15).

Unlike the burning of incense, the libation was not restricted
to the Israelite priesthood. The libation or drink offering was a ritual
act of pouring a liquid, usually oil or wine, onto the ground. The
drink offering was often a secondary sacrifice in that it accompanied
other types of sacrifices and offerings (with the Firstfruits sacrifice,
Lev. 23:13; or the Feast of Weeks [Pentecost] sacrifice, Lev. 23:18).

This sacrifice by ritual pouring was a part of the regular offerings
of the basic classes of foodstuffs cultivated and processed by the Israelites: livestock, fruit, cereal, etc. The drink offering also served to
consecrate and commemorate events of divine revelation associated
with particular places (Gen. 35:4; Num. 6:15, 17) or as the symbolic
acknowledgment of God's goodness in sustaining the Hebrews with
the bounty of produce from the land of covenant promise (Num.
29:6, 11, 16).[17]

Tithing. The tithe was the giving of a tenth part of the agricultural
produce, livestock, merchandise, and the like to the worship of a
deity or to the priests. Tithing was an ancient religious custom in
the biblical world, practiced widely among Israel's neighbors (the
Egyptians, Assyrians, Babylonians, and Canaanites). Nowhere however, was the application of a system of tithing more specific and
comprehensive than in ancient Israel. Tithing or the ritual giving
of a tenth began with the Hebrew patriarchs. After his victory over
the kings of the plain of Sodom and the rescue of Lot, Abram gave

a tithe of all his spoil to Melchizedek, king and priest of Salem (Gen. 14:18–20; Heb. 7:4–10). The purpose of the tithe was manifold. According to Proverbs 3:9, tithing is an act of worship that honors God. According to Mosaic legislation, the tithe had both a didactic and a practical function. Practically speaking, the tithe supported the Levitical priesthood since they had no tribal inheritance. In return for their service in the tent of meeting the Levites were allowed to keep a portion of the tithe to ensure their livelihood (Num. 21:21–26). By way of instruction the tithe taught Israel the fear of the Lord by reminding them that the covenant blessing of agricultural prosperity was God's gift to Israel (Deut. 14:23).

Elsewhere, Mosaic legislation specified those items to be tithed, including the seed of the ground, the fruit of the tree, and animals of the flocks (Lev. 27:30–32). These tithes were to be taken "to . . . the place the LORD your God will choose . . . to put his Name" (Deut. 12:5–7), that is, the place where his sanctuary resides, ultimately Jerusalem. Should distance require, the worshiper might take his tithe in the form of money equivalent to the worth of the tithe (Deut. 14:22–27). Additionally, every third year the whole tithe was given to the Levites and the socially disadvantaged—orphan, widow, aliens—as a form of charity (Deut. 26:12).

Regrettably, on several occasions the Old Testament prophets had to remind the Israelites that the giving of the tithe to the Lord in no way circumvented the covenant obligations to maintain social justice (Amos 4:4; 5:11–15). Neither was the tithe to be understood mechanically, like a type of "cosmic lotto." The giving of the tithe was motivated by love for God and his people (Deut. 14:23–29). Only then may tithing as a sign of covenant obedience prompt the blessing of God (Mal. 3:8, 10).

Purification rites. We have already learned that the doctrine of God's absolute holiness shaped the Hebrew worldview (see Chapter 2). The divine command "Consecrate yourselves and be holy, because I am holy" permeated all facets of Hebrew life (Lev. 11:44). When ceremonial or moral purity was violated or defiled, purification rites were necessary for restoring holiness in the community. These purification rites were symbolic public acts of cleansing. In some cases the ritual purification was part of the process of repentance and cleansing from sin and guilt or ceremonial impurity. It resulted in the restoration of the worshiper to fellowship in the community and participation in public worship. In others, the purification ritual was an act of consecration or sanctification setting aside someone or something for exclusive service to the Lord. The ceremonies related to ritual purification were another way the ancient Israelites attempted to order their relationship to the natural world in such a way as to reflect God's holiness.

Specific Old Testament examples of this symbolic ritual cleansing included the purification of the Levites for service in the sanctuary by shaving off body hair, the sprinkling of water, and appropriate offerings (Num. 8:5–13), cleansing after bodily discharges making a person "unclean" (like semen, menstrual flow, and even childbirth, Lev. 12:1–8; 15:1–33), cleansing from contamination by contact with unclean people, food, or dead bodies (Lev. 11:24–27; Num. 19:1–22), and purification from guilt as part of the process of repentance and atonement for sin (Exod. 19:9–15; Job 9:30; Ps. 73:13). In his lament over his sexual sin with Bathsheba (Ps. 51:6–17), David clearly was instructed in the rites of purity, as his references to being "purged with hyssop" and "washed" (Ps. 51:7) call to mind the symbols of hyssop and ceremonial bathing associated with the cleansing of leprosy (Lev. 14:8–9, 51–53). Yet David recognized that this was essentially an inward act of renewal. More than the proper animal sacrifice required for ritual purification, David knew cleansing was a matter of the heart and spirit, and only God himself could blot out David's sin, cleanse his heart, and renew his spiritual life (Ps. 51:9–10).

Penitential rites. Related to the Old Testament purification rituals are the penitential rites or symbolic acts signifying personal and/or corporate repentance of sin. Repentance in the Old Testament was a process beginning with the expression of genuine sorrow and grief over personal or community sin. This expression of sorrow motivated a return to God and a reorientation of the whole person to the way of godliness. This in turn led to the resolve of unqualified obedience to the will and word of Yahweh. The result was spiritual renewal (a new heart and a new spirit, Ezek. 18:31; 36:26), and restoration to fellowship and worship in the covenant community.

Ritual acts of penitence and mourning rites for the dead were closely connected in the ancient world. Death, plague and famine, devastation by war, sickness, divine curse, and threat of judgment were all reasons for expression of great grief and sorrow for the peoples of the Old Testament world. Likewise, one grieved over the consciousness of sin and guilt, whether personal or community sin, as if one were sorrowing over a death in the immediate family. Since sin severed relationship with God, sin may have indeed been tantamount to death in the mind of the righteous Hebrew. Conventional mourning and penitence rites practiced in the Old Testament by Hebrew and non-Hebrew alike include prayer, fasting, covering with sackcloth, sitting in ashes, and formal lamentation by professional mourners (Esther 4:12; Amos 5:16; Jon. 3:5). Even liturgies of lamentation and repentance have been identified in the Old Testament (Isa. 63:7—64:12; Dan. 9:4–19; Hos. 6:14). Basically, ritual acts of penitence and mourning were symbols acknowledging human feebleness and frailty before God. These culturally recognized means of permitting catharsis of emotion in situations of dire distress also were pleas for divine aid and merciful intervention. The New Testament understands penitential rites as the "fruit of repentance" (Matt. 3:8; Luke 3:8). The fruit of repentance includes both the outward acts of penitence and the inward change of heart and mind leading to renewed relationship with God. The visible signs of repentance were intended to demonstrate the sincerity of one's return to God, as well as confirm the individual in his or her intentions to faithfully heed the word of the Lord. There were many penitential rituals practiced by the Hebrews during Old Testament times, the more prominent ones are catalogued here:

- Tearing the clothes, donning sackcloth, sitting in ashes, and throwing dust on the head (1 Kings 20:31–32; 21:27; 2 Kings 34:27; 2 Chron. 34:27; Neh. 9:1; Dan. 9:3).
- Tearing out the hair and beating one's breast (Neh. 2:7; Isa. 32:12; Ezek. 23:34; Luke 18:13).
- Weeping and wailing (2 Kings 22:19; Ezra 10:1; Neh. 8:9; Job 16:20; Pss. 6:6; 137:1; Jer. 4:8; Mic. 1:8).
- Shaving the head bald (Job 1:20; Isa. 22:12; 32:11; Jer. 41:5; 48:37; Ezek. 27:31; Mic. 1:2).

• Sad, mournful looks (1 Sam. 1:8; Job 9:27).
• Fasting, including prayers and laments (Lev. 16:29; Judg. 20:26; 1 Sam. 7:6; 1 Chron. 10:12; Neh. 9:1; Dan. 6:18; 9:3; Joel 1:14).[18]
• Ritual washing (Isa. 1:16; Jer. 2:22; 4:14).

Artistic response. The playing of musical instruments was a vital part of Hebrew worship. King David actually appointed Levites to organize four thousand Levitical priests into minstrel groups, including cymbals, harps, lyres, trumpets, and other musical instruments (1 Chron. 15:16; 16:42; 23:5; 25:6–7).

These musicians, along with the singers, were an integral component of the worship associated with the temple liturgy (2 Chron. 5:11–14; Neh. 12:27–47). Vestiges of the Israelite musical heritage are scattered throughout the Old Testament, especially the Psalms. Here one may find references to an array of accompanying instrumentation: stringed, woodwind, brass, and tympanic (Ps. 150). In addition, psalmic collections are identified by the musical guilds of the composer (Psalms of Asaph, Pss. 76—83 and Psalms of Korah, Pss. 84—89). The introductions to certain psalms include musical notations and technical terms indicating tune, instrumentation, and performance cues (Pss. 4:1; 9:1; 16:1; 22:2; 32:1; 39:1; 45:1; see Appendix E).

It appears that both joyful noise and skillfully played music were incorporated into Hebrew liturgy. For instance, some celebrations called for "loud noise" from the instruments (1 Chron. 15:16; 23:5; Ps. 150:5). And yet the musicians, teachers and pupils alike, trained in schools so that skillful playing of musical instruments might characterize the music of temple worship (1 Chron. 25:7; 2 Chron. 34:12; Ps. 33:3).

Dance was another way the Hebrews celebrated the Lord in worship (Ps. 30:11; Eccles. 3:4; Lam. 5:15, where dancing is the antithesis of mourning). Dance is most often mentioned in a military context where a processional of women heralded victory in battle (Exod. 15:20; 1 Sam. 18:6; 21:11; 29:5). Elsewhere dancing was part of the Hebrew religious festivals (Judg. 21:16–24; 2 Sam. 6:14; 1 Chron. 15:29; Jer. 31:4, 13). It seems likely there was even a dance troupe associated with Hebrew temple worship (Ps. 87:7).

The Old Testament words used to describe this ritual dancing denote "twisting, turning" and "whirling." Hence this religious dancing is generally understood as the round dance, an artistic worship response recalling divine victory in battle and the deliverance of the Hebrews.

Other forms of artistic response in worship included the building of memorials and dramatic reenactments. The memorial was a monument, usually stone, erected to commemorate specific events of divine revelation, covenant renewal, or miraculous deliverance by God. The theological significance of these teaching memorials has been discussed in Chapter 5.

According to Robert E. Webber, "Drama reenacts and thus conveys a historical event through visible, tangible, and concrete symbols."[19] The dramatic re-creation of divine acts of revelation and redemption in Israelite history symbolically represents the relationship between God and the worshiper. It also serves to proclaim the meaning or significance of that event to the worshiper. Thus dramatic reenactment in worship both stimulates the memory of the religious community as to its spiritual legacy and imparts important theological instruction to the youth of the next generation. Classic examples of ritual reenactment in the Old Testament include the Levitical animal sacrifices, the Passover meal, and the Day of Atonement ceremony. Animal sacrifice was in reality a daily theological object lesson to the Hebrew people. The worshiper's identification with the animal slaughtered by the priest portrayed in symbol the removal of guilt and atonement for sin (see Lev. 1—7). The purpose of the Levitical animal sacrifices was didactic in that the enactment of the atonement ritual was designed to instruct the Israelites in the principles of God's holiness, human sinfulness, substitutionary death to cover human sin, and the need for repentance leading to cleansing and renewed fellowship within the community and with Yahweh.

Likewise, the yearly observance of the Passover meal celebrated the exodus event as both the supreme act of divine judgment and divine deliverance in Hebrew history. The memorial meal reenacted Yahweh's mercy in accepting the Passover blood for the Hebrew firstborn and the hasty night flight out of Egypt to freedom. The symbolic meal was also an object lesson for Israelite children, recalling the bitterness of slavery, teaching the faithfulness of God in keeping covenant promises made to Abraham, and instilling hope in the next generation of Israelites for a new beginning (Exod. 13:3–10).

Finally, the elaborate ceremony performed by the high priest during the annual Day of Atonement ritual graphically demonstrated the reality of community and personal sin before a righteous and holy God (Lev. 16:1–28). The emergence of the high priest from the Holy of Holies in the tabernacle (and later the temple) signified that the Lord in his mercy had accepted the sacrificial atonement for the sins of the entire congregation (Lev 16:11–19). The scapegoat segment of the ceremony symbolically removed sin and guilt from the people and assured divine pardon (Lev. 16:20–22).

Other worship expressions. Dedications, a common feature of Old Testament religious practice, were a formal and public act consecrating and separating someone or something for divine service. Almost anything might be dedicated to the Lord, including a house (Lev. 27:14; Deut. 20:5), a field (Lev. 27:16), the temple (2 Chron. 2:4), vessels and implements of various sorts (Exod. 35:22; 2 Sam. 8:10–11), spoil won in battle (1 Chron. 26:27), an altar (Num. 7:10), even the wall of Jerusalem (Neh. 12:27). On occasion people, including children, were set apart exclusively for God's service in special dedicatory rituals (Samuel, 1 Sam. 1:24–28). Oftentimes this kind of public act of consecration included anointing the person (Exod. 29:7) or the object (Num. 7:1, 10) with a ritually poured liquid (usually oil, Ps. 133:2). In reality, the act of dedication or consecration was the acknowledgment that possessions and children were gifts from God. Thereby the worshiper admitted that he or she was but a steward of divine resources for the glory of the Lord.

Marvin Wilson reminds us that even our study ought to be an act of worship.[20] In Jewish tradition study, like prayer, is service to the Lord (see Chapter 1). As we have previously learned in our analysis of Old Testament worship, the ideas of work and worship are closely related since all of life is united. Rather than activity divorced from worship, the service of study simply constitutes another aspect of our whole-person response to God (in this case the life of the mind, Ps. 16:8).

Life-style worship means the will of the attitude and spirit, the activities of the body, and the energies of the mind are given to the glory of God ("Do it all for the glory of God," 1 Cor. 10:31). Concerning the service of study, Rabbi Abraham Heschel summarized this way: "Genuine reverence for the sanctity of study is bound to invoke in the pupils the awareness that study in not an ordeal but an act of edification, that the school is a sanctuary, not a factory; that study is a form of worship."[21]

Ironically, rest also constitutes a worship response to God. In our discussion of active and participatory worship, it is important for us to remember the Old Testament Sabbath imperative regarding rest (Exod. 20:8–11). But this rest is not synonymous with inactivity. While Sabbath rest is freedom from labor and its attendant anxieties, more important to the biblical idea of Sabbath rest is meditation on God and the goodness of his creation, reflection on one's work and labor bringing the virtue of divine perspective to vocation in life, time devoted to prayer and study, and time devoted to family, friends, and community (see Chapter 6).

Recitation and Ritual Drama in Worship Today

What does all this prescribed worship activity of the ancient Israelites mean for me as a Christian or for the Christian church? Aren't we functioning under grace in the new covenant? Of course, Jesus Christ came to abolish the sacrificial system and offer for all time a single sacrifice for sin (Heb. 10:1–14). And yet the apostle Paul affirmed that the Old Testament Scriptures were written for our instruction (Rom. 15:4). So if we affirm, along with Leslie Flynn, that "real worship is something you do—not something you watch,"[22] then the worship responses of the Hebrews to God during the age of the old covenant offers much instruction for participatory worship today. This is true both for general worship principles and specific worship practices.

Worship Principles

Ultimately, the purpose of congregational participation in worship is to permit the expression of "full giftedness" for every believer-priest in the church. Or, as Robert E. Webber succinctly and passionately pleads, if worship is a meeting between God and his people, then return worship to the people.[23] Whether this participation is spontaneous or structured, sequential or simultaneous, congregational action depends on two basic ingredients: correct knowledge—the congregation must understand what they are doing, and correct intention—the congregation must desire to make the responses appropriate to worship. Apart from the specific participatory actions, gestures, and responses utilized in worship, a framework for participatory worship is essential. Again, Webber notes that worship is best understood when the worshiper participates in a sequence of related events. He suggests this outline: (1) preparation for worship, (2) ritual recitation—reading and preaching the Word, (3) ritual drama—holy Communion, and (4) the dismissal—including the response of obedience.[24]

We have already defined worship as the expression of a loving relationship between God and his people. Retaining vitality in any relationship requires communication. Several principles emerge from this study of recitation and ritual drama in the Old Testament that may contribute to our understanding and enrichment of worship as dialogue.[25] Our short list of Old Testament worship principles for worship renewal in the Christian church include

- the worshiper must consciously prepare for corporate worship;
- private and family worship are a complement to corporate public worship;
- the worshiper and local church leadership must recognize that worship requires whole-person responses to God;
- nonverbal communication is important to our dialogue with God (that is, worship is active and participatory);
- worship is directly connected with the redemptive acts of God in human history;
- symbolism is important to worship, both aesthetically and didactically;
- observing a liturgical calendar may enhance our worship, since it heightens our anticipation of and participation in ritual reenactment; and
- a life-style of obedience in service to God completes the integrity of our worship.

Worship Practices

This chapter does not pretend to be a how-to manual for adapting Hebrew participatory worship responses for Christian worship traditions. Any attempt to do so would likely inhibit individual initiative and creativity and unnecessarily limit the working of the Holy Spirit in the prompting of genuine worship of God.

In some cases, that work has already been done anyway. For example, Robert Schaper in his book *In His Presence*, offers readers a complete survey of liturgical practices in outline form for the ancient and Orthodox churches, the medieval and Roman Catholic churches, the Lutheran and Anglican churches, the Reformed and Methodist churches, and the Baptist and Congregational churches. He also provides practical suggestions for participatory worship in the general categories of preparation, praise, prayer, Scripture reading, preaching, and giving.[26]

Another useful guide is the catalog of nearly twenty liturgical postures and gestures prepared for the purpose of encouraging participatory worship.[27] The issue here is recognition of the importance of nonverbal communication as a supplement to recitation in worship. Erickson aptly summarizes,

> Liturgical gestures and signs are nonverbal communicators that give rich expression to, intensify, and provoke the deepest religious instincts. They give to the liturgy a power to prompt the human spirit to an awareness of the presence of God. Nonverbal gestures and signs are the distinguishing components of Multisensate Participation. Worship that utilizes nonverbal communication engages the spirit through the senses. It integrates the full range of human faculties—body, mind, senses, imagination, will, emotion, and memory. It is worship "with heart and hands and voices."[28]

The question of which of these participatory responses of Hebrew worship any given church should appropriate as a part of its worship renewal remains a valid one. Leslie Flynn offers a minimalist approach when he limits what he calls the physical side of worship to those Old Testament worship responses connected with the apostolic church. So he endorses worship practices like kneeling, standing, prayer with outstretched arms, and hand clapping in singing, but he rejects ritual dancing.[29]

The maximalist approach may be represented by the worship

characteristic of messianic Jewish congregations. These Jewish Christians acknowledge *Y'shua*, Jesus, as Messiah but retain their Jewish identity by observing the liturgical calendar of the Old Testament and Judaism and by keeping many of the worship practices found in the Old Testament and the synagogue of later Judaism.[30]

Perhaps Craig Erickson's approach to participatory worship is most balanced, at least for gentile Christians. While he affirms the Bible as the primary source for liturgical signs and gestures and participatory worship responses, he also recognizes the validity of liturgical theology in the traditions of church history. For Erickson, only those participatory responses "subject to the gospel and . . . informed in a way that is consonant with and supportive of biblical faith" hold value for Christian worship.[31] Specifically, Erickson endorses these liturgical postures and gestures: physical presence, processions, standing erect, praying with uplifted hands, raising of the eyes, kneeling, genuflection, bowing, prostration, sitting, the striking of the breast, the kiss of peace, the reverencing of sacred objects, the laying on of hands, the folding of hands, and the sign of the cross.

Conclusions

Our understanding and appropriation of these Hebrew principles and practices has the potential for revitalizing contemporary Christian worship. Indeed, we have already witnessed a renaissance of sorts within the worship traditions of Christianity. In his book *Dynamics of Spiritual Life*, Richard Lovelace identifies the preconditions, primary elements, and secondary elements necessary for spiritual renewal in the church.[32] The preconditions of renewal include awareness of God's holiness and the depth of human sin. Among the primary elements of renewal are justification (acceptance by God) and sanctification (freedom from bondage to sin). Finally, the secondary elements include prayer (individual and corporate) and community (union with macro- and micro-communities, especially church and family).

Recall the outline of Old Testament worship as set forth in Psalm 95 and discussed in Chapter 4: entrance (95:1), enthusiastic praise (95:1-5), humble worship and reverent silence (95:6-7), and obedience as worship response (95:7-11). Now compare these steps in the order of Hebrew worship with Lovelace's preconditions and elements of renewal. Both exuberant praise and humiliation before God in silent worship contribute to the preconditions necessary for renewal, namely the holiness of God and the reality of human sinfulness. Both reverent worship and the response of obedience foster the ideas of acceptance by God and release from sin's death grip. Naturally prayer—praise, thanksgiving, and petition—along with a keen desire to participate in the community of faith flow out of this worship experience.

In fact, George Mallone suggests this response of obedience actually "completes the integrity of our worship."[33] He further develops the complementary aspects of worship renewal and spiritual renewal by observing that God speaks to the worshiper about personal obedience or piety in the context of congregational worship.[34] Mallone contends that the praise, worship, and obedience liturgy of Psalm 95 liberates the believer-priest to the full expression of giftedness. As worship renewal feeds spiritual renewal and spiritual renewal prompts more profound worship renewal, "real church growth would soon develop. Hundreds of new churches would be springing up. Not obese churches, but stronger churches through division and multiplication."[35] Those churches which have taken the risk and accepted the challenge of worship renewal have experienced the reality of the dynamic relationship of worship renewal and spiritual renewal.

◆ 8 ◆

A Priestly Kingdom and Holy Nation

The Priest and King in Old Testament Worship

THE OLD TESTAMENT APOCRYPHAL BOOK of Sirach or Ecclesiasticus (ca. 200 B.C.) immortalizes Aaron and the Levitical priesthood in a lengthy hymn honoring the famous figures of Hebrew history. That text praising Aaron and his priestly descendants also offers an appropriate summary of the history and purpose of the Old Testament priesthood. (The segment of the praise hymn devoted to Aaron is reproduced at the end of this chapter in Fig. 8.3.)

The hymn celebrates various aspects of Aaron's priesthood, including his appointment by God (Ecclus. 44:6–7a), the splendor of the priestly garments (Ecclus. 44:7b–13), the symbolism represented in the priestly vestments (Ecclus. 44:8–9, 11), the twofold duty of the priesthood—sacrificial worship and religious instruction (Ecclus. 44:14–17), the blessing of eating from the sacrificial foods (Ecclus. 44:20–21), and the stress upon the Lord and not the land as the inheritance of the priesthood (Ecclus. 44:22).

Like the praise hymn of Sirach, this chapter highlights the essence of priestly ministry in the Old Testament. In addition, this chapter discusses the implications of that priestly ministry for Christian worship in the contemporary church.

The Old Testament Priesthood

We have already learned that no organized Hebrew priesthood functioned during the patriarchal period of Israelite history. Rather, the patriarch or elder of the Hebrew family and/or clan served as the priest for that group of people (see Chapter 3). The sole exception was Abraham's encounter with the priest-king of Salem, Melchizedek, as recorded in Genesis 14. The New Testament identifies this enigmatic Old Testament figure as the prototype of the later Levitical priesthood of the Mosaic covenant and ultimately the prototype of the Messianic priesthood fulfilled by Jesus of Nazareth (Heb. 7:1–27; cf., Ps. 110:4).

The Mosaic covenant enacted at Mt. Sinai legislated the establishment of a formal Hebrew priesthood to serve God in worship. This priesthood represented before the Lord the entire Israelite community who constituted a kingdom of priests and a holy nation (Exod. 19:5–6; 29:1–37). The Hebrew priests were a professional class of religious leaders, basically the counterpart of the clergy today. They were born into their priestly roles as descendants of Levi, the fifth son of the patriarch Jacob by Leah (Gen. 29:31–35).

The Hebrew priests were employed in the service of Yahweh full time and were supported in their ministry by the tithes, offerings, and portions of the sacrificial offerings of the Israelite community (Lev. 7:28–36; Deut. 14:22–29). The period of service for the Israelite priests was twenty years, from age thirty to age fifty (Num. 4:47). It appears that the priests were trained for their duties during a five-year apprenticeship, from age twenty-five to thirty (Num. 8:24–26).

Perhaps most significant, unlike the other Hebrew tribes the Levitical priesthood received no inheritance of land in Palestine, the land of covenant promise (Gen. 12:1–3). Instead, the priests and Levites were allotted forty-eight cities in which to live (Num. 35:1–5). This grant of cities to the Levitical priesthood was a pragmatic social and economic provision. The Aaronic priesthood and Levites were denied territorial rights since the Lord God and service to Israel in his name was their inheritance (Num. 18:20; Deut. 10:9–10).

The sprinkling of Levitical cities across the Israelite tribal territories served both religious and political purposes. It seems likely that in addition to their regular rotation of priestly duties in the tabernacle (and later the temple) the priests and Levites served both as teachers and enforcers of covenant law among the people of God (1 Chron. 26:20–32; 2 Chron. 17:7–9). They also may have performed an important political function during the days of tribal league and the monarchical period living as "model citizens" and "lobbyists" among the general populace in loyal support of Yahweh's anointed judge or king.

In addition, six of these Levitical cities served a special purpose in the administration of Hebrew civil law. These so-called cities of refuge, three on either side of the Jordan River, were places of asylum for those guilty of accidental manslaughter in accordance with the prescriptions of Mosaic Law (Num. 18:20–33; 35:9–15; Deut. 19:1–13; Josh. 20:1–9). This network of refuge cities was designed to prevent further death by interrupting the cycle of blood vengeance commonly practiced in the ancient Near East—the obligation of the nearest male relative of the deceased to avenge the death of his kinsman. The institution of refuge cities was unique in the ancient world.[1]

The selection of a fixed worship site, Jerusalem, during the reign of King David and the erection of a permanent worship center, the temple, by King Solomon prompted a significant shift in the function of the Levitical priesthood. While the Aaronic priests continued to oversee the sacrificial and festival worship, the Levites were assigned new duties. The permanence and immobility of the temple edifice necessitated this restructuring of responsibilities, since the Levites were no longer needed as porters for Yahweh's sanctuary. According to the Chronicler, it was King David who reorganized the Levitical priesthood and prescribed their new tasks (1 Chron. 23—24).[2]

Priestly Orders

Only Hebrew males descended from Levi were permitted to hold priestly office according to the Law of Moses (Num. 3:5ff.).[3] Of course, the practice of the Israelites often deviated from the divine ideal during Old Testament history. The priesthood was no exception, as both non-Levites and non-Hebrew pagan priests held office at times during Israel's history (1 Kings 12:31; 2 Kings 23:5, 20). And yet, a Levitical pedigree was no guarantee of appropriate priestly ministry, as the Levitical priesthood frequently became slack and even corrupt in their role as religious leaders of Israel (1 Sam. 3:10–14).

The Hebrew priesthood established by Mosaic Law in the Sinai covenant essentially consisted of two orders or divisions. The priests were descendants of Aaron, Israel's first priest (Exod. 29:1–37; Lev. 8:1–36; 21:1). One from among the Aaronic lineage was chosen and ordained as the high priest or chief priest in Israel for life.[4]

In addition to the high priest and Aaronic priests, the Levites were also part of the priesthood in ancient Israel. Broadly speaking, the term Levite may refer to the entire Hebrew priesthood, since Aaron and his sons belonged to the tribe of Levi as well (Gen. 46:11; Exod. 3:16–20). More specifically though, the Levites were those members of the tribe of Levi who were not descendants of Aaron but functioned in the service of the sanctuary in subordinate and nonpriestly roles. Three divisions or clans of Levites are recognized in the Old Testament, taking their names from the three sons of Levi: Gershon, Kohath, and Merari (Num. 3—4).[5]

Priestly Duties

Priestly duties basically fell into two categories: superintending tabernacle/temple worship, including representing the Israelite community before the Lord as mediator and intercessor, and instructing the people of God in the Law of Moses—especially personal and corporate holiness and covenant obedience and the declaration of the will of God to his people through oracles and the handling of the Urim and Thummim (Exod. 28:30; Lev. 8:8; Deut. 33:8–10). The specific duties of the high priest, the Aaronic priesthood, and the Levites are outlined below.

The high priest. The high priest was the exalted member of all the priesthood (Lev. 21:10). He was responsible for ministering and directing the sacrificial worship of the sanctuary, either personally, as in the case of the sin offering (Lev. 4:3–21), or in a supervisory role (Num. 3:3–7). The high priest was the only priest permitted to enter the Holy of Holies in the Lord's sanctuary and then only once a year on the Day of Atonement (Lev. 16:1–9). The high priest was both Israel's representative before God and God's mediator between him and his covenant people. As such the high priest was to be the model of holiness and purity for the rest of the priesthood and all the Israelites. For this reason, the high priest was obligated to abide by a more strict code of holiness laws (Lev. 21:1–24; especially vv. 10–15). The high priest was responsible for the Urim and Thummim, peculiar

Fig. 8.1 The Role of the Worshiper in Old Testament Sacrificial Ritual

The procedural order of sacrificial worship outlined below is a reconstruction based on the prescriptions for offerings and sacrifices explained in Leviticus 1—5. Details may vary given the specific type of sacrifice being presented, whether offerings of expiation, offerings of consecration, or offerings of fellowship. On the role of both worshiper and priest in Levitical sacrificial worship, see further Roland de Vaux, *Ancient Israel: Religious Institutions, Vol. 2* (New York: Macmillan, 1965), 415–423.

Tabernacle Worship

1. The person offering the sacrifice must be ceremonially clean. Ritual purity was secured by washing one's clothes and bathing, and in some cases special offerings were presented to the priest (Num. 19:17–21).
2. The worshiper approaches the tabernacle with his/her offering.
3. The officiating priest receives the worshiper, takes the sacrificial animal, and leads the worshiper to the altar of burnt offering in the tabernacle courtyard. The family of the worshiper may have watched from the gate or followed the two into the court area to observe from a better vantage point.
4. After a statement of confession or prayer or praise, (depending on the type of offering, the worshiper placed his hand on the animal's head and slit its throat with a knife. (Here the priest would collect the blood for use in the sacrifice.)
5. The worshiper, perhaps with the priest's help, would then skin and cut the sacrificial animal into quarters. (Once the sacrifice is brought into contact with the altar of burnt offering the formal priestly duties commence.)
6. The worshiper witnesses the priestly activity, including the burning of the sacrifice on the altar. It is possible that the worshiper may have responded to the priestly activity in some way, for instance with prayer, silent reflection and meditation, or chanting or singing of liturgical responses (depending on the nature of the sacrifice).
7. After the sacrifice was consumed by fire on the altar, the priest formally dismissed the worshiper with some type of blessing or benediction. In some instances, the worshiper ate a fellowship meal with the priest from the remnant of the sacrificial animal upon completion of the burnt offering. In other cases, the remainder of the sacrificial animal was taken home and eaten by the worshiper and his family. The remaining portions of the sacrifice were to be eaten within two days or destroyed by fire (Lev. 19:5–8).

objects worn in a pouch on the breastplate of the high priest's vestments and used for determining the will of God in certain instances (Num. 27:21; Deut. 33:8; 1 Sam. 14:41; 28:6).[6]

Aaronic priesthood. As mediators between God and the covenant people of Israel, the rest of the Aaronic priesthood were also subject to the holiness requirements of the Mosaic legal code, although to a somewhat lesser degree than the high priest (for example, mourning the death of a loved one, cf. Lev. 21:1–9, 16–24 with 21:2–11). The priests officiated sacrificial worship in the sanctuary under the direction of the high priest, especially the altar of burnt offering sacrifices and the manipulation of blood during the sin/guilt offerings (Lev. 4—5). The priests also led the congregation of Israel in corporate and festival worship and blessed the people at the corporate gatherings (Deut. 10:8; 21:5). The Hebrew priests were also responsible for transporting the ark of the covenant during the days of the portable sanctuary (Deut. 10:8; 31:9). In addition, the Aaronic priesthood was responsible for assessing, treating, and enforcing Mosaic legislation related to issues of ritual purity (childbirth, leprosy, Lev. 13—14). Perhaps most important, the Aaronic priesthood was charged with the duty of religious education in Israel. In particular the priests instructed the people in the Mosaic law and interpreted that law, thereby supplementing the training in covenant obedience taking place at home in families (Deut. 6:2–9). Only by obedience to the stipulations of Yahweh's covenant could the Israelites participate in the blessings of covenant relationship to him, hence the primacy of priestly instruction (Deut. 27:9–10; and the blessings and curses section in Deut. 28). Finally, the priests served as advisers to judges, kings, and other civic leaders of Israel as to God's will for the Hebrew covenant community (Deut. 20:2; Judg. 18:18–19; 1 Sam. 14:36–37; 21:6–9). By the time of the prophet Jeremiah (ca. 600 B.C.), three classes of officials were prominent in Hebrew society: the priest, the prophets, and the sages (Jer. 18:18). The primary function of each group is aptly summarized by one word—*oracles* for the prophets, *counsel* for the sages, and *instruction* for the priests. While sacrificial worship and temple ritual were important to ancient Israel, religious education was paramount for ancient Israel since autonomous existence was conditioned by obedience to the demands of Yahweh's covenant. Covenant obedience was dependent on Israelite knowledge of God and his covenant stipulations (Hos. 6:3). The responsibility for instructing the Hebrews in the knowledge of God lay with the priests, hence their status in ancient Hebrew society. Of course, Jeremiah anticipated a day when priests would no longer be necessary for religious instruction because everyone would teach each other the knowledge of God (Jer. 31:34).

The Levites. Originally, the non-Aaronic priests or Levites were designated as subordinates or assistants to the Aaronic priesthood and porters of the tabernacle. This Levitical assistance included doing service at the tabernacle, having charge of the sanctuary and its furnishings, and attending to the duties of the Israelites (Num. 3:5–8). According to Gordon Wenham, these ambiguous phrases describe two primary functions of the Levite: to keep guard of the sanctuary and its grounds and to do the heavy work of dismantling, transporting, and erecting the tabernacle.[7] Upon King Solomon's construction of a permanent sanctuary in Jerusalem, the Levitical duties were reorganized since they were no longer required as porters for the moveable sanctuary. According to the Chronicler, King David was responsible for reassigning the Levitical priests to new duties (1 Chron. 23—24). This shift in responsibilities included assisting the Aaronic priesthood in temple worship, cleaning and maintaining the temple and its furnishings, miscellaneous duties of service, baking and displaying the showbread, assisting in the grain offering, securing and storing supplies for the showbread and grain offerings, and participating daily in services of praise and thanksgiving in connection with the morning and evening sacrifices (1 Chron. 9:28–32; 23:26–32).

Priestly Dress and Ornamentation

Mosaic Law legislated special clothing for the Hebrew priesthood. These priestly uniforms were designed for the glorious adornment of the Israelite priests (Exod. 28:2, 40). In addition, the priestly vestments were highly symbolic in nature, depicting both the beauty and holiness of God and the delight of serving in his name, and highlighting the priestly role as mediator between God and covenant people (Heb. 5:1).[8]

The dress for the high priest signified his unique status as chief among the priests of the Lord. The elaborate turban was made of fine linen and fitted with a gold diadem engraved with the inscription "Holy to Yahweh" (Exod. 28:36–38; 39:30–31). The high priest's robe was a sleeveless garment woven of blue material fringed along the hem with alternating bells of gold and yarn pomegranates in blue, purple, crimson, and gold (Exod. 28:31–35; 39:22–26). Over this robe the high priest were the ephod, a vestlike article of clothing made of fine twined linen in blue, purple, crimson, and gold (Exod. 28:6–8; 39:2–5). Two shoulder pieces containing stones engraved with the names of the twelve tribes of Israel and a belt or sash were attached to the ephod (Exod. 28:9–14, 39). The breastplate hung at the front of the ephod and was woven in a fashion similar to the ephod (Exod. 28:15–30; 39:8–21). The breastplate was set with twelve precious stones, representing the twelve tribes of Israel.

Special clothing was ordered for the rest of the Aaronic priesthood as well, though much less ornate than the vestments of the high priest. This priestly wardrobe consisted of a tunic or robe, a sash or belt, and a headdress (Exod. 28:40–43). Specific detail regarding these garments is lacking in the Old Testament but presumably they were also woven of linen in color schemes similar to that of the high priest's—blue, crimson, purple, and gold. Additionally, all priests were required to wear linen undergarments of a particular design (Exod. 28:42). No specific dress is specified for the Levites, although presumably they too were identified by distinct types of clothing.

Priestly ministry, however, required more than a Levitical pedigree and special clothing. The priests of Israel were consecrated for service in complex ordination services lasting seven days (Exod. 29; Lev. 8—9). The ordination ritual included sacrificial offerings for the sins of the priestly family, anointing with oil, and the ceremonial sprinkling of blood upon the priests and their garments (especially Lev. 8; cf., Ps. 133). Furthermore, daily ritual washings were required for priestly service in the sanctuary (Exod. 30:17–22), and strict laws concerning ritual purity and cleanness were enforced against the Hebrew priests so they did not profane God's name (Lev. 22:1–16).

Significance of the Hebrew Priests
for Old Testament Worship

God's covenant with Israel declared the Hebrew people Yahweh's treasured possession, a priestly kingdom, and holy nation (Exod. 19:4–6). The Levitical priesthood was established and conse-

Fig. 8.2 Priestly Duties Associated with the Tabernacle

The legislation found in the Pentateuch assigned numerous duties to the Hebrew priests and Levites. Chief among them were the maintenance and transportation of the tabernacle (Num. 3—4) and the performance of the rituals and liturgies associated with Hebrew worship in the sacred sanctuary (Exod. 28—29). It is likely that some of these duties were determined by lot and discharged on a rotating basis (1 Chron. 23—24). The priestly role in the more prominent worship rituals of the tabernacle are outlined below:

Bronze Basin or Laver

The priests were to wash their hands and feet at the laver upon entering the tent of meeting (tabernacle proper) and before ministering at the altar of burnt offering (Exod. 30:17–21).

Altar of Burnt Offering

The national, festival, daily, and individual sacrifices took place at the altar of burnt offering. Mosiac Law instructed the priests to prepare the sacrifice—a year-old lamb in the morning and evening—on a daily basis. This burnt offering was to be accompanied by grain and drink offerings (Exod. 29:38–46; Num. 28:1–8).

The Mosiac legislation prescribing the five basic sacrifices offered to God by the people of Israel is found in Leviticus 1—7. Three types of sacrifices were required: offerings of expiation, offerings of consecration, and offerings of fellowship.

The offerings of expiation included a six-part ritual, three acts performed by the worshiper and three acts performed by the priest. The worshiper brought his offering to the gateway of the tabernacle (perhaps in the forecourt of the north side of the altar of burnt offering). He then laid his hand(s) on the sacrificial victim and confessed sin and guilt. The worshiper slaughtered the sacrificial animal. The priest then cut the victim into pieces, arranged the sacrifice on the altar, and ignited the burnt offering. During this process the priest collected the blood of the victim in a basin and dashed it against the four sides of the altar. The priest and his family, or the priest and the worshiper, ate the remaining portions of the offering as a sacrificial meal.

Nonanimal sacrifices were prepared by the worshiper, including anointing the offering with oil and frankincense and in some cases baking without leaven. The worshiper brought the sacrifice to the entrance of the tabernacle. There the priest received the sacrifice and burned a portion of it on the altar of burnt offering. The priest was permitted to retain the remaining portion of the offering as a sacrificial meal for his family (Lev. 2:1–10).

Specific ritual sacrifice was also prescribed for the national and festival worship gatherings. Especially prominent were the Passover, Feast of Firstfruits, Pentecost, and the Day of Atonement. Sacrificial instructions for these and other national and festival holy days are outlined in Exodus 12, 13, 29; Leviticus 16, 23; and Numbers 28:29. The instructions of the priests for keeping the fire of the altar of burnt offering burning are found in Leviticus 6:8–13.

Table of Showbread and Lampstand

The priests were charged to keep the lampstand (or menorah) burning during the hours of darkness—evening until morning—on a daily basis (Lev. 24:1–4).

The priests also prepared twelve loaves of bread to be arranged on the table of showbread in two rows of six loaves each. The loaves were to be garnished with frankincense and were replaced by the priests every Sabbath (Lev. 25:5–8).

Altar of Incense

The priests were commanded to burn incense twice daily on the altar of incense, which stood before the curtain of the tabernacle separating the Most Holy Place from the Holy Place. The incense offerings coincided with the sniffing out of the lampstand in the morning and lighting of lampstand in the evening (Exod. 30:1–10).

Once a year sacrificial blood was sprinkled on the altar of incense to purify it as part of the Day of Atonement ceremony (Lev. 16:18–19).

Curtain or Veil of the Tabernacle

The curtain was made of wool, dyed blue, purple, and scarlet. It was also embroidered with cherubim. The curtain divided the tent of meeting into two sections: the Holy Place and the Most Holy Place. Once a year, on the Day of Atonement, the high priest was permitted to go beyond the curtain into the Most Holy Place (Exod. 26:31–35).

Ark of the Covenant

The ark of the covenant was the visible symbol of God's presence and covenant relationship with Israel. The ark of the covenant contained the tokens of Israel's redemption from slavery in Egypt—the stone tablets of God's Law, a bowl of manna, and Aaron's rod. It resided in the Most Holy Place. Once a year, on the Day of Atonement, the high priest appeared before the ark to burn incense and sprinkle the blood of the sacrifice on the mercy seat resting on the top of the ark. The ritual made atonement for the tabernacle, cleansing the sanctuary of Israel's uncleanness and transgressions (Lev. 16:11–19).

crated to represent the entire Israelite nation as priests in service to Yahweh (Exod. 29:44). In addition to the service of worship the Levitical priests mediated God's presence among and his communication with the Israelites (Exod. 29:45–46). Finally, the Levitical priesthood was charged to instruct the Hebrews so that they might know God and imitate his holiness (Lev. 10:3; 11:44; Hos. 6:3).

The various priestly roles important to the service of worship in the Old Testament are outlined below:

- Organize, orchestrate, and lead the Israelites in corporate worship, including the place(s), time(s), forms, and order of public worship (Exod. 40:12–15; Lev. 1—10).
- Perform the service of worship for the Israelite community, especially the sacrificial worship and the manipulation of blood in the sin/guilt offerings—thus making atonement for sin in the community, and the ministry of intercession (see Figures 8.1 and 8.2).
- Serve as mediator between God and the Israelites as his covenant community, including representing the Hebrews before God, as in the Day of Atonement ceremony (Lev. 16) and

representing Yahweh to his people by making known God's will (1 Sam. 8).

* Adjudicate the Mosaic legal code, thus protecting the holiness and purity of the Israelite community and safeguarding covenant relationship with Yahweh (Lev. 11—15; Num. 5; Lev. 18:24–30).
* Interpret the Law of Moses and instruct the Hebrew people in holiness and covenant obedience (Deut. 17:8–13). Otherwise the Israelites risked the penalty of covenant curses, including the loss of their inheritance of the land of the covenant (Lev. 18:24–20). This eventually happened, and the prophetic indictment against the Levitical priesthood centered on the people's lack of the knowledge of God because the priests had failed in their role as religious educators (Hos. 4:4–6; 6:9; Mic. 3:11; Zeph. 3:4; Mal. 2:4–9).
* Function as adviser and counselor for the people and the divinely appointed civic leaders of the Israelites, in part fulfilling the role of sage which developed later during the period of Hebrew kingship (2 Kings 11—12; 22:13; Jer. 18:18).
* Serve as models and examples of faith, holiness, covenant obedience, and proper worship for the heads of tribes, clans, and families, ensuring the continuity and integrity of biblical instruction and private worship and devotion in the Hebrew home (Deut. 6:2–9).[9]

The Royal Priesthood in the Old Testament

The Old Testament depicts the king of Israel as a worship leader on several occasions. For instance, King David builds an altar for Yahweh in Jerusalem, where his worship averted a plague on Israel (2 Sam. 24:24–25). King Solomon commissioned the building of the temple and then led the dedicatory worship ceremony (1 Kings 5—8). Elsewhere the Hebrew king had the authority to nominate and dismiss priests (2 Sam. 8:17; 20:25; 1 Kings 2:26–27), enact laws regarding temple procedures and maintenance (2 Kings 12:5–9), and initiate and enforce reforms in temple worship (2 Kings 22—23).

Even further, the Old Testament records Hebrew kings personally performing priestly acts of worship. Examples here include King David offering animal sacrifices (2 Sam. 6:13–18) and King

Solomon both offering sacrifice and pronouncing priestly blessings upon the people (1 Kings 3:4, 15; 8:54–66). Interestingly, these acts of priestly worship executed by Israelite kings are approved without protest by the biblical historians. Yet King Saul was denied a royal dynasty, and King Uzziah was struck with leprosy as punishment for performing priestly acts of worship (1 Sam. 13:5–15; 2 Chron. 26:16–21).

How are we to explain the inconsistency in divine response to priestly worship performed by Hebrew kings? First, the Old Testament does specify that only descendants of Levi may hold priestly office (Num. 3:6; Deut. 10:9). No doubt this separation of the priestly role in Israel to the tribe of Levi and the royal office of king to the tribe of Judah (Gen. 49:10; 2 Sam. 7:12–13) was designed to prevent the unhealthy and unholy marriage of religion and politics in ancient Israel (cf., the reign of King Ahab where such a union brought disastrous results to the Northern Kingdom of Israel; 1 Kings 16:29—21:26).

Second, the Hebrew king was chosen and adopted by God when he was anointed and crowned (Deut. 17:14–15; Ps. 45:1–9). According to Roland de Vaux, he thus became a "sacred person" and was empowered to perform religious functions.[10] The issue seems to be one of authority and sanction and not the king's participation in the religious duties of the priests. It appears that the king had the right to function as a priest in Israel as long as he did so with the blessing and under the jurisdiction of the Levitical priesthood (Ps. 110:4). Note in the cases of kings Saul and Uzziah, they both usurped priestly function without priestly authority. Thus they performed priestly acts of worship independently rather than in conjunction with the divinely ordained priesthood (1 Sam. 13:13; 2 Chron. 26:18).

The stipulations of Mosaic Law for kingship in Israel indicate that the king functioned as a religious educator in addition to being the high judge of the land. He was to know and presumably teach the commandments of God to his people (Deut. 17:18–20). Again, the biblical text connects the king and his knowledge of the law with the supervision of the Levitical priesthood (Deut. 17:18).[11] Despite his personal sin and failings with his children, King David was a man after God's own heart (Acts 13:22) because he loved the law of the Lord (Ps. 19:7–10).

While the Hebrew king technically served as God's chief spiritual minister, his role was primarily that of religious figurehead rather than religious functionary. As Yahweh's covenant servant and partner the king was proxy for the people even more so than the Levitical priesthood (2 Sam. 7:6–16).[12] Throughout the history of Hebrew kingship the religious life of the Israelite people mirrored that of the monarch, whether obedient to Yahweh's covenant or apostate in serving the pagan idols. Such was the case that the biblical historians characterized the Israelite kings and the nation as a whole on the basis of their personal relationship to Yahweh (1 Kings 14:21–24). More crucial to the Israelite people was the impact of divine judgment against them as a result of the king's disobedience to God's covenant stipulations, including the punishment of covenant curses and ultimately exile from the land of covenant promise (Lev. 18:24–30; Deut. 28:36–37).

Priesthood in the New Testament

The Jewish Priesthood

By the time of Christ the Hebrew priesthood represented both the Jewish religious establishment as servants to the temple and Jewish vested political interests as power brokers to the Roman overlords. For this reason the New Testament writers portray the Jewish priests in a negative fashion since they co-opted their position of leadership for economic and political gain. And rightly so, given the fact that the Jewish priests opposed the ministry of Jesus (Matt. 16:21; 21:15; John 1:19), helped crucify him (Matt. 27:1–20; Mark 15:10–11; Luke 19:47), and persecuted the early church (Acts 4:1–4; although some Hebrew priests later converted to Christianity, Acts 6:7). But the response of the Jewish priests to Jesus Christ and Christianity was understandable because Jewish temple religion was viable only as long as the Jews remained subservient to Rome. A rebel messianic figure like Jesus of Nazareth was a political liability to the religious status quo in the minds of the priests (note the statement of Caiaphas in John 18:13–14).

The priesthood was the chief political power in Jerusalem and

Judea from the time of the Maccabees (160 B.C.) to the fall of Jerusalem (A.D. 70). The political ties between the Jewish priesthood and the civic officials of the Roman occupation proved to be a two-edged sword. On the one hand, the high priest was often able to sway Roman policy decisions in Palestine since he functioned as an adviser to the Roman procurator. But on the other, this union of Jewish religion and the governmental officials of the Roman occupation led to compromise and corruption within the Jewish religious hierarchy. (This is one reason the party of the Pharisees was so popular with the grassroots population; they espoused separation and not collusion.) Small wonder Jesus condemned the priests and Levites as the epitome of religious hypocrisy in his parable about the good Samaritan (Luke 10:25-37).

The New Testament period also witnessed a growing complexity in the ranks and divisions of the Hebrew priesthood. The high priest was still chief among the priests, but orders in high priestly rank were established—vested, anointed, and retired. This became necessary because the office of high priest could be filled by an appointment of the Roman authorities or sold to the highest Jewish bidder, and at times the high priest did not serve a lifetime term in office but retired (John 11:59).[13]

Other priestly offices included, by order of rank, captain of the temple (Acts 4:1), directors of the weekly ministry course (twenty-four priests), director of the daily ministry course (one hundred fifty-six priests), temple overseers (seven priests), treasurers, ordinary priests, and finally the Levites. The majority of priests did not belong to the priestly aristocracy, rather they were ordinary priests who served weekly stints in temple service twice a year (cf., Zechariah, Luke 1:8). The Levites were responsible for the music of temple worship and performed subordinate duties in assisting the priests in the worship rituals, cleaning, and policing the temple precinct. According to scholarly estimates there were about eighteen thousand priests and ten thousand Levites serving the temple complex during the time of Christ.[14]

The destruction of the second temple during the sack of Jerusalem by the Roman general Titus in A.D. 70 brought an end to the traditional role of the priest and Levite in Judaism. According to Peter Craigie, "Their principal reason for existence had been the religion of the temple. Without the temple their purpose was gone, and their role as religious leaders with the community passed into the hands of the rabbis, just as the temple was replaced by the centrality of the synagogue."[15]

The Priesthood of Christ

The priestly ministry of Jesus Christ is developed in the New Testament only in the book of Hebrews, sometimes called the Epistle of Priesthood. Here the writer explains the life, teachings, and public ministry of Jesus as the typological fulfillment of the Old Testament priesthood. By typological I mean the understanding of the sacrificial worship of the tabernacle and the priesthood of the Old Testament as foreshadowing a spiritual reality brought to fruition in the person and work of Jesus Christ (Gal. 3:24, "so the law was put in charge to lead us to Christ"; see also Chapter 12).

Specifically, the Old Testament sacrificial system required animal sacrifice for the atoning or covering of sin. The Hebrew priesthood officiated as mediator in the sacrificial worship between the Holy God of Israel and the lawbreaker within the covenant community. In the case of sacrificial worship under the old covenant the lawbreaker was represented by the unblemished and innocent animal victim substituted in his or her place (Lev. 3:1–5). According to the book of Hebrews, Jesus Christ fulfilled the role of priest, even high priest, since he acted as go-between for his Holy Father and sinful humanity (Heb. 9:23–28). Not only is Jesus Christ the great high priest, but he was also the perfect and innocent victim since he was tempted in every way yet remained sinless and perfect (Heb. 4:4–16; 7:27–28). Further, he offered himself as a once-for-all sacrifice for sin (Heb. 9:11–14), and thus he became the mediator of a new and better covenant (Heb. 9:15–22).

The book of Hebrews goes on to compare the priesthood of Jesus Christ with that of Melchizedek in the Old Testament (Gen. 14; Heb. 7:11–30). More than this, the writer acknowledged the priesthood of Christ as superior to the Levitical priesthood in every way, including the divine oath by which Jesus took office (Heb. 7:20–21), the eternality of Christ's priesthood—unbroken by genealogical beginning or end (Heb. 7:1–3), the subservience of Levi to Melchizedek—demonstrated in Abraham's recognition of Melchizedek's priesthood (Heb. 7:4–10). The Old Testament promise of a greater priest stands as an indictment against the permanence and perfection of the Levitical priesthood (Ps. 110:4). The ministry of Christ's priesthood was accomplished in a once-for-all event—the Cross—not continually, as in the daily sacrificial ministry of the Old Testament priests (Heb. 9:11–14; cf., 9:6–10). Christ's priesthood was established by an indestructible and eternal life and not in human weakness and resultant death (Heb. 7:15–25).[16]

The Priesthood of the Believer in Christ

The apostle Peter applied the "royal priesthood and holy nation" of Exodus 19:5–6 to the church of Jesus Christ (1 Pet. 2:5, 9). This universal Christian priesthood belonging to all those joined to Jesus Christ through faith is called the priesthood of all believers. The New Testament understands the church of Christ to be the typological fulfillment of the Old Testament people of God (1 Pet. 2:9–10).

The priesthood of the believer is more a corporate concept than an individual one. It is true that the believer in Christ presents herself or himself as a "living sacrifice" in service to God (Rom. 12:1–2). However, it is the corporate nature of the local church or larger body of Christ that fulfills the twofold function of the priesthood of the believer. This dual ministry of the Christian priesthood includes offering spiritual sacrifices of praise and thanksgiving in worship (1 Pet. 2:5) and proclaiming Christ's redemption through word and deed (1 Pet. 2:9).

The ministry of the priesthood of the believer is not redemptive. Rather, the believer's priestly role is the service of worship offered to God through Jesus Christ (1 Pet. 2:5). Hence, the book of Hebrews identifies this spiritual priestly service as the offering of praise and worship, the proclamation of Christ's gospel, and the ministry of doing good to others in the name of Christ (13:15–16). So then, the service of the priesthood of the believer, both corporately and individually, is the response of gratitude to God for the perfect and all-sufficient sacrifice of Jesus Christ for human sin (1 Cor. 5:7–8), and the ministry of bold proclamation to the world of this great redemption (1 Pet. 2:9; cf., Col. 4:2–4).[17]

The priesthood of the believer was an issue during the Protestant Reformation because through the course of Roman Catholic church history the office of the priest had been invested with church authority to administer the sacraments (dispense grace), hear prayers (make intercession), and hear confession (absolve sins). Generally speaking, the Reformers rejected the office of the priesthood in the church on two grounds: (1) the issue of church authority connected with the office of priest in the Roman church undermined biblical teaching about the authority of Christ over his church; and (2) the sacerdotal nature of Christ's priesthood "rendered all other priestly mediators eternally obsolete."[18]

The office of priest is retained in several church traditions today, including the Roman Catholic, the Orthodox, and the Anglican (Episcopal) churches. Each tradition varies by degree in its understanding of the priest as spiritual mediator and authority figure in the church. Most Protestant church traditions have followed the New Testament in recognizing the office of elder/bishop as the spiritual leader of the local congregation(s), while acknowledging certain priestly functions inherent to the office.[19]

Implications for Christian Worship

Striking by its absence is the application of the term *priest* to individual Christians in the New Testament. The Jewish priests continue to superintend the temple ritual, but the New Testament church has no sacerdotal priesthood. Rather, the New Testament identifies Jesus Christ as the great high priest of the church and his followers as the priesthood of believers.

As mentioned earlier, the Old Testament priesthood is analogous in some ways to the professional clergy of the church today. The New Testament paradigm for at least certain aspects of Old Testament priestly ministry is found in the biblical teachings regarding the church office of elder or bishop (1 Tim. 3:1–7; 2 Tim. 3:10–17; Titus 1:5–9).[20] Primary among the parallels between Old Testament priest and New Testament elder-bishop are the roles of worship leader, religious instructor, and pastoral overseer.

Servants of Covenant Relationship
Peter Craigie condensed the Hebrew religion of the Old Testament into a single word—relationship. By that he meant "the

relationship existing between God and Israel that was given formal expression in the covenant."[21] The Old Testament priests were servants of that covenant relationship in that they served as mediators representing both God and his people. In the new covenant Jesus Christ, the supreme high priest, now serves as the sole mediator between God and his people (1 Tim. 2:5–6).

For this reason the New Testament office of elder-bishop no longer parallels the Old Testament priesthood's role of mediator. The priesthood of Christ has made human priestly mediators of divine redemption obsolete. Yet there are many ways the New Testament elder-bishop still functions as a servant of covenant relationship in the church. Several of these parallels between the Old Testament priest and the New Testament elder-bishop as servants of covenant relationship are developed below.

- Like the Old Testament priest, the New Testament elder-bishop functions as a divine messenger bringing words of instruction, exhortation, admonition, and counsel to the people of God (2 Tim. 4:1–5).
- The New Testament elder-bishop serves as a trained interpreter of Holy Scripture for the church, instructing the congregation in faith, love, holiness, service, and covenant obedience (1 Tim. 1:3–11).
- The elder-bishop is the New Testament counterpart to the Old Testament priest as the model of faith, holiness, purity, and service for the religious community. Even as Christians are charged to be a light to the world, so the elder-bishop is a light to the Christian community (2 Cor. 12:15).[22]
- Like the Old Testament priest, the New Testament office of elder-bishop is a highly visible position of leadership in the religious and civic community, hence the elder-bishop serves as sage for the people of God and adviser to the appointed and elected civic officials. This means that the elder-bishop should be proactive in the social and political spheres of the community (1 Pet. 2:11–17).
- The New Testament elder-bishop functions as the worship role model for the church, demonstrating proper reverence and

worship of God to the church by personal example ("holy" or "devout," Titus 1:8).

These priestly roles of the New Testament elder-bishop are specifically connected to corporate worship in the church in three ways. First, personal piety is a necessary complement to congregational worship. As local church leadership models biblical piety they lay groundwork vital to dynamic corporate worship. Second, as a worship role model the elder-bishop leads, instructs, and encourages worship and the worship response of service in the local church. And third, as stewards of covenant relationship with God, the elder-bishop fosters and facilitates true worship among the people of God because worship is our response to God's gracious initiative in establishing the new covenant relationship with the church of Jesus Christ.

Worship Leader
As worship director the Old Testament priest led the congregation of Israel in corporate worship (the Day of Atonement ceremony, Lev. 16) and facilitated individual participation in sacrificial worship (see Figures 8.2 and 8.3). Curiously, apart from the proclamation of the word, there are no specific biblical texts identifying the elder-bishop as the worship leader in the New Testament church (1 Tim. 4:11–16). The role of the elder-bishop as worship leader in the church appears to be assumed, given the authority invested in this official. As overseer in the church the supervision of the elder-bishop naturally extends to the corporate worship of the congregation.

By analogy to the example of the Old Testament priesthood there are at least four distinct responsibilities the elder-bishop must discharge as worship leader of the church. Here it may be helpful to visualize the role of the elder-bishop as worship leader by appealing to Robert Webber's outline of worship as practiced in the early church. See diagram on page 157.

The first duty of the worship leader concerns the administration of church worship. This involves planning, organizing, and superintending the worship liturgy. Whether or not one adopts Webber's diagram of preparation, worship, and response, the worship leader must develop a form that provides the framework for the meeting between God and his people.

Next, the worship leader is responsible for instructing the congregation in worship, especially the form of worship characteristic of the church's worship tradition or denominational affiliation. In addition, this worship instruction should include teaching on the history, theory, and practice of worship in the Christian church generally. Finally, the training of lay worship leaders by the elder-bishop ensures the continuity of the worship tradition and congregational participation.

Third, the elder-bishop and the church have been charged to proclaim the word of God through the reading and exposition of Scripture and symbolically through the rite of the Eucharist or Lord's Table. This proclamation is intended for both the edification of believers and evangelizing of unbelievers. Most important, this proclamation focuses on the person and work of Jesus Christ and is grounded in the truth of God's revealed Word, the Holy Bible.

And fourth, as worship leader the elder-bishop is responsible for facilitating congregational participation in corporate worship so that all the gifts of the priestly community are employed in the service of worship to the glory of God. The worship leader's role as facilitator also includes encouraging and providing opportunity for the worship response of service to the body of believers and a world in great need.

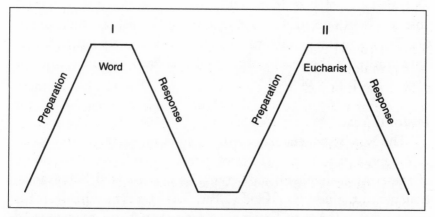

Robert E. Webber, *Common Roots: An Evangelical Call to Maturity.* Grand Rapids: Zondervan, 1978, p. 101. Used by permission.

Religious Education or Instruction

The priests were charged to instruct the people in the knowledge of God (Hos. 6:3). Specifically this meant tutoring the people of God in both the history and particular content of Yahweh's covenant with Israel (Ezek. 22:23–31; Hos. 4:4–6). Thus, the Old Testament priesthood was responsible for the welfare of the Israelites as messengers of God. True instruction on the part of the Israelite priests led to life and well-being for the people; but corrupt teaching caused the people to stumble, short-circuited the covenant relationship with Yahweh, and brought about Yahweh's wrath against his people in the form of the covenant curses (Mal. 2:4–9).[23]

Much like the Old Testament priesthood, the New Testament elder-bishop must be an able teacher (1 Tim. 3:2; here there is clear overlap between the church office of elder-bishop and the office gift of pastor-teacher in Eph. 4:11). Paul also reminded Timothy that a good servant of Christ gives instruction to the church (1 Tim. 4:6). This instruction is rooted in the Holy Scriptures and includes both teaching and exhortation (1 Tim. 4:11–13).

Especially important is the teaching of sound doctrine (Titus 2:1–2), that is, biblical teaching consistent with the words of Jesus Christ (1 Tim. 6:2–3) and his apostles (2 Tim. 1:13). Sound Christian doctrine in the church is crucial to right belief and the refutation of error (2 Tim. 4:3–5; Titus 1:9, 13). But important to our study is right worship predicated upon sound doctrine (Col. 2:6–19). Only this kind of worship rooted in the truth of Scripture is acceptable to God (John 4:24). And much like the priestly teaching of Old Testament times, only instruction in sound doctrine permits the harmonizing of the realms of religion and daily experience in the lives of the people of God.[24]

Pastoral Ministry

The New Testament exhorts the elder-bishop to serve the church as a shepherd would tend a flock of sheep. The two prescribed duties of these under-shepherds are serving as overseer and living as an example to the people of God (1 Pet. 5:1–7). Raymond Brown has suggested that the New Testament elder-bishop is similar to the Old Testament priest in that "he is predominantly a residential figure, living among the congregation for whom he cares."[25] As pastoral overseer, "his is the task of organizing, stabilizing, and preventing dangerous innovation (Titus 1:9)."[26]

We have already discovered that worship is an attitude as well as an act (see Chapter 2). The pastoral ministry of the elder-bishop is also the blending of attitude and action. According to the instruction of the apostle Peter, the actions of exercising oversight, teaching, and serving as an example to God's flock must be demonstrated with an attitude of submission to authority, humility, and an eagerness to serve God and others (1 Pet. 5:1–5). All three are foundational to the biblical understanding of worship.

Priestly Ministry and the Individual Christian

We have already learned that the individual Christian is part of the priesthood of believers, the church of Jesus Christ. This means the priestly ministry of Old Testament times has implications for the laity in the church too. The New Testament outlines two specific duties of the priesthood of believers: (1) to continually offer spiritual sacrifices of praise and thanksgiving to God (Heb. 13:15–16); and (2) proclaim redemption in Christ to the world through word and deed (1 Pet. 2:5, 9).[27]

More precisely, the offering of spiritual sacrifices includes the employment of individual spiritual gifts in the service of corporate worship. "In the liturgical gathering of the priesthood of the church, roles are apportioned according to gifts . . . the church acknowledges the diversity of these gifts by the setting aside of individuals for special aspects of liturgical leadership."[28] This continual offering of spiritual sacrifices also implies that the Christian develops a discipline of personal piety that manifests an attitude of private worship resulting in a worship life-style.

Peter Craigie noted that the priestly function was one of relationship in that the priests and Levites were the servants of covenant relationship with Yahweh for Israel.[29] Thus, the Christian's spiritual sacrifice of proclamation should emphasize the idea of reconciliation. Indeed, according to the apostle Paul, all believers in Christ have been given the ministry of reconciling the world to God

(2 Cor. 5:16–21). This proclamation aimed at reconciliation must be demonstrated with the spiritual sacrifices of good deeds done in the name of Christ (Heb. 13:16). The worship of works of righteousness motivated by love for Christ and others both honors God and validates the Christian proclamation (Eph. 2:10; Col. 1:10; Heb. 10:24; James 2:17).

Conclusions

The lesson for us in all this is obvious. Both the Old and New Testaments place a premium on godly character and uncompromising integrity in leadership (Exod. 29; Num. 20:12; 1 Tim. 3:2; Titus 1:7). The Israelites were obedient to Yahweh's covenant so long as they had role models of obedience to God in positions of religious and civic leadership (Gideon, Judg. 8:33–35; cf., 2 Kings 15:3; 17:8). Likewise, the Christian church remains pure in doctrine, worship, and service so long as its leadership imitates and implements the teaching of Christ and his apostles (note the apostle Paul's admonition: "Be imitators of me, as I am of Christ," 1 Cor. 11:1 NRSV).

The same principle holds true for worship leadership and meaningful corporate worship in the church—worshipers need worship role models! The quality of the worship experience for the people of God often occurs in direct proportion to the vitality and biblical grounding of the worship leadership. This means local church leadership must elevate the issue of worship leadership to a place of priority on the church's administrative agenda. It also means the professional clergy must be involved in ongoing training of lay worship leaders for service in the church. In addition, some kind of worship training should be instituted for all the members of the local congregation so the biblical principles of worship permeate the private worship and devotion in the home. Only then can the church effectively carry out the mission of priestly ministry to which it is called in behalf of the world. And only then can the church be assured of a new generation of believers who understand, appreciate, and become involved in the worship of proclamation and service.[30]

Fig. 8.3 Jewish Hymn in Honor of Ancient Ancestors

This selection extolling the Aaronic priesthood represents one section of a lengthy treatise praising well-known figures of Old Testament and intertestamental Jewish history (Ecclus. 44:1—50:21). The poetic epithet provides further insight on the character and ministry of the Hebrew priesthood.

6 He exalted Aaron, a holy man like Moses
who was his brother, of the tribe of Levi.
7 He made an everlasting covenant with him,
and gave him the priesthood of the people.
He blessed him with stateliness,
and put a glorious robe on him.
8 He clothed him in perfect splendor,
and strengthened him with the symbols of authority,
the linen undergarments, the long robe, and the ephod.
9 And he encircled him with pomegranates,
with many golden bells all around,
to send forth a sound as he walked,
to make their ringing heard in the temple
as a reminder to his people;
10 with the sacred vestment, of gold and violet
and purple, the work of an embroiderer;
with the oracle of judgment, Uʹrim and Thumʹmim;
11 with twisted crimson, the work of an artisan;
with precious stones engraved like seals,
in a setting of gold, the work of a jeweler,
to commemorate in engraved letters
each of the tribes of Israel;
12 with a gold crown upon his turban, inscribed like a seal with "Holiness,"
a distinction to be prized, the work of an expert,
a delight to the eyes, richly adorned.
13 Before him such beautiful things did not exist.
No outsider ever put them on, but only his sons
and his descendants in perpetuity.
14 His sacrifices shall be wholly burned
twice every day continually.

15 Moses ordained him
and anointed him with holy oil;
it was an everlasting covenant for him
and for his descendants as long as the heavens endure,
to minister to the Lord and serve as priest
and bless his people in his name.
16 He chose him out of all the living
to offer sacrifice to the Lord,
incense and a pleasing odor as a memorial portion,
to make atonement for the people.
17 In his commandments he gave him
authority and statutes and judgments,
to teach Jacob the testimonies,
and to enlighten Israel with his law.
18 Outsiders conspired against him
and envied him in the wilderness,
Dāʹthan and A·bīʹram and their followers
and the company of Kōʹrah, in wrath and anger.
19 The Lord saw it and was not pleased,
and in the heat of his anger they were destroyed;
he performed wonders against them
to consume them in flaming fire.
20 He added glory to Aaron
and gave him a heritage;
he allotted to him the best of the first fruits,
and prepared bread of first fruits in abundance;
21 for they eat the sacrifices of the Lord,
which he gave to him and his descendants.
22 But in the land of the people he has no inheritance,
and he has no portion among the people;
for the Lord himself is his portion and inheritance.

Sirach 45:6–22 (NRSV). Used by permission.

• 9 •

I Will Live
with My People!
The Tabernacle and Temple in Hebrew Worship

ONE OF THE EARLY SCENES in Genesis depicts the Creator God walking in the Garden of Eden seeking fellowship and communion with humankind (Gen. 3:8). Regrettably, and tragically, that first pair was banished from the divine presence that permeated original creation. They had believed the tempter's lie, sinned against God, and lost paradise (Gen. 3:14–19). The rest of the biblical narrative, in one sense, is the story of getting humanity "back to the garden" and back into the presence of God.[1] This is the great apocalyptic expectation of the prophets Ezekiel (37:27) and Zechariah (2:10–11). Indeed, the closing scene of the Bible envisions the realization of this long-awaited event—the home of God among mortals and the divine presence permeating the new creation (Rev. 21:1–4).

The intervening biblical books chronicle salvation history from the Hebrew exodus to the Advent of Jesus of Nazareth and the Easter resurrection of Jesus the Messiah. However, the biblical story is not one of humanity "getting themselves" back to the garden. Rather the biblical story is one of God restoring humanity to the garden through divinely initiated covenant relationship. And further, this "garden" was not a geographical space of peace and tranquility, but the garden of God's presence.

The Old Testament tabernacle and temples are important stages in the pilgrimage of humanity back to the very presence of God. The purpose of the Mosaic tabernacle was to enable God to live among his people and meet with them regularly (Exod. 25:8; 29:43). The glory of God, which filled Solomon's temple, affirmed this signal theological truth and prefigured the day when the greater glory of God in the person of Jesus Christ filled the Jerusalem temple (Luke 2:25–32). While the neighbors of ancient Israel also had their temples and holy sanctuaries, only the Hebrews had a theology that incorporated the idea of the divine presence in their midst (divine immanence) and the inability of the heavens to contain the Sovereign Lord of Creation (see Chapter 5).

This chapter offers an overview of the history and significance of the Old Testament tabernacle and temples for ancient Hebrew religion. Visual inserts have been included to illustrate more fully the grandeur and mystery of these worship centers. The overview concludes with a series of principles derived from the study of these Israelite religious institutions outlining the implications of tabernacle and temple structure and liturgy for Christian worship. I have deliberately avoided the often fanciful and sometime erroneous Christological allegorizing and spiritualizing of these Old Testament sanctuaries, choosing instead to emphasize the principles of biblical theology pertinent to Christian worship implicit in the text of Scripture.[2]

The Mosaic Tabernacle

The portable tent-sanctuary ordained by God and constructed by the Israelites under the supervision of Moses is known by several names in the Old Testament. The more frequently used terms include dwelling place or tabernacle (Hebrew *mishkān*, Lev. 15:31), tent; (Hebrew *'ōhel*, Exod. 26:36), and sanctuary (Hebrew *miqdāsh*, Exod. 25:8 or Hebrew *qōdesh*, Exod. 38:24).

At times these terms are used in combination with other descriptive words. For example, the tabernacle is often called the Tent of Meeting (Exod. 27:21), since this was the place where God convened with his people. Elsewhere, expressions like "the tabernacle of the Testimony" (since the tabernacle housed the ark of testimony, Exod. 38:21), "the tabernacle of the LORD" (Lev. 17:4), "the Tent of Meeting" (Num. 8:24), and even "the tabernacle, the Tent of

Meeting" (Exod. 39:32) are used to identify this portable sanctuary dedicated to the Israelite worship of Yahweh.

The New Testament makes reference to the Mosaic tabernacle with phrases like the "tent of witness" (Acts 7:44 NRSV), or the "first tent" (Heb. 9:8 NRSV), or simply "the tent" (Heb. 8:5; 9:21 NRSV). Significant wordplay on the term *tent* occurs in John 1:14, where the gospel writer depicts Jesus Christ as "the Word who *tented* among us." Here the New Testament Greek word *skēnē* is the same term used in the Septuagint, the Greek translation of the Old Testament, to render the Hebrew word *tabernacle* or *Tent of Meeting*. "That John means us to recall God's presence in the tabernacle in the wilderness scene is clear from the immediate reference to 'glory'. . . because the glory of the Lord filled the tabernacle."[3]

Design and Construction

The idea of a portable sanctuary or tent-shrine was not unique to the Hebrews. Similar religious structures in the ancient Near East are attested by way of extrabiblical literary parallel and archaeological discovery. For example, tent-shrines were a part of third millennium B.C. Egyptian culture and mid-second millennium B.C. Canaanite culture at Ugarit.[4] All this points to the fact that the Hebrew wilderness tabernacle was not a recent literary construct as some biblical scholars have proposed. Rather, the Israelite tent sanctuary "must now take its legitimate place as a genuine cultic phenomenon of the second millennium B.C., fulfilling the purpose and objectives described in connection with it by the narrative of Exodus."[5]

The tabernacle was a rectangular wooden-frame structure some ten cubits wide and thirty cubits long, according to the biblical dimensions, or approximately fifteen feet by forty-five feet. The tabernacle proper was divided into two rooms by a veil. The outer room or Holy Place was ten cubits by twenty cubits, or approximately fifteen feet by thirty feet, and the inner room or Most Holy Place was ten cubits by ten cubits, or approximately fifteen feet by fifteen feet. The Most Holy Place housed the ark of the covenant, and the Holy Place contained the lampstand, the table of the bread of presence, and the altar of incense. The tent-shrine was centered in a fenced courtyard some fifty cubits wide and one hundred cubits long, or

Fig. 9.1 The Mosaic Tabernacle

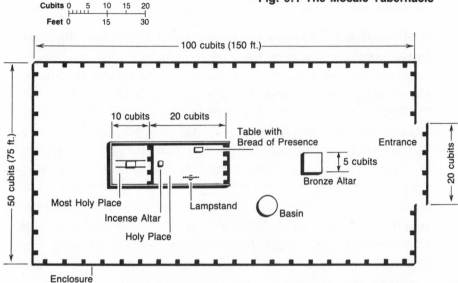

Cubits 0 5 10 15 20
Feet 0 15 30

100 cubits (150 ft.)

50 cubits (75 ft.)

10 cubits   20 cubits

Table with
Bread of Presence

Entrance

20 cubits

5 cubits

Bronze Altar

Most Holy Place

Incense Altar

Lampstand

Basin

Holy Place

Enclosure

The tabernacle was a "tent of meeting," the place where God met with his people (Exod. 27:21). This tent-shrine was portable and symbolized Yahweh's living presence among the Hebrews (Exod. 25:8). The tabernacle was designed to memorialize key experiences and theological ideas of the Mt. Sinai theophany. Primary among these key concepts embodied in the structure and furnishings of the tent was God's holiness, transcendence, and presence.

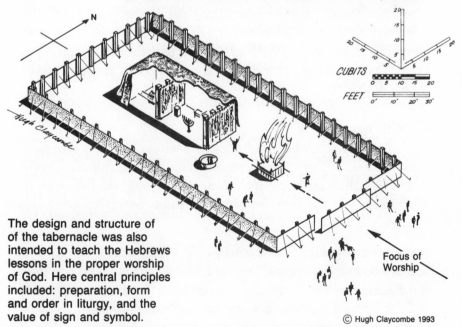

N

CUBITS

FEET

The design and structure of of the tabernacle was also intended to teach the Hebrews lessons in the proper worship of God. Here central principles included: preparation, form and order in liturgy, and the value of sign and symbol.

Focus of Worship

© Hugh Claycombe 1993

approximately seventy-five feet by one hundred fifty feet. Entrance to the sanctuary was from the east court with the bronze laver or basin and the altar of burnt offering set in the courtyard between the courtyard entrance and the tabernacle itself. (See Figure 9.1.)

The materials for the construction of the tabernacle were secured by offerings from the people (Exod. 25:3; 35:20–29). So much so that Moses had to restrain the people from giving gifts for the building of the sanctuary (Exod. 36:6–7). The construction materials gathered included gold, silver, bronze, linen and colored yarns, leather and animal skins, acacia wood, oil and incense, and precious stones. It has been suggested that the precious metals and gemstones were procured from the Egyptians (Exod. 12:35–36), while the Israelite flocks provided animals skins and leather (Exod. 12:38), and the linen, dye, oil, and incense could have been purchased from caravan traders.[6]

Actual construction of the tabernacle was supervised by Bezalel and Oholiab, who were filled "with the Spirit of God, with skill, ability and knowledge in all kinds of crafts" (Exod. 31:3). In addition, all the craftsmen were given skill to make everything for the tabernacle according to the divinely revealed blueprint (Exod. 31:6). God's directives for the tabernacle were part of the Mt. Sinai revelation given in the third month of the first year after the exodus from Egypt (Exod. 19:16; 24:19; 32:1, 15). The tent-shrine was completed on the first day of the first month in the second year after the Exodus (Exod. 40:1, 16).

Furnishings

The tabernacle was furnished with a series of items described in Exodus 25—30. The most sacred of these was the ark of the covenant. All the tabernacle furnishings are catalogued below in sequence as they are described in the exodus narrative. (See also Figures 8.2, 9.1, and 9.4.[7])

Ark of the covenant (Exod. 25:10–22). This rectangular chest of acacia wood was the centerpiece of Israelite religion. The box measured 2.5 cubits long by 1.5 cubits high and 1.5 cubits wide (roughly 3.75' x 1.5' x 1.5'). The ark was overlaid with gold and rested on four short legs equipped with rings for transporting on a set of

Fig. 9.2 The Ark of the Covenant

This rectangular chest of acacia wood was the centerpiece of Israelite religion. The box measured 2.5 cubits long by 1.5 cubits high, and 1.5 cubits wide (roughly 3.75' x 1.5' x 1.5'). The Ark was overlaid with gold and rested on four short legs equipped with rings for transporting on a set of wooden poles also overlaid with gold. Atop the Ark was a lid of pure gold called the "mercy seat"—since it was here blood was sprinkled on the Day of Atonement (see below).

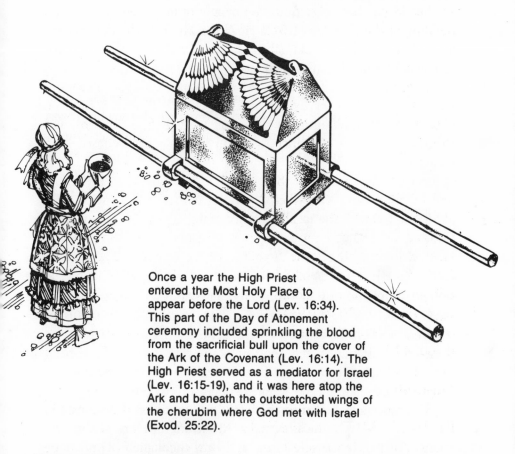

Once a year the High Priest entered the Most Holy Place to appear before the Lord (Lev. 16:34). This part of the Day of Atonement ceremony included sprinkling the blood from the sacrificial bull upon the cover of the Ark of the Covenant (Lev. 16:14). The High Priest served as a mediator for Israel (Lev. 16:15-19), and it was here atop the Ark and beneath the outstretched wings of the cherubim where God met with Israel (Exod. 25:22).

The Ark contained the stone tablets of the Decalogue, prompting the name "Ark of the Covenant" (Deut. 10:5). The tablets of God's law delivered to Moses at Mt. Sinai functioned as the constitution for the Israelite nation. Later a jar of manna from the desert wandering (Exod. 16:33), and Aaron's rod (Num. 10:5) were stored in the Ark as symbols of God's deliverance.

wooden poles also overlaid with gold. Atop the ark was a lid of pure gold called the mercy seat. Here blood was sprinkled on the Day of Atonement (Lev. 16:14; see also Chapter 7). Fixed at the ends of this lid were two cherubim facing each other with wings outstretched. The ark and its carrying poles were the only pieces of furniture in the Most Holy Place. The ark contained the stone tablets of the Decalogue (hence the name for this sacred chest—"ark of the covenant," Deut. 10:5), a jar of manna from the desert wandering (Exod. 16:33), Aaron's rod (Num. 17:10), and later a complete book of the law (Deut. 31:26).

Table of the bread of presence (Exod. 25:23–30). Like the ark of the covenant, the table of the bread of presence or showbread was made of acacia wood and overlaid with gold. The table measured 2 cubits long by 1 cubit wide and 1.5 cubits high (roughly 3' x 1.5' x 1.5'). Affixed to each of its four legs was a ring for the insertion of the gold-overlay acacia poles used to transport the table. The table was located on the north wall of the Holy Place. Gold plates, dishes, ladles, and bowls adorned the table (Exod. 37:10–15), and it was perpetually stocked with fresh bread symbolizing the meal of covenant fellowship the tribes of Israel enjoyed with Yahweh.

Lampstand (Exod. 25:31–40). The lampstand was located on the south wall of the Holy Place and was made of pure gold. It consisted of seven lamps or bowls, one on the central shaft and one on each of the three branches stemming from the two sides of the central shaft. In addition, three "cups like almonds" were designed into the branches of the lampstand. Implements made of pure gold for snuffing the lamps and trimming the wicks accompanied the lampstand (Exod. 37:17–24). The lampstand functioned practically as the source of light for the tabernacle and held theological significance as a symbol of the light of divine revelation.[8]

Curtains (Exod. 26:1–14). The tabernacle covering was a series of ten woven curtains measuring twenty-eight cubits by four cubits (about forty-two feet by six feet) and clasped together to form a single tapestry twenty-eight by forty cubits in dimension (roughly forty-two feet by sixty feet). This would easily cover the tabernacle frame itself (ten by thirty cubits), leaving the front end open. The curtains were made of fine linen, with woolen figures of cherubim, dyed blue, purple, and crimson, embroidered into the curtains. This tabernacle curtain was protected by two additional layers of covering, one made of rams' skins and the other of goatskins. These extra coverings both protected the fine linen covering from the elements and camouflaged the beauty and costliness of the tabernacle curtain and furnishings from bandits and marauders. The coverings were held in place by cords and bronze pegs staked into the ground (Exod. 27:19; 35:18). (See Figure 9.1.)

Framework (Exod. 26:15–30). The tabernacle coverings lay upon a wooden frame structure of acacia wood. These frame sections measured 10 cubits high by 1.5 cubits wide (roughly 15' x 2.25'), were overlaid with gold, and rested in twin silver bases. Considerable scholarly debate continues over the exact form of the tabernacle frames; were they hollow, solid, interlocking?

Veil (Exod. 26:31–35). The tabernacle sanctuary was divided into two rooms by a woolen veil dyed blue, purple, and crimson. The ten-by-ten cubit veil (about fifteen feet by fifteen feet) was suspended from four acacia poles overlaid with gold on a series of golden hooks. The supporting pillars were set in silver pedestals. (The equivalent of this veil in Herod's temple was torn in two from top to bottom at the death of Jesus Christ [Matt. 27:51].)

Screen (Exod. 26:36–37). Since the tabernacle covering left the east end of the structure open, a screen was erected at the sanctuary entrance. Presumably the screen was similar in size to the veil, approximately ten by ten cubits or about fifteen by fifteen feet. The screen was suspended from five acacia pillars overlaid in gold and set in bronze bases.

Altar of burnt offering (Exod. 27:1–8). This square altar measured five cubits by five cubits and was three cubits high (roughly 7.5' x 7.5' x 4.5'). The altar was made of acacia wood and overlaid with bronze. Horn-like ornaments projected from its four corners. A step or ledge of 1.5 cubits (about 2.25') in height encircled the altar. This step was supported by a bronze grating. Bronze implements for tending the altar included ash shovels, ash pots, basins, tongs, and firepans (Exod. 38:3–8). The altar was located in the east courtyard between the entrance and the tabernacle proper. Animal sacrifices were performed here, and the altar fire was to burn continually (Lev. 6:8–13).

Courtyard (Exod. 27:9–19). The tabernacle was enclosed in a courtyard measuring one hundred cubits (approximately one hundred fifty feet) on the north-south perimeter and fifty cubits (approximately seventy-five feet) on the east-west perimeter. The linen curtains of the courtyard wall were five cubits high. This linen "fence" was suspended on silver hooks from pillars of wood—twenty pillars each on the north-south walls and ten pillars each on the east-west walls. The linen hangings were anchored with bronze pegs, and the wooden support poles were set in bronze bases and decorated with silver capitals (Exod. 35:18).

Altar of incense (Exod. 30:1–10). The altar of incense was located in the Holy Place, along with the table and lampstand, in front of the veil. The altar was one cubit square and two cubits in height (roughly 1.5' x 1.5' x 3') and was made of acacia wood and overlaid with gold. Horn-like ornaments projected from the corners of the altar and rings were fixed just below the rim or molding of the top of the altar for insertion of the transport poles (Exod. 37:28). (See Figure 9.2.)

Laver (Exod. 30:17–21). A bronze laver or basin was located between the courtyard entrance and the altar of burnt offering. Here the priests carried out their daily ritual washings.

History

The instructions for designing and constructing a Tent of Meeting, and implementing worship of Yahweh there, were part of the covenant legislation revealed by God to Moses at Mt. Sinai (Exod. 25:9). According to Exodus 40:1, 16, the tabernacle was completed in the second year after the exodus from Egypt, a little less than a year after the revelation was given to Moses at Sinai (Exod. 19:16). The cloud of the glory of the Lord that filled the tent sanctuary then guided the Israelites in the stages of their desert trek to Canaan, the land of covenant promise (Exod. 40:34–38). The three clans of Leviti-

Fig. 9.3 The Tabernacle

This elaborate tent served as Yahweh's portable
sanctuary ''in all the travels of the Israelites'' (Exod. 40:36).

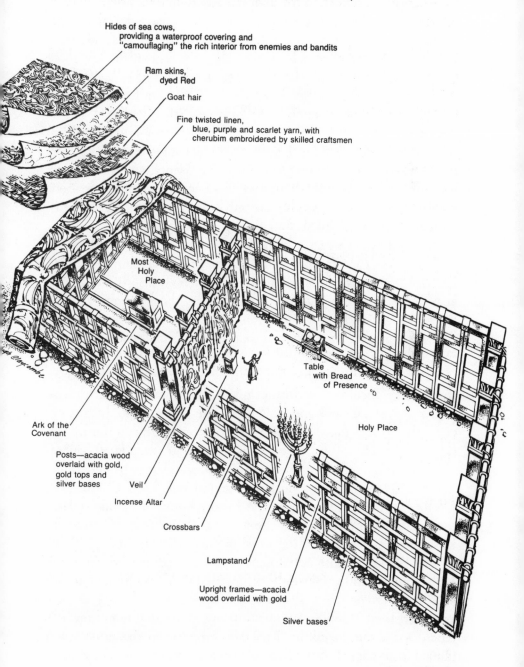

Hides of sea cows,
providing a waterproof covering and
''camouflaging'' the rich interior from enemies and bandits

Ram skins,
dyed Red

Goat hair

Fine twisted linen,
blue, purple and scarlet yarn, with
cherubim embroidered by skilled craftsmen

Most
Holy
Place

Table
with Bread
of Presence

Ark of the
Covenant

Holy Place

Posts—acacia wood
overlaid with gold,
gold tops and
silver bases

Veil

Incense Altar

Crossbars

Lampstand

Upright frames—acacia
wood overlaid with gold

Silver bases

© Hugh Claycombe 1993

cal priests—the Kohathites, Gershonites, and Merarites—were responsible for transporting the Tent of Meeting (Num. 3—4).

Little mention is made of the Mosaic tabernacle during the period of the judges, after the conquest and settlement of Palestine. Scattered biblical references suggest that the tent-shrine was more or less permanently erected at Shiloh (Josh. 18:1; 19:51; 22:19; Judg. 18:3). Here the tabernacle served as the focal point for the worship and political administration for the Hebrew tribal league.

By the time of the priest-judge Samuel the tabernacle still remained at Shiloh (1 Sam. 1:3, 9). Although some biblical scholars have understood the reference to the Lord's sanctuary as a *house* to indicate that the portable tent had now become a more permanent structure, perhaps the term *house* only signifies the repair and reinforcement of worn building materials.[9]

It was during this same historical time frame that the ark of the covenant was captured by the Philistine armies (1 Sam. 4:10–18). Later, during the reign of King Saul, the Hebrew priests are located at Nob and apparently attending a sanctuary there (1 Sam. 21:1–9; 22:9–19). While the words *tent* or *tabernacle* are not used to describe the worship center, it is assumed that the Lord's tabernacle had been shifted to this new site.

Difficulties increase as biblical scholars attempt to reconstruct the history, location, and function of the tabernacle during the reigns of Kings David and Solomon. The Chronicler's history records that the Lord's tabernacle was located at Gibeon during the rule of both David and Solomon (1 Chron. 16:39; 21:29). Subsequently the Tent of Meeting and its furniture and utensils were transferred to Solomon's temple in Jerusalem (1 Kings 8:4; 2 Chron. 5:5).

Yet the court historian in the history books of Samuel relates that David pitched a tent for the ark of the covenant in Jerusalem, which became a functioning worship center (2 Sam. 6:17; 12:20; 15:25). David's "house of the Lord" must be distinguished from the Mosaic tabernacle at Gibeon (1 Kings 2:28–30). David's tent-shrine possibly served only as a temporary house for the ark of the covenant as a witness to Yahweh's role in the capture of Jerusalem from the Jebusites and the founding of Davidic kingship in the new capital (2 Sam. 5:6–16; 6:1–19). His tent-sanctuary, built upon the threshing floor of Araunah, symbolically marked the site as sacred unto the Lord until such time as a permanent temple structure might be built (2 Sam. 6:17; 24:18–25; 1 Kings 8:14–21).

Purpose and Function

The tabernacle was not primarily a gathering place for the Israelites as the people of God, although there were times when the Hebrew community met together before God at the tabernacle (Num. 14:10). Instead, the basic intent of the tabernacle was to provide a dwelling place for God so that he might live in the midst of his people. For this reason the tabernacle was designed to be a portable dwelling place since God would have to move with his people as they traveled toward the land of covenant promise. Indeed God's home and his presence symbolized in the cloud and fire actually led the Israelites to Canaan (Exod. 40:36–37).

The tabernacle also functioned as the worship center for ancient Israel. Here the Hebrew priesthood led the people in worship and gave instruction in covenant obedience to Yahweh. But the tabernacle was more than God's dwelling place and Israel's worship center. It stood as a life-sized object lesson in the middle of the Israelite camp, vividly portraying the nature and character of God to the Hebrew people. Through sign, symbol, color, and liturgy the tabernacle served to instruct the Hebrews in God's holiness, transcendence, immanence, wrath and mercy, justice and grace, and covenant love and faithfulness. (On the specifics of tabernacle worship see Chapters 4 and 5.) All individual and corporate worship at the tabernacle was officiated by the Levitical priesthood. (The Hebrew priestly orders and duties are discussed in detail in Chapter 8, including the biblical instruction regarding the transportation of the tabernacle and its furnishings.) Tabernacle worship was not only highly structured in space, but also in time. (The Hebrew religious calendar is outlined in Chapter 6 and Appendix C.)

Solomon's Temple

History

The book of Deuteronomy forecasted a permanent site for the worship of Yahweh, a place chosen by the Lord God (Deut. 12:5, 11, 14, 18, 21, 26; etc.). That place was the threshing floor of Arau-

Fig. 9.4 Solomon's Temple
(ca. 960-587 B.C.)

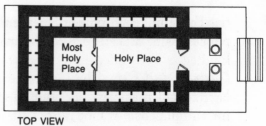

TOP VIEW

King Solomon achieved fame as the builder of Yahweh's temple in Jerusalem. The elaborate building project took seven years to finish. The temple symbolized God's presence and was a "house of prayer" for Israel (1 Kings 8:27–32).

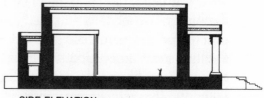

SIDE ELEVATION

The permanence of the temple structure testified to God's covenant faithfulness (1 Kings 8:15). The temple retained the same floor plan of the Tabernacle, but redesigned the sanctuary vertically—emphasizing God's transcendence (1 Kings 8:27–30).

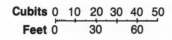

Cubits 0 10 20 30 40 50

Feet 0 30 60

The artwork on pages 174 and 176 (Figs. 9.4 and 9.5) has been drawn to the same scale for comparative purposes.

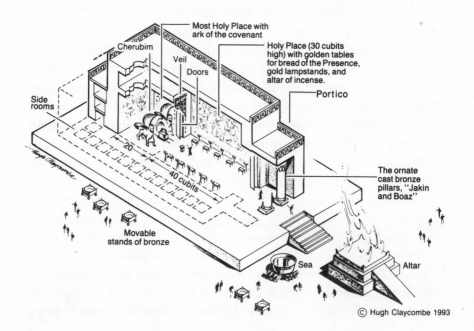

Most Holy Place with ark of the covenant

Cherubim

Veil

Doors

Holy Place (30 cubits high) with golden tables for bread of the Presence, gold lampstands, and altar of incense.

Portico

Side rooms

20

40 cubits

The ornate cast bronze pillars, "Jakin and Boaz"

Movable stands of bronze

Sea

Altar

© Hugh Claycombe 1993

nah the Jebusite, purchased by King David at the command of God's prophet (2 Sam. 24:18-25). David then erected an altar there and kindled a burnt offering to avert the Lord's plague against Israel (2 Sam. 24:21, 25). The Chronicler's record indicates that David later bought the entire tract of land surrounding the threshing floor for the purpose of permanently establishing God's sanctuary (1 Chron. 21:28—22:1). (See also Chapter 5.)

It was customary in the ancient Near East for the king to build a temple for the gods as a demonstration of his gratitude and loyalty in response to the divine grant of kingship (2 Sam. 7:17).[10] David also had such intentions; however, God overruled David's plan because he was a man of war and bloodshed (2 Sam. 17:18-29; 2 Chron. 22:6-9). Despite this divine prohibition against actually building a temple for Yahweh, King David did make arrangements for its construction, including the gathering of materials and supplies to ensure his son Solomon's success in erecting a house for the name of Yahweh (2 Chron. 22:2-19).

The reign of King Solomon is described as the golden age of ancient Hebrew history. His kingship ushered in an unprecedented era of peace, prosperity, and international prominence for Israel (1 Kings 10:14-29). Solomon also achieved fame as a master builder, the temple of Yahweh his architectural centerpiece. The temple-building project took seven years to complete (1 Kings 6:37-38). The elaborate edifice was ornately constructed in stone and cedar, much of it overlaid in gold (1 Kings 6:1-36; 2 Chron. 3:1-14; 4:1-10). Although the temple followed the floor plan of the desert tabernacle—entrance, Holy Place, and Most Holy Place—the blueprint confirmed by Solomon probably reflected Phoenician design in both size and tiered or storied structure (see 1 Kings 5, which recounts the importation of materials, labor, and technical skill from King Hiram of Tyre).[11] (See also Figure 9.4.)

Upon completion of the temple Solomon had the ark of the covenant and the tabernacle furniture installed in the sanctuary (1 Kings 8:1-11). Then all Israel participated in a ceremony of dedication led by the king himself. The dedication festival lasted seven days and included a royal speech of thanksgiving in recognition of the divine grant of kingship to the Davidic family (1 Kings 8:14-21), Solomon's dedicatory prayer (1 Kings 8:22-53), a royal blessing

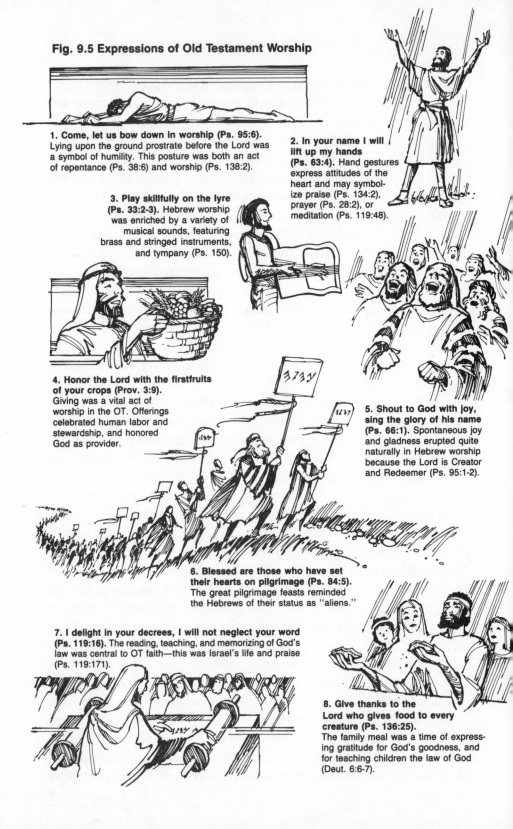

Fig. 9.5 Expressions of Old Testament Worship

1. Come, let us bow down in worship (Ps. 95:6). Lying upon the ground prostrate before the Lord was a symbol of humility. This posture was both an act of repentance (Ps. 38:6) and worship (Ps. 138:2).

2. In your name I will lift up my hands (Ps. 63:4). Hand gestures express attitudes of the heart and may symbolize praise (Ps. 134:2), prayer (Ps. 28:2), or meditation (Ps. 119:48).

3. Play skillfully on the lyre (Ps. 33:2-3). Hebrew worship was enriched by a variety of musical sounds, featuring brass and stringed instruments, and tympany (Ps. 150).

4. Honor the Lord with the firstfruits of your crops (Prov. 3:9). Giving was a vital act of worship in the OT. Offerings celebrated human labor and stewardship, and honored God as provider.

5. Shout to God with joy, sing the glory of his name (Ps. 66:1). Spontaneous joy and gladness erupted quite naturally in Hebrew worship because the Lord is Creator and Redeemer (Ps. 95:1-2).

6. Blessed are those who have set their hearts on pilgrimage (Ps. 84:5). The great pilgrimage feasts reminded the Hebrews of their status as "aliens."

7. I delight in your decrees, I will not neglect your word (Ps. 119:16). The reading, teaching, and memorizing of God's law was central to OT faith—this was Israel's life and praise (Ps. 119:171).

8. Give thanks to the Lord who gives food to every creature (Ps. 136:25). The family meal was a time of expressing gratitude for God's goodness, and for teaching children the law of God (Deut. 6:6-7).

pronounced upon the people of Israel (1 Kings 8:54–61), and a multitude of sacrificial offerings as part of the worship and praise of Yahweh (1 Kings 8:62–66). But most important, the cloud of God's glory filled the new temple, symbolizing his living presence among his covenant people Israel (1 Kings 8:10–11).

The later history of Yahweh's temple in Jerusalem mirrors that of kingship in Judah after the split of Solomon's empire. The fate of the holy sanctuary rose and fell in accordance with the covenant obedience, or lack thereof, demonstrated by the ruling royal family. As kings turned from the Lord God to serve idols, the temple too experienced decline, often falling into disrepair and usually given over to religious apostasy. Examples here include the pagan altar built in the temple by King Ahaz (2 Kings 16:10–16) and the idolatry and cult prostitution housed in the temple during the reign of King Manasseh (2 Kings 21:1–9).[12]

Conversely, those few kings who served Yahweh and obeyed his covenant stipulations initiated policies that secured renewal and reform in temple worship. Here the illustrations of covenant loyalty demonstrated by acts of faithfulness toward God and his temple include the extensive reparations of the temple complex by King Jehoash (2 Kings 12:1–16) and the great religious reforms of Kings Hezekiah and Josiah (2 Kings 18:1–18; 23:1–20).[13]

Sadly, these reform movements only delayed the inevitable. Yahweh's abandonment of his temple, witnessed by the prophet Ezekiel, was but a portent of the approaching storm of divine wrath (Ezek. 10). As punishment for the habitual transgression of his covenant in the worship of foreign gods, Yahweh disowned his sanctuary (Lam. 2:7), rejected his people (Lam. 1:15; 5:20), and scattered them in pagan lands in accordance with earlier Mosaic warnings (Ps. 137; Lev. 18:24–30). All that remained of the splendor of Solomon's temple was the memory after the Babylonian hordes reduced Jerusalem and the temple to ashes and rubble in 587 B.C. (2 Kings 25:1–21; Lam. 1—5).[14]

Religious Significance

The sanctuary of the Lord as a symbol of God's presence in the midst of his people was retained in the shift from desert tabernacle to urban temple (1 Kings 8:57). This is seen both in the prominence given to the temple as the place for housing the ark of the covenant and as the place where the name of the Lord resided (1 Kings 8:18–21). However, a new theological emphasis surfaces in King Solomon's prayer of dedication. Whereas the Mosaic tabernacle pictured Yahweh's holy presence in the midst of his people (Exod. 25:8), Solomon's temple now embodied the fulfillment of divine promises regarding the Davidic covenant and perpetual dynastic kingship (1 Kings 8:14–21).[15]

While the temple remained the center of Israelite sacrificial and festival worship officiated by the Levitical priesthood, it was also consecrated as a house of prayer. Again, King Solomon's dedicatory prayer reveals the temple stood as a monument to the God of Israel who heard and answered the prayers and petitions of his people (1 Kings 8:27–40, 44–54). But not only for the Hebrews, as the Sovereign Lord also responds to aliens and foreigners (1 Kings 8:41–43). In fact, the idea of prayer is so entwined with Solomon's temple that this house of the Lord now becomes the direction of prayer for the pious Hebrew (1 Kings 8:35).

In addition, the newly erected temple served as a token of Israel's vow of covenant obedience to Yahweh (1 Kings 8:56–61) and a witness to the sovereignty of God over all creation and his election of Israel (1 Kings 8:41–43). The permanence of the temple structure was a testimony to God's faithfulness in keeping his covenant promise to give his people rest in the land bequeathed to the patriarch Abraham (Gen. 12:1–3). Finally, the temple was a tangible reminder of God's transcendence and glory—the true God who does not dwell in a house made by human hands (1 Kings 8:27–30).

By the time of the prophet Jeremiah (ca. 627–580 B.C.), this lofty "temple theology" had been forgotten or so corrupted by religious syncretism with the surrounding paganism as to be unrecognizable. The temple had become a fetish or talisman for the people of Judah (Jer. 7:1–11). No longer a symbol of God's divine presence and a monument to his sovereignty, the temple was now equated with God's actual presence and regarded as the ultimate spiritual reality by the Hebrews. The mere association of Yahweh's temple with Jerusalem and the people of God insured protection, security, and covenant blessing. Jeremiah indignantly condemned this misplaced trust in the physical structure and predicted its eventual destruction (Jer. 7—10).[16]

Political Significance

The association of Solomon's temple with Davidic kingship brought the institutions of Israelite state and religion into a close and potentially harmful alliance. The ideal of a check-and-balance system between king and priest, state and temple, could easily degenerate into political power mongering by either side. Even a cursory reading of the Old Testament historical records reveals that this scenario proved to be the rule and not the exception for Hebrew kingship.

As early as King Saul, the loyalty of the priesthood was recognized as an essential ingredient for stable and effective royal rule. This was tragically demonstrated in Saul's brutal massacre of the Israelite priesthood at Nob in retaliation for their support of his political rival David (1 Sam. 22:6–19). Neither was King David above playing politics with Israelite religion in the appointment of his sons—not from the tribe of Levi—as priests (2 Sam. 8:18).

Prior to the building of the temple, King Solomon banished the priest Abiathar and anointed his rival Adonijah (1 Kings 1:7; 2:26–27). He then appointed Zadok as the new high priest (1 Kings 2:35). After the split of Solomon's empire Jeroboam soon learned the value of state-controlled religion in building a political power base. To secure the loyalty of the northern tribes and prevent their regular pilgrimages into Jerusalem and the Southern Kingdom of Judah, King Jeroboam erected twin temples at Dan and Bethel, housing golden bull-gods, supposedly as symbols of Yahweh (1 Kings 12:25–33). In addition, he appointed a spurious priesthood to officiate the new religious cult (1 Kings 12:31). Again, the Old Testament historians identified this attempt to control the political fate of the Northern Kingdom of Israel through an alternative "religion of Yahweh" as the fatal blunder of the kings of the northern empire (2 Kings 17:21–23).

A study of later Hebrew history uncovers similar and even more blatant manipulation of Hebrew religion by the kings of both the monarchies of Judah and Israel. Micah's diatribe against such practices (in this case the rulers of the Northern Kingdom of Israel enlisting priest and prophet on the royal payroll) characterizes both the political history of the divided monarchy period and the prophetic response to such behavior:

> Her leaders judge for a bribe,
> her priests teach for a price,
> and her prophets tell fortunes for money.
> Yet they lean upon the LORD and say,
> "Is not the LORD among us?
> No disaster will come upon us." (Mic. 3:11)

The Second Temple

History

The first wave of Jewish emigrants to Jerusalem from exile in Babylonia were led by Shesh-bazzar (Ezra 1:5–11). He was a prince of Judah who became the first governor of the restoration community in Jerusalem. This return by former captives was made possible by the decree of King Cyrus of Persia, which permitted conquered peoples who had been deported by the Babylonians to return to their homelands (Ezra 1:1–4). The foundation for a new temple was laid during the early stages of Shesh-bazzar's administration (Ezra 5:16). However, the meager project was abandoned as the vision of Ezekiel's "temple-state" quickly faded amid the stark reality of Persian domination.

Work on the second temple resumed some seventeen years later at the prompting of the prophets Haggai and Zechariah. The primary purpose of their message was to inspire the rebuilding of God's temple (Hag. 2:8; cf., Ezra 5:1–2) The renewal of sacrificial and festival worship in the restoration community of Judah was intended to symbolize the renewal of God's covenant promises to his people (Zech. 8:1–17). The construction project began in 520 B.C. and was completed sometime in 516 or 515 B.C. The second temple was but a shadow of its predecessor, to such a degree that those who remembered the former temple lamented the inferiority of the new edifice (Ezra 3:12–13).[17]

Several decades later, during the mid-fifth century B.C., Ezra and Nehemiah initiated reforms in Jerusalem that included the rehabilitation of the priesthood (Ezra 10:18–44) and the reinstitution of the temple ritual and Sabbath observance (Neh. 8:13-18; 13:15-22). In addition, the temple tithe was enforced to ensure that the temple personnel received the portion necessary for their livelihood (Neh. 13:4-14; Mal. 3:8-12). As in the case of Solomon's temple, the mere presence of a building dedicated to Yahweh was no guarantee of God's covenant favor for Israel. The divine formula for Israel's success had not changed; loving obedience to the stipulations of God's covenant was still mandatory.

Religious Significance

The period of the second temple had considerable impact on the development of Israelite religion. While temple ritual and animal sacrifice remained at the core of the Jewish religious experience, the dispersion of Jews across the Mediterranean world prompted the rise of a competing religious institution—the synagogue. Synagogue worship emphasized personal piety and the spiritual sacrifices of prayer, fasting, and almsgiving. The Jerusalem temple still drew Jews to the great pilgrimage festivals, but increasingly the institution of the temple was identified with the Hellenized Jewish aristocracy of Jerusalem. Thus the synagogue grew in importance as the worship place of the grassroots population, especially among those Jews outside the environs of Jerusalem. (See also Chapter 12.)

The zealous but misguided appeal to the Law of Moses for the restructuring of Hebrew society eventually led to a pharisaical legalism that ruthlessly tithed spice seeds but ignored the very heart of Torah—faith, justice, and mercy (Matt. 23:23). In addition, the fear of another exile spawned the creation of a supplemental legal tradition in the Jewish religion—the oral law (Matt. 15:1-9). This secondary law code, originally intended to guarantee obedience to the Law of Moses by hedging it in at every point, later supplanted the primary Mosaic law. Jesus decried this form of Judaism as a religion that had abandoned divinely revealed truth for the sake of clinging to human tradition (Mark 7:1-9).

Certain apocalyptic connotations and ideas were also attached to the second temple. Unlike Solomon's temple, there is no record of any visible demonstration of the presence of God returning to reside in the temple after the Babylonian exile. Whether symbolized in a cloud of glory or otherwise, the Old Testament prophets predicted that the Lord would return to his temple (Mal. 3:1). By New Testament times there was a growing anticipation of this apocalyptic event, spurred by the longed-for judgment of the nations associated with God's appearance in his temple (Hag. 2:20–23; Zech. 14:12–19). Of course, Jesus identified John the Baptist as the Elijah-like forerunner (Matt. 11:13–14), and he himself, as Son of God and Son of David, was the glory of the second temple (John 1:19–28), perhaps fulfilling Haggai's prophecy that the glory of the second temple would surpass that of Solomon's temple (Hag. 2:9). And his appearance in the temple did indeed inaugurate that great apocalyptic event—the kingdom of God (Luke 2:25–35).

Last, and perhaps most significant, the second temple period witnessed the metamorphosis of the priestly office from teacher of the law to that of religious and political bureaucrat. By the time of Christ a professional class of scribes and lawyers had usurped the priestly role of biblical interpreter and teacher.[18] The very thing that originally constituted the essence of the priestly endeavor according to Mosaic legislation was now delegated to a group of lawyers and academicians who enjoyed parading about in long robes, holding the conspicuous seats in the synagogue, prayed pretentiously, and devoured widows' houses (Mark 12:38–40).

Social and Political Significance

Israel's identity as the people of God took on new characteristics during the post-exilic period. The rebuilt temple and the reorganized priesthood replaced the state and king as the stabilizing institutions of Hebrew society. As a result of the reforms of Ezra and Nehemiah the Law of Moses became the charter by which society was restructured and redefined. Religious, social, and economic policy was now determined by Old Testament law. The attendant emphases of exclusiveness and separatism from the Gentiles and their polluted world order was shaped by two main concerns: preventing another exile and preserving Israelite ethnic identity.

The long-term ramifications of this reordering of Hebrew society along the principles of legalism becomes evident in the New Testament, especially in the encounters between Jesus and the Jewish religious leaders. By the time of Christ the unhealthy preoccupation in Judaism with the minutiae of law-keeping and separation from the

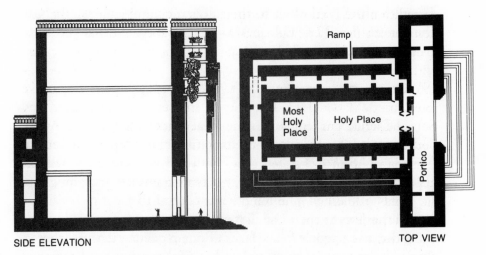

Fig. 9.6 Herod's Temple
(20 B.C. — A.D. 70)

Ramp

Most Holy Place

Holy Place

Portico

SIDE ELEVATION

TOP VIEW

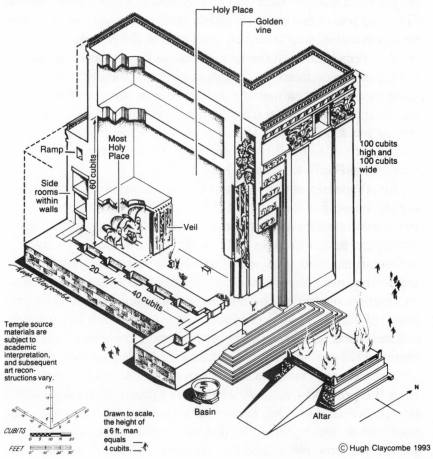

Holy Place

Golden vine

100 cubits high and 100 cubits wide

Ramp

Most Holy Place

Side rooms within walls

60 cubits

Veil

20

40 cubits

Temple source materials are subject to academic interpretation, and subsequent art reconstructions vary.

CUBITS

FEET

Drawn to scale, the height of a 6 ft. man equals 4 cubits.

Basin

Altar

N

© Hugh Claycombe 1993

Gentiles blinded the Jews to their divine commission as a light to the nations (Isa. 42:6; Luke 2:32) and their own spiritual and moral bankruptcy (Luke 5:27–31; 10:25–27).[19]

The Temple in the New Testament

The Jerusalem temple was the focal point of Judaism during the New Testament era. Indeed, the rabbinic tradition preserved in the Mishnah (*Aboth* i.2) stated that the world was sustained by three things: the Torah (law of Moses), the temple service, and almsgiving (or deeds of mercy). The temple was central to Judaism because it linked the Jews to their Old Testament covenant heritage, thus unifying them as a people in the face of Roman occupation and persecution. As the place of sacrificial and festival worship the temple was pivotal to Jewish destiny since divine blessing in the future was contingent on obedience to Mosaic legislation in the present. While the temple symbolized both the religious and ethnic roots of Judaism, it was far more significant as the sole institution that afforded Judaism some measure of political and judicial autonomy from the Roman overlords. For this reason Christianity posed a lethal threat to Judaism in the minds of the Jewish religious leaders because the new covenant fulfilled in Christ made sacrificial worship, and hence the temple, obsolete.[20] (See also Chapter 8.)

Jesus showed great respect for the institutions of Judaism, including the synagogue and temple (Matt. 4:23; Mark 1:39; John 10:22–23). He condemned the hypocrisy of the religious leaders associated with these institutions but not the institutions themselves nor the biblical injunctions on which they were founded (e.g., Jesus' teaching on the tithe; Matt. 23:23–24). For example, at age twelve Jesus was found teaching in the temple, a place he called his "Father's house" (Luke 2:41–51). Twice Jesus cleansed the temple in his zeal for the institution as a house of prayer and not a commercial exchange (John 2:13–16; Matt. 21:12–13; cf., Ps. 118:26). Elsewhere the New Testament records that Jesus regularly taught in the temple (Matt. 24:1; Mark 14:49; Luke 19:47; 20:1) and even predicted its destruction (Matt. 24:1–2; Mark 13:1–2; Luke 21:5–6). However, it was the veiled statement of Jesus regarding the destruction and rebuilding of the temple in three days that incited the religious Jews (John 2:18–22). They mistook his teaching and accused him of blasphemy. Of course, Jesus was referring to himself as the ultimate reality of what the temple symbolized—God's presence among his people.[21]

The early chapters of the book of Acts indicate that the Jerusalem temple was important to the development of the early church. The newly constituted church met daily for prayer and worship at the temple (Acts 2:46; 3:1). The apostles also evangelized within the temple precincts by performing miracles and preaching Jesus as the Christ (Acts 3:11—4:2). This daily preaching and teaching of Jesus as the Messiah in the temple did not cease despite the persecution of the Sadducees and priestly temple officials (Acts 5:17-39, 42). It appears that the early church continued to worship, pray, preach, and teach in the temple until the persecution of Christians in Jerusalem associated with the stoning of Stephen, who, according to the Jewish council, blasphemed Moses, God, and the temple (Acts 6:11-14).[22]

The book of Hebrews interprets the tabernacle, and later the temple, typologically as the first tent (Heb. 9:8). This worship sanctuary was only a symbol of the perfect and eternal redemption secured by Jesus Christ, the Great High Priest (Heb. 9:11-14). The contrast here is between the tent of this creation and the heavenly and perfect tent of the Godhead (Heb. 9:11). The one illustrated the new order as an object lesson; the other fulfills the new order mediated by Jesus Christ with his blood (Heb. 9:12, 14). (See also Chapter 12.)

Last, the book of John's revelation understands the temple of God as the church of Jesus Christ. The community of believers confessing faith in Christ and practicing obedience to his word now comprises the spiritual temple of God (Rev. 3:12). John also had a vision of God's heavenly temple after which the earthly tabernacle-temple was patterned (Heb. 9:8-10). This heavenly temple is a symbol of both divine self-revelation and judgment (Rev. 11:19; 14:15, 17; 15:5-8). John's concluding vision of the New Jerusalem depicts no physical temple in the city of God, because Almighty God and Christ the Lamb are its temple (Rev. 21:22). God is truly and finally in the midst of his people; Eden is restored.

Theological Significance

Old Testament Tabernacle Period

The Mosaic tabernacle teaches important theological truths about God and his worship. The primary purpose of the tent-sanctuary was to provide a dwelling place for Yahweh so that he might live with his people. This conception of God's divine presence among the Hebrews was essentially a reenactment of the Mt. Sinai theophany, when Yahweh met with the Israelites after the Exodus to establish covenant relationship with them.[23]

The design and construction of the tabernacle, as well as the prescriptions for the worship liturgy performed there, all reinforced key theological emphases. For example, the tension between divine immanence and divine transcendence, seen in the boundaries set for the people around Mt. Sinai, is replicated in the floor plan of the tabernacle, which restricts the Israelites to the courtyard (Exod. 19:12; Lev. 1:1–13; see also Figure 9.1).

In turn, the limits imposed on the Israelites for approaching God underscored both Yahweh's holiness and the need for cleansing and purity on the part of his worshipers (Exod. 19:10–11, 14–15, 23–24). The bronze laver or basin located in the tabernacle courtyard symbolized this aspect of worship preparation, as the priests were required to purify themselves by means of ritual washing there on a daily basis (Exod. 30:17–21).

Likewise, entry into the presence of God required mediation. Even as Moses mediated the Sinai covenant between Yahweh and Israel, so the Hebrew priesthood served as mediators for the people of God in tabernacle worship (Lev. 5:6, 10, 13; etc.). The strict form and order of tabernacle worship finds its parallel in the careful stipulations of the Sinai covenant code. This Law of God tested the sincerity of Israelite loyalty to Yahweh, instructed them in divine holiness and the fear of the Lord, and guarded them from sin (Exod. 20:20).

Worship and covenant relationship in the Old Testament were similar in that both were conducted strictly on God's terms. Here Stephen Westerholm reminds us that although the central theme of the tabernacle narrative remains God's desire to live and commune with his people, this divine presence in no way suggested "that human beings . . . have gained the means of manipulating God and guaranteeing His favor for their own endeavors."[24]

Last, the tabernacle introduced the use of sign and symbol for inspiring worship and conveying theological education to God's people. The awesome majesty, glory, holiness, and power of God displayed at the quaking mountain in the Sinai wilderness was recreated by the artistry and craftsmanship employed in the design and construction of the tabernacle and its furnishings. The inscription on the golden plate of the high priest's turban summarizes the motivation behind and the intent of all the artistic expression associated with the Mosaic tabernacle—"HOLY TO THE LORD" (Exod. 39:30).

Old Testament Temple Period

The erection of Solomon's temple in Jerusalem as the permanent dwelling place of God's divine presence with his people injected new emphases into Israelite theology and worship. Primary among these was the idea of the royal priesthood emerging from the Davidic kingship covenant pronounced by the prophet Nathan (2 Sam. 7:1–17). Of course, this notion of a king-priest later became important to the Old Testament and later Jewish messianic expectation (Ps. 110; see Chapter 8).

God's sanctuary as the place of prayer, instruction in covenant obedience, and divine revelation are also prominent theological developments associated with Solomon's temple. Perhaps most important however was the shift from portable tent-shrine to permanent temple, which proved a mixed blessing for Israel. The unpredictable and mysterious nature of Yahweh represented in the Mosaic tabernacle now gave way to an accessible and familiar God. In a sense God had been "tamed." Sadly, the ideal of Yahweh's holiness and sovereignty portrayed in the desert-tent was gradually replaced by the twisted reality of an accommodating and handicapped God confined within the walls of a sophisticated and urbane edifice and served by a smug constituency who had religion all figured out (Jer. 7).[25]

New Testament Temple Period

The New Testament renews this theme of God's presence among humankind with the announcement found in John's gospel that "the word became flesh and lived [or tabernacled] among us" (John

1:14; cf., Isa. 7:14). The return of the divine presence in the New Testament shifts the focus from the building, the temple, to the person, Jesus Christ (Matt. 12:6; John 2:19). After Pentecost and the beginning of the church, God dwells with his people in the new covenant by means of his indwelling Holy Spirit. The apostle Paul can then write that the believer in Christ is now the temple of God (1 Cor. 3:16–17; 6:19–20).[26]

This means the church of Jesus Christ forms his spiritual temple and constitutes the dwelling place of God's Holy Spirit (Eph. 2:21). The church of Christ is now that "spiritual house of God" which bears witness to the presence of God in a dark world (1 Pet. 2:5). But eventually, God's divine presence will pervade the restored creation, with his very throne found among humanity (Rev. 21:1–4). According the John's vision, there is no longer any need for a temple structure as the Godhead is the temple (Rev. 21:22).[27]

Implications for Christian Worship

What does our study of the portable tent-shrine and the temple sanctuary, central to the Hebrew worship of Yahweh, mean for us, for Christian worship? How do these ancient Israelite religious institutions impact the Christian church? I have concluded this chapter by outlining several ways corporate worship in the Christian church might be enhanced given the foregoing overview of Old Testament teaching on the Israelite tabernacle and temples. Interestingly, these suggestions coincide with certain of Robert E. Webber's "nine proposals" for worship renewal.[28] These parallels have been used as referents for the sake of clarity in the organization of the Old Testament materials.

The basic purpose of the tent-shrine and the later temple of Jerusalem was to enable God to live among his people. The focus was primarily on God's meeting with his people and participating in their daily lives. The physical structure was merely a vehicle to facilitate and appropriately order this encounter between the divine and the human. It is important for us to remember that redeemed people comprise the church of Jesus Christ, the holy temple of the Lord (Eph. 2:21). It is equally important to remember in this age of multimillion-dollar church-building programs that people—not steel, concrete, and glass structures—worship God.

Both tabernacle and temple worship emphasized the importance of preparation on the part of the worshiper or congregation before meeting with a holy God (Exod. 19:9–15; Ps. 15). This preparation for worship included ritual washing symbolizing the internal and spiritual washing of penitence, confession, and purification on the part of the worshiper (Ps. 24:3–6). Implicit in this preparation for meeting with God in worship is education. This mirrors Webber's first proposal, which calls for evangelicals to "study the biblical, historical, and theological sources of Christian worship."[29]

The highly detailed and precise biblical prescriptions for construction of and worship in the Old Testament sanctuaries dedicated to Yahweh indicates that the Hebrews worshiped God on his terms, not theirs. This principle reinforces Webber's fourth proposal for worship renewal: "Orient worship toward God rather than human beings . . . for this reason more care should be given to the planning of the service so that a vertical focus be regained."[30]

The design and construction of the Old Testament sanctuaries, the dress and service of the priesthood, and the worship liturgy all served to highlight the person and character of God—particularly his sovereignty, majesty, glory, and holiness. The Old Testament worshiper was overpowered with a sense of awe, reverence, mystery, and divine transcendence in his or her meeting with God. This truth constitutes the essence of Webber's worship proposal five: "Create a sense of the holy."[31]

The floor plan, arrangement of the furnishings, and the order of worship in the Old Testament sanctuaries were all intended to lead the worshiper through a sequence of experiences that culminated in a close encounter with the holy God. Step by step the Old Testament worshiper was taken from the ordinary and mundane world of daily living into the realm of the holy, and then the most holy—the very presence of God. This movement from the so-called secular or ordinary to the holy and even the most holy in the worship of the God who created all things, redeemed Israel from Egypt, and established covenant with them at Sinai echoes Webber's sixth proposal, which calls for recovering a Christ-centered focus in worship through the reenactment of the Christ event.[32]

If nothing else, our study of Old Testament tabernacle and temple has revealed the participatory nature of the Hebrew worship experience. The liturgy of the sanctuaries dedicated to Yahweh engaged the worshiper's whole person, mind, emotions, and body. Again, Webber's proposal seven represents the logical outcome of this Old Testament teaching—the restoration of congregation involvement in the church's worship service. He observes, "If worship is an action done by the entire congregation and is offered to God as a communal act, then more attention must be given to the involvement of the entire congregation in worship."[33]

The premium on beauty and craftsmanship in the design and construction of the Old Testament sanctuaries suggests artistic expression and an aesthetically pleasing environment inspire worship and complement the liturgy. Important too is the use of sign and symbol in artistic expression to convey theological truths. These principles derived from the expression of the arts in Old Testament worship roughly correspond to Webber's eighth proposal—the need to balance form and freedom in liturgy in order to attain spontaneity in worship.[34] (See also Chapters 4 and 11.)

Finally, the Old Testament sanctuaries dedicated to the worship of Yahweh occupied center stage in the life of the ancient Hebrews, spatially, artistically, religiously, and socially. The reality of God living with his people in Old Testament times necessitated a covenant code that stressed spiritual and moral purity and holiness in all aspects of daily living, even down to the food one ate and the mildew in the corner of one's house (Exod. 19—24; Lev. 11; 14). This brings us to Webber's ninth and last proposal for worship renewal: "Restore the relationship of worship to all of life. . . . worship is not an isolated aspect of the Christian life, but the center from which all life is understood and experienced."[35] Worship is life and life is worship in the Old Testament; the same is no less true today for the New Testament church.

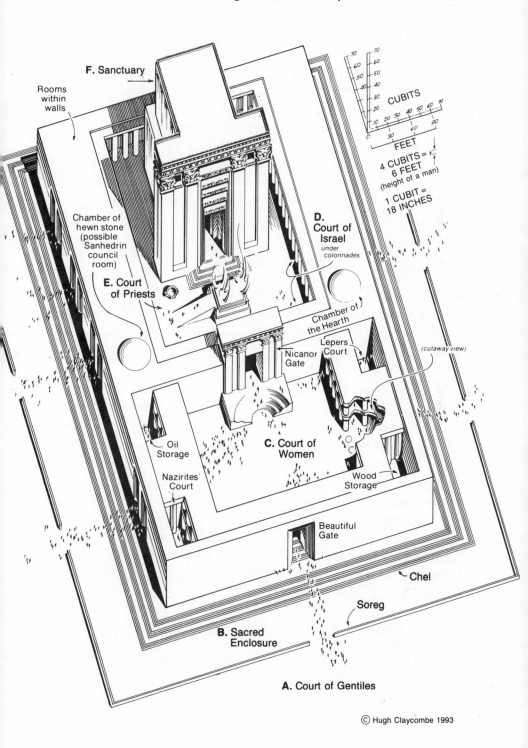

Fig. 9.7 Herod's Temple and Outer Courts

F. Sanctuary

Rooms within walls

Chamber of hewn stone (possible Sanhedrin council room)

E. Court of Priests

D. Court of Israel
under colonnades

CUBITS

FEET

4 CUBITS = 6 FEET
(height of a man)

1 CUBIT = 18 INCHES

Chamber of the Hearth

Lepers Court

Nicanor Gate

(cutaway view)

Oil Storage

C. Court of Women

Wood Storage

Nazirites Court

Beautiful Gate

Chel

Soreg

B. Sacred Enclosure

A. Court of Gentiles

© Hugh Claycombe 1993

The Jerusalem temple was the focal point of Judaism during the NT era. Expansion of the temple complex by King Herod reinforced architecturally certain theological emphases: separation from the Gentiles, the transcendence of God, and Jewish exclusiveness. These developing perspectives in NT Judaism are outlined in the descriptions of the Outer and and Inner temple courts below.

A. Court of the Gentiles
This rectangular expanse outside the boundary wall or soreg limited the approach of non-Jews to the temple complex.

B. Sacred Enclosure
Restricted to Jewish men and women, and containing sets of steps to the Inner Courts.

C. Court of Women
This raised terrace was the first of the Inner Courts and Jewish women were restricted to this precinct. The Levitical choirs and instrumentalists performed on the fifteen semi-circular steps leading to the Court of Israel.

D. Court of Israel
This narrow and roofed court was reserved exclusively for Jewish males.

E. Court of Priests
This open court rose above the Court of Israel and was restricted to the ministering priests and levites.

F. Sanctuary
Another set of steps led to the entrance of the temple proper, containing the Holy Place and the Most Holy Place.

The series of elevated courts and the further increase in the temple's height all spoke to the notion of God's transcendence. Further, the elevated courts underscored the ethnic and gender distinctions important

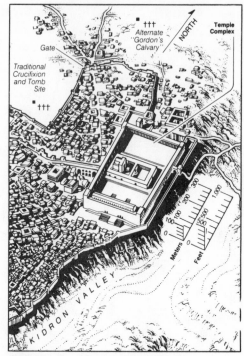

Fig. 9.8 Overview of the Temple Complex During New Testament Era

to Jewish religion. Finally, the network of courts and gates emphasized the restrictive nature of Hebrew worship.

The New Covenant established by Jesus Christ brought radical changes to biblical worship practices. The entire church constitutes a priesthood unto God (Rev. 1:6), and sacrifices of praise and good deeds have replaced animal sacrifice (Heb. 13:15-16). The Outer Court wall of partition between Jews and Gentiles no longer restricts access to to God (Eph. 2:14). Exclusiveness and separation have given way to universalism and community (Col. 3:11), and the temple of God is now an internal reality (1 Cor. 6:19). Indeed, the old has gone and the new has come! (2 Cor. 5:17)

◆ 10 ◆

Let Me Live That I May Praise You!
The Psalms in Hebrew Worship

LIFE AND DEATH ISSUES literally fill the pages of our newspapers, news magazines, and air time on radio and television newscasts: the right to die with dignity and the right to live the way "I want"; the right to help a cancer patient commit suicide and the right to an active and wholesome life for the handicapped; the right to choose life for ourselves and the right to choose death for others, unborn or otherwise! All this and much, much more currently occupy center stage in the public forum. Of course, this raises the ultimate question for many people today: "What is life, anyway?"

Why do you want to live? Why do I want to live? What motivates people to press on? I am sure there is no single answer to these questions. However, some people have unattained goals, while others desire to drink their fill of life's pleasure and experiences, since they believe that's all there is. Still others live to accumulate or dominate or "-ate" in any of a variety of ways. Some even live to learn, to improve, or to serve others. And no doubt, many people live simply because they fear death.

The Psalms are about life, and the psalmist points us to a more noble reason for being. He exclaims, "Let me live that I may praise you" (Ps. 119:175). I hope this study of the Psalms will redirect our desires to live, so that like the Hebrew poet we delight in praising God seven times a day (Ps. 119:164). Interestingly, as we praise God we fulfill his divine mandate for creation (Isa. 43:7) and enjoy an unsurpassed quality of life (Pss. 63:3–4; 84:4, 10).

The Psalms in the Old Testament

Literary Development

The composition of the Old Testament book of Psalms spans as many as ten centuries. The collection of Hebrew poetry contains the ancient Song of Moses (Ps. 90; middle or late second millennium B.C.) and psalms that clearly originate during the post-exilic period of Israelite history, after 539 B.C. (Ps. 146). The book of Psalms, then, is a collection or anthology of individual poetic compositions written by several different authors. Over the years these poetic compositions were preserved, grouped into smaller collections, and eventually arranged to create the larger literary work we now know as the book of Psalms.

At least seven authors are identified by name in the Psalter. They include Moses, David, Solomon, Heman, Ethan, Asaph, and the sons of Korah. It appears that Asaph, Heman, and Korah represent musical guilds associated with the temple (2 Chron. 25:1–5). These titles may signify the source of a given psalm only, as in the label of the guild producing the psalm, and not necessarily authorship. Almost one-third of the Psalms are anonymous compositions. The breakdown of psalmic authorship may be catalogued as follows:

MOSES—1 (Ps. 90)
DAVID—73 (Pss. 3—9; 11—32; 34—41; 51—63; 65; 68—
    70; 86; 101; 103; 108—110; 122; 124; 131; 133; 138—
    145)
SOLOMON—2 (Pss. 72; 127)
ASAPH—12 (Pss. 50; 73—83)
SONS OF KORAH—11 (Pss. 42; 44—49; 84—85; 87—88)
HEMAN—1 (Ps. 88)
ETHAN—1 (Ps. 89)
UNKNOWN—49 (Pss. 1—2; 10; 33; 43; 66—67; 71; 91—
    100; 102; 104—107; 111—121; 123; 125—126; 128—
    130; 132; 134—137; 146—150)

It is important to distinguish between the individual authors of the Psalms and the editors who compiled and arranged the poetic compositions at a later date. Probably members of the Asaph, Korah, and Heman musical guilds served as both authors and editors of parts of the Psalms (1 Chron. 16:4–7; 25:6–8). Some have suggested the Psalter was edited in its final form by the musicians of the second temple period during Nehemiah's governorship in Jerusalem (Neh. 7:73; 12:44–46). The dedication of the rebuilt walls of Jerusalem may have been the event that prompted the final edition of the Hebrew Psalms (Neh. 12:27–43).

Several smaller psalmic collections have been identified in the larger corpus of the Psalms, including First Davidic Group (3–41), First Korah Group (42–49), Second Davidic Group (51–65), Asaph Group (73–83), Second Korah Group (84–88), First Congregational Praise Group (95–100), Hallelujah Group (111–117), Songs of Ascent to Jerusalem (120–134), Third Davidic Group (138–145), and the Second Congregational Praise Group (146–150).

These smaller collections were eventually spliced into the present five-book structure recognizable in the Psalms. Bernhard Anderson outlines the structure of the Hebrew songbook like this:[1]

BOOK 1: *Psalms 1–41*
    CONCLUDING DOXOLOGY, Ps. *41:13*
BOOK 2: *Psalms 42–72*
    CONCLUDING DOXOLOGY, Ps. *72:18–19*
BOOK 3: *Psalms 73–89*
    CONCLUDING DOXOLOGY, Ps. *89:52*
BOOK 4: *Psalms 90–106*
    CONCLUDING DOXOLOGY, Ps. *106:48*
BOOK 5: *Psalms 107–150*
    CONCLUDING DOXOLOGY FOR ENTIRE PSALTER, Ps. *150*

Literary Structure

Recently, John Walton has offered the most convincing argument for understanding the particular literary arrangement of the poetic collections in the Psalter.[2] He suggests the theological agenda motivating the editor(s) who combined the psalmic collections into a unified literary work was the Davidic covenant, the covenant of kingship in ancient Israel.

By analogy to Old Testament historical literature the "psalms use the arrangement of liturgical composition to reflect on the nature of God and the response of the individual."[3] According to Walton, the product of this arrangement resembles a cantata about the nation of Israel represented by King David.

A Cantata About the Davidic Covenant

| Introduction Psalms 1—2 | | Ps. 1. Ultimate vindication of the righteous Ps. 2. God's choice and defense of Israelite king |

Book	Seam	Theme	Content
Book 1	41	David's conflict with Saul	Many individual laments; most psalms mention enemies
Book 2	72	David's kingship	Key psalms: 45, 48, 51; 54–65 mostly laments and "enemy" psalms
Book 3	89	Eighth-century Assyrian crisis	Asaph and Sons of Korah collections; key psalm: 78
Book 4	106	Introspection about destruction of temple and exile	Praise collection: 95–100; key psalms: 90, 103–105
Book 5	145	Praise/reflection on return from exile and beginning of new era	Halleluyah collection: 111–117; Songs of Ascent: 120–134; Davidic reprise: 138–145; key psalms: 107, 110, 119

| Conclusion 146–150 | Climatic praise to God |

From Andrew Hill & John Walton, *A Survey of the Old Testament*. Grand Rapids, Zondervan, 1991, p. 279. Used by permission.

The twofold theme of the cantata is introduced in Psalms 1 and 2: ultimately God will vindicate the righteous, and he alone will choose and defend the Israelite king. The "seam" psalms connect the five books of the Psalter historically and theologically. The seam psalm of Books 1–2, Psalm 41, shows the transition of kingship from Saul to David, and the seam psalm of Books 2–3, Psalm 72, bridges the monarchies of David and Solomon. "Psalm 89, the seam between Books III–IV, shows a covenant in disarray and a people under siege; and the last seam, Psalm 106, is a litany of the failure of Israel and a plea to regather the people from exile."[4]

This understanding of the Psalms as a liturgical composition for the second temple or post-exilic period also fits the historical and theological milieu of the era. On a national level the psalmic recitation of the Davidic covenant affirmed God's intention to remember his covenant and vindicate Israel by returning to Jerusalem (Zech. 8:3). This gave the fledgling Persian satellite hope that one day Israel would shake off the yoke of foreign oppression and again enjoy freedom and security under a Davidic monarch (Hag. 2:20–23; cf., Ezek. 34:23–24; 37:24–28). Practically speaking, the wisdom theme of the vindication of the righteous finds its fulfillment in the renewed emphasis on the "law of the Lord" in the post-exilic reforms of Ezra and Nehemiah (Neh. 8—10; cf., Ps. 119).

Literary Types

For decades biblical scholars have been attempting to isolate the historical situation giving rise to each psalm.[5] Others have assumed that some kind of liturgical occasion, Israelite or otherwise, lay behind the origin of each psalmic composition.[6] These theories remain highly speculative and largely unsubstantiated by biblical or extra-biblical evidence. It makes more sense to admit that the psalms were inspired by a variety of circumstances, some historical (Ps. 3), some liturgical (Ps. 121), and some simply reflecting personal devotional thoughts prompted by life experiences (Ps. 51).

The identification of literary types or genres in the Psalms has proven more helpful. Although divergent opinion exists as to the exact literary classification of particular psalms, fairly well-defined genre categories have been established.[7] Recognizing the literary type of each psalm is important to appreciating psalmic structure as well as understanding or interpreting psalmic content.[8] I have cataloged the basic psalmic types below, including outlines of distinctive structural features where appropriate[9]:

- Hymn. Exuberant praise of God in general, a song that extols his glory and greatness as it is revealed in nature and history. The hymn is often framed in this three-part outline:
  1. Call to worship, usually introduced with an imperative verb (Ps. 95:1–8);
  2. Main section, containing the motive for praise (95:9–11); and

   3. Recapitulation, renewed summons to praise God, echoing
      the opening of the psalm (95:12).
 • Community lament. National expression of distress and
   mourning at God's apparent abandonment of his people and
   covenant promises. The community lament is sometimes characterized by this four-part outline:
   1. Call to remember God's past faithfulness (Ps. 44:1–3);
   2. Summons to worship (44:4–8);
   3. People's lament proper (44:9–22); and
   4. Plea for deliverance (44:23–26).
 • Individual lament. A personal expression of honest doubt
   about God's goodness and an appeal to God's grace and compassion for intervention in a desperate situation. The community and individual lament may overlap; the individual lament
   is often cast in this distinctive form:
   1. Address to God (Ps. 56:1);
   2. Complaint (56:2, 5–6);
   3. Confession of trust (56:3–4);
   4. Petition (56:7);
   5. Words of assurance (56:8–11);
   6. Vow of praise (56:12–13); and
 • Community song of thanksgiving. The song of thanksgiving
   expands the vow of praise found at the end of many laments.
   The community song of thanksgiving is a corporate praise response to God in gratitude for a specific act of deliverance experienced by the nation (Ps. 124).
 • Individual song of thanksgiving. A personal confession of gratitude and praise for God's providential intervention in a time
   of need, delivering the suppliant from a specific trial, distress,
   or illness. The outline for the community and individual song
   of thanksgiving is similar:
   1. Introduction—including an invocation and expression of
      intent to offer thanks to God (Ps. 116:1–2);
   2. Recitation of worshiper's experience—the suppliant recalls
      past distress and cries for help and divine deliverance
      (116:3–9); and
   3. Conclusion—recapitulation of God's gracious deliverance and
      prayer for future help or a confession of faith (116:10–19).

- Wisdom/Torah. Essentially meditations on the righteous life, instruction in the fear of Lord, and admonitions to good conduct rooted in obedience to the Torah, sometimes contrasting the righteous and the wicked (Pss. 1; 112).
- Songs of trust. Emphasize the nearness of God, his compassion, and saving power; often make reference to formal worship—singing, dancing, offering sacrifice, etc. (Pss. 11; 16).
- Royal. Exaltation of the Israelite king and/or the Davidic covenant of kingship, emphasizing the divine appointment and protection of the Hebrew king (Ps. 2).
- Liturgy. Reflections on aspects of ancient Hebrew worship and ritual, especially formal entrance to the temple and covenant renewal ceremonies (Pss. 15; 24).
- Remembrance or storytelling. Recitation of Yahweh's past redemptive acts on behalf of Israel, presented as a confession of faith (Ps. 106).

Catalog of Psalmic Types

The accompanying table identifying the Psalms according to literary type is based on Berhnard Anderson's classifications (some psalms are a "mixed type," or a hybrid of psalmic genres, and are listed under more than one literary category).

HYMN: 8; 19; 29; 33; 36; 46—48; 66; 76; 84; 87; 89; 93; 95—100; 103—104; 111; 113—114; 117; 122; 145—150

INDIVIDUAL SONG OF THANKSGIVING: 18; 30; 32; 34; 40; 66; 92; 116; 118; 138

COMMUNITY SONG OF THANKSGIVING: 65; 67; 75; 107—108; 124

INDIVIDUAL LAMENT: 3—7; 9—10; 13; 14 (=53); 17; 22; 25—28; 31; 35; 38—43; 51—52; 53 (=14); 54—57; 59; 61; 64; 69—71; 77; 86; 88—89; 102; 108—109; 120; 130; 139—143

COMMUNITY LAMENT: 12; 44; 58; 60; 74; 79—80; 83; 85; 90; 94; 123; 126; 129; 137

SONG OF TRUST: 11; 16; 23; 27; 62—63; 91; 121; 125; 131

WISDOM *(including Torah)*: 1; 19; 36—37; 49; 73; 112;
    119; 127—128; 133
REMEMBRANCE *(storytelling)*: 78; 105—106; 135—136
LITURGY: 15; 24; 50; 68; 81—82; 115; 132; 134
ROYAL: 2; 20—21; 45; 72; 89; 101; 110; 132; 144

Messianic and Imprecatory Psalms

Two additional psalmic types deserve mention: messianic psalms and imprecatory psalms. A messianic psalm is any psalm that anticipates the Messiah or, more normally understood, any psalm that makes predictions or prophetic statements about the Messiah.[10] A Christian reading of the Hebrew Psalms may result in one of two extremes, either regarding all psalms as anticipating Jesus of Nazareth as Messiah or none of the psalms as exclusively predictive of Jesus' life and ministry as Messiah.

I prefer a middle ground, which identifies as messianic those psalms, the New Testament writers apply to the life and ministry of Jesus as the Christ by direct quotation or strong allusion. The precedent for this kind of Christian reading of the Psalms stems from the text in Luke's gospel, where Jesus gave the disciples a Christ-centered understanding of the Law of Moses, the Prophets, and the Psalms (24:44). Those psalms having direct connections to the life and ministry of Jesus of Nazareth as Messiah according to the New Testament writers include Psalms 2; 8; 16; 19; 22—24; 28; 31; 40; 47; 62; 69; 72; 89; 91; 96; 98; 103; 107; 109—111; and 118.

The so-called imprecatory psalms are more difficult to analyze. So much so, C. S. Lewis labeled these psalms "terrible" and "contemptible."[11] He viewed the writers of imprecatory psalms as reactionaries who were "profoundly wrong."[12] Perhaps we can forgive Lewis for his erroneous understanding of the nature and purpose of the imprecatory psalms, given his theological naiveté.[13] However, the ethical and interpretive problems associated with these "cursing psalms" remains.

By definition, imprecatory psalms are those psalms containing passages that seek the hurt of someone else by invoking curses or revengeful punishments against them as enemies. Examples include Psalms 5; 12; 35; 55; 58—59; 69—70; 83; 109; 137; and 139—140.

Any formulation of a biblical apologetic for the cursing of one's enemies in imprecatory psalms must include the following data:

* The Psalter reflects the reality of life, all of life, including godless enemies.
* All imprecatory psalms are prayers rooted in the plea for vindication of the righteous in the face of continuing (and even triumphant) wickedness.
* The righteous cry of the oppressed for justice is expected in any age of history.
* By means of imprecation the righteous acknowledge that they hate what God hates—sin and the sinner (Ps. 5:5; Prov. 8:13).
* True imprecation recognizing vengeance belongs to God alone (Pss. 5:6; 7:4).
* Imprecation implies an obedient faith toward God and an unretaliatory spirit toward others.
* The goal or purpose of imprecation is the vindication of God's name and character (Pss. 9:19; 83:16–17).
* Imprecation understands the theological principle of retribution, that is, God judges sin in this life and the next (Pss. 109:13; 137:9). The imprecatory psalm simply asks God to be consistent with his own character as a holy, righteous, and just God.[14]

The Psalms in Israel's Worship

The Psalms represent, in part, the creative literary energies of the ancient Hebrews. The word *psalm* derives from the Greek *psalmos* which means "psalm, hymn of praise." The use of the term *psalm* in the English versions translates two Hebrew words, *mizmôr* (melody, psalm) and *maskîl* (contemplative poem, cultic song). The musical nature of the Hebrew psalms is confirmed by other words describing the compositions, especially derivatives from the roots *zāmar* (sing, praise, play an instrument) and *shîr* (sing). In addition, these psalms are poetic pieces characterized by a particular type of rhythmic feature called parallelism. As in the case with psalmic genres, knowledge of Hebrew parallelism in poetry is important to the understanding of the Psalms.[15]

Interpretive approaches to the Psalms have primarily focused on the life setting of the poetic compositions, with attention given to the literary character and type of the individual psalms. Heavy emphasis has been placed on the function of the Psalms in the formal religious life of the ancient Hebrews. While these approaches offer some benefit to the study of the Psalms, they remain hypothetical constructs and are usually applied indiscriminately across the entire psalmic collection.[16]

The approach to the function of the Psalter in Hebrew worship in this study is essentially one of biblical theology, letting the text of the Old Testament speak for itself. Where appropriate I have adapted the sociological approach of Erhard Gerstenberger, who recognized the importance of the family unit in ancient Hebrew worship.[17]

Daily Life

The composing and reciting of poetry was a common response to life experiences in the ancient world. The Hebrew culture was no exception. This poetry both reflected and addressed the array of emotions associated with the events and situations of daily living. Poetic compositions were no doubt perpetuated by oral tradition in families, clans, and tribes, and by the bards of that day. Some of this poetry was eventually set to writing, primarily for the purpose of preservation. Of course, these written collections of poetic works later served liturgical purposes as well, like our book of Psalms. Four specific uses of psalmic poetry in daily life during Old Testament times are explored here: spontaneous worship, private devotion, life-event responses, and entertainment.

Peter Craigie marks the beginning of psalmody in Israel with the exodus from Egypt.[18] The exodus event, that great act of divine redemption in the Old Testament, prompted both the song of Moses (Exod. 15:1–19) and the song of Miriam (Exod. 15:21–21) as worship responses to Yahweh. Acts of divine deliverance and providential care were often celebrated and commemorated with spontaneous worship responses of psalm (or song) and singing. Examples here include the song of thanksgiving raised up in gratitude for the divine provision of water at Be'er (Num. 21:16–17), the song of Moses as covenant affirmation at Mt. Nebo (Deut. 31:19, 21; 31:30—32:47), the prophetess Deborah's victory song praising God for rescue from the Canaanites (Judg. 5:1–31), and even the spontaneous "night songs" of the righteous exalting God as Creator (Job 35:10). In fact, the psalmist encourages this kind of spontaneous worship song because it is always fitting to praise God (Pss. 98:4; 147:1).

Many of the psalms were originally private prayers and devotional responses to God; only later did they become public songs of worship. These personal prayers, songs, hymns, and laments included cries for deliverance from enemies (Ps. 57), confession of faith (Ps. 56), confession of sin (Ps. 51), affirmation of true worship (Ps. 50), songs of thanksgiving for providential help (Ps. 40), and heartfelt praise and adoration of God (Ps. 33). Examples of personal devotional response to God is found outside the Psalter as well. Especially well-known are Hannah's song of thanksgiving over the birth of Samuel (1 Sam. 2:1–10) and David's deathbed poetic oracle (2 Sam. 23:1–7). This tradition of raising song to God in private devotion for his grace and goodness continues in the New Testament with Mary's song of praise, the Magnificat (Luke 1:46–55) and Zechariah's hymn, the Benedictus (Luke 1:67–79).

There are a few Old Testament texts that indicate the ancient Hebrews enjoyed musical poetry of some sort sheerly for pleasure. As early as the time of Moses, Israel employed ballad singers who preserved historical moments in music (Num. 21:27). The Hebrew kings gathered choirs of male and female singers for entertainment in the royal court (Eccles. 2:8). Elsewhere, the prophet Amos condemned minstrels specializing in Davidic-like improvisations because the idle songs contributed to Israelite debauchery and revelry (Amos 6:5–7), and Ezekiel's prophetic message received the same hearing as the love songs of contemporary singers (Ezek. 33:32).

Liturgical Life

The precedent for singing psalms and hymns as part of formal Hebrew worship in Old Testament times can also be traced to the exodus. The divine deliverance from slavery in Egypt was the redemptive event that prompted worship in song throughout all Israelite history. The song of Moses and the song of Miriam are the precursors of later praise hymns and songs of thanksgiving celebrating Yahweh's activity in history (Exod. 15:1–21). In addition, another song of Moses was sung as an oath of witness or testimony to covenant renewal with God (Deut. 31:19; 31:30—32:47). Thus, singing was connected with Hebrew liturgy from its inception.

David's role as the organizer of the musical guilds responsible for the music of the temple liturgy comes as no surprise (1 Chron. 6:31–32; 25:1–31). He accounted for nearly half of the songs in the Psalter and was remembered as the "sweet psalmist" of Israel (2 Sam. 23:1 RSV). David even commissioned the writing of psalms for special events, such as the return of the ark of God to Jerusalem (1 Chron. 16:7; cf., 13:8). The singing of psalms was also a part of the temple dedication (Ps. 30), the Sabbath (Ps. 92), temple worship (2 Chron. 29:28, 30; Ps. 100:2; Amos 8:3), and other special festivals (Isa. 30:29). The technical notes preserved in the Psalter regarding musical scores and instrumentation further demonstrate the Psalms as "the hymnbook of the temple."[19]

It is assumed the use of the Psalms in the liturgy of the second temple largely mirrored that of the earlier era. The books of Ezra and Nehemiah do indicate singing was an important feature of the worship of God in the post-exilic period. Ezra records that two hundred male and female temple singers were among the returning Hebrew exiles from Babylon (Ezra 2:65, 70). Elsewhere, the Israelites celebrated the laying of the second temple foundation with the responsive singing of psalms (Ezra 3:11); Nehemiah reports that the dedication of the rebuilt walls of Jerusalem included songs of thanksgiving (Neh. 12:8, 27, 46). A study of the Apocrypha reveals a similar pattern of usage of the Psalms during the intertestamental period of Jewish history (Jth. 15:13; 16:1, 2, 13; Ecclus. 39:15; 1 Macc. 4:54; 13:51; 3 Macc. 7:16).

The later rabbinic traditions of Judaism indicate the Psalms were used in the daily temple service at the time of the morning and evening sacrifices (Exod. 29:38–46; Num. 28:1–8). The Levites were instructed to sing psalms appropriate to the occasion after the offering, such as:

Day One—Psalm 24 (Creation)
Day Two—Psalm 48 (Song of Mount Zion)
Day Three—Psalm 82 (Song of Deliverance)
Day Four—Psalm 94 (Song of Divine Vengeance)

Day Five—Psalm 81 (Song of God's Goodness to Wayward Israel)
Day Six—Psalm 93 (Completion of Creation)
Day Seven—Psalm 92 (Sabbath Song)

Additionally, select psalms were incorporated into the festival liturgies. For example, the Hallelujah psalms (113—118) were used in conjunction with the New Moon, Passover, Pentecost, Tabernacles, and Dedication feasts. The Feast of Purim included Psalm 7, the New Year's celebration Psalm 47. Select penitential psalms for the Day of Atonement and the Songs of Ascents were associated with the three great pilgrimage festivals (Pss. 120—134; cf., Exod. 23:14-17).[20]

Although outside the scope of this study, it is worth noting that psalmody in Israel also developed within the prophetic tradition. Especially prominent are hymns and hymn fragments and laments (Isa. 5:1-7; Lam. 1—5, Jon. 2:2-9). Some of this prophetic literature may have been borrowed from the temple liturgies; other materials were no doubt generated by individual creativity and prophetic inspiration. In either case these prophetic psalms were used to rebuke, warn, instruct, and call Israel to repentance (Isa. 42:10-20; Amos 5:1-2).

The Psalms in New Testament Times

The Synagogue
The Jewish synagogue is a place for teaching the Torah of Moses and transmitting the customs and traditions of Judaism. The origins of the institution are obscure. It is likely the synagogue evolved from some kind of informal gathering or association of Hebrews during the Babylonian exile. Development continued and perhaps was even spurred by the reforms of Ezra and Nehemiah rooted in the Torah during the mid-fifth century B.C. The oldest testimony of a Diaspora synagogue is an inscription dated to the reign of Ptolemy III Euergetes (247—221 B.C.), found at Schedia in Egypt.

During New Testament times the synagogue stood alongside the temple as an equal religious institution. After the destruction of the second temple by the Romans in A.D. 70, the synagogue was considered a full substitute for the temple. The synagogue was a lay institution; officiating priests were not mandatory. (See Chapter 12.)

It has been assumed that synagogue worship largely reflected the temple liturgy.[21] This means the Psalms would have been incorporated into the daily and festival synagogue liturgies.[22] John Lamb has identified six specific ways the Psalter was used in the synagogue service:

1. The reading and singing of complete psalms (using the Psalter as a hymnbook).
2. The use of proper psalms—all or parts of select psalms ascribed to specific holy days and occasions.
3. The recitation of versicles—select psalms or psalmic portions recited as a response to the Torah and Prophetic readings.
4. Brief psalmic responses to prayers and readings.
5. Extensive appeal to the Psalms for the phraseology of the liturgical prayers.[23]

The psalms continue to form an important part of the worship service in the modern synagogue, especially in the prayers, congregational responses, and festal singing.

The Early Church (First to Third Centuries)

Most biblical scholars acknowledge some continuity in psalmody between the Jewish synagogue and the Christian church.[24] Massey Shepherd actually documents the similarities and differences in the liturgical use of the Psalms in synagogue and church.[25] He concludes that both synagogue and church had cantors sing the psalms (not choirs), both used the psalms as congregational responses, and both sang or chanted the psalms without musical accompaniment, employing a similar monotone cadence in the recitations and chanting. By contrast, the church used the Psalms as responses between the Old and New Testament lessons, whereas this practice is not attested in the synagogue until the eighth century A.D. The daily office of morning and evening prayers in the church included the recitation of the entire Psalter in cycle; Jewish worship appealed to the Psalter on a selective basis only.

The importance of the Psalms for the New Testament church is evidenced by the extensive appeal to the Psalter by the New Testament writers. The New Testament contains more than four hundred quotations and allusions to the Psalms, second only to the book of Isaiah.[26] Only three New Testament texts actually make reference to the singing of psalms in public worship: 1 Corinthians 14:26; Ephesians 5:18–19; and Colossians 3:16. In each case the joyous singing of psalms is connected with the edification of the church body. There are two instances where the singing of a psalm or hymn occurs in the context of private worship: in Matthew 26:30 and Mark 14:26 and in James 5:13.

The tradition of singing the Psalms as part of worship in the early church is confirmed by the writings of the ante-Nicene church fathers (before the Council of Nicea, A.D. 325). For example, Clement of Alexandria, Origin, and Tertullian all spoke of the singing of psalms and hymns as an integral part of the early Christian liturgy.[27]

Especially important to the liturgy of the early Christian church was the development of new psalmody. According to Ralph Martin, "the Christian church was born in song."[28] This was not unexpected, given the spiritual vitality released by the Holy Spirit at Pentecost. Many fragments of these early Christian psalms and hymns celebrating the gospel of Jesus Christ are scattered throughout the New Testament (Phil. 2:6–11; Col. 1:15–20; 1 Tim. 4:16). Among the more well-known New Testament songs are Mary's Magnificat (Luke 1:46–55), Zechariah's Benedictus (Luke 1:68–79), the Gloria in Excelsis (Luke 2:14), and Simeon's Nunc Dimittis (Luke 2:29–32).[29]

Later Church History

I have attempted to highlight the salient points on the use of the Psalms under two major headings: (1) the forms of psalmic use in Christian worship, and (2) the methods of psalmic use in Christian worship.[30]

Forms of psalmic use. Over the centuries complex worship forms incorporating the Psalms into Christian liturgy developed. These forms varied from church to church, region to region, and era to era. However, certain standardized liturgical uses of the Psalms did

emerge in church history. The more prominent forms are outlined
here:

- Proper psalms—psalms selected for special occasions because
  the psalmic content was appropriate to the event or festival;
  examples include the use of Psalm 63 as the morning prayer
  psalm and Psalm 141 as the evening prayer psalm, Psalm 34
  as preparation for the Lord's Table, Psalm 22 for Good Friday,
  and Psalm 118 for Easter Sunday.[31]
- The gradual—a fixed responsorial psalm read, chanted, or sung
  by the congregation after the Old Testament lesson in the liturgy of the Western church.[32]
- The introit, offertory, and communion—antiphonal use of
  fixed psalms—halves of the congregation, or two choirs, or a
  choir and the congregation alternately reciting psalmic
  verses—was used in conjunction with the introit (the priestly
  processional from the vestry to the altar). The offertory included the consecration of the elements of the Eucharist with
  select psalms, and the Eucharist (communion or the Lord's Table) was celebrated with the singing of select psalms.[33]
- Daily office of prayer—a six- or sevenfold daily prayer rhythm
  adapted from Judaism and established in the early church; this
  was reduced to two offices, morning and evening, as part of the
  Counter-Reformation. The daily office includes fixed cycles of
  morning and evening psalms and dialogic versicles with responses—short segments of psalms employed as invocations,
  biddings, or petitions by the worship leader with brief psalmic
  responses by the suppliant.[34]
- Church year—many church lectionaries and prayer books as-
  sign select psalms to the principal festival cycles, seasons, and
  holy days of the Christian liturgical calendar. In addition,
  there is a fixed schedule for reading the psalms during the
  church year.[35]
- Special occasions—sometimes called the Occasional Offices,
  special services for baptism, confirmation, marriage, ordination, burial, etc.—that may incorporate versicles or select
  psalms into the liturgy.[36]

The writings of Augustine show that the Psalms were sung at any time during the worship service, apart from those times when other aspects of worship were in process (*Epistle 55* the, xviii). Eventually the use of the Psalms in the Sunday liturgy was limited primarily to the entrance processional, the call to worship, Scripture lesson responses, and the celebration of the Lord's Table or Eucharist.

The Reformation witnessed the revision of the daily office of prayer in the Roman Catholic Church and the Anglican Church. Protestant traditions repudiated the offertory, and in some cases the introit and gradual. For the most part the Reformers abandon the church year, so the use of fixed psalms for special days and seasons was discarded. Yet the Psalms were an important part of the Protestant worship tradition as attested by the publication of the Geneva Psalter (1562) and its inclusion in part in the Scottish *Book of Common Order* (1564).[37]

Methods of psalmic use. The history of Christian liturgy shows that the psalms were read, recited, chanted, and sung as part of the church's worship response to God from the beginning. Also, it should be remembered that since the psalms are basically prayers, the praying of the Psalms has always been a part of Jewish and Christian private devotion and public worship.[38]

An array of participants may be responsible for using the Psalter in formal Christian worship, including an individual reader or soloist (cantor or singer), a choir or choirs, and segments or all of the congregation. Gender issues may surface here in some church circles. Regarding the singing of psalms in worship, I concur with John Chrysostom, who wrote that women and men, young and old, could be united in Spirit like the melody in the psalms.[39]

Finally, John Lamb has identified five specific methods for rendering the Psalms in Christian worship.[40] These five are reading, reciting, chanting, or singing the Psalms

- in unison—by the congregation as a whole.
- in solo—by one individual with all others listening.
- alternately (by verse or half-verse)—antiphonally with two choirs or halves of the congregation.

- alternately (by verse or half-verse)—responsorially with the congregation responding to the reader or soloist.
- alternately—with the congregation responding to the individual reader or singer with a fixed liturgical response like "Amen!" "Alleluia!" or "His mercy endures forever!" (a variation of the responsorial).

Other combinations are possible, and were no doubt used by the church, given the importance of the Psalms in Christian liturgy.

• 11 •

Play Skillfully
on the Strings!
The Arts and Hebrew Worship

THERE IS A CHRISTIAN HYMN that begins "Let the the whole creation cry . . ." and ends with the line "In this worship bear their parts. . . ."[1] One of the stanzas of this praise hymn based on Psalm 148 contains the phrase "those to whom the arts belong." This chapter introduces the role of artistic expression in Old Testament worship and encourages the appropriation of the arts for contemporary Christian worship.

We have already learned that the Psalter was poetry set to music and functioned as the hymnbook of ancient Israel (see Chapter 10). Here the psalmist elicits new psalmody from the righteous for the worship of God and specifically commands skillful artistry on the musical instruments used in temple worship (Ps. 33:2–3). In commenting on this text Derek Kidner notes "the call in that verse [Ps. 33:3] is for freshness and skill as well as fervor; three qualifications rarely found together in religious music."[2]

I trust this brief study of the place of the arts in worship will help each one of us renew our freshness and fervor for artistic expression in our private and corporate worship, and help us reclaim our Christian heritage among "those to whom the arts belong."

The Arts in Old Testament Worship

Art Among the Ancients

For the ancients artistic skills were practiced in professional guilds, and artists were essentially craftsmen and artisans. Art was daily life for the ancients, whether temples or tombs, palace murals or painted pottery, inscribed monumental stelae or engraved cylinder seals. Art was functional in that it related directly to the experience of daily existence and expressed a worldview that was basically religious. Artistic expression in the ancient world tended toward the symbolic—physical images portray corresponding spiritual reality, but representational art—art that imitates life—and abstract art—art that represents nothing beyond itself—were not unknown. The arts for the ancients, including the Hebrews, may be organized under the broad headings of visual art, music, literature, and architecture.[3]

Although, the Old Testament has no specific word for "art" or "aesthetics," there are more than a dozen terms in the Hebrew vocabulary of the Old Testament used to describe various types of artistic expression. Prominent among these are the Hebrew terms for discernment or insight (*bînâ*, 1 Chron. 25:7), technical skill or aptitude (*ḥokmâ*, 1 Chron. 28:21), craftsman (*ḥārāsh*, Gen. 4:22), invent or design (*ḥāshab*, Exod. 35:35), knowledge (*da'at*, 1 Sam. 16:16), intelligence or cleverness (*śekel*, 2 Chron. 30:22), beauty or beautiful (*yāpeh*, Jer. 10:14), and artistic skill or aptitude (*tĕbûnâ*, 1 Kings 7:14).

Thus, the ancient Hebrew culture had a developed approach to the arts in the sense of expressing the beautiful, arranging space and color, engaging in skilled workmanship, honing technical crafts and polished performances, and implementing imaginative design. Archaeology attests flourishing artistic traditions across the ancient Near East. Unfortunately, little remains of the material evidence for these flourishing arts in ancient Hebrew culture.[4]

Aesthetics in the Old Testament

The word *aesthetic* means "having a sense or appreciation of the beautiful" or "characterized by a love of beauty." In Old Testament teaching all sense of beauty is rooted in the personal character of God.[5] Indeed, one of God's perfections is beauty (Pss. 27:4; 96:6), and thus God is the source of all beauty. This divine beauty and perfection is reflected in God's works of creation (Gen. 1:4, 10, 12, 18, 21, etc.) and his sovereign rule of history (Ps. 78:72). In fact, the Hebrew poets acknowledged that God has made everything beautiful in its own time (Eccles. 3:11), and that the beauty of God's creation shouts his glory and beauty to all the world (Ps. 19:1–4).[6]

Aesthetic appreciation was part of the endowment given to humanity created in the image of God for the purpose of artistic expression, along with a creative spirit or imagination (Gen. 1:26). Logically then, implicit in the divine mandate for humankind to subdue the earth is the cultivation of this inherent sense of beauty (Gen. 1:28–30). The practical outworking of this mandate is seen in the command to build an aesthetically pleasing worship center for Yahweh (Exod. 25:8–9) and in the precepts of the sage for enjoying all aspects of life as God's gift (Eccles. 2:24–26; 5:18–20). Ultimately, the cultivation of this divinely bestowed sense of beauty serves to beautify or glorify God as Creator and Redeemer and foreshadows the beauty of his righteous King (Isa. 33:17; 43:7).

The Old Testament attributes artistic expression to two distinct sources: innate talent or ability resident within the individual (Exod. 35:25–26; 1 Chron. 28:21; 2 Chron. 30:22), and a special endowment of God's Spirit for specific purposes and tasks (Exod. 31:2–11; 30:30–35). Yet this artistic ability could also be taught (Exod. 35:34). After the time of Kings David and Solomon artistic expression associated with Hebrew temple worship took on characteristics of fine art as professional guilds were established and tutoring occurred in the given art required (1 Chron. 25).[7]

Sadly, humanity's sense of beauty was perverted in the Fall.[8] Interestingly, even that first temptation played upon humankind's sense of beauty, since the fruit was "pleasing to the eye" (Gen. 3:6). Hence, artistic expression in the Old Testament was employed both for noble purposes like the worship of God (1 Chron. 16) and aesthetic pleasure (1 Sam. 16:16, 18) and base purposes like idleness and debauchery (Amos 6:4–7) or even false worship and idolatry (Isa. 44:9–20).[9]

Artistic expression is frequently cited in connection with tabernacle and later temple architecture and worship in the Old

Testament. Here is a list of arts, skills, and crafts employed in the service of worship by the ancient Hebrews:

1. Visual art
    engraving (Exod. 28:9, 11; 39:6, 14, etc.)
    metalworking (Exod. 31:1–11; 35:30–35; 1 Kings 8:14; 2 Chron. 2:7)
    woodworking (Exod. 31:1–11; 35:30–35)
    stonecutting (1 Kings 5:18; 6:7)
    textiles, including weaving and embroidery (Exod. 26:1; 28:6, 8, 27–28; 36:8, 35)
    artisans (1 Chron. 22:15)
    perfumers' art (Exod. 30:25, 35; 37:29; 2 Chron. 16:14)
    painting (not mentioned in the Old Testament but certainly a part of artistic expression in Hebrew life) (4 Macc. 17:7)
2. Music
    singing (1 Chron. 25:7)
    making and playing musical instruments (1 Chron. 16:7; 23:5; 2 Chron. 34:12; Ps. 33:3)
    new psalmody (Pss. 33:3; 96:1; 98:1; 144:9; 149:1; Isa. 42:10)
    dance (Pss. 149:3; 150:4)
    lamentation (Jer. 9:17; Amos 5:16)
3. Others
    architecture and design (Exod. 31:4; 35:35; 38:23; 1 Chron. 28:21)
    service in worship (2 Chron. 30:22)
    wisdom and knowledge (Prov. 1:2–7; Dan. 1:17; cf., the role of the sage in Jer. 18:18)
    God's law, including oration and interpretation (Ezra 7:6)
    literature and storytelling, including imagery and various poetic and literary devices and features (Pss. 23; 114)
    drama and symbolic action (Exod. 12—14)
    imagination and creativity (cf., the beginnings of civilization in Genesis 4:20–22 and the references for architecture and design in 1. Visual Art, above).

Toward an Old Testament Theology of Art and Worship

Why is artistic expression linked to Hebrew worship in the Old Testament? How do the arts contribute to biblical worship? Listed below are several key principles for developing a biblical understanding of the place of the arts in Old Testament worship:

- As Creator and Redeemer, God both deserves and demands our whole-person worship response, including artistic expression (Ps. 150).
- The arts both mirror and convey God's personality and attributes as Creator and Redeemer—his power, wisdom, glory, majesty, honor, holiness, creativity. Thus artistic expression not only affirms the image of God in human beings as his creatures but also serves as a mandate for imitating God in creating (Gen. 1:26–31; Ps. 8:5–9).
- Any sense of beauty manifest in humanity originates in the beauty of God's person and character (Pss. 27:4; 96:6; James 1:17–18; cf., Wisd. of Sol. 13:3, 5).
- The arts directly celebrate God and creation. The diversity of artistic expression reflects the manifold variety of God's created order and of his creatures made in his image, whether they acknowledge it or not. The arts may be employed to celebrate God and divine redemption in a worship context (Pss. 19:1–4; 89:5–12; 104).
- Artistic expression and the arts bridge the natural and spiritual world. The arts permit creatures to explore and express the mystery of divine transcendence and immanence (Pss. 96:11–12; 97:5–6; 148; Isa. 55:12; the discussions in Job 34; 36; 38; and 39).
- The arts belong to God, since it is God who both made human beings and endowed them with capacities for artistic expression (Wisd. of Sol. 7:16).
- Intrinsic to the arts is the potential to inspire and enhance the worship of God (Exod. 26:1; 28:2, 39).

The Arts and Contemporary Christian Worship

What Is Art, Anyway?

Just what constitutes *art*? How is *art* defined? What do we mean by the phrase "the arts"? A survey of art history, at least in the West, reveals two theories on the definition of art. The first essentially identifies art as the imitation of reality, whereas the second explains art as the artifact itself—an alternative reality created by the artist.[10]

Today the dominant aesthetic theory is that of explaining art by the artifact—art for its own sake or as an end in itself. For our purposes an adaptation of Gene Veith's broad understanding of art is sufficient. He identifies "art" as "all aesthetic forms," or paraphrased, "all manner of human expression resulting in beauty."[11]

For Leland Ryken the definition of art as only the imitation of reality or life, even the imitation of divine truth and beauty from Christian perspectives, is inadequate. He suggests that a truly Christian definition of art includes both the imitation of life and the artifact itself, but it must extend beyond that to underscore the idea of human creativity and imagination as affirmed in the doctrine of creation and the image of God in humanity.[12] From a Christian perspective then, art is human creativity applied to the expression of the idea of beauty.

Our definition of art must be carried a step further. According to H. R. Rookmaaker, "art became fine art" during the Age of Reason or the Enlightenment of the eighteenth century.[13] This movement away from the crafts of artistic guilds began in parts of Europe during the Renaissance (fourteenth to sixteenth centuries). Rookmaaker contended that this development of "high art" in contrast to "low" or commercial art brought about a curse upon the arts that still plagues modern society—art became "a kind of irreligious religion."[14]

This distinction between "popular art" and "fine art" remains embedded in contemporary culture, especially among those who consider themselves fine artists. Yet Gene Veith reminds us that art is within the will of God, artistic ability is a gift of God, art is a vocation for God, and the whole creation is called to praise God.[15] Thus, he, and others such as Rookmaaker and Francis Schaeffer, agree that artistic expression in the church should not be limited to fine art.[16] Rather, the arts in the broadest sense should be employed by the Christian church for worship, instruction, and evangelism. In fact, Schaeffer argues poignantly that the entire Christian life should be our greatest work of art, expressing truth and beauty to the glory of God in a lost and dark world.[17]

What Is the Value or Purpose of Art?

Our technological culture craves the practical and the functional. Today we ask, "How is this relevant for me?" This question, with the emphasis on *relevant* and *me*, forms the basis for much of the life response in contemporary society. While it is true the arts are utilitarian to some degree, they are much more. The following distillation of the value or purpose of the arts is derived from many sources; several are cited for those interested in pursuing the topic in detail. Frank E. Gaebelein has noted "that art inescapably affects us."[18] Here is an outline of the key features of that inescapable impact the arts have on humanity:

- The arts are intrinsically valuable simply because they can be enjoyed on their own merits of beauty and pleasure—a sense of sheer aesthetics. In turn, this sense of beauty has value because beauty is a quality of the Godhead, and the beauty inherent to art permits and encourages leisure and recreation among humanity.[19]
- The arts are valuable for the truth they convey—truth about human values and truth about the realities of life.[20]
- The arts have great merit as a statement of our "creatureliness"—men and women created in God's image—since "the desire and ability to make things" is a primary characteristic shared by God and humanity.[21]
- The arts also have utilitarian value in that they may be didactic, expressing truth in general terms and ultimate terms framed in a worldview.[22]
- The arts possess great value because they remind us that the claims of truth extend to the realms of creativity and imagination, heightening the perception of reality.[23]
- The arts hold value for humanity because they remind us of our common heritage as part of humanity—our "corporate identity." They also remind us of God's "common grace," endowing all people with gifts, abilities, good qualities, and natural blessings; ultimately, this reminds us that all truth belongs to God, and we can appropriate it regardless of the source.[24]
- The arts are purposeful because they help us perceive and appreciate the "aesthetics of the infinite" in nature and human history. Of course, this has profound theological implications, certain of which are developed in the following section.[25]

Categories of Artistic Expression for Worship

Robert E. Webber cogently summarizes the controversy in Protestantism over the place of the arts in Christian worship by appealing to the teachings of the two great reformers John Calvin and Martin Luther.[26] According to Calvin, only what is explicitly taught in the New Testament was permissible in worship; whereas Luther believed that whatever was not explicitly rejected by Scripture was permissible for worship. Here I humbly echo Webber's call for the Protestant church to take another look at how the arts may be utilized to inspire and enhance Christian worship.[27]

Robert Webber suggests several categories from which the church might draw to increase artistic expression in Christian worship. These include

- music—including new psalmody and hymnody for inspiring worship and reinforcing theological instruction;
- art—including painting and drawing, sculpture, textiles and ceramics, video-film, photography, engraving, and calligraphy;
- drama—including oratory and pantomime in addition to stage theatrics as a part of reenactment in worship;
- dance—as a part of whole person worship and celebration in worship;
- space—especially design fostering congregational participation in worship; and
- color—used both to create moods for worship and mnemonically to teach theological truth.[28]

To these categories I would add

- literature—including renewed awareness of story, poem, vision, and letter as the primary genres for conveying biblical truth and an emphasis on original prose and poetry written for liturgical purposes;
- leisure and recreation—essential for developing biblical attitudes toward enjoyment and worship;
- imagination/creativity—the imagination has a unique way of expressing truth and reality—a reality which transcends the

physical world, thus preventing art from being reduced to "realism" only; and

• numerology—perhaps a subset of color, since both the Old and New Testaments use numbers symbolically in artistic design and mnemonically to teach biblical truths.

The Bibliography offers the reader an entry into the theory, history, and practice of artistic expression in Christian worship.

The Arts and Christian Worship: Theological Implications

Our study of artistic expression in the Old Testament has demonstrated close connections between the arts and the worship of God. In fact, Leland Ryken has noted, "The arts permeate all of life, and they are meant to be a central ingredient in the worship of God."[29] What then are the theological implications of the arts for Christian worship? These summary observations and related principles are offered as a first step toward integrating the arts and Christian worship:

• The arts celebrate truth and beauty. The Bible teaches that God is the source of truth and beauty; hence, the arts play a significant role in worship.
• The arts celebrate the gifts of God's "common grace" to all humanity. How much more might the arts be employed in the celebration of God's provision of "special grace" through the divine person and redemptive work of Jesus Christ (Isa. 6:1–3; Rev. 4:1–11)?
• The arts celebrate the "creatureliness" of humanity created in God's image. We have already learned that a key ingredient for biblical worship is a recognition of our place as creatures before the Almighty Creator (see Chapter 4).
• The arts express and speak to us as whole persons. "The arts can mediate the message of Christ and minister to . . . the depth of [our] being."[30] I concur with Robert E. Webber, who forecasts that the arts hold great promise for the continuing development of participatory worship in the Christian church.
• Even as the arts permeate all of life, so they offer inspiration and instruction for biblical worship that engulfs the entire Christian experience.

- The varieties of artistic expression mirror the diversity of God's creation. Two important principles emerge from this truth: first, God may be appropriately worshiped in a variety of ways; and second, we should embrace this vast diversity since God shows no partiality (James 2:1–7).
- Artistic expression combines creativity, imagination, and the interpretation of the human experience. True biblical worship is practiced in spirit and truth (John 4:24); the arts may offer a paradigm for worship responses that are spiritual—imagined and conceived in submission to Christ—and truthful—interpreting life's experiences from God's perspective and responding to God accordingly.
- The arts function as a catalyst for the mind, and ultimately for worship, because artistic expression is rooted in a worldview that affords the Christian the opportunity to apply his or her mind to the practice of biblical principles in daily life.
- Artistic expression has not escaped the effects of the Fall. The arts may be perverted and corrupted and used toward base and evil purposes. Even as the Christian is exhorted to test the spirits to see whether they are of Christ (1 John 4:1–6), so too the Christian and the Christian church must continually consider and critically evaluate the role of the arts and artistic expression in worship, measuring them against the supreme standard of truth and beauty, Jesus Christ.

◆ 12 ◆

A Shadow of the Good Things to Come

Toward Worship in the New Testament

EVEN A CURSORY READING of the New Testament reveals early Christianity was essentially Jewish. Jesus Christ was a Jew from Nazareth in Galilee (Matt. 1:1). The twelve apostles were all Jewish (Mark 3:13–19). The gift of the Holy Spirit at Pentecost was largely a Jewish event (Acts 1:15; 2:1–5), and the initial missionary outreach of the church focused on the Jew first (Acts 6:7; 13:5; etc.). In sum, the early church was comprised of Christian Jews. All this prompts Roger Beckwith to observe that Christianity owed its existence to Judaism and that "from the outset, the originality of Christianity is seen in its worship, but so is the traditional, Jewish character of Christianity."[1]

This continuity between early Christianity and Judaism in the first century A.D. is directly linked to the Holy Scriptures of Judaism—the Old Testament. As noted in the Introduction, the Old Testament was the Bible for the early church. Jesus Christ, by word and deed, demonstrated himself as the fulfillment of the old covenant promises made to God's people Israel (Acts 2:14–36; 9:22). The Jewish-Christian authors of the New Testament understood the church of Jesus Christ would be the new Israel (Rom. 4:16–24; 9:11–27; Gal. 3:19–29). Thus, although the Holy Bible contains two covenants, the old and the new, it is one continuous record of divine redemption in human history.[2]

It is only natural then that we seek the origins of early Christian worship in Jewish temple and synagogue worship. My purpose in this concluding chapter is twofold: first, to introduce the primary sources spawning early Christian worship, and second, to instruct in the Jewish heritage of Christianity in order to develop an appreciation for its Jewish roots and to enrich the Christian worship experience by a conscious reclamation of traditions and principles of the Judeo-Christian heritage pertinent to contemporary Christian faith.[3]

Three specific Jewish sources of early Christian worship are examined here: the Jewish religious literature of the intertestament period—the Old Testament Apocrypha, ancient synagogue worship, and the methodology of first-century Jewish biblical interpretation—typology.[4]

What Is the Apocrypha?

The word *apocrypha* means "hidden." As applied to the collection of intertestamental Jewish religious literature, the word has two connotations: writings that are "hidden away" because of their mysterious and esoteric nature, or writings that are "hidden away" because they were spurious and never recognized as canonical by the Hebrews.

The Old Testament Apocrypha is an anthology of fourteen (or fifteen, depending on numeration) books composed by pious Jewish writers between 200 B.C. and A.D. 100. These books were originally composed in the Hebrew, Greek, and Aramaic languages, and they have been preserved in the Greek, Latin, Ethiopic, Coptic, Arabic, Syriac, and Armenian languages. The Apocrypha contains six different types of literature, including legendary, prophetic (both epistolary and apocalyptic), historical, didactic, romantic, and religious literature.

The contents of the Old Testament Apocrypha may be outlined as shown in the chart on the opposite page.

As the books of the Apocrypha were written they were added one by one to later editions of the Septuagint, a Greek translation of the Hebrew Old Testament. This translation, necessitated by the impact of Hellenism on Judaism, was completed about 250 B.C. Initially, these additional books were separated from the Hebrew Scriptures and were not considered a part of the Old Testament canon.

Unfortunately, most Jewish scribes made no notations to this fact, which led to confusion among the Greek-speaking Christians who had adopted the Septuagint as their Bible. The problem became acute after A.D. 100, since subsequent copies of the Septuagint were transmitted by Christian scribes.

During the early centuries of church history there were conflicting opinions on the value and canonicity of the apocryphal books. Some church fathers, such as Eusebius and Athanasius, made clear distinctions between Apocrypha and the Old Testament canon. Yet, others, such as Irenaeus and Tertullian, quoted the Apocrypha as "Scripture" in their writings, and the Synod of Hippo (A.D. 393) authorized the use of the Apocrypha as canon. The debate over the canonicity of the books of the Apocrypha was heightened with the publication of Jerome's Latin Vulgate (A.D. 405). Despite his attempts to carefully distinguish Apocrypha and Old Testament in the

Type of Book	Revised Standard Version	Catholic Versions
Didactic	1. The Wisdom of Solomon (c. 30 B.C.)	Book of Wisdom
	2. Ecclesiasticus (Sirach) (132 B.C.)	Ecclesiasticus
Religious	3. Tobit (c. 200 B.C.)	Tobias
Romance	4. Judith (c. 150 B.C.)	Judith
Historic	5. 1 Esdras (c. 150–100 B.C.)	3 Esdras* or 1 Esdras‡
	6. 1 Macabees (c. 110 B.C.)	1 Machabees
	7. 2 Maccabees (c. 110–70 B.C.)	2 Machabees
Prophetic	8. Baruch (c. 150–50 B.C.)	Baruch chaps. 1–5
	9. The Letter of Jeremiah (c. 300–100 B.C.)	Baruch chap. 6
	10. 2 Esdras (c. A.D. 100)	4 Esdras* or 2 Esdras‡
Legendary	11. Additions to Esther (140–130 B.C.)	Esther 10:4–16:24†
	12. The Prayer of Azariah (second or first century B.C.) (Song of Three Young Men)	Daniel 3:24–90†
	13. Susanna (second or first century B.C.)	Daniel 13†
	14. Bel and the Dragon (C. 100 B.C.)	Daniel 14†
	15. The Prayer of Manasseh (second or first century B.C.)	Prayer of Manasseh*

* Books not accepted as canonical at the Council of Trent, A.D. 1546.
† Books not listed in Douay table of contents because they are appended to other books.
‡ Numbering depends on whether Ezra and Nehemiah are titled 1 and 2 Esdras or Ezra and Nehemiah.

From David Ewert, *A General Introduction to the Bible.* Grand Rapids: Zondervan, 1990, p. 75. Used by permission.

"popular edition" Latin Bible, later recensions of Jerome's Vulgate failed to retain these clear distinctions. Soon most Latin readers understood no difference between the Old Testament and the Apocrypha.

The Protestant Reformation again brought the issue of the Old Testament Apocrypha to the forefront of church debate. As the Reformers translated the Old Testament into the languages of their constituencies, they discovered that the Hebrew Bible omitted the books of the Apocrypha. Following the example of the ancient Hebrews, they either excluded from the Old Testament canon or appended as a separate and inferior collection in the Protestant Bibles these "lesser books".

The Roman church responded to the Reformers at the Council of Trent (1545–1564). There the church fathers reaffirmed the Vulgate as the Bible of the true church and pronounced the Apocrypha equivalent to canonical books. Today this collection of apocryphal books is usually called the Deutero-Canon, and it was confirmed as such by the Vatican Council of 1870. The Roman Catholic Church does make some appeal to the Deutero-Canon for doctrine, including the concepts of Purgatory, merit for good works, and the practice of prayers for the dead (Tob. 12:9; 2 Macc. 12:43–45; 2 Esd. 8:33; 13:46; Ecclus. 3:30).

The Westminster Confession of 1647 rejected the inspiration and authority of the apocryphal books and refused to grant the collection canonical status. Thus, the Protestant churches have generally adopted this position of regarding the Apocrypha as uncanonical literature. Although not widely appreciated or observed today, Martin Luther's assessment of the Apocrypha remains valid. He held that the books of the Apocrypha are not equal to Scripture but are profitable to read and valuable for personal edification.[5]

Worship in the Old Testament Apocrypha

The scattered references to temple worship and personal devotion in the Apocrypha demonstrate considerable continuity with the worship patterns of the Old Testament. On several occasions the Apocrypha records fairly detailed descriptions of entire religious ceremonies and worship rituals, for example, Josiah's Passover in 1 Esdras 1; Nehemiah's sacrifice of dedication in 2 Maccabees 1; the temple dedication of Ezra in 1 Esdras 5—7; and the Maccabean re-dedication of the temple in 1 Maccabees 4. These accounts highlight the role of the priesthood in leading the Hebrew community in worship, the importance of animal sacrifice and the temple liturgy, and the significant role of congregational participation in worship.[6]

More specifically, the Apocrypha mentions an array of worship responses, including

- raising the hands and prostration in worship (1 Esd. 9:47; Ecclus. 50:17; 1 Macc. 4:55; Jth. 6:18; 13:17);
- pilgrimages to Jerusalem and festival worship (Tob. 1:6; 5:13);
- prayer, including certain postures and places (Tob. 12:8; 13:1; Jth. 13:10; Sir. 7:14; 28:2; 2 Macc. 10:27; 2 Esd. 9:25; 1 Macc. 11:17);
- repentance and confession, including fasting and the donning of sackcloth and ashes (1 Esd. 8:91; 2 Esd. 16:2; Jth. 4:10–14; Tob. 12:8; Bar. 1:5; 4:20);
- music and singing, including praise hymns and new psalmody (1 Macc. 4:24, 54; 2 Macc. 1:30; Ecclus. 39:14, 35; 50:18–21; Jth. 16:1–17; Rest of Esther 13:17; Song of Three Children 1:29–68); and
- temple worship, including daily sacrifice and festival worship (Jth. 4:14; 16:16–18; 1 Esd. 5:50–53; 2 Macc. 1:8; 3:33; Ecclus. 7:29–31; 35:1–13; Bar. 1:10).

Equally important in the literature of the Apocrypha is emphasis upon personal piety as the foundation for worship and upon works of righteousness as the by-product of worship. This personal devotion is rooted in obedience to the Law of Moses and is essential for proper worship (4 Macc. 5:24). In addition, the fear of the Lord (Jth. 16:15; Ecclus. 1:11–20; 7:29–31) and a right heart are accorded prominence in the worship of God (2 Macc. 1:3–4; 15:27; Sir. 1:12; 21:6; 38:10; Sus. 1:35).[7]

Likewise, worship as service to others in a life-style of good deeds is regarded as a natural complement to the worship of God (3 Macc. 3:4). For the intertestamental Jew charity and almsgiving to the poor and the socially disadvantaged are understood to atone for sin and deliver from death (Ecclus. 3:30; Tob. 4:11; 12:9; cf., Ecclus. 17:22; 29:12; 40:17, 24).

The Book of Tobit and New Testament Worship

The apocryphal book of Tobit is an anonymous literary work of the intertestamental period of Jewish history, probably written between 200 and 170 B.C. The book is usually classified as moralizing short story. The introduction to Tobit in *The Oxford Annotated Apocrypha* describes the books as "a fascinating amalgam of *Arabian Nights* romance, kindly Jewish piety, and sound moral teaching."[8]

The book of Tobit was written for Jews of the Dispersion, exhorting them to practice a righteous life-style based on obedience to the Law of Moses as they lived among the Gentiles outside Palestine. Obvious historical errors in Tobit show that the book is a work of fiction, but its popularity is attested by the wide reading it still receives in Jewish (and some Christian) circles.

The story of Tobit purports to take place during the Assyrian exile of the Israelites of the Northern Kingdom (eighth century B.C.). The plot centers on the fortunes of two Jewish families, that of Tobit (with wife Anna and son Tobias) and his cousin Raguel (with wife Edna and daughter Sarah). Despite Tobit's zealous piety and generous charity, he becomes poor and blind, and Raguel's daughter Sarah is tormented by demons. God uses Tobias, Tobit's son, to answer the prayers of both Tobit and Sarah. Through a series of unusual circumstances and angelic help, Tobit's eyesight and fortune are restored, and Sarah is freed from the demons that haunted her, thus she is able to find love and happiness in her marriage to Tobias.[9]

The book of Tobit is important for biblical study because of its portrayal of Jewish daily life and religion just prior to the New Testament era. The more negative side of this picture of intertestamental Jewish life includes the excessive emphasis on angels and demons, folklore, and magic (3:16–17; 5:21; 6:15–17). On the plus side, the book does stress participation in corporate worship and tithing (1:6–8), prayer (3:1–6), a righteous life-style (2:3–10), and charity or social concern (4:7–11).

The book of Tobit has been called the Jewish counterpart to John Bunyan's *Pilgrim's Progress*.[10] Tobit recognizes the spiritual warfare bound up in life's pilgrimage and the importance of personal piety in steering a prudent course through the stormy seas of human existence. Significant for our study is the nexus in Tobit between corporate worship (1:6–9), private devotion fostering a life filled with praise to God (13:3–4, 6), and the worship response of a life-style of service in charity and good deeds to others (12:6–10).

The key ingredient for inspiring this participation in corporate worship and a life-style of praise to God and service to others is personal piety and private devotion to God. Here the book of Tobit is consistent with what we have learned elsewhere in the Old Testament about the role of personal piety in worship (see Chapter 2). Personal piety in Tobit is rooted in the fear of the Lord (4:21; 14:2, 6) and is demonstrated by three distinct religious practices: prayer, sometimes combined with fasting, and almsgiving (4:5–11; 12:8–15). In fact, these three acts of piety became known as the "three pillars of Judaism" in later Jewish religious practice.[11]

All this brings us to the New Testament and the Sermon on the Mount (Matt. 5:1—7:29). A portion of this discourse by Jesus to his disciples is really a theological commentary on the three pillars of Judaism—almsgiving, prayer, and fasting (6:1–18).[12] Here Jesus called attention to the abuse of these contemporary Jewish practices of religious piety. His teaching on personal piety served as a bridge between the Mosaic faith of the Old Testament and current religious practices in Judaism as taught by the rabbis. Jesus' teaching also lays the groundwork for what will become New Testament worship in the Christian church. A synopsis of this teaching is outlined below.

- Jesus affirms the importance of personal piety as a catalyst for a worship life-style. (Note that he does not condemn prayer, fasting, and almsgiving but seeks to correct abuses associated with the practices.)
- Jesus affirms the complementary relationship between worship and service to others.
- Jesus instructs his followers on true piety versus hypocrisy, since in each case he contrasts religious hypocrites with the truly pious (public hypocrisy versus individual and private piety). The word *hypocrite* here (Matt. 6:1–18) means one who pretends or "playacts."

• Jesus instructs his followers to practice a piety characterized by an attitude of humility toward God and others and a total lack of pretense, even secrecy, in the outward demonstration of religious acts of piety.

Notice how the teaching of Jesus on personal piety brings us full circle to the essence of personal religion in the Old Testament:

"He has showed you, O man, what is good.
And what does the LORD require of you?
To act justly and to love mercy and to walk humbly with your God."
(Mic. 6:8)

The Jewish Synagogue

The origins of the Jewish institution known as the synagogue are obscure. The synagogue probably evolved from some kind of informal gathering or association of Hebrews during the Babylonian exile. Development continued and perhaps was even spurred by the Torah-based reforms of Ezra and Nehemiah during the mid-fifth century B.C.

Wherever Jews settled in the Diaspora (the voluntary and/or involuntary scattering of Jews from Palestine across the Gentile world) a synagogue was established. In fact, according to the Jewish historian Josephus, it was difficult to find a place without a synagogue (*Antiquities* 14.115). More than one hundred fifty known ruins of ancient synagogues dot the Mediterranean world from Galilee and Syria to Asia Minor and Greece, Italy, Gaul, Spain, North Africa, and Egypt.[13]

The New Testament cites the synagogue as a place of prayer, reading and teaching and preaching the Old Testament Scriptures, almsgiving, exhortation, and fellowship (Acts 4:21; 13:15; etc.). These New Testament-era synagogues were local Jewish congregations scattered throughout Palestine and beyond and were apparently under the jurisdiction of Jerusalem as the religious power center (Acts 9:1-2). The synagogue was also the site for judgment and punishment in matters of Jewish law (Mark 13:9; Acts 22:19). Jesus taught, healed, and preached in the synagogues, often attacking the abuses associated with the institution and not the institution itself (Mark 1:21; 3:1; Luke 4:16–24). The book of Acts indicates the synagogue was the primary focus of early Christian missionary outreach (Acts 9:20; 13:5, 14–15; 14:1; etc.). Jewish Christians apparently stayed within the synagogue congregation for the first several decades of church history, until the Jew–Gentile issue split the two groups (Acts 15:1–35; 18:26; 19:8; 22:19). During New Testament times the synagogue stood alongside the temple as an equal religious institution in Judaism. After the destruction of the second temple by the Romans in A.D. 70, the synagogue was considered its full regime.[14]

Architecture

Three types of ancient synagogue architecture have been identified: the Galilean or basilical (oriented toward the short wall), the broadhouse (oriented toward the long wall), and the apsidal (with the apse pointing in the direction of Jerusalem).[15] According to Jewish tradition, the synagogue was to be built on the highest point of the city (obviously not always possible), have windows, and face Jerusalem—the direction of prayer (Talmud Berakot 4.8bc; 31a; cf., Dan. 6:10–11; 2 Chron. 6:34, 38).

Naturally, synagogue architecture and decoration evolved over the centuries from the simple to the more complex and ornate. However, specific features of synagogue design and furnishing were standardized. Among these were the Torah shrine or ark of the Torah, in which the sacred scrolls of Old Testament Scripture were kept (originally portable, but later the shrine was fixed permanently at the end of the structure facing Jerusalem), the bema or platform (a raised stage or platform for the ark of the Torah), the bema furniture (including a reading table for the Old Testament scrolls, a lectern or podium for the readings and sermon, a chair or throne for the head of the synagogue [the Moses seat], and chief seats for those participating in the service), seats for the congregation (benches along the walls or pews arranged across the building and facing the bema), the shofar (trumpet), and lampstands, including a candelabra or menorah.

The influence of synagogue architecture and furnishings on the early Christian church may be seen in the use of the bema or raised platform, including an altar (replacing the ark of the Torah) and a pulpit or podium. In addition, seating the worship participants on the platform and arranging the congregation in rows facing the platform are Christian adaptations of synagogue design. During the Byzantine period of church history the orientation of church architecture to the east, or Jerusalem, was common, since the light of the gospel came from the east.[16]

Officers

Several different officers were either appointed or elected to positions of leadership in the ancient synagogue. Premier among them was the head of the synagogue (Matt. 5:22). This officer presided over the synagogue worship and was responsible for handling the Scripture scrolls. Other duties included maintaining order during the synagogue services, supervising building maintenance, and inviting guests speakers to address the congregation. Inscriptional evidence indicates both men and women were synagogue leaders in the Diaspora.[17]

The minister, or *hazzan*, was a paid officer of the synagogue who served as overseer of the building and its contents. The minister announced the Sabbath and sacred festivals with the blowing of the ram's horn (*shofar*). The minister was also responsible for distributing and replacing the scrolls in the ark of the Torah for the Scripture readings and lessons. At times the minister of the synagogue read the Scripture lessons and occasionally led the congregation in the prayers. Finally, the *hazzan* assigned roles for the worship participants, signaled the proper time for the recitation of the benedictions during the service, and frequently functioned as the synagogue tutor and interpreter.

Other prominent offices in the synagogue included the elders—the spiritual patriarchs of the congregation from whom the leader of the synagogue was chosen, the interpreter—who not only translated but also explained the Scripture lessons and sermon, the messenger of the benediction or delegate—who led in the prayers for congregational participation, heralds of the *Shema*—members of the congregation selected to recite the *Shema* with the congregation before the recitation of the cycle of prayers, and the almoners—members of the congregation selected to gather (usually two almoners) and distribute (usually three almoners) alms or charitable gifts.[18]

Again, similarities may be identified in the functions of the ancient synagogue officers and the officers of the early Christian church. For example, the Christian office of bishop or overseer combines some of the duties of the head of the synagogue, the minister, and even the interpreter (1 Tim. 3:1–13; 5:17—6:2; Titus 2:5-9). The concept of spiritual patriarchs or ruling elders in the synagogue congregation carries over into the early church as well (Acts 11:30; 15:4, 6, 23; 16:4; 20:17; etc.). Lastly, the first deacons of the Christian church functioned much like the almoners of the ancient Jewish synagogue (Acts 6:1-7).

Liturgy

The purpose of the synagogue was to teach the Torah of Moses through reading, instruction, and exposition. In addition, the synagogue became a primary institution for transmitting the culture and traditions of Judaism. During New Testament times prior to A.D. 70, the synagogue stood alongside the temple as an equal religious institution. After the destruction of the second temple by the Romans in A.D. 70, the synagogue was considered a full substitute for temple worship. Later, the synagogue developed into the Jewish community center, serving as a school, town hall for community meetings and legal proceedings (including the redemption of slaves), and even a hospice for Jewish travelers.[19]

The Jewish synagogue service was patterned in part after the daily and Sabbath temple liturgy. An outline of a typical synagogue liturgy (both ancient and modern) follows:

> Call to Worship. The ruler of the synagogue invites a member of the congregation to commence the service with a psalmic blessing.
>
> Cycle of Prayers. The cycle of prayers included the Yotzer, prayers emphasizing the theme of God as Creator, and the 'Ahabah, prayers emphasizing God's covenant love for Israel.
>
> Recitation of the Shema. This congregational recitation is both a confession of faith and a benediction and includes Deuteronomy 6:4-9, emphasizing God's oneness, Deuteronomy 11:13-21, emphasizing obedience to God's law, and Numbers 15:37-41, emphasizing tassels on garments.

Second Cycle of Prayers. The minister summons someone from the congregation to lead in the recitation of the Eighteen Benedictions, prayers ranging over a variety of themes and including praise and petition.

Scripture Lessons. The Scripture lessons included reading, translation if necessary, and exposition of a passage from the Torah, one from the Prophets, and perhaps a selection from the Psalms.

Benediction. Often a psalmic selection.

Sermon. Based on the Scripture readings of the day.

Congregational Blessing and Amen. Often a psalmic selection.[20]

Influence on Early Christian Liturgy

By way of general principle the influence of the Jewish synagogue on the worship of the early church may be seen in the church's commitment to prayer and instruction in the Scriptures by means of reading and exposition (Acts 2:42). This development was only natural, given the fact the early church was essentially Jewish (Acts 15:1–35).[21] In addition, we have already learned that the reading, chanting, and singing of the Psalms held a prominent place in early Christian liturgy (see Chapter 10). Thus, much like the Jewish synagogue, the worship of the early Christian church was founded on praise, prayer, and biblical exposition.[22]

More specifically, W. O. E. Oesterley has identified particular parallels between the Jewish synagogue and early Christian liturgies.[23] His catalog of influences includes

- the call to worship—often a psalmic blessing inviting the worshiper to consider and respond to God's glory, majesty, steadfast love, marvelous works.[24]
- affirmation of faith—through creedal recitation that paralleled the recitation of the Shema in Jewish liturgy.
- reading and exposition of Scripture—this hallmark of Jewish worship was accorded equal prominence in Christian worship.
- prayer—including praise, thanksgiving, intercession, and petition. Here Oesterley cites many direct parallels in thought and language between the Jewish prayers of the Yotzer, 'Ahaba, and Eighteen Benedictions.[25]
- confession—including liturgical confession of sin in prayer and congregational confession as part of the worship liturgy.[26]

- the liturgical use of "Amen" (1 Cor. 14:16; 2 Cor. 1:20).[27]
- the parallels between the Passover Feast and the Eucharist.[28]
- the parallels between the Jewish *Chaburah*, the weekly Jewish social meal, and the Eucharist and Agape Feast of the early church.[29]

To this list I would add the notion of covenant community gathering for worship, baptism, the concept of corporate personality in the relationship between the one and the many in the congregation (1 Cor. 5:1–8), alms collection and monetary offerings, liturgical benedictions, and the idea of lay leadership and congregational participation.[30]

Of course, Christian worship continued to develop in distinct worshiping communities through the centuries of church history. Naturally the form and practice of Christian liturgy changed over time. Christian worship gradually drifted away from its close ties to Jewish worship, especially as the church became an increasingly Gentile enterprise. The official schism between the two groups, Judaism and Christianity, occurred in the second century A.D.[31] The point here is simply to recognize the importance of synagogue worship for the early church and appreciate the Jewish roots of our Christian heritage.[32]

Typology in the Book of Hebrews

This final installment in the analysis of Old Testament worship examines the understanding of Israelite religious practice, including the priesthood, the sanctuary, and sacrificial worship, recorded in the New Testament book of Hebrews. In fact, the focus of our attention is "the law [especially Old Testament ceremonial law regarding the worship of God] [that] has but a shadow of the good things to come" (Heb. 10:1 RSV). This study points us toward New Testament worship, the continual sacrifice of praise and doing good (Heb. 13:15–16).

Jewish Allegory and Christian Typology

Typology is one of several hermeneutical or interpretive approaches to the Old Testament employed by Christian interpreters through the centuries of church history.[33] John Goldingay defines typology as "the way in which the redemptive events and other realities of Old Testament times may implicitly foreshadow the Christ event" (2 Cor. 1:20).[34]

More specifically, formal typology is a method of biblical exegesis seeking to establish historical correspondence between Old Testament events, person, objects, or ideas and similar New Testament events, persons, objects, and ideas by way of analogy or prototype. Usually the Old Testament correspondent is identified as the "type," while the New Testament corresponded expressing the Old Testament truth is regarded as the "anti-type" (e.g., Rom. 5:14, where Paul identifies Adam as the type and Christ as the anti-type).[35]

The book of Hebrews uses the typological method of interpreting the Old Testament to unveil the reality behind the Old Testament symbols of worship.

The typological understanding of the Old Testament that characterizes the book of Hebrews originated within an exegetical tradition common to both Jews and Christians in the first century A.D.— namely, allegory (Gal. 4:21–31). However, the writer of Hebrews is not developing an allegorical interpretation of the Old Testament similar to that of Philo of Alexandria. Philo, a prominent member of the Jewish-Platonist school of Alexandria, Egypt, during the lifetime of Christ, combined monotheistic Judaism and Greek philosophy (especially Stoicism and Platonism) in his understanding of the Old Testament, yielding an allegorical interpretation of Hebrew history. An allegorical interpretation assumes the text contains a deeper, hidden meaning beyond the intent of the literal wording. Philo's used allegory to demonstrate the viability of Judaism as a world religion to Hellenistic culture.[36]

However, the interpretive approach of Hebrews is a distinctive hybrid of several exegetical methods, better understood as historical typology rooted in the correspondence of the work of Jesus Christ with the Israelite exodus from Egypt and the Passover Feast. F. F. Bruce described this treatment of the Old Testament in Hebrews as "a mashal, a parable or mystery which awaits explanation, and the explanation given in the pages of the epistle takes the form of messianic typology."[37]

Two specific emphases characterize this typological approach:

first, the writer of Hebrews considered the Old Testament incomplete and imperfect (Heb. 8:13; cf., Jer. 31:31–37), and second, the writer understood the Old Testament from a Christocentric perspective—recognizing Jesus Christ as the fulfillment of the redemptive promises in the Old Testament (Heb. 10:11–18). Thus, despite this highly individualized understanding of the Old Testament, the book of Hebrews should be considered just another facet of Christian interpretation well within the accepted exegetical traditions of the early church.[38]

The New Testament book of Hebrews is an anonymous literary epistle (as opposed to the personal epistle) of instruction and exhortation written to Jewish Christians shortly before the fall of Jerusalem and the destruction of the temple by the Romans in A.D. 70. The occasion and destination of the letter remain unknown, although the imminent destruction of Jerusalem may have prompted the writing. The purpose was to demonstrate the superiority of Jesus Christ and his new covenant over Moses and the designed obsolescence of the Mosaic covenant. The writer also affirms Christianity as the consummation of the Mosaic covenant, thereby encouraging his readers to persevere in the present distress and maintain hope for the future (Heb. 10:23, 32–38).

Four specific typological interpretations of Hebrew religious form and practice are pertinent to our study of Old Testament worship:

1. The priesthood of Melchizedek (Aaron and Levi) correspondent to the priesthood of Jesus Christ (Heb. 4—7).
2. The Mosaic covenant of the Old Testament correspondent to the better covenant of Jesus Christ in the New Testament (Heb. 8).
3. The sanctuary of the Mosaic covenant (the tabernacle and later the temple) correspondent to the greater and perfect sanctuary, not made with hands, of the new covenant (Heb. 9:1–23).
4. The sacrificial worship of the Mosaic covenant correspondent to Christ's offering of his body as the single sacrifice for all time initiating the new covenant (Heb. 9:23—10:18).[39]

In each case the writer of Hebrews avows the superiority of Jesus Christ and the new covenant to the religious leaders, forms, and institutions of the Mosaic covenant. Further, the writer emphasizes the gradual and built-in obsolescence of the Mosaic covenant and the finality, perfection, and permanence of the new covenant established by Jesus Christ. Jesus Christ is identified as the anti-type, or reality, to the Old Testament types of priesthood, sanctuary, and sacrificial offering (Heb. 9:11).

Significance of the Old Testament Typology for New Testament Worship

Like any literary methodology, the typological approach to Old Testament interpretation may yield helpful or distorted results, depending on how the methodology is applied to the biblical text. Again, John Goldingay offers helpful suggestions as controls limiting (and legitimizing) the typological approach to Old Testament interpretation. These safeguards to proper biblical interpretation include working from the New Testament anti-type back to the Old Testament type, recognizing the selective nature of typological interpretation, and the need to utilize the typological method only within the historical boundaries of overall Christian revelation.[40] More important to our study are the values of the typological approach for Old Testament interpretation and Christian worship. Here Goldingay cites two significant outcomes of this methodology: the ability of historical typology to illuminate the Christ event, and the intrinsic capacity of the typological method to prompt a more complete understanding of the biblical text.[41]

By way of application to Old Testament worship the typological approach to Old Testament interpretation holds great significance for contemporary Christian worship.

Appreciating and understanding the Old Testament as the promise Jesus Christ fulfilled permits the enrichment of worship by drawing attention to God's sovereignty and grace, his redemptive plan accomplished in the lives of many different Old Testament characters through centuries of history, his revelation of that plan to humanity through Israel, and Jesus Christ as the ultimate or final Word from God (Heb. 1:1–4). So then, even as the Israelites sacrificed the Passover lamb prior to the exodus from Egypt (Exod. 12:21), Christ our Passover lamb has been sacrificed for us (1 Cor. 5:7; cf., John 1:14, 18, 29).

The typological approach to Old Testament interpretation gives us a greater sense of the meaning of Scripture. This is especially true for the Old Testament forms and practices of worship and subsequent prophetic commentary on ancient Hebrew religion. For example, Moses' appeal to Israel to choose life by obeying the commandments of God out of a heart motivated by love for God becomes more intelligible in light of John's exhortation to keep the "old commandment" (Deut. 30:11–20; cf., 1 John 2:7–17). Likewise, the Old Testament prophetic charge to do justice and love mercy instead of offering animal sacrifice takes on new meaning in light of Paul's command to the believer in Christ to be a living sacrifice (Hos. 6:6; Amos 5:21–24; cf., Rom. 12:1–2).

Thus, the typological approach to the Old Testament refined in the book of Hebrews provides a window into the spiritual principles implicit in Old Testament worship.

> But when Christ came as a high priest of the good things to come . . . [and] offered for all time a single sacrifice for sins, he sat down at the right hand of God. For this reason he is the mediator of a new covenant. . . . Therefore, since we are receiving a kingdom that cannot be shaken, let us give thanks, by which we offer to God an acceptable worship with reverence and awe. (Heb. 9:11; 10:12; 9:15; 12:28 NRSV)

Epilogue

I BEGAN THIS STUDY of Old Testament worship and its implications for the Christian church by affirming A. W. Tozer's observation that worship is the "normal employment" of human beings. My premise, adapted from that of John Naisbitt in *Megatrends,* has been education or instruction on the nature and character of Old Testament worship will change our expectations and participation in Christian worship. And I certainly pray that God's Holy Spirit may use this text to accomplish the goal of improving us in our "employment" of worshiping him as Creator and Redeemer.

Yet too often well-intended words of instruction and application get lost in the maze of the writer's verbiage or are drowned out by competing voices forcing readers to "listen too hard." Like the Teacher who summarized the wisdom of Ecclesiastes, we need to hear the conclusion of the whole matter (Eccles. 12:12–14). Perhaps the sum of the whole matter for us is—"just doing it!" That is, consciously act on what St. Augustine described as the God-given instinct and desire inherent within humanity—to praise God the Creator (*Confession* Book 1, Chapter 1, 1–4).

In fact, this was the directive given to John by the angel: "Worship God! Let . . . the righteous still do right, and the holy still be holy" (Rev. 22:9–11). So then, go in peace and just worship God!

Notes

PREFACE

1. Leith Anderson, *Dying for Change* (Minneapolis: Bethany House, 1990), especially pp. 123–138.
2. For a helpful synopsis of academic approaches to the study of religion see Douglas Davies, "The Study of Religion," *Eerdmans' Handbook to the World Religions*. R. P. Beaver, et. al., eds. (Grand Rapids: Eerdmans, 1982), 10–18.

INTRODUCTION

1. John Naisbitt, *Megatrends* (New York: Warner Books, 1982), 95–96.
2. John Naisbitt and Patricia Aburdene, *Re-Inventing the Corporation* (New York: Warner Books, 1985), 79–80.
3. A. W. Tozer, "Worship, The Missing Jewel of the Evangelical Church," *The Best of A. W. Tozer*. W. W. Wiersbe, comp. (Grand Rapids: Baker Books, 1978), 217.
4. Robert N. Schaper, *In His Presence* (Nashville: Thomas Nelson, 1984), 13.
5. Evelyn Underhill, *Worship* (Scranton: Harper & Row, 1936), 3.
6. John Huxtable, *The Bible Says* (Richmond, VA: John Knox Press, 1962), 109.
7. Leslie B. Flynn, *Worship: Together We Celebrate* (Wheaton, IL: Scripture Press, 1983), 21.
8. Robert E. Webber, *Worship Old & New* (Grand Rapids: Zondervan, 1982), 11.
9. Robert G. Rayburn, *O Come, Let Us Worship* (Grand Rapids: Baker Books, 1980), 20–21.
10. Schaper, *In His Presence*, 15–16.
11. Geoffrey Wainwright, "Focus on Worship," *Christianity in Today's World*. R. Keeley, ed. (Grand Rapids: Eerdmans, 1985), 123.
12. Robert E. Webber, *Worship Is a Verb* (Nashville: Star Song, 1992), 7–8.
13. Wainwright, "Focus on Worship," 126.
14. James F. White, *Christian Worship in Transition* (Nashville: Abingdon, 1976), 132–142.
15. Ibid., 7–8.
16. A. S. Herbert, *Worship in Ancient Israel* (Richmond, VA: John Knox, 1959).
17. For discussion of the cosmic nature of the contest between Moses and Pharaoh and the plagues as judgment against the Egyptian pantheon, see John J. Davis, *Moses and the Gods of Egypt* (Grand Rapids: Baker & BMH Books, 1971), 79–152.

18. Herbert, *Worship in Ancient Israel*, 9.

19. Elmer A. Martens, *God's Design: A Focus on Old Testament Theology* (Grand Rapids: Baker, 1981), 65–79.

20. George E. Mendenhall, *The Tenth Generation* (Baltimore: Johns Hopkins, 1973), 200.

21. F. W. Grosheide, "First Corinthians," *New International Commentary on the New Testament* (Grand Rapids: Eerdmans, 1953), 225. See also, Walter C. Kaiser, *The Uses of the Old Testament in the New* (Chicago: Moody, 1985).

22. Webber, *Worship Old & New*, 17.

23. A. R. van de Walle, *From Darkness to the Dawn* (Mystic, CT: Twenty-third Publications, 1985), 152.

24. See the discussion of "Person" in Hans W. Wolff, *Anthropology of the Old Testament*. M. Kohl, trans. (Philadelphia: Fortress Press, 1974), 21–25.

25. On Hebraic vs. Hellenic perspectives of anthropology see Thorleif Boman, *Hebrew Thought Compared with Greek*. J. L. Moreau, trans. (New York: Norton, 1970), 74–89.

26. Gordon Dahl, *Work, Play, and Worship in a Leisure Oriented Society* (Minneapolis: Augsburg Press, 1972).

27. Herbert, *Worship in Ancient Israel*, 47.

28. See Conrad Antonsen, "Jewish Sources of Christian Worship," *Modern Liturgy* 3/4, 1976, 4–6.

CHAPTER 1

1. Peter Funk, "It Pays to Enrich Your Word Power," *Reader's Digest* (Apr 1990): 145–146.

2. See the discussion of the power of the word in the ancient Orient, including the Old Testament Hebrews, in Thorleif Boman, *Hebrew Thought Compared with Greek*. J. L. Moreau, trans. (New York: Norton, 1960), 58–67. For a more technical linguistic analysis of the idea of the word in the ancient Near East and the Old Testament, see J. Bergman, H. Lutzmann, and W. H. Schmidt, "DBR; *dābār*," *Theological Dictionary of the Old Testament*. G. Johannes Botterweck and Helmer Ringgren, eds., J. T. Willis, G. W. Bromiley and D. E. Green, trans., Vol. III (Grand Rapids: Eerdmans, 1978), 84–125. By contrast, note Richard J. Foster's contemporary discussion of the power of silence as a spiritual discipline. According to Foster, learning silence frees one from the need to control other people, since we are accustomed to relying on our words to control others (*The Freedom of Simplicity* [New York: Harper & Row, 1981], 57–58).

3. R. B. Edwards, "Word," *International Standard Bible Encyclopedia: Revised*. G. W. Bromiley, gen. ed., Vol. 4 (Grand Rapids: Eerdmans, 1988), 1102–1103.

4. With one exception *Worship as Nearness to God* this catalog of Old Testament terms represents the Hebrew words translated "worship" in English in *The Eerdmans Analytical Concordance to the Revised Standard Version of the Bible*,

Richard E. Whitaker, comp. (Grand Rapids: Eerdmans, 1988), 1238–1239. For introductory-level theological discussions of these Old Testament worship terms, see Robert B. Girdlestone, *Synonyms of the Old Testament* (Reprint) (Grand Rapids: Eerdmans, 1974), 215–225; and R. Laird Harris, ed., *Theological Wordbook of the Old Testament*, Vol. I (Chicago: Moody, 1980), 198, 267–269, 399–400, and Vol. II, 553–554, 617, 639–641, 914–915, 958.

5. James L. Crenshaw, *Old Testament Wisdom: An Introduction* (Atlanta: John Knox, 1981), 95.

6. See the theological discussion of ŠHH by H. D. Pruess, "ḤWH," *Theological Dictionary of the Old Testament*. G. Johannes Botterweck and Helmer Ringgren, eds., David E. Green, trans. Vol. 4 (Grand Rapids: Eerdmans, 1980), 248–256.

7. Interestingly, the Arabic cognate word for SGD (*sĕgid*) also connotes prostration in prayer, as the noun "masjid" means "mosque"—the Muslim "house of prayer."

8. For an excellent statement on the active nature of Christian worship, see Robert E. Webber, *Worship Is a Verb* (Nashville: Star Song, 1992).

CHAPTER 2

1. William Dyrness, *Themes in Old Testament Theology* (Downers Grove, IL: InterVarsity Press, 1979), 161.

2. J. I. Packer, "Piety," *New Bible Dictionary: Revised*. J. D. Douglas, ed. (Wheaton, IL; Tyndale House, 1982), 939.

3. Elmer A. Martens, *God's Design: A Focus on Old Testament Theology* (Grand Rapids: Baker, 1981), 179.

4. Dyrness, *Themes in Old Testament Theology*, 162.

5. Martens, *God's Design*, 169.

6. Ronald Youngblood, *The Heart of the Old Testament* (Grand Rapids: Baker, 1971), 87–88.

7. Dyrness, *Themes in Old Testament Theology*, 163.

8. On the relationship between faith and obedience in both the Old and New Testaments, see also Thomas E. McComiskey, *The Covenants of Promise* (Grand Rapids: Baker, 1985), 36–38, 64–65, 123–128.

9. Youngblood, *The Heart of the Old Testament*, 96. This is not to suggest that faith in the Old and New Covenant is identical. For a cogent summary of the differences betweem Old and New Testament faith see John Goldingay, *Approaches to Old Testament Interpretation* (Downers Grove, IL: InterVarsity Press, 1981), 29–37.

10. For example, Solomon's affirmation of Israel's separateness at the dedication of the temple (1 Kings 8:53), and the reforms of Ezra and Nehemiah in restoring the Hebrews to their place as a separate people are high-water marks in Israel's history (Ezra 9:1; 10:11; Neh. 9:2; 10:28; 13:3). And yet the Hebrews failed miserably to maintain this priestly holiness (the golden calf episode in Exodus 32—34 and the incident at Baal-Peor in Numbers 25).

11. Cf., A.W. Tozer, *The Knowledge of the Holy* (New York: Harper & Row, 1978).

12. Dyrness, *Themes in Old Testament Theology,* 165.

13. Gerhard von Rad, *Old Testament Theology.* D. M. G. Salker, trans., Vol. 1, (New York: Harper & Row, 1962), 370.

14. Richard J. Foster, *Celebration of Discipline* (Revised) (New York: Harper & Row, 1988), 30.

15. Walter L. Liefeld, "Prayer," *International Standard Bible Encyclopedia: Revised.* G. W. Bromiley, gen. ed., Vol. 3 (Grand Rapids: Eerdmans, 1986), 931.

16. J. G. S. S. Thomson, "Prayer," *New Bible Dictionary: Revised,* 958; see also Richard J. Foster, *Prayer: Finding the Heart's True Home* (New York: Harper Collins, 1992).

17. Dyrness, *Themes in Old Testament Theology,* 167.

18. Walther Eichrodt, *Theology of the Old Testament.* 6th Edition. J. A. Baker, trans., Vol. 1 (Philadelphia: Westminster, 1967), 175.

19. Volkmar Hernrich as cited in Otto Kaiser, "Isaiah 1—12," *Old Testament Library.* R. A. Wilson, trans. (Philadelphia: Westminster, 1972), 79.

20. C. S. Lewis, *Reflections on the Psalms* (New York: Harcourt, Brace, & World, 1958), 97.

21. Stuart R. Imbach, "Syncretism," *Evangelical Dictionary of Theology.* W. A. Elwell, ed. (Grand Rapids: Baker, 1984), 1062–1063.

22. David A. Hubbard, "Hypocrisy," *Evangelical Dictionary of Theology,* 539.

23. Willard Sperry, "Reality in Worship," *The Fellowship of Saints: An Anthology of Christian Devotional Literature.* Thomas S. Kepler, ed. (New York: Abingdon-Cokesbury Press, 1963), 685, as cited in Richard J. Foster, *Celebration of Discipline* (Revised) (New York: Harper & Row, 1988), 149.

24. See discussion on "Worship in Spirit and Truth" in John MacArthur, *The Ultimate Priority* (Chicago: Moody Press, 1983), 115–126.

25. See the discussion on "Holiness" in Gordon J. Wenham, *The Book of Leviticus* (New International Commentary on the Old Testament) (Grand Rapids: Eerdmans, 1979), 18–25.

26. Cf., J. I. Packer, *God's Words: Studies of Key Bible Themes* (Downers Grove, IL: InterVarsity Press, 1981), 173–177.

27. See the excellent discussion of and exhortation to practical holiness in Jerry Bridges, *The Pursuit of Holiness* (Colorado Springs: NavPress, 1978).

28. Packer, *God's Words,* 174.

29. Dyrness, *Themes in Old Testament Theology,* 125.

30. Ibid. See further the helpful discussion of the theological implications of covenant for the sacred and secular in Elmer A. Martens, *God's Design: A Focus on Old Testament Theology* (Grand Rapids: Baker, 1981), 187–188.

CHAPTER 3

1. Gordon J. Wenham, "Genesis 1—15," *Word Bible Commentary #1* (Waco, TX: Word, 1987), 280. See his "Religion of the Patriarchs," *Essays on the Patriar-*

chal Narratives. A. R. Milliard and D. J. Wiseman, eds. (Winona Lake, IN: Eisenbrauns, 1983), 161–195.

2. Walter Brueggemann, *Genesis* (Interpretation) (Atlanta: John Knox, 1982), 192.

3. Ralph P. Martin, "Worship," *International Standard Bible Encyclopedia: Revised.* G. W. Bromiley, gen. ed., Vol. 4 (Grand Rapids: Eerdmans, 1988), 1118; "The History and Character of Israelite Religion," *Ancient Israelite Religion.* Patrick D. Miller, Paul D. Hanson, and S. Dean McBride, eds. (Philadelphia: Fortress, 1987), 303–644; and the older classic by A. Z. Idelsohn, *Jewish Liturgy and Its Development* (Reprint) (New York: Schocken Books, 1960).

4. At issue here is the occurrence of the name *YHWH* in the Genesis records. Some biblical scholars have assumed the Hebrew patriarchs did not know the name Yahweh for God. They argue the name Yahweh was written after the fact into the text of Genesis or else the book is a compilation of later written sources that included the divine name. In contrast, those biblical scholars committed to the antiquity and integrity of the Pentateuch have asserted it is more reasonable to understand that the patriarchs knew the name Yahweh and were unfamiliar with the radical new dimension of theological meaning for the name stemming from Israel's exodus experience. See Roland de Vaux, "The Revelation of the Divine Name *YHWH,*" *Proclamation and Presence,* 2nd edition. J. I. Durham and J. R. Porter, eds. (Macon: Mercer University Press, 1983), 48–75.

5. F. F. Bruce, *Israel and the Nations,* 2nd edition (Grand Rapids: Eerdmans, 1969), 15. See also Ronald Youngblood, "Monotheism," *The Evangelical Dictionary of Theology.* W. A. Elwell, ed. (Grand Rapids: Baker, 1984), 731–732.

6. William J. Dumbrell, *The Faith of Israel* (Grand Rapids: Baker, 1988), 37.

7. Standard resources on baalism include: William F. Albright, *Yahweh and the Gods of Canaan* (London: Univ. of London Press, 1968); Jack Finegan, "Canaanite Religion," *Myth & Mystery* (Grand Rapids: Baker, 1989), 119–154; and Helmer Ringgren, "West Semitic Religion," *Religions of the Ancient Near East.* J. Sturdy, trans. (Philadelphia: Westminster, 1973), 124–176.

8. For example, see Albert H. Baylis, *On the Way to Jesus* (Portland, OR: Multnomah, 1988), 221–223, on the significance of Elijah's contest with the priests of Baal for demonstrating the superiority of the Hebrew religion of Yahweh over Canaanite baalism.

9. On the Davidic collections and the growth of the Psalter consult Bernard W. Anderson, *Out of the Depths* (Revised) (Philadelphia: Westminster, 1983), 25–28.

10. For a digest of the reigns of the kings of Israel and Judah, see Andrew E. Hill, *Baker's Handbook of Bible Lists* (Grand Rapids: Baker, 1981), 205–207.

11. On the prophetic reaction to Hebrew worship, see also James M. Ward, "Worship and Idolatry," *The Prophets* (Nashville: Abingdon, 1982), 88–114.

12. See also the fine summary of post-exilic Hebrew religion in Donald E. Gowan, *Bridge Between the Testaments*, 2nd edition (Allison Park, PA: Pickwick Press, 1984), 249–287.

CHAPTER 4

1. For example, see the first page of H. J. Kraus, *Worship in Israel*. G. Buswell, trans. (Richmond: John Knox, 1966); or H. H. Rowley, *Worship in Ancient Israel* (Philadelphia: Fortress Press, 1967).
2. I. Hexham, "Cults," *The Evangelical Dictionary of Theology*. W. A. Elwell, ed. (Grand Rapids: Baker, 1984), 289.
3. William Dyrness, *Themes in Old Testament Theology* (Downers Grove, IL: InterVarsity Press, 1979), 143.
4. Craig D. Erickson, *Participating in Worship* (Louisville: W/JKP, 1989), 14.
5. Dyrness, *Themes in Old Testament Theology*, 144.
6. A. S. Herbert, *Worship in Ancient Israel* (Richmond, VA: John Knox Press, 1959), 15.
7. Walther Eichrodt, *Theology of the Old Testament*. J. A. Baker, trans., Vol. 1 (London: SCM Press, 1961), 99.
8. Dyrness, *Themes in Old Testament Theology*, 144.
9. Ibid., 145.
10. Jacques Ellul, *The Subversion of Christianity*. G. W. Bromiley, trans. (Grand Rapids: Eerdmans, 1986), 65.
11. Herbert, *Worship in Ancient Israel*, 16.
12. Franz Kafka, *Parables and Paradoxes* (New York: Schocken Books, 1961), 92–93.
13. Erickson, *Participating in Worship*, 16.
14. Ibid.
15. Ibid., 25.
16. C. S. Lewis, *Reflections on the Psalms* (New York: Brace & World, 1958), 94–95.
17. Erickson, *Participating in Worship*, 24.
18. Ibid., 25.
19. Ibid., 36.
20. George Mallone, *Furnace of Renewal* (Downers Grove, IL: InterVarsity Press, 1981), 55.
21. Erickson, *Participating in Worship*, 37.
22. Robert Schaper, *In His Presence* (Nashville: Thomas Nelson, 1984), 160.
23. Ibid., 161–162.
24. Vernon H. Kooy, "Symbol," *The Interpreter's Dictionary of the Bible*. G. A. Buttrick, ed., Vol. 4 (Nashville: Abingdon, 1962), 472.
25. Victor R. Gordon, "Sign," *The International Standard Bible Encyclopedia: Revised*. G. W. Bromiley, gen. ed., Vol. 4 (Grand Rapids: Eerdmans, 1988), 506.
26. W. Stewart McCullough, "Sign in the Old Testament," *The Interpreter's Dictionary of the Bible*, Vol. 4, 345–346.

27. Kooy, "Symbol in the Old Testament," 473.
28. Ibid., 472–472; also.
29. Kooy, "Symbol in the Old Testament," *The Interpreter's Dictionary of the Bible,* Vol. 4, 472.
30. F. J. Helfmeyer, "'*ot*" ("sign"), *The Theological Dictionary of the Old Testament.* G. J. Botterweck & H. Ringgren, eds., J. T. Willis, trans. (Grand Rapids: Eerdmans, 1974), 177. See also the concise summary statement of biblical symbols in E. H. Van Olst, *The Bible and Liturgy.* J. Vriend, trans. (Grand Rapids: Eerdmans, 1991), 20–33.
31. See Bernhard W. Anderson, "Signs and Wonders," *The Interpreter's Dictionary of the Bible,* Vol. 4, 350.
32. Andrew Blackwood, *The Fine Art of Public Worship* (Nashville: Abingdon-Cokesbury Press, 1939), 8.
33. Robert C. Rayburn, *O Come, Let Us Worship* (Grand Rapids: Baker, 1980), 139.
34. Robert E. Webber, *Worship Old & New* (Grand Rapids: Zondervan, 1982), 109–113.
35. Ibid., 112.
36. Ibid.
37. Erickson, *Participating in Worship,* 15.

CHAPTER 5

1. William Dyrness reminds us that the response of fear to encounters with God at sacred places in Old Testament times was appropriate and necessary. The meeting with God must first involve judgment before it offers joy. The sacred place must first be a place of cleansing and forgiveness. *Themes in Old Testament Theology* (Downers Grove, IL: InterVarsity Press, 1979), 148.
2. See Vergilius Ferm, ed., *Ancient Religions* (New York: Citadel Press, 1965), 121.
3. T. C. Hammond, *In Understanding Be Men.* D. F. Wright, ed. (London: Inter-Varsity Press, 1968), 44–46.
4. For a survey of salvation history in the Old Testament, see Eric Sauer, *The Dawn of World Redemption.* G. H. Lang, trans. (Grand Rapids: Eerdmans, 1951).
5. On pilgrimages in the Old Testament, see J. A. Wharton, "Pilgrimage," *Interpreter's Dictionary of the Bible,* G. A. Buttrick, gen. ed., Vol. 3 (Nashville: Abingdon, 1962), 814–815.
6. Abraham Bloch, *The Biblical and Historical Background of the Jewish Holy Days* (New York: KTAV, 1978), 39–40.
7. On the theme of divine presence in the Old Testament see Samuel Terrien, *The Elusive Presence* (New York: Harper & Row, 1978).
8. On the theme of divine abandonment see Daniel I. Block, *The Gods of the Nations* (ETSMS #2) (Jackson, MS: Evangelical Theological Society, 1988), 129–161.

9. Dyrness, *Themes in Old Testament Theology*, 148.

10. R. K. Harrison, *Jeremiah & Lamentations* (TOTC) (London: Tyndale, 1973), 85–86.

11. Robert E. Webber, *Worship Old & New* (Grand Rapids: Zondervan, 1982), 117–122.

12. Ibid., 118.

13. Ibid., 120–121.

14. See *The Way of the Cross* (Baltimore: Barton-Colton, Inc., 1965) or A. Bonetti, *The Way of the Cross* (New York: Pueblo Publications, 1980).

15. On the history and theological significance of the Christian pilgrimage see E. R. Labande, "Pilgrimages," *The New Catholic Encyclopedia*. W. J. MacDonald, ed., Vol. 11 (New York: McGraw-Hill, 1967), 362–372; and Victor W. Turner, *Image and Pilgrimage in Christian Culture* (New York: Columbia University Press, 1978).

16. On the value of teaching memorials for contemporary biblical education see Walter Brueggemann, *The Creative Word: Canon as a Model for Biblical Education* (Philadelphia: Fortress, 1980), 91–117. On the education of children generally in the ancient world see William Barclay, *Educational Ideals in the Ancient World* (Reprint) (Grand Rapids: Baker, 1974), especially 234–262; and Robert E. Webber, *The Majestic Tapestry* (Nashville: Thomas Nelson, 1986), especially 155–171.

17. Brueggemann, *The Creative Word*, 16.

18. Ibid., 16.

19. For examples of these kinds of Christian teaching memorials see Ceil and Moishe Rosen, *Christ in the Passover* (Chicago: Moody, 1978); D. A. Carson, ed., *From Sabbath to Lord's Day* (Grand Rapids: Zondervan, 1982); Dean Moe, *Christian Symbols Handbook* (Minneapolis: Augsburg, 1985); George W. Benson, *The Cross: Its History & Symbolism* (Reprint) (New York: Hacker, 1976); Walter L. Nathan, *Art and the Message of the Christian Church* (Philadelphia: Westminster, 1961); Johannes Troyer, *The Cross as Symbol & Ornament* (Philadelphia: Westminster, 1961); Othmar Keel, *The Symbolism of the Biblical World* (New York: Seabury, 1978).

20. J. B. Phillips, *Your God Is Too Small* (New York: Macmillan, 1958).

21. Ibid., 19–23.

22. Ibid., 37–41.

23. Malcolm Muggeridge, *Jesus Rediscovered* (Wheaton, IL: Tyndale, 1971), 134.

24. Ibid., 136.

CHAPTER 6

1. Steve Winwood, "The Finer Things." On *Back in the High Life* (New York: Island Records, 1986).

2. Richard E. Whitaker, comp., *Revised Standard Version Analytical Concordance* (Grand Rapids: Eerdmans, 1980), 1118–1121.

3. The serious student is directed to the classic essay by James Barr, "Biblical Words for Time," *Studies in Biblical Theology*, Series 1, #33 (London: SCM Press, 1962); and the comprehensive but technical study of time and history in the Old Testament by Simon J. DeVries, *Yesterday, Today and Tomorrow* (Grand Rapids: Eerdmans, 1975), especially 31–54.

4. M. H. Cressey, "Time," *The New Bible Dictionary*. J. D. Douglas, ed., 2nd edition (Wheaton: Tyndale, 1982), 1199.

5. Clark H. Pinnock, "Time," *The International Standard Bible Encyclopedia: Revised*. G. W. Bromiley, gen. ed., Vol. 4 (Grand Rapids: Eerdmans), 853.

6. Ernst Jenni, "Time," *The Interpreter's Dictionary of the Bible*. G. A. Buttrick, ed., Vol. 4 (Nashville: Abingdon, 1962), 647.

7. Ibid., 648.

8. Thorleif Boman, *Hebrew Thought Compared with Greek*. J. L. Moreau, trans. (New York: Norton, 1970), 137; note his section "Israelite Conception of Time," 129–153; for another perspective on the Hebrew worldview, including time and history, see Marvin R. Wilson, *Our Father Abraham* (Grand Rapids: Eerdmans, 1989), 135–165.

9. Abraham J. Heschel, *The Sabbath: Its Meaning for Modern Man* (Philadelphia: Jewish Publication Society, 1952), 7.

10. Ibid., 8.

11. Michael Card, "The Final Word." On *The Final Word* (Nashville: Sparrow Corp., 1987).

12. Ralph P. Martin, *Colossians* (Grand Rapids: Zondervan, 1972), 138.

13. Peter G. Cobb, "The History of the Christian Year," *The Study of Liturgy*. C. Jones, G. Wainwright, & E. Yarnold, eds. (New York: Oxford, 1978), 403–419.

14. Robert E. Webber, *Worship Old & New* (Grand Rapids: Zondervan, 1982), 166–168. For a more detailed sketch but popular treatment of the historical development of the church year see Theodore J. Kleinhans, *The Year of Our Lord* (St. Louis: Concordia Publishing House, 1967); and Peter G. Cobb, "The History of the Christian Year," *The Study of Liturgy*. C. Jones, G. Wainwright, and E. Yarnold, eds. (New York: Oxford, 1978), 403–418.

15. The Eastern Orthodox church continues to celebrate Easter on the Jewish Passover, the fourteenth day of Nisan.

16. Specifically, the Western church year begins with the first Sunday of Advent (always the nearest Sunday to the feast of St. Andrew, November 30). There are four Sundays in the Advent season of preparation for Christmas. The seasons of Advent and Christmas conclude with the Feast of Epiphany (January 6). This first season of the church year is sometimes called "The Cycle of Light." The second season of the church year includes Lent and Easter, sometimes called "The Cycle of Life." Easter Sunday was set on the first Sunday to follow the new moon, which occurs on or after the spring equinox, as determined by the Council of Nicea, A.D. 325). Lent commences on Ash Wednesday, forty weekdays (Sundays excluded) prior to Easter Sunday. The

Lenten and Easter festival cycle ends with the Feast of Pentecost, or Whitsunday, the seventh Sunday after Easter. For a complete church year calendar, see L. W. Cowie and J. S. Gummer, *The Christian Calendar* (Springfield, MA: Merriam Co., 1974). On the Eastern church calendar, see *The Festal Menaion*. M. Mary & A. K. Ware, trans. (London: Faber & Faber, 1969), 40–66; and *The Lenten Riodion*. M. Mary & A. K. Ware, trans. (London: Faber & Faber, 1978).

17. Terence J. German, "Christian Year," *The Evangelical Dictionary of Theology*. W. A. Elwell, ed. (Grand Rapids: Baker, 1984), 218.

18. See Webber, *Worship Old & New*, 165.

19. An example of the sacred vs. secular tension in the church year may be seen in the apologetic statements often put forward in explanations of "ordinary time," usually attempting to affirm ordinary time as special time in some roundabout way; Robert E. Webber, *The Book of Family Prayer* (Nashville: Thomas Nelson, 1986), 74–75.

20. Jacques Ellul, *The Subversion of Christianity*. G. W. Bromiley, trans. (Grand Rapids: Eerdmans, 1986), 63.

21. Useful overviews include Abraham Millgram, *Jewish Worship* (Philadelphia: Jewish Publication Society, 1971), 161–198; K. Strand, ed., *The Sabbath in Scripture and History* (Washington, D.C.: Review and Herald Publishing Co., 1982); especially Part I: "Sabbath and Sunday in the Biblical Period," 21–131; and Tamara C. Eskenazi, ed., *The Sabbath in Jewish and Christian Tradition* (New York: Crossroad, 1991).

22. Abraham J. Heschel, *The Sabbath: Its Meaning for Modern Man* (Philadelphia: Jewish Publication Society, 1952).

23. Ibid., 7.

24. Ibid., 8.

25. Ibid., 10.

26. Ibid., 19.

27. Ibid.

28. Ibid., 75.

29. E. H. Van Olst, *The Bible and Liturgy*. J. Vriend, trans. (Grand Rapids: Eerdmans, 1991), 38.

30. A. S. Herbert, *Worship in Ancient Israel* (Richmond, VA: John Knox, 1959), 42–43.

31. Roland de Vaux, *Ancient Israel: Religious Institutions*, Vol. II (New York: McGraw-Hill, 1965), 468.

32. Van Olst, *The Bible and Liturgy*, 39.

33. William Dyrness, *Themes in Old Testament Theology* (Downers Grove, IL: InterVarsity Press, 1979), 148.

34. Dyrness, *Themes in Old Testament Theology*, 151; Webber, *Worship Old & New*, 163, develops the emphasis on prophecy in the Hebraic concept of time.

35. Robert Banks, *The Tyranny of Time* (Downers Grove, IL: InterVarsity Press, 1983), 169–170.

36. Banks, *The Tyranny of Time*, 171.
37. Already in the *Didache* or *Teaching of the Twelve Apostles* (early second century A.D.), the injunction to the believer is to gather on the Lord's Day and frequently at other times (but not daily); see J. B. Lightfoot, *The Apostolic Fathers* (Reprint) (Grand Rapids: Baker, 1956), 128–129.
38. For example, the Anglican church *Book of Common Prayer* (ca. 1544) was published in part to guide in their morning and evening prayers those Christians who could not attend the daily parish services. See G. J. Cuming, *A History of Anglican Liturgy* (New York: Macmillan, 1969).
39. See also D. R. DeLacey, "The Sabbath/Sunday Question and the Law in the Pauline Corpus," *From Sabbath to Lord's Day*. D. A. Carson, ed. (Grand Rapids: Zondervan, 1982), 159–196; and Willy Rordorf, *Sunday*. A. A. K. Graham, trans. (Philadelphia: Westminster, 1968); "The Sabbath Problem," 45–153.
40. See also R. J. Bauckham's essays "The Lord's Day," and "Sabbath and Sunday in the Post-Apostolic church," *From Sabbath to Lord's Day*, D. A. Carson, ed. (Grand Rapids: Zondervan, 1982), 221–298; and Roger Beckwith & Wilfrid Stott, *The Christian Sunday* (Grand Rapids: Baker, 1978), especially Part II: "The Evidence of the Fathers," 50–139.
41. Niels-Erik Andreasen, *The Christian Use of Time* (Nashville: Abingdon, 1978), 19.
42. See Banks, *The Tyranny of Time*, Chapter 19: "The Primacy of Becoming Over Doing," 204–212.
43. C. S. Lewis, *Mere Christianity* (New York: Macmillan, 1952), 188.
44. Heschel, *The Sabbath*, 28; on the Christian heritage of sanctifying time, see further Marion J. Hatchett, *Sanctifying Life, Time and Space* (New York: Seabury, 1976).
45. Richard Foster, *Freedom of Simplicity* (New York: Harper & Row, 1981), 57.
46. Ibid.
47. Gordon Dahl, *Work, Play, and Worship in a Leisure Oriented Society* (Minneapolis: Augsburg, 1972), 95–101.
48. Dahl, *Work, Play, and Worship in a Leisure Oriented Society*, 105–106; for an example of Christian responsibility to the world of space, see Loren Wilkinson, ed., *Earthkeeping: Christian Stewardship of Natural Resources* (Grand Rapids: Eerdmans, 1980), and Art and Jocele Meyer, *Earthkeepers* (Scottsdale, AZ: Herald Press), 1991.
49. Dahl, *Work, Play, and Worship in a Leisure Oriented Society*, 115.
50. See John Marsh, "Christian Worship: Human and Divine Transcendence of Time," *The Divine Drama in History and Liturgy* (Essays in Honor of Horton Davies) (Allen Park, PA: Pickwick, 1984), 123–130.
51. George Mallone, *Furnace of Renewal* (Downers Grove, IL: InterVarsity Press, 1981), 56.
52. Robert Schaper, *In His Presence: Appreciating Your Worship Tradition* (Nashville: Thomas Nelson, 1984), 200.

53. Ibid., 213.
54. Jacques Ellul, *The Presence of the Kingdom*. O. Wyon, trans. (New York: Seabury Press, 1967), 27.
55. See all five of Robert Webber's principles of time for worship, *Worship Old & New*, 173.
56. Ibid., 165.
57. Ibid., 165–173; Mary I. Hock, *Worship Through the Seasons* (Portland, OR: Resources Publications, 1987).
58. Robert Lee, *Religion and Leisure in America* (Nashville: Abingdon, 1964), 188.
59. For an excellent discussion of creative silence in worship, including the silence of preparation, the silence of centering on God, the silence of confession, the silence of listening, the silence of adoration, the silence of communion, and the silence of engagement, see Craig D. Erickson, *Participating in Worship* (Louisville: Westminster/John Knox, 1988), 40–53.
60. Foster, *Freedom of Simplicity*, 57; see his discussion on renouncing speech to learn compassion, pp. 57–58; and his chapter on the discipline of solitude in *Celebration of Discipline* (New York: Harper & Row, 1978), 84–95.
61. For practical suggestions on implementing Sabbath rest and worship in a "rhythm of life," see Tilden Edwards, *Sabbath Time* (New York: Seabury, 1982), Chapter 7: "Sabbath Rest," pp. 44–61, and Chapter 8: "Sabbath Worship," pp. 62–72.
62. Ibid., 65.
63. Lee, *Religion and Leisure in America*, 128–138.
64. Edwards, *Sabbath Time*, 73.
65. Ibid., 76.
66. Ellul, *The Presence of the Kingdom*, 44–49; for an example of this kind of revolutionary Christianity committed to social justice, see Ronald J. Sider, *Rich Christians in an Age of Hunger* (Downers Grove, IL: InterVarsity Press, 1977).

CHAPTER 7

1. See Robert E. Webber, *Worship Is a Verb* (Nashville: Star Song, 1992); Craig D. Erickson, *Participating in Worship: History, Theory, and Practice* (Louisville: W/JKP, 1989).
2. For example, see A. A. Anderson, *Psalms 1–72* (NCBC) (London: Marshall, Morgan, and Scott, 1972), 455–457; or D. Kidner, *Psalms 1–72* (TOTC) (Downers Grove, IL: InterVarsity Press, 1973), 224–225.
3. Patrick D. Miller, *Deuteronomy* (Interpretation) (Louisville: W/JKP, 1990), 103.
4. Jacques Ellul, *The Subversion of Christianity*. G. W. Bromiley, trans. (Grand Rapids: Eerdmans, 1986), 65.
5. Leslie B. Flynn, *Worship: Together We Celebrate* (Wheaton, IL: Scripture Press, 1983), 42.

6. Robert E. Webber, *Worship Old & New* (Grand Rapids: Zondervan, 1982), 97–99.

7. A. S. Herbert, *Worship in Ancient Israel* (Richmond, VA: John Knox Press, 1959), 15–24.

8. Webber, *Worship Old & New,* 99.

9. Ibid., 97.

10. W. Liefeld, "Prayer," *International Standard Bible Encyclopedia: Revised,* G. W. Bromiley, gen. ed., Vol. 3 (Grand Rapids: Eerdmans, 1986), 937.

11. Implicit examples of unconditional vows in the Old Testament include confessions or affirmations of obedience in response to covenant renewal ceremonies (Exod. 24:7; Josh. 24:16–22).

12. On Jephthah's vow at dedication to tabernacle service, see Leon J. Wood, *The Distressing Days of the Judges* (Grand Rapids: Zondervan, 1975), 287–295; on Jephthah's vow as human sacrifice see Arthur E. Cundall, *Judges & Ruth* (TOTC) (Downers Grove, IL: InterVarsity Press, 1968), 146–147.

13. On the importance and reliability of oral tradition in the ancient world, see "Tradition, Oral," *The Baker Encyclopedia of the Bible,* W. A. Elwell, ed., Vol. 2 (Grand Rapids: Baker, 1988), 2094.

14. William Dyrness, *Themes in Old Testament Theology* (Downers Grove, IL: InterVarsity Press, 1979), 153–154.

15. For a detailed study of the exodus Passover, Passover at the time of Christ, the contemporary Passover, and the relationship of the Old Testament Passover to the life of Jesus Christ and the new covenant, see Ceil and Moishe Rosen, *Christ and the Passover* (Chicago: Moody Press, 1978).

16. Robert N. Schaper, *In His Presence* (Nashville: Thomas Nelson, 1984), 28.

17. In the New Testament, Paul uses the drink offering or libation as a metaphor for his impending martyrdom, Philippians 2:7; 2 Timothy 4:6.

18. There are two types of fasts in later Judaism, the "less strict," which lasts from sunrise to sunset with no food or drink but washing and anointing are permitted. The "strict fast" lasts from one sunset to the next (when the stars appear), and everything is prohibited, including salutations.

19. Webber, *Worship Old & New,* 103.

20. Marvin R. Wilson, *Our Father Abraham* (Grand Rapids: Eerdmans, 1989), 309–311.

21. Abraham J. Heschel, *The Insecurity of Freedom* (New York: Schocken Books, 1972), 42.

22. Flynn, *Worship,* 38–39.

23. Webber, *Worship Old & New,* 127–128.

24. Ibid., 128.

25. On worship as dialogue see Schaper, *In His Presence,* 174–176.

26. Ibid., 85–199.

27. Erickson, *Participating in Worship,* 155–176.

28. Ibid., 153.

29. Flynn, *Worship,* 41–42.

30. Individuals or churches seriously interested in developing a participatory worship model that incorporates Old Testament Hebrew practices in recitation and ritual drama would do well to visit a messianic Hebrew congregation. See also Arnold G. Fruchtenbaum, *Hebrew Christianity: Its Theology, History, and Philosophy* (Washington, D.C.: Canon Press, 1974); Daniel C. Juster, *Jewishness and Jesus* (Downers Grove, IL: InterVarsity Press, 1977); Edith Schaeffer, *Christianity Is Jewish* (Wheaton: Tyndale House, 1977).

31. Erickson, *Participating in Worship*, 155.

32. Richard F. Lovelace, *Dynamics of Spiritual Life* (Downers Grove, IL: InterVarsity Press, 1979), 75.

33. George Mallone, *Furnace of Renewal* (Downers Grove, IL: InterVarsity Press, 1981), 45.

34. Ibid., 50.

35. Ibid., 56. Other books helpful on the topic of worship renewal include James F. White, *Introduction to Christian Worship* (Revised) (Nashville: Abingdon, 1990); H. L. Hickman, D. E. Saliers, L. H. Stookey, and J. F. White, *Handbook of the Christian Year* (Nashville: Abingdon, 1986).

CHAPTER 8

1. See Andrew E. Hill, *Baker's Handbook of Bible Lists* (Grand Rapids: Baker Books, 1981), 159–161.

2. The full history and development of the Hebrew priesthood was a long and complex process. The complete documentation of that process lies outside the scope of our study. For a synopsis the reader is encouraged to follow up on the topic of priests and Levites in any basic Bible dictionary or encyclopedia (e.g., W. O. McCready, "Priests and Levites," *The International Standard Bible Encyclopedia: Revised*. G. W. Bromiley, gen. ed., Vol. 3 [Grand Rapids: Eerdmans, 1986], 965–970; for more detailed and technical analysis the reader may consult Roland De Vaux, *Ancient Israel: Religious Institutions*. Darton, Longmann & Todd, trans., Vol. 2 [New York: Macmillan, 1965], 345–405; Aelred Cody, *A History of the Old Testament Priesthood*. Analecta Biblical 35 [Rome: Pontifical Biblical Institute, 1969]).

3. On the role of women in Old Testament Hebrew religion, see Phyllis Bird, "The Place of Women in the Israelite Cultus," *Ancient Israelite Religion*. P. D. Miller, P. D. Hanson, and S. D. McBride, eds. (Philadelphia: Fortress, 1987), 397–420.

4. Roland de Vaux, *Ancient Israel: Religious Institutions*. Vol. 2, 397–403; see also Hans-Joachim Kraus, *Worship in Israel*. G. Buswell, trans. (Richmond: John Knox, 1966), 93–111.

5. de Vaux, *Ancient Israel: Religious Institutions*, Vol. 2, 358–371.

6. Ibid., 352.

7. Gordon J. Wenham, *Leviticus* (Tyndale Old Testament Commentaries) (Downers Grove, IL: InterVarsity Press, 1981), 70.

8. On the priestly dress, see C. W. Slemming, *These Are the Garments* (Revised) (Chicago: Moody, 1955). Sections of the work are helpful despite the author's excessive and sometimes inaccurate allegorizing and spiritualizing of the Old Testament priestly clothing.

9. See Walter Brueggemann, *The Creative Word: Canon as a Model for Biblical Education* (Philadelphia: Fortress, 1982), especially Chapter 2: The Discourse of "Binding," 14–39.

10. Roland de Vaux, *Ancient Israel: Social Institutions.* Darton, Longmann & Todd, trans., Vol. 1 (New York: Macmillan, 1965), 113–114; A. R. Johnson, *Sacral Kingship in Ancient Israel,* 2nd edition (Cardiff: University of Wales Press, 1967).

11. John H. Eaton, *Kingship and the Psalms* (Studies in Biblical Theology, 2/32) (London: SCM Press, 1976), 172–177.

12. Ibid., 181–182.

13. F. F. Bruce, *New Testament History* (New York: Doubleday, 1972), 56–68.

14. Joachim Jeremias, *Jerusalem in the Time of Jesus.* F. H. and C. H. Cave, trans. (Philadelphia: Fortress, 1969), 147–221.

15. Peter C. Craigie, "Priests and Levites," *The Evangelical Dictionary of Theology.* W. A. Elwell, ed. (Grand Rapids: Baker, 1984), 877.

16. See Philip E. Hughes, *A Commentary on the Epistle to the Hebrews* (Grand Rapids: Eerdmans, 1977), especially Chapter 4: "Christ Superior to Aaron," 169–404.

17. According to Craig Erickson (*Participating in Worship: History, Theory, and Practice* [Louisville: W/JKP, 1989], 127–147), the corporate and missionary emphasis of the priesthood of believers necessitates employment of the spiritual gifts given to the church.

18. Bruce Milne, *Know the Truth* (Downers Grove, IL: InterVarsity Press, 1982), 225; Geoffrey W. Bromiley, *Historical Theology: An Introduction* (Grand Rapids: Eerdmans, 1978), 210–228.

19. See the helpful discussion on the office of bishop/elder in J. N. D. Kelly, *The Pastoral Epistles* (Black's New Testament Commentaries) (London: Black, 1963), 70–80, 229–233; and on the history of the office of priest in the church, see Bernhard Lohse, *A Short History of Christian Doctrine.* F. E. Stoeffler, trans. (Philadelphia: Fortress, 1978), 132–155.

20. Notice here I distinguish the church office of bishop-elder from the church "office-gifts" of apostle, prophet, pastor-teacher, and evangelist (Eph. 4:11).

21. Craigie, *The Evangelical Dictionary of Theology,* 877.

22. Raymond Brown, *Priest and Bishop: Biblical Reflections* (New York: Paulist Press, 1970), 9. Though Roman Catholic in orientation, this work offers much to the Protestant reader as well.

23. See de Vaux, *Ancient Israel: Religious Institutions,* Vol. 2, 353–355.

24. Brown, *Priest and Bishop,* 8.

25. Ibid., 35.

26. Ibid., 36.

27. Here Erickson lists seven ways the individual Christian acts in a priestly role, including having direct access to God through prayer (James 5:16), offering spiritual sacrifices (Rom. 12:1), proclaiming God's word (1 Pet. 2:9), baptizing new believers in Christ (Matt. 28:18–20), forgiving sins (Matt. 18:18), partaking of the Lord's Table (1 Cor. 11:23–26), and serving as mediator for the world (1 Tim. 2:1–4) (*Participating in Worship*, 128–129).

28. Ibid., 129.

29. Peter C. Craigie, *The Evangelical Dictionary of Theology*, 877.

30. Erickson, *Participating in Worship*, 146.

CHAPTER 9

1. On the subject of divine presence, see Samuel Terrien, *The Elusive Presence* (New York: Harper & Row, 1978).

2. For example, see I. M. Haldeman, *The Tabernacle, Priesthood, and Offerings* (Old Tappan, NJ: Revell, 1925); Stephen F. Olford, *The Tabernacle: Camping with God* (Neptune, NJ: Loizeaux Brothers, 1971).

3. Leon Morris, *The Gospel According to John* (New International Commentary on the New Testament) (Grand Rapids: Eerdmans, 1971), 103.

4. R. K. Harrison, "Exodus, Book of," *The International Standard Bible Encyclopedia: Revised*. G. W. Bromiley, gen. ed., Vol. 2 (Grand Rapids: Eerdmans, 1982), 230.

5. Harrison, *The International Standard Bible Encyclopedia: Revised*, Vol. 2, 230.

6. Umberto Cassuto, *Commentary on the Book of Exodus*. I. Abrahams, trans. (Jerusalem: Magnes Press, 1967), 325–327.

7. For color photographs of a complete reconstruction of the Mosaic tabernacle, see Moshe Levine, *The Tabernacle: Its Structure & Utensils* (New York: Soncino Press, 1969).

8. See Carol L. Meyers, *The Tabernacle Menorah* (American Schools of Oriental Research Dissertation Series #2) (Missoula, MT: Scholars Press, 1976).

9. Stephen Westerholm, "Tabernacle" in *The International Standard Bible Encyclopedia: Revised*, Vol. 4 (Grand Rapids: Eerdmans, 1988), 704.

10. R. J. McKelvey, *The New Temple* (Oxford: Oxford University Press, 1969) 1–2; cf. Henri Frankfort, *Kingship and the Gods* (Reprint) (Chicago: Univ. of Chicago Press, 1978).

11. John Bright, *A History of Israel*, 3rd edition (Philadelphia: Westminster, 1981), 211–223; R. E. Clements, *God and Temple* (Philadelphia: Fortress, 1965), 40–62.

12. See also Eugene H. Merrill, *Kingdom of Priests* (Grand Rapids: Baker, 1987), 391–402.

13. Ibid., 409–430, 441–446.

14. Standard works on the history and liturgy of Solomon's temple include Menahem Haran, *Temples and Temple Service in Ancient Israel* (Reprint) (Winona Lake, MN: Eisenbrauns, 1985); Andre Parrot, *The Temple of Jerusalem*, 2nd edition, B. E. Hooke, trans. (New York: Philosophical Library, 1955),

15–60; H. H. Rowley, *Worship in Ancient Israel* (London: S.P.C.K., 1967), 71–110.

15. See Bright, *A History of Israel*, 223–228.

16. Ibid., 331–339.

17. J. Stafford Wright, *The Building of the Second Temple* (London: Tyndale Press, 1958); Parrot, *The Temple of Jerusalem*, 68–75.

18. For a detailed discussion of the scribe in the Old and New Testaments, see N. Hillyer, "Scribe," *The New International Dictionary of New Testament Theology*. C. Brown, ed., Vol. 3 (Grand Rapids: Zondervan, 1978), 477–482.

19. See also Andrew E. Hill and John H. Walton, *A Survey of the Old Testament* (Grand Rapids: Zondervan, 1991), 235–236.

20. See W. von Meding, C. Brown, and D. H. Madvig, "Temple," *The New International Dictionary of New Testament Theology*. C. Brown, ed., Vol. 3 (Grand Rapids: Zondervan, 1978), 781–798.

21. See Morris, *The Gospel According to John*, 196–200; Alfred Edersheim, *The Temple: Its Ministry and Services as They Were in the Time of Christ* (Reprint) (Grand Rapids: Eerdmans, 1975).

22. Ralph P. Martin, *Worship in the Early Church* (Grand Rapids: Eerdmans, 1974), 18–27.

23. Clements, *God and Temple*, 63.

24. Stephen Westerholm, "Temple," *The International Standard Bible Encyclopedia: Revised*, Vol. 4, 775.

25. On "divine abandonment" in the Old Testament see Hill & Walton, *A Survey of the Old Testament*, 337–338.

26. The ministry of the indwelling Holy Spirit is implicit already in the Old Testament. While the indwelling of the Holy Spirit takes on new significance after Pentecost the key development in the doctrine of the Holy Spirit after Pentecost is the universal bestowment of spiritual gifts in fulfillment of Joel's prophecy (Joel 2:28–32). See also Leon J. Wood, *The Holy Spirit in the Old Testament* (Grand Rapids: Zondervan, 1976), 64–77.

27. Whereas in the New Testament and Christianity the idea of temple shifted from a building to the person of Jesus Christ and the believer in Christ, in later Judaism the institution of temple was transferred to the Jewish home. Thus the Jewish home became a miniature temple. See further Marvin R. Wilson, *Our Father Abraham* (Grand Rapids: Eerdmans, 1989), 214–217.

28. Robert E. Webber, *Worship Old & New* (Grand Rapids: Zondervan, 1982), 193–196.

29. Ibid., 193.

30. Ibid., 194.

31. Ibid., 194–195.

32. Ibid., 195.

33. Ibid.

34. Ibid., 195–196.

35. Ibid., 196. For suggestions on discovering and developing the relationship between doing and hearing, liturgy and ethics, and the celebrating church in a suffering world, see E. H. Van Olst, *The Bible and Liturgy*. J. Vriend, trans. (Grand Rapids: Eerdmans, 1991), 135–159.

CHAPTER 10

1. Bernhard Anderson, *Out of the Depths: the Psalms Speak for Us Today* (Revised) (Philadelphia: Westminster, 1983), 22.
2. Andrew E. Hill & John H. Walton, *A Survey of the Old Testament* (Grand Rapids: Zondervan, 1991), 274–285; see also John H. Walton, "The Psalms: A Cantata About Davidic Covenant," *Journal of the Evangelical Theological Society* 34 (1991), 21–31.
3. Hill & Walton, *A Survey of the Old Testament*, 280.
4. Ibid., 279.
5. This idea has been advanced by Hermann Gunkel, *The Psalms*. T. M. Horner, trans. (Philadelphia: Fortress Press, 1967); and popularized by Claus Westermann, *The Psalms: Structure, Content and Message*. R. D. Gehrke, trans. (Minneapolis: Augsburg Press, 1980); *Praise and Lament in the Psalms* (Atlanta: John Knox, 1981).
6. For example, Sigmund Mowinckel, *The Psalms in Israel's Worship*. D. R. AP-Thomas, trans., 2 Vols. (Nashville: Abingdon, 1962). See especially Vol. 1, 23 where Mowinckel states "A cultic interpretation—and a real understanding of the Psalms means setting each one of them in relation to the definite cultic act—or the cultic acts—to which it belonged." Cf. Kenneth A. Kitchen, *Ancient Orient and Old Testament* (London: InterVarsity Press, 1966), 102–106.
7. These are not rigid categories of identification, as some overlap exists (between the hymn and song of thanksgiving), and some psalms are "mixed types" (i.e., they may combine elements of two or more psalmic types); see further Tremper Longman, *How to Read the Psalms* (Downers Grove, IL: InterVarsity Press, 1988), 20–36.
8. On the importance of genre identification for the interpretation of the Psalms, see Gordon D. Fee & Douglas Stuart, *How to Read the Bible for All It's Worth* (Revised) (Grand Rapids: Zondervan, 1993), 187–205; and Patrick D. Miller, *Interpreting the Psalms* (Philadelphia: Fortress Press, 1986), 3–47.
9. The catalog of psalmic types represents a distillation of Anderson's discussion of the various literary forms in the Psalter, *Out of the Depths*, Chapters 2–7.
10. See also Longman, *How to Read the Psalms*, 67.
11. C. S. Lewis, *Reflections on the Psalms* (New York: Harcourt & Brace, 1958), 21–22.
12. Ibid., 26.
13. Ibid., 1; the author offers this caveat: "This is not a work of scholarship."
14. The idea of imprecation is not limited to the Old Testament, as Jesus (Matt 23:13) and Paul (Gal. 1:18) used such maledictions. Even the prayer at the

end of the book of Revelation is imprecatory ("Amen, come, Lord Jesus!" 22:20), since the second coming of Christ includes judgment. See also, Anderson, *Out of the Depths*, 87–93; and C. Hassell Bullock, *An Introduction to the Old Testament Poetic Books*, 2nd edition (Chicago: Moody, 1988), 139–141.

15. On parallelism in Hebrew poetry, see Longman, *How to Read the Psalms*, 95–110.

16. On the strengths and weaknesses of the various approaches, see Miller, *Interpreting the Psalms*, 3–11; and W. H. Bellinger, *Psalms: Reading and Studying the Book of Praises* (Peabody, MA: Hendrickson, 1990), 15–32.

17. Erhard Gerstenberger, *Psalms 1* (Forms of Old Testament Literature: 14) (Grand Rapids: Eerdmans, 1988), 21–22. I would expand Gerstenberger's thesis to include the psalmic categories other than laments.

18. Peter C. Craigie, "Psalms 1—50" *Word Biblical Commentary* (Waco: Word, 1983), 25.

19. George S. Gunn, *Singers of Israel* (New York: Abingdon, 1963), 18.

20. See also John A. Lamb, *The Psalms in Christian Worship* (London: Faith Press, 1962), 1–17; Duncan Lowe, "Biblical Worship: The Place of the Psalms," *The Book of Books* (Essays in Honor of Johannes G. Vos), J. H. White, ed., Nutley, N.J.: Presbyterian and Reformed, 1978), 73–88; Abraham Millgram, *Jewish Worship* (Philadelphia: Jewish Publication Society, 1971), 59–63; Mowinckel, *The Psalms in Israel's Worship*, Vol. 1, 1–22; Marie Pierik, *The Psalter in the Temple and the Church* (Washington D.C.: Catholic Univ. Press of America, 1957); H. H. Rowley, *Worship in Ancient Israel: Its Forms and Meaning* (Philadelphia: Fortress, 1967), 176–212.

21. Millgram, *Jewish Worship*, 63.

22. See Massey H. Shepherd, *The Psalms in Christian Worship: A Practical Guide* (Minneapolis: Augsburg, 1976), 26; Eric Werner, *The Sacred Bridge* (New York: Columbia Univ. Press), 1959.

23. Lamb, *The Psalms in Christian Worship*, 12–17.

24. The Latin church father Tertullian (A.D. 155–223) states that the Psalms were appropriated from the synagogue liturgy and were used widely in Christian churches (*The Apology*, xxxi.3).

25. Shepherd, *The Psalms in Christian Worship*, 26–27.

26. On the New Testament use of the Old Testament, see Andrew E. Hill, *Baker's Handbook of Bible Lists* (Grand Rapids: Baker, 1981), 102–103.

27. Lamb, *The Psalms in Christian Worship*, 26–27.

28. Ralph P. Martin, *Worship in the Early Church* (Grand Rapids: Eerdmans, 1974), 39.

29. See Martin, *Worship in the Early Church*, 39–52; Shepherd, *The Psalms in Christian Worship*, 28–31.

30. A full study of the usage of the Psalms through the post-Nicene, Medieval, Reformation, and Enlightenment periods of church history proves impossible here. The reader is recommended to special studies on the subject. Two

are especially helpful: Lamb, *The Psalms in Christian Worship*. (A somewhat ponderous and technical study of the history of the Psalms in Christian worship, this work offers thorough treatment of the subject and copious references to primary sources, and discusses both the Eastern and Western church traditions.) A second is Shepherd, *The Psalms in Christian Worship*. This is a readable summary of the development of psalmody in Christian liturgy, which emphasizes contemporary use of the Psalms in church liturgy and private devotion. It includes extensive bibliographies, including musical settings for the Psalms.)

31. See Lamb, *The Psalms in Christian Worship*, 35–36.
32. See Shepherd, *The Psalms in Christian Worship*, 36–39.
33. See Lamb, *The Psalms in Christian Worship*, 85–89; and Shepherd, *The Psalms in Christian Worship*, 40–43.
34. See Shepherd, *The Psalms in Christian Worship*, 61–65.
35. Ibid., 80–83; see also Shepherd, *A Liturgical Psalter for the Christian Year* (Minneapolis: Augsburg, 1976).
36. See Lamb, *The Psalms in Christian Worship*, 120–127; Shepherd, *The Psalms in Christian Worship*, 100–103.
37. See Lamb, *The Psalms in Christian Worship*, 133–159; Shepherd, *The Psalms in Christian Worship*, 48–52, 69–73.
38. On chanting and singing the Psalms, see the bibliography in Shepherd, *The Psalms in Christian Worship*, 124–125.
39. John Chrysostom, *Homily on Psalm 145*.
40. Lamb, *The Psalms in Christian Worship*, 38.

CHAPTER 11

1. "Let the Whole Creation Cry," written by the English churchman Stopford A. Brooke (1832–1881), with arrangement by Robert Williams (1781–1821).
2. Derek Kidner, "Psalms 1–72," *Tyndale Old Testament Commentaries* (Downers Grove, IL: InterVarsity Press, 1973), 136.
3. See also W. S. LaSor, "Art," *The International Standard Bible Encyclopedia: Revised*. G. W. Bromiley, gen. ed., Vol. 1 (Grand Rapids: Eerdmans, 1979), 299–306.
4. Piere Amiet, *The Art of the Ancient Near East* (New York: Abrams), 1980.
5. Here I still like the expression "beauty of His holiness" used in the King James Version (1 Chron. 16:29; 2 Chron. 20:21; Ps. 96:9). The NIV reads "splendor of his holiness," and the NRSV reads "holy splendor."
6. The Apocryphal book of the Wisdom of Solomon, condemns the worship of nature instead of God; but admits to the great beauty of God's creation (13:1–9).
7. See Gene E. Veith's discussion of the gifts of Bezalel—filled with the Holy Spirit, filled with ability, and filled with intelligence—in *The Gift of Art: The Place of the Arts in Scripture* (Downers Grove, IL: InterVarsity Press, 1983), 17–28.

8. On the fall of humanity and the arts, see Frank E. Gaebelein, *The Christian, the Arts, and Truth* (Portland, OR: Multnomah, 1985), 74–77, 109–114.

9. See also Leland Ryken, *Culture in Christian Perspective* (Portland, OR: Multnomah, 1986); especially Chapter 2: "What the Bible Says About the Arts," 41–64; Veith, *The Gift of Art*, 43–77.

10. Ryken, *Culture in Christian Perspective*, 67–68.

11. Veith, *The Gift of Art*, 9.

12. Ryken, *Culture in Christian Perspective*, 68.

13. H. R. Rookmaaker, *Art Needs No Justification* (Downers Grove, IL: InterVarsity Press, 1978), 9.

14. Ibid., 13.

15. Veith, *The Gift of Art*, 18–21.

16. Ibid., 107–126; Rookmaaker, *Art Needs No Justification*, 12–14; and Francis Schaeffer, *Art & the Bible* (Downers Grove, IL: InterVarsity Press, 1973), 33.

17. Schaeffer, *Art & the Bible*, 63.

18. Gaebelein, *The Christian, the Arts, and Truth*, 102.

19. See also, Ryken, *Culture in Christian Perspective*, 88–94; Schaeffer, *Art & the Bible*, 33–34; Veith, *The Gift of Art*, 121.

20. See also, Frank E. Gaelelein, "What Is Truth in Art?" *The Christian Imagination*. Leland Ryken, ed. (Grand Rapids: Baker, 1981), 99–109.

21. Dorothy Sayers, *The Mind of the Maker* (Reprint) (Elnora, NY: Meridian Books, 1951), 34.

22. See also Ryken, *Culture in Christian Perspective*, 140–148; Schaeffer, *Art & the Bible*, 38–39, 56–59.

23. See also Clyde S. Kilby, "Christian Imagination," *The Christian Imagination*, 37–46.

24. See also Ryken, *Culture in Christian Perspective*, 148–150.

25. See also Gaebelein, *The Christian, the Arts, and Truth*, 94–97.

26. Robert E. Webber, *Worship Is a Verb* (Nashville: Star Song, 1992), 175–177; see also the discussion of icons and iconoclasts—art as veneration or idolatry—in church history, in Veith, *The Gift of Art*, 11–16.

27. Webber, *Worship Is a Verb*, 177.

28. Ibid., 179–195.

29. Ryken, *Culture in Christian Perspective*, 62.

30. Webber, *Worship Is a Verb*, 195.

CHAPTER 12

1. Roger Beckwith in C. Jones, G. Wainwright, and E. Yarnold, eds., *The Study of Liturgy* (New York: Oxford Univ. Press, 1978), 39.

2. See D. L. Baker, *Two Testaments: One Bible* (London: InterVarsity Press, 1976).

3. On the Judeo-Christian heritage of the church, see also Marvin R. Wilson, *Our Father Abraham: The Jewish Roots of the Christian Faith* (Grand Rapids: Eerdmans, 1989).

4. This selective treatment of Jewish backgrounds of the New Testament and New Testament worship may be supplemented by appeal to any one of a number of standard resources on the topic, for example: Ralph P. Martin, *New Testament Foundations* (Grand Rapids: Eerdmans, 1975), Vol. 1, 53–118; Jacob Neusner, *First Century Judaism in Crisis* (New York: KTAV, 1982); Ronald H. Nash, *Christianity & the Hellenistic World* (Grand Rapids: Zondervan, 1984); and Edwin Yamauchi, *Harper's World of the New Testament* (New York: Harper & Row, 1981).

5. See also Bruce M. Metzger, *An Introduction to the Apocrypha* (New York: Oxford Univ. Press, 1957); Bruce M. Metzger, ed., *The Oxford Annotated Apocrypha* (New York: Oxford Univ. Press, 1977). For an introduction to the entire corpus of intertestamental Jewish religious literature, see Leonhard Rost, *Judaism Outside the Hebrew Canon*. D. E. Green, trans. (Nashville: Abingdon, 1976); and for complete English translations of these documents see James H. Charlesworth, ed., *The Old Testament Pseudepigrapha* (New York: Doubleday), (Vol. 1 1983), (Vol. 2 1985).

6. On the development of Jewish religion in the Intertestamental period, see Donald E. Gowan, *Bridge Between the Testaments* (Pittsburgh: Pickwick Press, 1984), 249–290; D. S. Russell, *Between the Testaments* (Philadelphia: Fortress, 1965), 41–57; Raymond F. Surburg, *Introduction to the Intertestamental Period* (St. Louis: Concordia, 1975), 53–71.

7. On personal piety in Judaism, see George F. Moore, *Judaism in the First Centuries of the Christian Era* (New York: Schocken, 1971), Vol. 1, 201–275.

8. Metzger, *The Oxford Annotated Apocrypha*, 63.

9. See Metzger's analysis of Tobit, *An Introduction to the Apocrypha*, 31–41; compare Frank Zimmermann, *The Book of Tobit* (New York: Harper Brothers, 1958).

10. Metzger, *An Introduction to the Apocrypha*, 40.

11. The idea of prayer, fasting, and almsgiving as the three pillars of later Judaism is an adaptation of the Jewish tradition that the world rested on three pillars— the Torah (knowledge of divine revelation), the temple cultus (the worship of God), and works of charity (deeds of lovingkindness to others); compare Moore, *Judaism in the First Centuries of the Christian Era*, Vol. 1, 35.

12. Compare W. D. Davies, *The Sermon on the Mount* (Cambridge: Cambridge Univ. Press, 1966), 87–90.

13. On the history of the synagogue, see further H. H. Rowley, *Worship in Ancient Israel* (Philadelphia: Fortress, 1967); L. I. Levine, ed., *Ancient Synagogues Revealed* (Jerusalem: Israel Exploration Society, 1982); I. Levy, *The Synagogue: Its History and Function* (London: Valentine & Mitchell, 1964).

14. Compare W. Scharge, "συναγωγή (synagogue)," *The Theological Dictionary of the New Testament*, G. Friedrich, ed., G. W. Bromiley, trans. (Grand Rapids: Eerdmans, 1971), Vol. 7, 798–853.

15. Eric M. Meyers and James F. Strange, *Archaeology, the Rabbis & Early Christianity* (Nashville: Abingdon, 1981), 140–154.

16. See also the discussion (with diagrams) in Robert E. Webber, *Worship Old & New* (Grand Rapids: Zondervan, 1982), 151–160.

17. The ancient synagogue was not ruled by rabbis (literally "great ones"), as the synagogue was a lay institution and officiating priests were not mandatory. Likewise, rabbis were not necessarily priests but scholastics devoted to the reading, teaching, and interpretation of the Law of Moses and accrued Jewish tradition.

18. On the officers of the synagogue see Moore, *Judaism in the First Centuries of the Christian Era*, Vol. 1, 289–290; W. S. LaSor, "Synagogue," *The International Standard Bible Encyclopedia: Revised*. G. W. Bromiley, gen. ed. (Grand Rapids: Eerdmans, 1988), Vol. 4, 681.

19. See Abraham Millgram, *Jewish Worship* (Philadelphia: Jewish Publication Society, 1971), 63–88, 336–366; Moore, *Judaism in the First Centuries of the Christian Era*, Vol. 1, 281–307.

20. Martin, *Worship in the Early Church*, 18–27; cf., Joseph Heinemann, The Literature of the Synagogue (New York: Behrman House, 1975); A. Z. Idelsohn, *Jewish Liturgy and Its Development* (Reprint) (New York: Schocken Books, 1960).

21. Webber, *Worship Old & New*, 51–53.

22. See Martin, *Worship in the Early Church*, 39–52; see also William W. Simpson, *Jewish Prayer and Worship: An Introduction for Christians* (London: SCM Press, 1965), for helpful instruction on appropriating Jewish prayer and liturgy for the enrichment of Christian worship.

23. W. O. E. Oesterley, *The Jewish Background of Christian Liturgy* (New York: Oxford Univ. Press, 1965), 111–154.

24. On the place of the call to worship in the order of the synagogue service, see Millgram, *Jewish Worship*, 110.

25. Oesterley, *The Jewish Background of Christian Liturgy*, 125–147.

26. On confession of sin in Jewish liturgy, see Millgram, *Jewish Worship*, 230–231 (cf., James 5:16).

27. The "amen corner" was an important part of Christian liturgy earlier in church history. The "amen corner" was a specific area off to one side of the pulpit where a group of worshipers led the congregation in responsive amens during the worship service. Later the term signified any special place in the church occupied by zealous worshipers; compare, G. Uhlhorn, "Liturgics," *The New Schaff-Herzog Encyclopedia of Religious Knowledge* (Reprint) S. M. Jackson, ed. (Grand Rapids: Baker, 1977), Vol. 6, 501.

28. Oesterley, *The Jewish Background of Christian Liturgy*, 156–179; compare, Marvin R. Wilson, *Our Father Abraham* (Grand Rapids: Eerdmans, 1989), 237–255.

29. Oesterley, *The Jewish Background of Christian Liturgy*, 194–204.

30. Compare Jones, Wainwright, and Yarnold, *The Study of Liturgy*, 39–50.

31. Webber, *Worship Old & New*, 51.

32. See further Wilson, *Our Father Abraham*, especially 19–51.

33. John Goldingay, *Approaches to Old Testament Interpretation* (Downers Grove, IL: InterVarsity Press, 1981). Goldingay outlines five basic approaches, including the Old Testament as covenant faith, as salvation history, as moral instruction, as typology, and as canon.

34. Ibid., 97.

35. See further Leonhard Goppelt, *Types, the Typological Interpretation of the Old Testament in the New Testament.* D. H. Madvig, trans. (Grand Rapids: Eerdmans, 1982).

36. Samuel Sandmel, *Philo of Alexandria: An Introduction* (New York: Oxford, 1979); on Philo's allegorical method, see A. B. Mickelsen, *Interpreting the Bible* (Grand Rapids: Eerdmans, 1963), 28–30.

37. F. F. Bruce, "Hebrews," *New International Commentary on the New Testament* (Grand Rapids: Eerdmans, 1964), 1.

38. Richard N. Longenecker, *Biblical Exegesis in the Apostolic Period* (Grand Rapids: Eerdmans, 1975), 184–185.

39. See Bruce, "Hebrews," xxiii–lii.

40. Goldingay, *Approaches to Old Testament Interpretation*, 97–109.

41. Ibid., 109–111.

APPENDIXES

1. Athanasius, "Letter to Marcellinus on the Interpretation of the Psalms," *St. Athanasius on the Incarnation.* (Crestwood, NY: St. Vladimir's Orthodox Theological Seminary, 1953), 105.

2. As cited in John Calvin, *Commentaries on Joshua-Psalms 1—35* (Reprint), H. Beveridge, trans. (Grand Rapids: Baker, 1979), Vol. 4, vii.

3. Athanasius, "Letter to Marcellinus on the Interpretation of the Psalms," 105.

4. Abraham Millgram, *Jewish Worship* (Philadelphia: Jewish Publication Society, 1971), 63.

5. As cited in John Calvin, *Commentaries on Joshua-Psalms 1—35*, Vol. 4, vii.

6. Compare Walter Brueggemann, *The Message of the Psalms* (Minneapolis: Augsburg, 1984).

7. John Chrysostom, *Homily on the Psalms*, vi.

8. Compare Tremper Longman, *How to Read the Psalms* (Downers Grove, IL: InterVarsity Press, 1988), 63–73.

9. St. Jerome, *Commentary on Ephesians*, 5:19.

10. John Chrysostom, *Homilies on Colossians*, ix.

11. "Letter to Marcellinus on the Interpretation of the Psalms," *St. Athanasius on the Incarnation*, 104.

12. See Longman, *How to Read the Psalms*, 75–85.

Old Testament Worship
Bibliography

This is A SELECT BIBLIOGRAPHY including those works in English that directly address the topic of Hebrew worship in the Old Testament and/or later Judaism. Not all the entries are theologically conservative or evangelical in nature. The reader is encouraged to explore the rich literature on Old Testament worship with "discerning openness" (cf. Prov. 18:15). Of course, additional titles of a more specialized nature may be found in the notes.

Baly, D. *God and History in the Old Testament.* New York: Harper and Row, 1976, pp. 133–158.

Birch, B. C. *Let Justice Roll Down: The Old Testament, Ethics, and Christian Life.* Louisville: W/JKP, 1991, pp. 179–197.

Bloch, A. P. *The Biblical and Historical Background of the Jewish Holy Days.* New York: KTAV, 1978.

———. *The Biblical and Historical Background of Jewish Customs and Ceremonies.* New York: KTAV, 1980.

Brueggemann, W. *Israel's Praise: Doxology Against Idolatry and Ideology.* Philadelphia: Fortress, 1988.

Dawn, M. J. *Keeping the Sabbath Wholly: Ceasing, Resting, Embracing, Feasting.* Grand Rapids: Eerdmans, 1989.

Dyrness, W. *Themes in Old Testament Theology.* Downers Grove, IL: InterVarsity Press, 1979, pp. 143–160.

Eichrodt, W. *Theology of the Old Testament.* J. A. Baker, trans. Philadelphia: Westminster, 1967, Vol. 1, pp. 98–177, 268–379.

Erickson, C. D. *Participating in Worship: History, Theory and Practice.* Richmond, VA: Westminster/John Knox, 1988.

Foster, R. J. *Celebration of Discipline.* Revised. New York: Harper & Row, 1988, pp. 138–149.

Gavin, F. *The Jewish Antecedents of the Christian Sacraments.* New York: KTAV, 1969.

Haran, M. *Temples and Temple-Service in Ancient Israel.* Oxford: Clarendon Press, 1978.

Herbert, A. S. *Worship in Ancient Israel.* Richmond, VA: John Knox, 1959.

Hill, A. E. & J. H. Walton. *A Survey of the Old Testament.* Grand Rapids: Zondervan, 1991, pp. 223–224.

Idelsohn, A. Z. *Jewish Liturgy and Its Development.* Reprint. New York: Schocken Books, 1960, especially pp. 3–35.

Jacob, E. *Theology of the Old Testament.* A. W. Heathcote and J. P. Allcook, trans. New York: Harper & Row, 1958, pp. 233–280.

Kaufmann, Y. *The Religion of Israel.* Abridged. M. Greenberg, trans. New York: Schocken, 1972.

Kidner, F. D. *Sacrifice in the Old Testament.* London: Tyndale Press, 1952.

Kraus, H. J. *Worship in Israel: A Cultic History of the Old Testament.* G. Buswell, trans. Richmond, VA: John Knox, 1966.

Law, P., (comp.) *Praying with the Old Testament.* London: Triangle, 1989.

Lehman, C. K. *Biblical Theology: Old Testament.* Scottdale, PA: Herald Press, 1971, pp. 134–171.

Levine, B. A. *In the Presence of the Lord: A Study of Cult and Some Cultic Terms in Ancient Israel.* Leiden: Brill, 1974.

Lewis, C. S. *Reflections on the Psalms.* New York: Harcourt, Brace and World, 1958.

MacArthur, J. *The Ultimate Priority.* Chicago: Moody Press, 1983.

Mallone, G. *Furnace of Renewal.* Downers Grove, IL: InterVarsity Press, 1981, pp. 43–60.

Martens, E. A. *God's Design: A Focus on Old Testament Theology.* Grand Rapids: Baker, 1981, pp. 47–59, 112–115, 224–229.

Martin, R. P. "Worship" in *International Standard Bible Encyclopedia: Revised.* G. W. Bromiley, gen. ed. Grand Rapids: Eerdmans, 1988, Vol. 4, pp. 1117–1133.

Matthews, V. H. *Manners and Customs in the Bible.* Peabody, MA: Hendrickson, 1988, pp. 26–28, 75–85, 138–144, 179–188, 251–262.

Micklem, N. (ed.) *Christian Worship*. Oxford: Clarendon, 1936, pp. 19–49.

Miller, P. D., P. D. Hanson & S. D. McBride. (eds.) *Ancient Israelite Religion*. Philadelphia: Fortress, 1987.

Millgram, A. E. *Jewish Worship*. Philadelphia: Jewish Publication Society, 1971.

Nicholls, W. *Jacob's Ladder: The Meaning of Worship*. Richmond, VA: John Knox, 1958, pp. 9–35.

Oesterley, W. O. E. "Worship in the Old Testament" in *Liturgy and Worship*. W. K. L. Clarke, ed. London: S. P. C. K., 1932, pp. 38–59.

Oesterley, W. O. E. & T. H. Robinson. *Hebrew Religion: Its Origin and Development*. 2nd Edition. New York: Macmillan, 1937.

Pierik, M. *The Psalter in the Temple and the Church*. Washington, D. C.: Catholic Univ. of America Press, 1958, pp. 1–58.

von Rad, G. *Old Testament Theology*. D. M. G. Stalker, trans. New York: Harper & Row, 1962, Vol. 1, pp. 355–459.

Rayburn, R. G. *O Come, Let Us Worship*. Grand Rapids: Baker, 1980, pp. 43–76.

Rowley, H. H. *Worship in Ancient Israel: Its Forms and Meanings*. Philadelphia: Fortress, 1967.

Schaper, R. N. *In His Presence*. Nashville: Thomas Nelson, 1984, pp. 21–47.

Simpson, W. W. *Jewish Prayer and Worship: An Introduction for Christians*. London: SCM Press, 1965.

Stallings, J. *Rediscovering Passover: A Complete Guide for Christians*. San Jose: Resource Publications, 1988.

Van Olst, E. H. *The Bible and Liturgy*. J. Vriend, trans. Grand Rapids: Eerdmans, 1991, pp. 1–46.

de Vaux, R. *Ancient Israel*. Darton, Longman and Todd, trans. New York: McGraw-Hill, 1961, Vol. 2, "Religious Institutions."

Wainwright, G. *Doxology: The Praise of God in Worship, Doctrine and Life: A Systematic Theology*. New York: Oxford, 1980.

Webber, R. E. *Worship Old & New*. Grand Rapids: Zondervan, 1982, pp. 23–32, 237–238.

_____. *Signs of Wonder*. Nashville: Star Song, 1992, pp. 29–42.

_____. *The Complete Library of Christian Worship: The Biblical Foundations of Christian Worship*. Nashville: Abbott-Martyn Press, 1993, Vol. 1.

Wenham, G. J. "Religion of the Patriarchs" in *Essays on the Patriarchal Narratives*. A. R. Millard and D. J. Wiseman, eds. Winona Lake, MN: Eisenbrauns, 1983, pp. 161–195.

Werner, E. *The Sacred Bridge: Liturgical Parallels in Synagogue and Early Church*. New York: Schocken, 1970.

White, J. F. *Introduction to Christian Worship*. Nashville: Abingdon, 1980.

Willimon, W. H. *Word, Water, Wine and Bread*. Valley Forge: Judson Press, 1980, pp. 9–19.

Winward, S. F. *The Reformation of Our Worship*. Richmond, VA: John Knox, 1965.

Wright, C. J. H. *An Eye for an Eye: The Place of Old Testament Ethics Today*. Downers Grove, IL: InterVarsity Press, 1983, pp. 206–208.

Youngblood, R. *The Heart of the Old Testament*. Grand Rapids: Baker, 1971, pp. 67–96.

Time . . . for Further Reading

The bibliography below contains a range of religious perspectives on time, not always evangelical. Topics addressed include time and worship, time in cross-cultural contexts, time management, and the relationship of time to work and leisure and everyday life. Brief annotations are offered to both stimulate and expedite your reading!

Andreasen, N. E. *The Christian Use of Time*. Nashville: Abingdon, 1978. Creative Christian perspectives on time management; see especially the suggestions for responding to holiness in time in Chapter 7: "Time for Worship," pp. 75–86.

Banks, R. *The Tyranny of Time*. Downers Grove, IL: InterVarsity Press, 1983. Biblical perspectives on time management emphasizing a dynamic and unified approach to understanding and utilizing time. Chapter notes contain a wealth of bibliographic information.

Boman, T. *Hebrew Thought Compared with Greek*. J. L. Moreau, trans. New York: Norton, 1970. A classic monograph on the differences between Greek and Hebrew worldviews; see especially the section "Israelite Conception of Time," pp. 129–153.

Custance, A. C. *Time and Eternity*. Grand Rapids: Zondervan, 1977. Philosophical and psychological considerations of time and eternity from a Christian perspective.

Dahl, G. *Work, Play, and Worship in a Leisure Oriented Society*. Minneapolis: Augsburg, 1972. Precocious essay calling the Christian to stop worshiping work, working at play, and playing at worship.

Edwards, T. *Sabbath Time*. New York: Seabury Press, 1982. Explores the ways in which Christians may apply the principles of Old Testament Sabbath to contemporary religious and social life.

Ellul, J. *The Presence of the Kingdom*. O. Wyon, trans. New York: Seabury Press, 1967. See especially Chapter II: "Revolutionary Christianity," on how the future or "eschatological time" shapes (or should shape) the Christian life-style.

Engstrom, T. W. & A. Mackenzie. *Managing Your Time: Practical Guidelines on the Effective Use of Time*. Grand Rapids: Zondervan, 1967. Small Christian classic on time management based upon the premise that one must learn to manage him or herself to manage time.

Exley, R. *The Rhythm of Time*. Tulsa: Honor Books, 1987. Christian time-management principles for the "overachiever," advocating a balance between work, play, worship, and rest. See especially Part III, "Worship," pp. 105–150.

Heschel, A. J. *The Sabbath: Its Meaning for Modern Man*. Philadelphia: Jewish Publication Society, 1952. Profound monograph examining the Jewish Sabbath tradition and its role in civilization, offers penetrating insights on Judaism as a religion of time.

Hummel, C. E. *The Tyranny of the Urgent*. London: InterVarsity Press, 1967. Brief and engaging essay calling the Christian to distinguish between the important and the urgent.

Jewett, P. K. *The Lord's Day*. Grand Rapids: Eerdmans, 1971. A historical and theological guide to the Christian day of worship.

Johnston, R. K. *The Christian at Play*. Grand Rapids: Eerdmans, 1983. A theology of play integrating the work-play aspects of time, see especially Section IV: "Play: The Hebraic Model," pp. 85–122.

Lee, R. *Religion and Leisure in America*. Nashville: Abingdon, 1964. Standard work on the history, meaning, and theological significance of leisure in Western culture; see especially Part IV: "Time: A Theological Resource for Leisure," pp. 119–264.

Markell, J. & J. Winn. *Overcoming Stress*. Wheaton: Scripture Press/Victor Books, 1982. See especially Chapter 12: "The Tyranny of Time," pp. 78–83.

Martimort, A. G. (ed.) *The Church at Prayer, IV: Liturgy and Time*. Collegeville, MN: Liturgical Press, 1985, especially pp. 151–272.

McConnell, W. T. *The Gift of Time*. Downers Grove, IL: InterVarsity Press, 1983. Cross-cultural study of time outlining implications for the Christian and the Christian church in America.

Ryken, L. *Work & Leisure in Christian Perspective*. Portland, OR: Multnomah, 1987. See especially Chapter 1: "Understanding Work and Leisure," pp. 19–42 and Chapter 8: "The Ethics of Leisure," pp. 207–230.

Torrance, T. F. *Space, Time, and Incarnation*. London: Oxford, 1969. Philosophical apologetic relating the incarnation of Christ to space and time; see especially Chapter 3: "Incarnation and Space and Time," pp. 52–90.

————. *Space, Time, and Resurrection*. Grand Rapids: Eerdmans, 1976. Philosophical apologetic relating the resurrection of Jesus Christ to space and time; see especially Chapter 8: "The Lord of Space and Time," pp. 159–193.

de Vries, S. J. *Yesterday, Today and Tomorrow*. Grand Rapids: Grand Rapids: Eerdmans, 1975. Detailed and technical study of the relationship between time and history in the Old Testament.

Webber, R. E. *Worship Old & New*. Grand Rapids: Zondervan, 1982. See especially the application of biblical principles of time to Christian worship in Chapter 14: "Worship and Time," pp. 161–174.

Wright, J. S. *Man in the Process of Time*. Grand Rapids: Eerdmans, 1956. A Christian assessment of the powers and functions of the human personality; see especially Chapter VI: "The Mind and Time," pp. 50–64.

Express Yourself! Resources for Those to Whom the Arts Belong

Here is a representative, not exhaustive, bibliography designed to help you and/or your church appropriate the arts for contemporary Christian worship. The catalog contains a range of evangelical perspectives on developing a biblical theology of the arts, as well as practical suggestions for implementing various forms of artistic expression in church liturgies.

Adams, D. *Congregational Dancing in Christian Worship*. Revised. North Aurora, IL: The Sharing Co., 1980.

Brown, F. B. *Religious Aesthetics: A Theological Study of Making and Meaning*. Princeton, NJ: Princeton Univ. Press, 1989.

Daniels, M. *The Dance in Christianity*. New York: Paulist Press, 1981.

Davies, J. G. *Liturgical Dance: An Historical, Theological, and Practical Handbook*. London: SCM Press, 1984.

Deitering, C. *The Liturgy as Dance and the Liturgical Dancer*. New York: Crossroad, 1984.

Dillenberger, J. *A Theology of Artistic Sensibilities: The Visual Arts and the Church*. New York: Crossroad, 1986. (The section on developing a theology of art in worship is especially helpful, pp. 231–256.)

_____. *The Visual Arts and Christianity in America*. New York: Crossroad, 1989. (A historical survey from the Colonial period to the present.)

Erickson, C. D. *Participating in Worship: History, Theory, and Practice*. Louisville: W/JKP, 1989 (especially the chapter on multi-sensate worship, pp. 149–179).

Gaebelein, F. E. *The Christian, the Arts, and Truth*. Portland, OR: Multnomah, 1985.

Hustad, D. P. *Jubilate!* Carol Stream, IL: Hope, 1981.

Johansson, C. M. *Music & Ministry: A Biblical Counterpoint*. Peabody, MA: Hendrickson, 1984.

Lamb's Players Staff. *Developing a Drama Group*. Minneapolis: World Wide Publications, 1989.

L'Engle, M. *Walking on Water: Reflections on Faith & Art*. Wheaton, IL: Shaw, 1980.

Paquier, R. *Dynamics of Worship*. D. Macleod, trans. Philadelphia: Fortress, 1967, especially Chapter 13: "Liturgical Vestments and Colors," pp. 135–145, and Chapter 14: "Singing and Music in Worship," pp. 146–154.

Pearson, K. (ed.) *Worship in the Round: Patterns of Informative & Participative Worship*. New York: Meyer Stone Books, 1982.

Rookmaker, H. R. *Art Needs No Justification*. Downers Grove, IL: InterVarsity Press, 1978.

Routley, E. *Church Music and Christian Faith*. Carol Stream, IL: Agape, 1978.

Ryken, L. (ed.) *The Christian Imagination: Essays on Literature and the Arts*. Grand Rapids: Baker, 1981.

———. *Culture in Christian Perspective: A Door to Understanding and Enjoying the Arts*. Portland, OR: Multnomah, 1986.

Sayers, D. *The Mind of the Maker*. Reprint. Elnora, NY: Meridian Press, 1956.

Schaeffer, F. A. *Art and the Bible*. Downers Grove, IL: InterVarsity Press, 1973.

Schaeffer, F. *Addicted to Mediocrity: 20th Century Christians and the Arts*. Westchester, IL: Cornerstone Books, 1981.

Schmitt, F. P. *Church Music Transgressed: Reflections on Reform*. New York: Seabury, 1977.

Smith, J. G. *26 Ways to Use Drama in Teaching the Bible*. Nashville: Abingdon, 1988.

de Sola, C. *The Spirit Moves*. Washington, D.C.: Liturgical Conference, 1977.

Taylor, M. F. *A Time to Dance: Symbolic Movement in Worship*. North Aurora, IL: The Sharing Co., 1967.

Van Olst, E. H. *The Bible and Liturgy*. J. Vriend, trans. Grand Rapids: Eerdmans, 1991, especially the section dealing with whole-person worship, pp. 108–127.

Veith, G. E. *The Gift of Art: The Place of the Arts in Scripture*. Downers Grove, IL: InterVarsity Press, 1983.

Webber, R. E. *Worship Old & New*. Grand Rapids: Zondervan, 1982, especially Chapter 12: "Worship and Space," pp. 151–160.

———. *Worship Is a Verb*. Waco, TX: Word, 1985, especially Chapter 9: "Rediscover the Arts," pp. 173–195.

White, J. F. *Protestant Worship and Church Architecture: Theological and Historical Considerations.* New York: Oxford Univ. Press, 1964.

White, J. F. & S. J. White. *Church Architecture: Building and Renovating for Christian Worship.* Nashville: Abingdon, 1988.

Wilson, J. *One of the Richest Gifts.* Edinburgh: Handsel Press, 1981. (A survey of the arts from a Christian perspective.)

Wolterstorff, N. *Art in Action: Toward a Christian Aesthetic.* Grand Rapids: Eerdmans, 1980.

Appendix A
Old Testament Chronology

SINCE THE BIBLE IS HISTORY and not myth, items like geographical features and sites, genealogical records, and chronological data are very important to the study of the Old Testament. The following outline of Old Testament chronology presents a general overview of Hebrew history. The outline lends perspective to the entire scope of Israelite history as preparation for the birth of Jesus Christ in the "fulness of time" (Gal. 4:4 KJV). It also provides the basic historical framework for assessing the development of Hebrew worship in the Old Testament.

Pre-patriarchal Period: Adam to Terah
(Creation to ca. 2000 B.C.)

As a precursor to God's election of and covenant with Abraham, the book of Genesis is careful to delineate the genealogical line of the seed of the promise made in Genesis 3:15. The rest of the Bible conscientiously preserves this genealogical line of the promise to ensure the identification of the coming one as the seed of Abraham, the Lion of Judah, and the Branch of David. Biblical genealogies find their completion in the birth of Jesus Christ. The gospel writers (Matthew 1 and Luke 3) reconstruct the ancient family tree and evince Christ as the fulfillment of Old Testament genealogical prophecy. Once Christ has been verified as the "Son of the promise," the biblical genealogies end because they have accomplished their intended function.

   A. *The generations from Adam to Noah, Gen. 5:1–32 Adam → Seth →
   Enosh → Kenan → Mahalalel → Jared → Enoch → Methuselah →
   Lamech → Noah*

B. The generations from Shem to Abram, Gen. 11:10–26 Noah →
Shem → Arphaxad → Shelah → Eber → Peleg → Reu → Serug →
Nahor → Terah → Abram

Patriarchal Period: Abraham to Moses (ca. 2000–1400 B.C.)

Despite the elaborate chronologies constructed for the Hebrew
patriarchs by some biblical scholars, it seems best to place the Israelite forefathers in the Middle Bronze Age of ancient history and leave
it at that (ca. 2100–1550 B.C.). Citing exact dates for the birth and
death of each patriarch is sheer speculation and proves misleading
given the uncertainties of pre-Mosaic chronology due to the scanti-
ness of specific biblical and extra-biblical materials.

One important datum emerging from the narratives about the
beginnings of Hebrew history is the entry of Jacob into the land of
Egypt (Gen. 46:1–7, 26–27). According to Exodus 12:40 the Israelites lived in Egypt for four hundred thirty years (Acts 7:6; Gal. 3:17).
If the Hebrew exodus from Egypt occurred in the fifteenth century
B.C., Jacob's entry into Egypt would have taken place in the nine-
teenth century B.C. If, however, the exodus from Egypt occurred in
the thirteenth century B.C., the date of Jacob's entry into Egypt
would be placed in the seventeenth century B.C.

A. The Family of Abraham, Gen. 16:15; 21:1–5; 25:1–4 Abraham/
Hagar → Ishmael; Abraham/Sarah → Isaac; Abraham/Keturah → Zim-
ran, Jokshan, Medan, Midian, Ishbak, Shuah
B. The Family of Isaac, Gen. 25:19–26 Isaac/Rebekah → Esau, Jacob
C. The Family of Esau, Gen. 36:1–14 Esau/Adah → Eliphaz; Esau/
Oholibamah → Jeush, Jalam, Korah; Esau/Basemath → Reuel
D. The Family of Jacob, Gen. 46:8–27 Jacob/Leah → Reuben, Simeon,
Levi, Judah, Issachar, Zebulun; Jacob/Zilpah → Gad, Asher; Jacob/
Rachel → Joseph, Benjamin; Jacob/Bilhah → Dan, Naphtali
E. The Family of Joseph, Gen. 41:50–52 Joseph/Asenath → Manasseh,
Ephraim

The Formative Period: Moses to Samuel (ca. 1440–1000 B.C.)

The exodus from Egypt. The date of the Hebrew exodus from Egypt
under the leadership of Moses remains a significant problem in the
study of Old Testament chronology. Two distinct positions on the

date of the Exodus have emerged from the voluminous past and present research. The traditional, early date for the Exodus is based on the literal interpretation of 1 Kings 6:1 and Judges 11:26. Here the annals of Israel date the exodus from Egypt to the four hundred eightieth year prior to King Solomon's fourth year of rule. Solomon's fourth year of rule is variously dated between 966 and 957 B.C. This places the Exodus in the fifteenth century B.C., somewhere between 1446 and 1437 B.C. (This book assumes the traditional date for the Hebrew exodus from Egypt.)

The so-called late-date theory for the Israelite flight from Egypt is based on a figurative interpretation of the numbers given in 1 Kings 6:1 and Judges 11:26. According to this view, the four hundred eighty years between the commencement of the building of the temple and the exodus from Egypt is a symbolic number representing twelve generations between the two events. A biblical generation is perceived to be nearer twenty-five years than forty, hence a period of about three hundred years intervenes between the Exodus and the events of 1 Kings 6. This, coupled with the weight of recent archaeological evidence, suggests a date for the Exodus sometime in the thirteenth century B.C. Actual dates range anywhere from 1290 to 1220 B.C.

For a detailed presentation of the arguments for the traditional or early Exodus date, the reader is directed to Leon J. Wood, "Date of the Exodus," in New Perspectives on the Old Testament, J. B. Payne, ed. (Waco, TX: Word Books, 1970), pp. 66–87. Kenneth A. Kitchen ably tenders the reasons supporting the late Exodus date in Ancient Orient and Old Testament (Downers Grove, IL: Inter-Varsity Press, 1966), 57–75.

The chronology of the judges. (Note that these events are not successive since many, if not all, the judgeships overlapped one another.)

The period of the judges extended from approximately 1350 to 1050 B.C. based on the traditional date for the Hebrew exodus from Egypt. Biblical scholars committed to the late-date Exodus compress the period of the judges into a time span of nearer two hundred years (ca. 1220–1050 B.C.).

> Joshua died at the age of one hundred ten, the elders ruled Israel (Judg. 2:8).
>
> Chushan-Rishathaim, king of Aram Naharaim, oppressed Israel for eight years (3:8).
>
> Othniel defeated Cushan-Rishathaim, Israel at peace for forty years (3:11).
>
> Eglon, king of Moab, oppressed Israel for eighteen years (3:14).
>
> Ehud delivered Israel from Eglon and Moab, Israel at peace for eighty years (3:30).
>
> Jabin, king of Canaan, oppressed Israel for twenty years (4:3).
>
> Deborah defeated the Canaanites, Israel at peace for forty years (5:3).
>
> Midianites oppressed Israel for seven years (6:1).
>
> Gideon delivered Israel from the Midianites, Israel at peace for forty years (8:28).
>
> Abimelek ruled in Shechem for three years (9:22).
>
> Tola judged Israel for twenty-three years (10:2).
>
> Jair judged Israel for twenty-two years (10:3).
>
> Philistines and Ammonites oppressed Israel for eighteen years (10:8).
>
> Jephthah defeated Ammonites and judged Israel for six years (12:7).
>
> Ibzan judged Israel for seven years (12:9).
>
> Elon judged Israel for ten years (12:11).
>
> Abdon judged Israel for eight years (13:1).
>
> Philistines oppressed Israel for forty years (13:1).
>
> Samson defeated Philistines and judged Israel for twenty years (15:20).
>
> Samuel judged Israel all the days of his life (1 Sam. 7:15).

The defeat of Israel at Shiloh by the Philistines (ca. 1055 or 1050 B.C.) marked the end of God's theocratic rule and the beginning of Israel's clamor to have a king, like all the neighboring nations who were oppressing them (1 Sam. 4:1–11; 8:1–9).

The Traditional or Monarchical Period (ca. 1050–600 B.C.)

A. The United Monarchy

Saul	?–1010 B.C.
Ishbaal	1010–1008
David	1010–970
Solomon	970–930

B. The Divided Monarchies (* indicates co-regency)

Judah		Israel	
Rehoboam	930–913 B.C.	Jeroboam I	930–910 B.C.
Abijah	913–911	Nadab	910–909
Asa	911–870	Baasha	909–886
Jehoshaphat	*873–848	Elah	886–885
Jehoram	*853–841	Zimri	885
Ahaziah	841	Tibni	885–880
Athaliah	841–835	Omri	*885–874
Joash	835–796	Ahab	874–853
Amaziah	796–767	Ahaziah	853–852
Azariah	*791–740	Joram	852–841
Jotham	*750–732	Jehu	841–814
Ahaz	*744–716	Jehoahaz	814–798
Hezekiah	*729–687	Jeroboam II	*793–753
Manasseh	*696–642	Zechariah	753–752
Amon	642–640	Shallum	752
Josiah	640–609	Menahem	752–742
Jehoahaz	609	Pekahiah	742–740
Jehoiakim	609–597	Pekah	*752–732
Jehoiachin	597	Hoshea	732–722
Zedekiah	597–587		
Judah falls to Babylonia		Israel falls to Assyria	

C. Prophets to the Kings of Israel and Judah

Samuel . . . . Saul
Nathan . . . . David
Gad . . . . David
Ahijah . . . . Solomon, Jeroboam I
Iddo . . . . Solomon, Rehoboam, Abijah
Shemaiah . . . . Rehoboam
Azariah . . . . Asa
Hanani . . . . Asa
Jehu . . . . Jehoshaphat, Baasha
Jahaziel . . . . Jehoshaphat
Elijah . . . . Ahab, Ahaziah, Jehoram
Micaiah . . . . Ahab
Eliezer . . . . Jehoshaphat

Zechariah .... Joash
Elisha .... Ahaziah, Jehoram, Jehu, Jehoahaz, Jehoash
Isaiah .... Azariah, Jotham, Ahaz, Hezekiah
Hosea .... Azariah, Jotham, Ahaz, Hezekiah, Jeroboam II
Amos .... Azariah, Jeroboam II
Micah .... Jotham, Ahaz, Hezekiah
Jonah .... Jeroboam II
Oded .... Pekah
Huldah .... Josiah
Zephaniah ...... Josiah
Jeremiah .... Josiah, Jehoahaz, Jehoiakim, Jehoiachin,
                 Zedekiah
Uriah .... Jehoiakim
Ezekiel .... (Exile of) Jehoiachin
Daniel .... Jehoiakim, Nebuchadnezzar, Belshazzar, Darius
                the Mede, Cyrus
Haggai .... Darius of Persia
Zechariah ...... Darius of Persia
Obadiah .... None Named
Joel .... None Named
Nahum .... None Named
Habakkuk .... None Named
Malachi .... None Named

The Exilic Period: Fall of Jerusalem
to the Decree of Cyrus (587–539 B.C.)

602 B.C.   Nebuchadnezzar, king of Babylon, besieged Jerusalem.
            Along with booty and others from the ranks of royalty
            and nobility, Daniel taken captive (Dan. 1:1–4).

597   Nebuchadnezzar again besieged Jerusalem. Ezekiel taken
            captive along with over ten thousand captives and the
            temple treasures (2 Kings 24:10–17).

587   Nebuchadnezzar conquered Jerusalem and deported the
            Israelites to Babylon (2 Kings 24:8—25:21; 2 Chron.
            36:1–21).

582   Nebuchadnezzar again raided Jerusalem and deported an-
            other forty-six hundred people in retaliation for the assas-

sination of Gedaliah, the Babylonian appointed governor (Jer. 52:24–30).

561   Evil-Merodach, king of Babylon, released Jehoiachin, king of Judah, from prison in the thirty-seventh year of his exile (2 Kings 25:27–30; Jer. 52:31–34).

539   King Cyrus of Persia defeated the Babylonians and issued an edict that permitted those taken captive by the Babylonians to return to their homelands (Ezra 1:1–4).

The Restoration or Post-Exilic Period:
The Decree of Cyrus to Alexander (539–332 B.C.)

539 B.C. Decree of Cyrus (Ezra 1:1–4).

538   Shesh-bazzar led a small group of Jews back to Jerusalem (Ezra 1:8–11).

522?   Zerubbabel and Jeshua led another group of Jews back to Jerusalem (Ezra 2:1–67).

520   Haggai prophesied (Hag. 1:1).

520–518 Zechariah prophesied (Zech. 1:1; 7:1).

516/515 Second temple reconstruction completed (Ezra 6:15).

500?   Malachi prophesied.

458   Ezra the scribe led a third band of Jews back to Jerusalem, where he helped organize the restored community around the Law of Moses (Ezra 7:7; 8:1–36; Neh. 8:1—9:25).

445   Nehemiah journeyed to Jerusalem and supervised the rebuilding of sections of the wall of Jerusalem and then remained as governor under Persian auspices for twelve years (Neh. 2:11–18; 5:14).

432   Nehemiah returned for a second stint as governor after an interval of a year or two (Neh. 13:6).

400?   The books of Chronicles written.

The restoration community in post-exilic Jerusalem enjoyed considerable autonomy but remained subject to Persian authority. This subjugation to Persian rule was the first (and perhaps most tolerant) in a series of Jewish capitulations to foreign powers. The Persians (539–332 B.C.) were followed in succession by Alexander the Great and the Greeks (332–323 B.C.), the Egyptian Ptolemies (323–198 B.C.), the Syrian Seleucids (198–165 B.C.), and finally the Romans

(63 B.C. to A.D. 135). Only during the brief Maccabean and Hasmonean age did Palestinian Jews enjoy a respite from harsh foreign oppression. Little wonder when the New Testament opens, the Jews of Jerusalem and its surrounding area are awaiting the arrival of a military-minded Messiah who will drive out the hated Gentiles, cleanse the land of pagan pollutions, and establish a Davidic-like kingdom of God on earth.

Admittedly, the names and numbers of this historical time line are less than scintillating. And yet, the Babylonian courtier Daniel found cause to worship God because he is Lord of the nations and the ruler of human history. Daniel's hymn of thanksgiving extols the God of heaven for his knowledge and control of the mystery of the times and seasons of earthly kingdoms (Dan. 2:20–23). Daniel's hymn also reminds us of Jesus' retort to Pilate, "You would have no power over me unless it had been given you from above" (John 19:11 RSV). This truth prompted the apostle Paul to charge Timothy to shun evil and aim at godliness because God is the only Sovereign, the King of kings and Lord of lords (1 Tim. 6:11–16).

For further reading, the following are standard histories of Israel:

Bright, John. A History of Israel. 3rd Edition. Philadelphia: Westminster, 1981.
Merrill, Eugene H. Kingdom of Priests. Grand Rapids: Baker, 1987.
Wood, Leon J. A Survey of Israel's History. Revised by David O'Brien. Grand Rapids: Zondervan, 1986.

Appendix B
Divine Names and Titles in the Old Testament

DURING OLD TESTAMENT TIMES, names described the being, existence, character, personality, reputation, and authority of individuals. Given this context, it is only natural God would choose to reveal himself to the Hebrews using a variety of divine names and titles. In order to know God, it is important to understand the names he used to communicate himself and his purposes to humankind. A list of the more prominent Old Testament divine names are included below. (For a complete catalog of divine names and titles in the Old Testament, see Herbert Lockyer, *All the Divine Names and Titles in the Bible* (Grand Rapids: Zondervan, 1975); for a more technical study of divine names in the Old Testament, see Tryggve N. D. Mettinger, *In Search of God*. F. H. Cryer, trans. (Philadelphia: Fortress Press, 1987).

1. El = God (Gen. 17:1). A general name for any deity in the ancient world. As applied to the God of the Hebrews it signified his majesty and authority.
2. Elohim = God (literally "gods"; Gen. 1:2). Often regarded "the plural of majesty" for God in the Old Testament.
3. El-Elyon = Most High God (Gen. 14:18–20). This name indicated God's superior position above all the other gods of the nations.
4. Jehovah (*YHWH*) = usually translated LORD (Exod. 3:14). The "I AM" God of the burning bush episode in Moses' call to deliver Israel. The name signified God would be an inexhaustible resource for accomplishing all that he had charged Moses to do.
5. Adonai = LORD (Josh. 3:11). Revealed God as owner and master of all his creation.

6. El-Shaddai = God Almighty (literally, "God of the mountains"; Gen. 17:1). The name recalled God's power in creating and sustaining all life. Later the name became associated with the awesome display of divine might at Mt. Sinai (Exod. 19).

7. El-Olam = God Everlasting (Gen. 21:33). This name emphasized God's immenseness and eternality.

8. El-Roeh = God, the One Who Sees (Gen. 16:13). Revealed God's beneficent omniscience, a God who saw the needs of his people and cared enough to respond with help and deliverance.

9. El-Berith = God of the Covenant (Judg. 9:46). Reminded Israel of God's immanence as a covenant maker with humanity, his faithfulness as a covenant keeper, and the security found in covenant relationship with God.

10. El-Elohe-Israel = God, the God of Israel (Gen. 33:19–20). This name attested God's sovereignty and providential watch and care over his elect, Israel.

11. Jehovah (YHWH)-Jireh = the LORD our Provision (Gen. 22:13–14). A name that witnessed God's ability to sustain the faithful in trial and testing.

12. Jehovah (YHWH)-Rapha = the LORD Heals (Exod. 15:26). Revealed God's potent curative powers to overcome sin and disease in the fallen creation.

13. Jehovah (YHWH)-Nissi = the LORD our Banner (Exod. 17:15). God himself goes before his people in battle—in life.

14. Jehovah (YHWH)-Shalom = the LORD is Peace (Judg. 6:24). The righteous may rest secure in God.

15. Jehovah (YHWH)-Raah = the LORD our Shepherd (Ps. 23:1). The most poignant of all the divine names—God tends to his people like the shepherd for his sheep.

16. Jehovah (YHWH)-Tsidkenu = the LORD our Righteousness (Jer. 23:6). Exalts the perfection and impeccable character of God.

17. Jehovah (YHWH)-Shammah = the LORD is Present (Ezek. 48:35). Affirmed the omnipresence of God as a personal Creator.

18. Jehovah (*YHWH*)-Sabaoth = the LORD of Hosts (1 Sam. 17:45). Designated God as the leader or general of the armies of heaven and of Israel.
19. Jehovah (*YHWH*)-Hoseenu = the LORD our Maker (Ps. 95:6). Celebrated the beauty of creation and the unique ability of the Creator.
20. Jehovah (*YHWH*)-Elohim = the LORD God (Zech. 13:9). Emphasized God as the majestic and omnipotent Creator and Ruler of creation.

Other divine titles and epithets include

21. Holy One of Israel (Ps. 71:22).
22. Father (Ps. 89:26).
23. Redeemer (Job 19:25).
24. Savior (Isa. 43:3).
25. Shield (Ps. 33:20).
26. Help (Ps. 33:20).
27. Rock (Isa. 30:29).
28. King (Ps. 24:7–8).
29. Living God (2 Kings 19:4).
30. First and Last (Isa. 44:6).
31. Mighty One (Isa. 9:6).
32. Amen God (Isa. 65:16).
33. Ancient of Days (Dan. 7:9).
34. Lawgiver (Isa. 33:22).
35. Fortress (Ps. 18:2).
36. Sun (Ps. 84:11).
37. God of Heaven (Jon. 1:9).
38. King of Heaven (Dan. 2:18).
39. Hope of Israel (Jer. 14:8).
40. Horn of Salvation (2 Sam. 22:3).

The Old Testament names and titles for God remain an important source of knowledge about his nature, character, personality, and redemptive purpose for creation. Today these names and titles for God might be employed in Christian private and corporate worship in a variety of ways. For example, even as selections from the

Proverbs are used on a weekly basis in many churches to instruct the congregation in the way of wisdom, so also the names of God could be used to instruct congregations in the knowledge of God. Or, the names of God might be used to order private or public prayer. For instance, when praying for the sick and infirm Jehovah-Rapha can be petitioned, when praying for those in urgent need or dire circumstances El-Roeh may be petitioned, and when offering thanksgiving to God for his bountiful provision the use of Jehovah-Jireh would be appropriate.

Appendix C
The Hebrew Religious Calendar

1. Equivalents of the Julian Calendar

Julian Calendar	Babylonian-Jewish Calendar
Mar/Apr	Nisan, pre-exilic Hebrew name 'Abib (Exod. 12:2)
Apr/May	Iyyar, pre-exilic Hebrew name Ziw (1 Kings 6:1)
May/June	Sivan
June/July	Tammuz
July/Aug	Ab
Aug/Sept	Elul
Sept/Oct	Tishri, pre-exilic Hebrew name 'Etanim (1 Kings 8:2)
Oct/Nov	Marhesvan, pre-exilic Hebrew name Bul (1 Kings 6:38)
Nov/Dec	Kislev
Dec/Jan	Tebeth
Jan/Feb	Shebat
Feb/Mar	Adar

2. Jewish Religious Calendar: Festivals

Month	Date	Festival
Nisan	1	New moon (Num. 10:10)
	10	Selection of Passover lamb (Exod. 12:3)
	14	Passover lamb killed (Exod. 12:6), Passover begins (Num. 28:16)
	15	First day of Unleavened Bread (Num. 28:17)

	16	Firstfruits (Lev. 23:10)
	21	End of Passover and Unleavened Bread (Lev. 23:6)
Iyyar	1	New moon (Num. 1:18)
Sivan	1	New moon
	6	Pentecost (fifty days after Firstfruits), Feast of Weeks (Lev. 23:15–21)
Tammuz	1	New moon
Ab	1	New moon
	9	Day of mourning for destruction of temple
Elul	1	New moon
Tishri	1	New moon, New Year, Feast of Trumpets (Lev. 23:24; Num. 29:1–2)
	10	Day of Atonement (Lev. 23:26–32; the fast in Acts 27:9)
	15–21	Feast of Tabernacles (Lev. 23:33–43)
Marhesvan	1	New moon
Kislev	1	New moon
	25	Feast of Dedication of the temple (1 Macc. 4:52ff.), Hanukkah or Feast of Lights, an eight-day festival (John 10:22)
Tebeth	1	New moon
Shebat	1	New moon
Adar	1	New moon
	14–15	Feast of Purim (Esther 9:21)

Jewish years are counted according to the World Era, beginning with the creation of man (estimated to be the year 3761 B.C.). Thus Israel became a nation in the Jewish year 5709 (A.D. 1948). Rather than counting time from the birth of Christ, Jewish people indicate the years before Christ as B.C.E. (Before Common Era); and the years following Christ's birth as C.E. (The Common Era). On ancient calendars see Jack Finegan, *Handbook of Biblical Chronology* (Princeton,

NJ: Princeton Univ. Press, 1964). For an in-depth discussion of the development of the events comprising the Hebrew religious calendar, see Abraham P. Bloch, *The Biblical and Historical Background of the Jewish Holy Days* (New York: KTAV, 1978); and Peter S. Knobel, ed., *Gates of the Seasons: A Guide to the Jewish Year* (New York: Central Conference of American Rabbis, 1983).

Appendix D

Sacrifice in the Old Testament

1. The Sacrificial System

The Sacrificial System

Name	Portion Burnt	Other Portions	Animals	Occasion or Reason	Reference
Burnt offering	All	None	Male without blemish; animal according to wealth	Propitiation for general sin, demonstrating dedication	Lev. 1
Meal offering or tribute offering	Token portion	Eaten by priest	Unleavened cakes or grains, must be salted	General thankfulness for first fruits	Lev. 2
Peace offering a. Thank offering b. Vow offering c. Freewill offering	Fat portions	Shared in fellowship meal by priest and offerer	Male or female without blemish according to wealth; freewill, slight blemish allowed	Fellowship a. For an unexpected blessing b. For deliverance when a vow was made on that condition c. For general thankfulness	Lev. 3 Lev. 22:18–30
Sin offering	Fat portions	Eaten by priest	Priest or congregation: bull; king: he-goat; individual: she-goat	Applies basically to situation in which purification is needed	Lev. 4
Guilt offering	Fat portions	Eaten by priest	Ram without blemish	Applies to situation in which there has been desecration or de-sacrilization of something holy or there has been objective guilt	Lev. 5:1–6:7

From John H. Walton, Chronological Charts of the Old Testament (Grand Rapids: Zondervan, 1978), p. 45. Used by permission.

2. Occasions for Sacrifice

Sacrifice and Offering

Animals to be offered	Bullocks	Rams	Lambs	Goats
Occasions for Offerings				
Daily (morning & evening)			2	
Additional offerings on the Sabbath			2	
New Moons	2	1	7	1
Annual Festivals				
Unleavened Bread (daily offering)	2	1	7	1
Total for 7 days	14	7	49	7
Weeks (Firstfruits)	2	1	7	1
1st day of 7th month	1	1	7	1
Day of Atonement	1	1	7	1
Tabernacles Day 1	13	2	14	1
Day 2	12	2	14	1
Day 3	11	2	14	1
Day 4	10	2	14	1
Day 5	9	2	14	1
Day 6	8	2	14	1
Day 7	7	2	14	1
Day 8	1	1	7	1
Total for 8 days	71	15	105	8

Numbers of animals to be offered at the public sacrifices, daily, weekly, and at festivals.

The two lambs on the Sabbath are additional to the usual daily 2.

The total for seven days refers to the seven days of the Festival of Unleavened Bread (i.e., 2 bullocks per day for 7 days = 14).

Similarly, the total for eight days refers to the eight days of the Feast of Tabernacles (i.e., 1 goat per day for 8 days = 8 goats).

Chart of the occasions laid down for public sacrifice and offerings (Num. 28—29).

From the *New Bible Dictionary,* J. D. Douglas, ed. 2nd Edition. Wheaton: Tyndale House, 1982, p. 1046. Used by permission.

Appendix E
Music in the Old Testament

Music in the Old Testament
1. Jubal is called the first of all musicians (Gen. 4:21).
2. Music was a part of family gatherings and celebrations (Gen. 31:27; cf. Luke 15:25).
3. Music accompanied the labor of harvesting and well-digging (Isa. 16:10; Jer. 48:33; Num. 21:17).
4. Music was a part of military strategy and victory celebrations (Exod. 32:17–18; Josh. 6:4–20; Judg. 7:18–20; 11:34–35; 1 Sam. 18:6–7).
5. Dancing was often part of musical merrymaking (Exod. 15:20; 32:19; Judg. 11:34; 21:21; 1 Sam. 18:6; 21:11; 29:5; 30:16).
6. Music was a part of worship and the temple ministry (1 Chron. 15:16; 23:5; 25:6–7; 2 Chron. 5:11–14; cf., Ezra 2:65 and Neh. 12:27–43).
7. Music was part of the court life of the kings (1 Sam. 16:14–23; 2 Sam. 19:35; Eccles. 2:8); and also a part of the enthronement celebrations (1 Kings 1:39–40; 2 Kings 11:14; 2 Chron. 13:14).
8. Music was associated with feasting and merrymaking (Isa. 5:12; 24:8; cf., Matt. 14:6).
9. Music expresses a wide range of human feelings (book of Psalms).
10. Music was a vital part of mourning and lament (2 Sam. 1:17–18; 2 Chron. 35:25; cf., Matt. 9:23).
11. Music was used for the restoration of prophetic gifts (2 Kings 3:15); and to soothe troubled individuals (1 Sam. 16:14–23).

12. Amos condemned idle music and feasting (Amos 6:5–6).

13. Singing and rejoicing are characteristic of the righteous man (Prov. 29:6).

14. Music will be a part of the new covenant (Jer. 31:7–13).

From *Baker's Handbook of Bible Lists*. Andrew E. Hill, compiler. Grand Rapids: Baker, 1981, pp. 221–226. Used by permission.

Musical Instruments in the Old Testament

1. musical instruments (*zmr'*) (Dan. 3:5)

2. flute (*ḥlyl*) (1 Sam. 10:5)·

3. trumpet (*ḥṣṣrh*) (2 Kings 11:14)

4. ram's horn (*ywbl*) (Lev. 25:13)

5. musical instruments (*kly*) (Ps. 71:22)

6. lyre (*knwr*) (Gen. 4:21)

7. stringed instruments (*mnym*) (Ps. 150:4)

8. sistrum or rattle (*mn'n'ym*) (2 Sam. 6:5)

9. small bell (*mṣlh*) (Zech. 14:20)

10. cymbals (*mṣltym*) (Ezra 3:10)

11. flute or pipe (*mšrwqy*) (Dan. 3:5)

12. stringed instrument, harp? (*nbl*) (Ps. 33:2)

13. string music (*ngynh*) (Lam. 5:14)

14. musical instrument (*swmpwnyh*) (Dan. 3:5)

15. flute (*'wgb*) (Ps. 150:4)

16. harp (*psnṭryn*) (Dan. 3:7)

17. bells (*p'mwn*) (Exod. 28:33; 39:25–26)

18. cymbals (*ṣlṣlym*) (Ps. 150:5)

19. lyre or lute (*qytrs*) (Dan. 3:5)

20. horn (*qrn*) (Josh. 6:5)

21. lyre (*śbk'*) (Dan. 3:7)

22. ram's horn (*šwpr*) (1 Kings 1:34)

23. lyre with three strings (*šlyš*) (1 Sam. 18:6)

24. tambourine, timbrel (*twp*) (Gen. 31:27)

The English translation of these alphabetized Hebrew terms is based on W. L. Holladay, *A Concise Hebrew and Aramaic Lexicon of the Old Testament* (Grand Rapids: Eerdmans, 1971).

Musical Notations of the Psalms

1. according to *'ylt hšḥr* ("the doe of the dawn"):
   22

2. for the flutes (*'l-hnḥylwt*):
   5

3. according to *'l-tšḥt* ("do not destroy"):
   57
   58
   59
   75

4. with stringed instruments (*bngynwt*):

4	61
6	67
54	76
55	

5. according to *gtyt* (an unknown musical term, suggested meanings: (a) a Gathite instrument; (b) "by the wine press" of the Feast of Tabernacles; (c) of the New Year's festival):
   8
   81
   84

6. higgaion (*hgywn*, an interlude for resounding music?):
   9

7. a petition (*hzkyr*):
   38
   70

8. for or according to *ydwtwn* (?):
   39
   62
   77

9. according to *ywnt 'lml rḥwqym* ("a dove on distant oaks"):
   56

10. for the choir director (*lmnṣḥ*):

4	13	31	45	54	61	69	84
5	14	36	46	55	62	70	85
6	18	39	47	56	64	75	88
8	19	40	49	57	65	76	109
9	20	41	51	58	66	77	139
11	21	42	52	59	67	80	140
12	22	44	53	60	68	81	

11. according to *mwt lbn* ("death of the son"):

9

12. psalm (*mzmwr*):

3	15	29	47	64	76	85	108
4	19	30	48	65	77	87	109
5	20	31	49	66	79	88	110
6	21	38	50	67	80	92	139
8	22	39	51	68	82	98	140
9	23	40	62	73	83	100	141
12	24	41	63	75	84	101	143
13							

13. according to *mḥlt* (with a sickness or after a sad tone?):

53

14. according to *mḥlt l'nwt* (after a sad manner, to make humble?):

88

15. miktam (*mktm*, a mystery poem or song of expiation?):

16	58
56	59
57	60

16. maskil (*mśkyl*, an unknown musical term, suggested meanings: (a) a cultic song; (b) a passage for learning; (c) a wisdom song put to music):

32	45	54	88
42	52	74	89
44	53	78	142

17. *selāh* (*selāh*, an unknown musical term, suggested meanings: (a) raising of the voice to a higher pitch; (b) "forever"; (c) a

pause for a musical interlude; (d) an acrostic indicating a change of voice or "da capo"):

3	32	50	61	76	85
4	39	52	62	77	87
7	44	54	66	81	88
9	46	55	67	82	89
20	47	57	68	83	140
21	48	59	75	84	143 (cf. Hab. 3:3, 9, 13)
24	49	60			

18. according to 'lmwt (young women or to be sung by young women?):

46

19. shiggaion (šgywn, an unknown musical term):

7 (cf. Hab. 3:1)

20. to the tune of "lilies" (šwšnym):

45
69
80

21. a song (šyr):

30	66	76	87
46	67	76	88
48	68	83	108
65			

22. a song of ascents (šyr hm'lwt):

120	123	126	129	132
121	124	127	130	133
122	125	128	131	134

23. a wedding song (šyr ydydwt):

45

24. a song for the Sabbath day (šyr lym hsbt):

92

25. according to šmynyt ("on the eight-stringed instrument"?):

6
12

26. according to ššn 'dwt ("the lily of the covenant"):

60
80

27. a psalm of praise (*thlh*):
     145
28. a prayer (*tplh*):
          17   102
          86   142
          90

The English translation of these alphabetized Hebrew musical notations is based on W. L. Holladay, *A Concise Hebrew and Aramaic Lexicon of the Old Testament* (Grand Rapids: Eerdmans, 1971).

Appendix F
Psalms for the Church Today

TWO QUESTIONS SERVE as the conclusion to this analysis of the place of the Psalms in Jewish and Christian worship. First, what have we learned about the Psalms and about worship from the survey of psalmic use in the Old Testament and church history? And second, how might we implement this instruction so that the Psalms may be used more effectively in our worship?

These questions not only climax our study of the Psalms and worship, they also serve as an invitation to the reader—an invitation to revitalize appreciation for the place of the Psalms in your current worship practices, or an invitation to reclaim the Judeo-Christian heritage of ascribing the Psalms a prominent place in private devotion and public worship.

What Have We Learned?

I have organized this study of the Psalms around a series of quotations from the stalwart church fathers and distinguished Jewish and Christian biblical scholars. My purpose is twofold: their commentary on the Psalms and the use of the Psalms in worship bring historical and theological perspective to our summary of the topic, and you, the reader, will probably remember their words much longer than mine.

The Psalms for life. "But in the Psalter . . . you learn about yourself."[1]

The church fathers from Tertullian to Calvin agreed that the Psalms speak *for* us, unlike the rest of Scripture which speaks *to* us. John Calvin described the Psalms as "an anatomy of all parts of the soul,"[2] and the Psalms do express the full gamut of human response to God's goodness and justice. We have learned that the Psalms depict the pilgrimage of faith not only for ancient Israel but also for

Christians today. Again, Athanasius counseled his friend Marcellinus, "The marvel with the Psalter is that . . . the reader takes all its words upon his lips as though they were his own. . . . the Psalms thus serve him who sings them as a mirror, wherein he sees himself and his own soul."[3]

The Psalms for Jewish worship. "The Psalms thus became the spiritual girders of the synagogue worship."[4]

What Millgram claims for synagogue worship was also true for temple worship in Old Testament times. Indeed, we have learned that the Psalms are the hymnbook of the Old Testament and the essence of the sacrifice of praise raised to God in the temple liturgies (Ps. 141:2). But more, the Psalms encapsulate the message of the entire Old Testament. Martin Luther, that great Reformer and Bible scholar, labeled the Psalms, "a little Bible, and a summary of the Old Testament."[5] And rightly so, as all the major themes of Old Testament theology are addressed in the Psalter, including covenant, divine presence, God's providential rule of history, divine kingship, God as Creator, God's Law, justice and mercy, redemption, blessings and curses, personal piety, and worship—to name a few.[6]

The Psalms for Christian worship. "If we keep vigil in the church, David comes first, last, and midst."[7]

We have learned that the Psalms were vital to personal devotional life and central to corporate worship through the entire course of church history. More than this, the Psalms anticipate Jesus Christ as the Son of God and the Son of David. The Christian reading of the Psalms permits both our appreciation of and entry into the passion of Jesus of Nazareth.[8]

The Psalms as a how-to book. "Do not sing psalms with your voices only, but sing praises in your heart to God."[9]

Just as Jerome adjured his readers to connect external and internal psalmody, we have learned the Psalms portray theology in the concrete and not the abstract. The Psalms instruct the reader in the array of ways in which the righteous may approach and speak—or better, sing to God. The Psalms also teach us about the important dynamic between the individual and the larger religious community.

The pragmatic Chrysostom even found virtue in the method of singing psalms as a pedagogical device, since reading was toilsome and
irksome.[10]

But more important is Athanasius's observation that the Psalter
is a "how to" book. The Psalms tell us how to obey biblical prohibitions, how to repent, and how to bear affliction. The Psalter tells
us how to pray, how to express our thanks, and how to praise God.
"We are bidden elsewhere in the Bible to bless the Lord and to acknowledge Him; here in the Psalms we are shown the way to do
it."[11]

How Might I or My Church Use the Psalms in Worship?

This final section of our study of the Psalms in worship is designed as a practical guide to implement psalmody in private devotion and public worship. The categories are not exhaustive but
representative. Be creative!

Again, the bibliography is not comprehensive but merely introduces the topic. Bibliographic entries represent a wide range of religious persuasion, and inclusion here is not necessarily endorsement
of the author's theological stand. (Unfortunately, not all the titles
cited remain in print. Check your local libraries and used book
stores.) The works have been selected as resources for both stimulat-
ing and personalizing the appropriation of the Psalms for Christian
worship. Be discerning!

Private devotion. Meditation is listening to God, communing with
God alone and sometimes in silence. Biblical meditation is both detachment from the material world and attachment to the spiritual
world. Meditation involves focused thought, concentration and reflection, and emotional involvement. Biblical meditation is an active practice of worship, spiritual renewal, mental refreshing, and
divine communion.

Yet biblical meditation is not necessarily a silent practice, as one
of the Hebrew words for "meditate" means "mutter, moan, growl,
read in an undertone, ponder by talking to oneself" (hāgâ; Ps. 1:2).
The content of biblical meditation is the person of God, his works,
and his Law as revealed in creation (Ps. 145:5) and Scripture (Ps.
119:97).

Biblical References to "Meditation":

NIV—Pss. 1:2; 19:14; 39:3; 48:9; 77:12; 104:34; 119:15, 23, 27, 48, 78, 97, 99, 148; 143:5; 145:5.

NRSV—Pss. 1:2; 19:14; 38:12; 49:3; 63:6; 77:3, 6, 12; 104:34; 119:15, 23, 27, 48, 78, 97, 99, 148; 143:5; 145:5.

Resources:

Bonhoeffer, D. *Meditating on the Word*. D. M. Gracie, trans. Cambridge: Cowley, 1986.

Downing, J. *Meditation: The Bible Tells You How*. Colorado Springs: NavPress, 1977.

Erickson, C. D. *Participating in Worship: History, Theory and Practice*. Louisville: W/JKP, 1989, 41–44.

Fenhagen, J. C. *More Than Wanderers: Spiritual Disciplines for Christian Ministry*. New York: Seabury Press, 1978, 41–71. (Useful suggestions for keeping a personal journal.)

Foster, R. J. *Celebration of Discipline*. New York: Harper & Row, 1978, 13–29.

Gorsuch, J. P. *An Invitation to the Spiritual Journey*. New York: Paulist Press, 1990, 81–96.

Kelsey, M. T. *The Other Side of Silence: A Guide to Christian Meditation*. New York: Paulist Press, 1976. (A comparative analysis of Eastern and Christian meditation.)

Merton, T. *Contemplative Prayer*. New York: Herder & Herder, 1969.

_____. *Spiritual Direction and Meditation* (Reprint). Collegeville, MN: Liturgical Press, 1960.

Prayer, praise, and worship. The Psalms represent the honest dialogue of faith, including thanksgiving, praise, and worship, as well as the expression of joy, hope, despair, pain, and doubt rooted in the experiences of daily life. The Psalms teach us to bring all our life responses to God—praise or lament—in a prayerful attitude.

You may find it helpful to use the outlines of psalmic types as a prayer guide, especially the lament since it takes the suppliant from complaint to praise. You may even experiment with writing your own psalms based on the outlines of the various psalmic forms. Regardless, learn to the make the Psalms a great resource for Christian prayer, and let your personal prayer, praise, and worship be as rich and varied as the Psalter itself.

Resources:

Bonhoeffer, D. *Psalms: The Prayer Book of the Bible*. 2nd Edition. J. H. Burtness, trans. Philadelphia: Augsburg Fortress, 1970.

Brueggemann, W. *Praying the Psalms*. Winona, MN: St. Mary's, 1986.

Clifford, P. *Praying with the Jewish Tradition*. London: Triangle, 1989.

Craghan, J. *Psalms: Prayers for the Ups, Downs, & In-Betweens of Life*. Wilmington, MD: M. Glazier, 1985.

Donin, H. H. *To Pray as a Jew*. New York: Basic Books, 1980.

Galley, H. (comp.) *Morning and Evening Prayer: With Selected Psalms and Readings for the Church Year*. New York: Seabury Press, 1983.

Hales, R. *Praying with the Church Through the Christian Year*. Minneapolis: Light & Life Publishers, 1989.

Klug, R. *Psalms: A Guide to Prayer & Praise*. Wheaton: Shaw, 1979.

Law, P. (comp.) *Praying with the Old Testament*. London: Triangle, 1989.

Link, M. *Psalms for Today: Praying an Old Book in a New Way*. Allen, TX: Tabor Publishers, 1988.

Lockyer, H. *All the Prayers of the Bible* Grand Rapids: Zondervan, 1959.

Magee, B. (comp.) *Psalm Prayers for Morning and Evening*. San Francisco: Ignatius Press, 1991.

Merton, T. *Bread in the Wilderness*. Philadelphia: Augsburg Fortress, 1986.

_____. *Praying the Psalms*. Collegeville, MN: Liturgical Press, 1956.

Oxford Book of Prayer. G. Appleton, ed. Oxford: Oxford Univ. Press, 1989.

Peterson, E. H. *Psalms: Prayers of the Heart*. Downers Grove, IL: InterVarsity Press, 1987.

Reid, J. C. *Prayer Journey Through the Psalms*. Nashville: Abingdon, 1987.

Shepherd, B. J. *Praying the Psalms: Daily Meditations on Cherished Psalms*. Louisville: W/JKP, 1978.

Simpson, W. W. *Jewish Prayer and Worship: An Introduction for Christians*. London: SCM Press, 1965.

Zim, R. *English Metrical Psalms: Poetry as Praise and Prayer*. Cambridge: Cambridge Univ. Press, 1987.

Life, life-style, and worldview. The continuing appeal of the Psalms resides in its ability to speak to the whole person, informing our intellect, arousing our emotions, and directing our will.[12] For this reason the Psalter plays an integral role in shaping Christian lifestyle and worldview. The following resources offer insight and help on the subject of a Christian response to life.

Resources:

Armerding, C. *Psalms in a Minor Key*. Chicago: Moody, 1973.

Brandt, L. *Psalms of Comfort*. St. Louis: Concordia, 1977.

———. *Psalms of Joy*. St. Louis: Concordia, 1977.

———. *Psalms of Praise*. St. Louis: Concordia, 1977.

———. *Psalms of Strength*. St. Louis: Concordia, 1977.

Brownlow, L. *Psalms in My Heart: Daily Devotionals from the Book of Psalms*. Fort Worth: Brownlow Publishing Co., 1989.

Brueggemann, W. *The Message of the Psalms*. Minneapolis: Augsburg, 1984.

Calvin, J. *Commentaries on the Psalms* (Reprint) H. Beveridge, trans. Vols. 4–6. Grand Rapids: Baker, 1979.

Goldingay, J. *Songs From a Strange Land* (Psalms 42–51). Downers Grove, IL: InterVarsity Press, 1978.

Limburg, J. *Psalms for Sojourners*. Philadelphia: Augsburg Fortress, 1986.

Luther, M. *The Works of Martin Luther: On the Psalms* Vols. 10–14. St. Louis: Concordia, 1974.

Psalms of Friendship. Collegeville, MN: Liturgical Press, 1991.

Psalms of Suffering. Collegeville, MN: Liturgical Press, 1991.

Psalms of Tenderness. Collegeville, MN: Liturgical Press, 1991.

Psalms of Trust. Collegeville, MN: Liturgical Press, 1991.

Robinson, H. *The Good Shepherd: Reflections on Psalm 23*. Chicago: Moody, 1987.

Spurgeon, C. H. *The Treasury of David*. D. O. Fuller, ed. Grand Rapids: Kregel, 1977.

Stedman, R. C. *Psalms of Faith: A Life-Related Study from Selected Psalms* (Revised). Glendale, CA: Regal Books, 1988.

Stephens, B. *Psalms for Recovery: Meditations for Strength and Hope.* San Francisco: Harper & Row, 1991.

Corporate Worship. Here is a summary of liturgical uses of the Psalms surveyed in our study of the place of the Psalms in Hebrew/Jewish and Christian worship:

* Entrance or processional and call to worship,
* Preparation for worship,
* Preparation for hearing the Word,
* Preparation for the Lord's Table or Eucharist,
* Confession,
* Prayers and praises,
* Praise singing and chanting,
* Congregational and choir singing,
* Responsorial and antiphonal uses,
* Dismissal or recessional and benediction, and
* Special occasions and church year.

Resources:

Abbot, J. & E. Bamberger. *The Abbey Psalter: The Book of Psalms Used By the Trapist Monks of Genesee Abbey.* New York: Paulist Press, 1981.

Allen, W. *Psalms and Hymns for Public Worship* (Reprint). Irvine, CA: Reprint Services, 1989.

Barrett, J. E. *The Psalmnary: Gradual Psalms for Cantor and Congregation.* Missoula, MT: Hymnary Press, 1982.

Book of Common Order (Church of Scotland). New York: Outlook, 1979.

Book of Common Prayer (Anglican/Episcopal). Oxford: Oxford Univ. Press, 1986.

Bower, P. C. (ed.) *Handbook for the Common Lectionary* (Presbyterian). Louisville: W/JKP, 1987.

Chamberlain, G. *Psalms for Singing: Twenty-six Psalms with Musical Settings for Congregation and Choir*. Nashville: Upper Room, 1984.

_____. *Psalms: A New Translation for Prayer & Worship*. Nashville: Upper Room, 1984.

Gelineau, J. *Psalms: A Singing Version*. New York: Paulist Press, 1968.

Hostetter, D. *Psalms & Prayers for Congregational Participation*. Series A, B. Lima: CSS of Ohio, 1983.

_____. *Psalms & Prayers for Congregational Participation*. Series C. Lima, OH: CSS of Ohio, 1985.

Leaver, R. *Ways of Singing the Psalms*. New York: Harper & Row, 1986.

Lutheran Book of Worship. Minneapolis: Augsburg Fortress, 1978.

Psalter Hymnal. Grand Rapids: CRC Publications, 1987.

Shepherd, M. H. *The Psalms for Christian Worship: A Pracitical Guide*. Minneapolis: Augsburg, 1976.

_____. *A Liturgical Psalter for the Christian Year*. Minneapolis: Augsburg, 1976.

Thomspon, B. *Liturgies of the Western Church*. Philadelphia: Fortress, 1980.

Van Olst, E. H. *The Bible and Liturgy*. J. Vriend, trans. Grand Rapids: Eerdmans, 1991, 135–159.

Author-Subject Index

Aaron, 6, 138, 141, 167
Abbot, J., 301
Abram/Abraham, xxvi, xxvii, 15, 30,
 31, 32, 33, 34, 56, 57, 58, 75, 126,
 132, 139, 152, 272
Accretion in religion, 52
Adams, D., 269
Adoration, 116
Affirmation of God's glory, the, 76
Agape feast, 233
Ahab, king, 149
Ahaz, king, 177
Ahijah, the prophet, 42, 58
Albright, W. F., 243
Alexander the Great, 278
Allegory, 234
Allen, W., 301
Almsgiving, 225, 227, 230–31
Altar, 32, 120; of burnt offering, 146,
 169; of incense, 147, 170
Amen, liturgical use, 113–14, 233
Amiet, P., 258
Anderson, A. A., 250
Anderson, B. W., 60, 195, 243, 245,
 256
Anderson, L., ix, 239
Andreasen, N. E., 101, 249, 266
Angels, 54
Anglican church, 93, 135, 154, 209
Antichrist, 61
Anti-formalism in religion, 53
Antonsen, C., 240
Apocrypha, 222–24; definition of,
 222; books of, 223
Armerding, C., 300
Arts, the, 61; annotated bibliography,
 269–271; aesthetics in the OT,
 212–14; definition of, 215–16;
 impact on humanity, 217; in

Christian worship, 218–220; value
 of, 216–17
Asaph, 194, 195
Athanasius, 223, 262
Atonement, 27, 121; day of, 121,
 123–24, 125, 132, 141, 156, 167
Augustine, 101, 107, 209, 238

Baal and baalism, 17, 24, 38, 39, 74,
 115
Baker, D. L., 259
Baly, D., 263
Bamberger, E., 301
Banks, R., 99, 248, 249, 266
Baptism, 77
Baptist church, 135
Barclay, W., 246
Barr, J., 247
Barrett, J. E., 301
Bauckhams, R. J., 249
Baylis, A. H., 243
Beckwith, R., 221, 249, 259
Bellinger, W. H., 257
Bema, 229
Benedictus, 203, 207
Benson, G. W., 246
Bergman, J., 240
Bezalel, tabernacle craftsman, 166
Bible, Holy, 2, 157; inspiration of, xxv
Birch, B. C., 263
Bird, P., 252
Bishop/elder, 155, 156, 158–59, 231
Blackwood, A., 61, 245
Bloch, A., 70, 245, 263, 286
Block, D. I., 245
Boman, T., 240, 247, 266
Bonetti, A., 246
Bonhoeffer, D., 298, 299
Bower, P. C., 301
Brandt, L., 300

Scripture Index

THE APOCRYPHA

THE NEW TESTAMENT